EDEXCEL
A LEVEL
HISTORY

*Active*Book included

endorsed for
Edexcel ▦

CW00542458

Paper 3:
Ireland and the Union, c1774-1923

Adam Kidson
Series editor: Rosemary Rees

ALWAYS LEARNING

PEARSON

Published by Pearson Education Limited, 80 Strand, London, WC2R 0RL.

www.pearsonschoolsandfecolleges.co.uk

Copies of official specifications for all Edexcel qualifications may be found on the website: www.edexcel.com

Text © Pearson Education Limited 2016

Designed by Elizabeth Arnoux for Pearson

Typeset and illustrated by Phoenix Photosetting, Chatham, Kent

Produced by Out of House Publishing

Original illustrations © Pearson Education Limited 2016

Cover design by Malena Wilson-Max for Pearson

Cover illustration © Mary Evans Picture Library/Epic/Tallandier

The rights of Adam Kidson to be identified as author of this work have been asserted by him in accordance with the Copyright, Designs and Patents Act 1988.

First published 2016

21

10 9

British Library Cataloguing in Publication Data

A catalogue record for this book is available from the British Library

ISBN 978 1 447 985389

Copyright notice

Printed in the UK by Ashford Colour Press Ltd.

Websites

Pearson Education Limited is not responsible for the content of any external internet sites. It is essential for tutors to preview each website before using it in class so as to ensure that the URL is still accurate, relevant and appropriate. We suggest that tutors bookmark useful websites and consider enabling students to access them through the school/college intranet.

A note from the publisher

In order to ensure that this resource offers high-quality support for the associated Pearson qualification, it has been through a review process by the awarding body. This process confirms that this resource fully covers the teaching and learning content of the specification or part of a specification at which it is aimed. It also confirms that it demonstrates an appropriate balance between the development of subject skills, knowledge and understanding, in addition to preparation for assessment.

Endorsement does not cover any guidance on assessment activities or processes (e.g. practice questions or advice on how to answer assessment questions) included in the resource nor does it prescribe any particular approach to the teaching or delivery of a related course.

While the publishers have made every attempt to ensure that advice on the qualification and its assessment is accurate, the official specification and associated assessment guidance materials are the only authoritative source of information and should always be referred to for definitive guidance.

Pearson examiners have not contributed to any sections in this resource relevant to examination papers for which they have responsibility.

Examiners will not use endorsed resources as a source of material for any assessment set by Pearson.

Endorsement of a resource does not mean that the resource is required to achieve this Pearson qualification, nor does it mean that it is the only suitable material available to support the qualification, and any resource lists produced by the awarding body shall include this and other appropriate resources.

Contents

How to use this book

STRUCTURE

This book covers Paper 3, Option 36.2: Ireland and the Union, c1774–1923 of the Edexcel A Level qualification.

You will also need to study a Paper 1 and a Paper 2 option and produce coursework in order to complete your qualification. All Paper 1/2 options are covered by other textbooks in this series.

EXAM SUPPORT

The examined assessment for Paper 3 requires you to answer questions from three sections. Throughout this book there are exam-style questions in all three section styles for you to practice your examination skills.

Section A contains a compulsory question that will assess your source analysis and evaluation skills.

Section B contains a choice of essay questions that will look at your understanding of the studied period in depth.

Section C will again give you a choice of essay questions but these will assess your understanding of the period in breadth.

The Preparing for your exams section at the end of the book contains sample answers of different standards, with comments on how they could be improved.

FEATURES
Extend your knowledge

These features contain additional information that will help you gain a deeper understanding to the topic. This could be a short biography of an important person, extra background information about an event, an alternative interpretation, or even a research idea that you could follow up. Information in these boxes is not essential to your exam success, but still provide insights of value.

Knowledge check activities

These activities are designed to check that you have understood the material that you have just studied. They might also ask you questions about the sources and extracts in the section to check that you have studied and analysed them thoroughly.

ACTIVITY
KNOWLEDGE CHECK

The importance of the textile industry

1 What were the main textile industries in Ulster?

2 How did these industries affect the province?

3 How secure were these industries?

4 Which industry was most important and in what way?

Summary activities

At the end of each chapter, you will find summary activities. These are tasks designed to help you think about the key topic you have just studied as a whole. They may involve selecting and organising key information or analysing how things changed over time. You might want to keep your answers to these questions safe – they are handy for revision.

ACTIVITY
SUMMARY

Trade unionism in Ireland

Using the material you have read together with your own knowledge, complete the following tasks.

1 Outline the reasons for the growth of trade unionism in Ireland between the years 1907 and 1914.

2 Using these reasons, answer the questions below.

a) How important was the role of the individuals in promoting a confrontation such as the Dublin lockout?

b) Why were the reasons you came up with insufficient to win the lockout by 1914?

c) In your opinion what was the main cause for the ITGWU's defeat by 1914?

Thinking Historically activities

These activities are found throughout the book, and are designed to develop your understanding of history, especially around the key concepts of evidence, interpretations, causation and change. Each activity is designed to challenge a conceptual barrier that might be holding you back. This is linked to a map of conceptual barriers developed by experts. You can look up the map and find out which barrier each activity challenges by downloading the progression map from this website: www.pearsonschools.co.uk/historyprogressionsapproach

progression map reference

THINKING HISTORICALLY Evidence (6b)

The strength of argument

Use Extracts 1–3 to complete this activity.

Answer the following.

1 Read Extract 1.

  a What is weak about this claim?

  b What could be added to it to make it stronger?

2 Read Extract 2.

  a Is this an argument? If yes, what makes it one?

  b How might this argument be strengthened?

3 Read Extract 3.

  a How have they expanded their explanation to make the claim stronger?

  b Can you explain why this is the strongest claim of the three extracts?

  c What elements make an historian's claims strong?

Getting the most from your online ActiveBook

This book comes with three years' access to ActiveBook* – an online, digital version of your textbook. Follow the instructions printed on the inside front cover to start using your ActiveBook.

Your ActiveBook is the perfect way to personalise your learning as you progress through your A Level History course. You can:

- access your content online, anytime, anywhere
- use the inbuilt highlighting and annotation tools to personalise the content and make it really relevant to you.

Highlight tool – use this to pick out key terms or topics so you are ready and prepared for revision.

Annotations tool – use this to add your own notes, for example links to your wider reading, such as websites or other files. Or, make a note to remind yourself about work that you need to do.

*For new purchases only. If the access code has already been revealed, it may no longer be valid. If you have bought this textbook secondhand, the code may already have been used by the first owner of the book.

Introduction
A Level History

WHY HISTORY MATTERS

History is about people and people are complex, fascinating, frustrating and a whole lot of other things besides. This is why history is probably the most comprehensive and certainly one of the most intriguing subjects there is. History can also be inspiring and alarming, heartening and disturbing, a story of progress and civilisation and of catastrophe and inhumanity.

History's importance goes beyond the subject's intrinsic interest and appeal. Our beliefs and actions, our cultures, institutions and ways of living, our languages and means of making sense of ourselves are all shaped by the past. If we want to fully understand ourselves now, and to understand our possible futures, we have no alternative but to think about history.

History is a discipline as well as a subject matter. Making sense of the past develops qualities of mind that are valuable to anyone who wants to seek the truth and think clearly and intelligently about the most interesting and challenging intellectual problem of all: other people. Learning history is learning a powerful way of knowing.

WHAT IS HISTORY?

History is a way of constructing knowledge about the world through research, interpretation, argument and debate.

Building historical knowledge involves identifying the traces of the past that exist in the present – in people's memories, in old documents, photographs and other remains, and in objects and artefacts ranging from bullets and lipsticks, to field systems and cities. Historians interrogate these traces and *ask questions* that transform traces into *sources of evidence* for knowledge claims about the past.

Historians aim to understand what happened in the past by *explaining why* things happened as they did. Explaining why involves trying to understand past people and their beliefs, intentions and actions. It also involves explaining the causes and evaluating the effects of large-scale changes in the past and exploring relationships between what people aimed to do, the contexts that shaped what was possible and the outcomes and consequences of actions.

Historians also aim to *understand change* in the past. People, states of affairs, ideas, movements and civilisations come into being in time, grow, develop, and ultimately decline and disappear. Historians aim to identify and compare change and continuity in the past, to measure the rate at which things change and to identify the types of change that take place. Change can be slow or sudden. It can also be understood as progressive or regressive – leading to the improvement or worsening of a situation or state of affairs. How things change and whether changes are changes for the better are two key issues that historians frequently debate.

Figure 1 Fragment of a black granite statue possibly portraying the Roman politician Mark Antony.

Debate is the essence of history. Historians write arguments to support their knowledge claims and historians argue with each other to test and evaluate interpretations of the past. Historical knowledge itself changes and develops. On the one hand, new sources of knowledge and new methods of research cause *historical interpretations* to change. On the other hand, the questions that historians ask change with time and new questions produce new answers. Although the past is dead and gone, the interpretation of the past has a past, present and future.

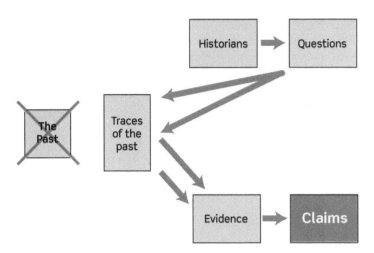

Figure 2 Constructing knowledge about the past.

THE CHALLENGES OF LEARNING HISTORY

Like all other Advanced Level subjects, A Level history is difficult – that is why it is called 'advanced'. Your advanced level studies will build on knowledge and understanding of history that you developed at GCSE and at Key Stage 3 – ideas like 'historical sources', 'historical evidence' and 'cause', for example. You will need to do a lot of reading and writing to progress in history. Most importantly, you will need to do a lot of thinking, and thinking about your thinking. This book aims to support you in developing both your knowledge and your understanding.

History is challenging in many ways. On the one hand, it is challenging to build up the range and depth of knowledge that you need to understand the past at an advanced level. Learning about the past involves mastering new and unfamiliar concepts arising from the past itself (such as the Inquisition, Laudianism, *Volksgemeinschaft*) and building up levels of knowledge that are both detailed and well organised. This book covers the key content of the topics that you are studying for your examination and provides a number of features to help you build and organise what you know – for example, diagrams, timelines and definitions of key terms. You will need to help yourself too, of course, adding to your knowledge through further reading, building on the foundations provided by this book.

Another challenge is to develop understandings of the discipline of history. You will have to learn to think historically about evidence, cause, change and interpretations and also to write historically, in a way that develops clear and supported argument.

Historians think with evidence in ways that differ from how we often think in everyday life. In history, as Figure 2 shows, we cannot go and 'see for ourselves' because the past no longer exists. Neither can we normally rely on 'credible witnesses' to tell us 'the truth' about 'what happened'. People in the past did not write down 'the truth' for our benefit. They often had clear agendas when creating the traces that remain and, as often as not, did not themselves know 'the truth' about complex historical events.

A root of the word 'history' is the Latin word *historia*, one of whose meanings is 'enquiry' or 'finding out'. Learning history means learning to ask questions and interrogate traces, and then to reason about what the new knowledge you have gained means. This book draws on historical scholarship for its narrative and contents. It also draws on research on the nature of historical thinking and on the challenges that learning history can present for students. Throughout the book you will find 'Thinking Historically' activities designed to support the development of your thinking.

You will also find – as you would expect given the nature of history – that the book is full of questions. This book aims to help you build your understandings of the content, contexts and concepts that you will need to advance both your historical knowledge and your historical understanding, and to lay strong foundations for the future development of both.

Dr Arthur Chapman
Institute of Education
University College London

Ireland and the Union, c1774-1923

Ireland has enjoyed a very chequered history and its relationship with Britain has been particularly troubled. Being in such close proximity to Britain – Dublin and Holyhead on the west coast of Wales for example have only 50 miles of water between them – Ireland has always occupied a position of strategic importance with regard to the perceived safety of the British mainland, and as such it has always been of interest to Britain. In the 16th century, this resulted in the conquest of Ireland by English troops so as to protect their western borders and assert control over the Irish nation.

The aggressive manner in which this conquest was achieved has affected the relationship ever since and, despite brief periods of quiet, it has often been violent and always strained. Even entering the 21st century, there are continuing difficulties between the two countries and this has been the result of policy decisions and personal agendas on both sides. No two countries have been so emotionally embroiled as Britain and Ireland. Throughout their long connection there has been a strong feeling of bitterness and betrayal on the part of Ireland, contrasted with suspicion and ingratitude from Britain. These feelings have often made reconciliation difficult and caused suffering on both sides. Within this topic, there is the opportunity to look more closely at some of the key themes and events that have informed these deep-seated attitudes and perhaps understand the reasons for such long-standing enmity.

The main key themes and events relate to the desire amongst substantial sections of Ireland's population to retain their own sense of autonomy following years of what nationalists regarded as oppressive rule. The period 1774–1923 saw the awakening of this desire most clearly amongst the Catholic community – a traditionally discriminated against segment of the population since Protestantism was the favoured faith. After the formal Act of Union in 1801, there was a marked increase in nationalist agitation – first through constitutional means and then more violently expressed, ultimately resulting in the War of Independence after 1919. The growth of nationalist opposition to British rule was encouraged by a difficult set of circumstances in Ireland; religious discrimination and particularly economic troubles produced unrivalled misery in the 1840s, but it should not simply be described as Ireland seeking freedom from an unrelentingly oppressive master. Throughout the years 1774–1923, British politicians attempted to ameliorate Irish concerns and gradually adopted more sympathetic attitudes which were intended to promote a better relationship and keep the two nations bound together. The extent to which this was a reaction to the nationalist agenda, or whether it encouraged nationalist action, is open to debate. The softening of British control certainly emboldened Irish activists, however it was greatly encouraged by a growing acceptance of Irish demands and a recognition of the power that nation could wield – especially following its growing voice in the British parliament after 1801. It is sufficient to suggest that both parties influenced one another and therefore share responsibility for the events that have determined the course of modern Irish history. In focusing upon such an informative period of this history, the topic offers the chance to understand the background to the sometimes strained relationship that exists between Britain and Ireland.

1782 – Constitution of 1782 is created

1801 – Act of Union with Britain

1829 – Catholic emancipation is granted

1842 – Blight comes to Ireland and famine begins

1867 – Fenian uprising takes place

1879 – Irish Land League is founded and the start of the three-year-long Land Wars

1913 – The Dublin lockout begins

1916 – Easter Rising

1921 – Anglo-Irish Treaty is signed and Ireland is partitioned

1798 — 1798 – United Irishmen uprising

1826 — 1826 – Belfast's first steamship is built by Ritchie and MacLaine

1830 — 1830 – Start of the three-year-long Tithe Wars

1848 — 1848 – Young Ireland uprising

1870 — 1870 – Gladstone's first Land Act is passed

1909 — 1909 – Larkin founds the Irish Transport and General Workers' Union

1914 — 1914 – Home rule bill is passed

1919 — 1919 – Start of the Irish War of Independence

1922 — 1922 – Civil war breaks out in Ireland

SOURCE 1 Ireland and its provinces c1844, drawn by Henry Schenck Tanner.

3.1 Irish nationalism: from agitation to civil war

KEY QUESTIONS

- How effective was Irish agitation before 1870?
- How did the campaign for Home Rule change Irish nationalism between 1870 and 1910?
- Why did the tensions in the years 1910–23 result in civil war?

INTRODUCTION

Ireland was Britain's oldest possession. There had been an English presence in the country since the Norman invasion, but in terms of real authority it was under Henry VIII that the two nations became more closely bound. In an attempt to secure his own crown, Henry embarked upon the conquest of Ireland so as to prevent his enemies from using the country as a staging post for a possible attack on England. By 1541 this policy had been so successful that the Irish parliament declared Henry to be 'King of Ireland'.

By the end of the 18th century, despite their long-standing relationship, Ireland and Britain did not enjoy a happy union. In matters of religion especially there was fundamental disagreement as Henry VIII's introduction of the Protestant faith jarred with the more traditional Catholicism of the indigenous Irish. The issue of religion was a regular source of contention and it was a prominent factor in the emergence of a distinctive Irish identity. By the late 1700s this was increasingly being used to support a burgeoning nationalist movement established around the ideas of American **republicanism** and an evolving desire for greater self-government.

The development of Irish nationalism marks the start of Ireland's struggle for constitutional change. Beginning first with the moderate demand for greater rights for the established Irish parliament, and then progressing towards more radical demands for **home rule** – self-government over domestic affairs and later independence – the demand for complete autonomy became more assertive in the 19th and 20th centuries. In making these demands, the nationalist movement not only transformed the political landscape in Ireland, but also its social and geographical topography. With foundations in religious discord, Irish nationalism divided the population along these lines. In the north of the country, where Protestant – and by extension British – influence was more keenly felt, there was a determined **loyalist** backlash to the nationalist agenda. Such was the forcefulness of this reaction that when independence was finally conceded in 1921 it was not a smooth transition of power. Ireland descended into bitter civil war and the country was partitioned – the south became independent and the north remained under British control.

KEY TERMS

Republicanism
A political concept that opposes power being held by a hereditary head of state and seeks to replace them with elected representatives.

Home rule
The right to self-government.

Loyalism
A general term describing the pro-British movement that emerged in the province of Ulster after 1886.

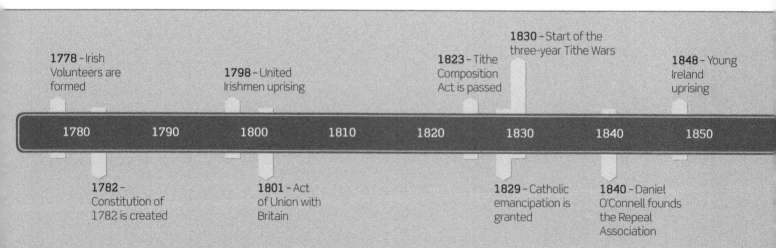

1778 – Irish Volunteers are formed

1782 – Constitution of 1782 is created

1798 – United Irishmen uprising

1801 – Act of Union with Britain

1823 – Tithe Composition Act is passed

1829 – Catholic emancipation is granted

1830 – Start of the three-year Tithe Wars

1840 – Daniel O'Connell founds the Repeal Association

1848 – Young Ireland uprising

1780   1790   1800   1810   1820   1830   1840   1850

HOW EFFECTIVE WAS IRISH AGITATION BEFORE 1870?

The demands of the Irish Volunteers and the United Irishmen

A dominant theme in Irish politics before 1774 was religion. Catholics were trying to achieve greater toleration of their religion following the passage of discriminatory Penal Laws after 1691 that restricted their political rights. Protestants were endeavouring to retain their dominant position following their co-religionist William III's ascension to the throne of England, which had established a **Protestant ascendancy**. The issue of legislative authority was largely irrelevant, since Britain retained a significant military presence in Ireland and therefore effectively governed the country despite the maintenance of a separate parliament in Dublin.

> **KEY TERM**
>
> **Protestant ascendancy**
> A period of Protestant domination in all aspects of Irish life beginning in the late 17th century and continuing in the early 20th century.

EXTEND YOUR KNOWLEDGE

Protestant ascendancy
This was a period of Protestant domination in political, economic and social life in Ireland lasting from the late 17th century into the early 20th century. It began after the victory of the Protestant William of Orange over Catholic James II in 1688 that saw William become William III of England and consequently paved the way for Protestant hegemony in Ireland where William was also pronounced King. With his ascension to the throne a series of discriminatory laws against Catholics were passed, called the Penal Laws, which denied political rights to members of the Catholic faith, such as sitting in parliament. In addition they favoured Protestant businesses and gave preferential treatment to them in an attempt to promote that religion in a country where Catholicism had been the prominent faith.

The existence of an Irish parliament gave the impression of autonomy. However, in reality the country was under the direction of the British government and any decision reached by the parliament had to be agreed by the **lord lieutenant** of Ireland who was, in effect, the chief representative of the monarch and head of the Irish **executive**. Under this arrangement Irish affairs were often administered according to the interests of Britain and its dominant Protestant Church.

The selective manner in which the country was administrated drew both support and antipathy in equal measure. From the Protestant community in Ireland there was a significant degree of agreement with Britain's policies – especially from the landowners who benefited greatly from the favourable economic environment that had been created through the discriminatory Penal Laws. At the same time, however, such prioritisation also encouraged a more critical opinion from Catholics and even liberally minded Protestants who saw little benefit in deliberately antagonising a substantial portion of the Irish population.

By the mid-1770s, therefore, Ireland was a country that quietly bridled under British authority. The presence of this slow-burning ember of discontent meant that the country was vulnerable to potential ignition should the right circumstances present themselves. In the late 1700s, such circumstances would start to emerge not in Ireland itself, but on the world stage – first in America and then France, where revolutions broke out, giving those nations new government and suggesting a different future for Ireland.

> **KEY TERMS**
>
> **Lord lieutenant**
> The chief representative of the British monarch in Ireland – also referred to as the 'viceroy'. Political decisions taken by the Irish parliament had to be agreed by the lord lieutenant before they were passed into law.
>
> **Executive**
> A term denoting the government or administrating body of a country.

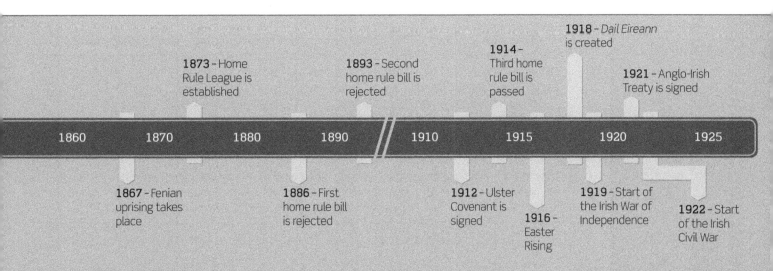

Timeline:

- **1867** – Fenian uprising takes place
- **1873** – Home Rule League is established
- **1886** – First home rule bill is rejected
- **1893** – Second home rule bill is rejected
- **1912** – Ulster Covenant is signed
- **1914** – Third home rule bill is passed
- **1916** – Easter Rising
- **1918** – Dail Eireann is created
- **1919** – Start of the Irish War of Independence
- **1921** – Anglo-Irish Treaty is signed
- **1922** – Start of the Irish Civil War

1860 1870 1880 1890 // 1910 1915 1920 1925

The Irish Volunteers

SOURCE

A black-and-white engraving by the English artist Francis Wheatley of the Dublin Volunteers saluting the statue of William III on College Green in Dublin, 4 November 1779. The engraving was made while Wheatley was visiting Dublin in 1779.

The American revolution (1775–83), with its emphasis upon rising up against the government of George III, had a profound effect upon Irish politics. In most part this was because of the perceived shared experience that Irish nationalists felt they enjoyed with the Americans: subjugation under British power and the fact that a large number of Irish men and women had emigrated to the American colonies in an attempt to pursue better fortune in the New World. This connection encouraged many in Ireland to watch the events unravelling in America with a close interest that quickly educated them in the notions of republicanism that were being pronounced, and also the success that could be enjoyed in the event of standing up to the British government.

In terms of the revolution's impact, two particular developments took place. The first was that it encouraged the growth of a more thoughtful and forceful nationalist perspective. Also, it saw the militarisation of the country as many Protestant supporters of Britain sought to defend Ireland's borders against potential enemies at a time when the mother country was away fighting. In the case of nationalism, successful revolutions in both America and France raised the prospect of greater

Irish political rights, and consequently ideas of republicanism began to filter into the country. More immediately, however, the French revolution placed Ireland in a vulnerable position as a result of its revolutionary government's war with Britain in 1793. Having emptied Ireland of troops for the prosecution of this war, there was a fear among Britain's politicians that French and Spanish rivals might use the opportunity to invade the country and exploit it as a staging port for an attack on Britain. This fear was given greater credibility since these countries had each openly sided with the Americans in 1778–79.

Due to this possibility, loyal-spirited Protestants in Belfast formed themselves into volunteer units of **militia** in 1778 so as to defend the island in the event of attack. Throughout the early 1780s volunteering became a popular endeavour and many units were established, resplendent in grand uniforms as gentlemen proudly used their ranks and titles as a mark of importance and loyalty. The Irish Volunteers, as they were known, regularly paraded and undertook military drills so that they might be ready for a potential invasion, and by 1782 there were more than 60,000 well-trained militia prepared to fight.

The existence of these units might be seen as a declaration of loyalty to Britain – defending its borders against possible attack. However, they are perhaps better seen as a demonstration of patriotic sentiment that in fact provided for an opportunity to begin challenging British authority. The frequent drilling and parades gave the volunteers a chance to meet regularly, and in the absence of attack they quickly became debating societies wherein members could discuss politics and other issues of concern. Foremost among these was the Act of 1720 declaring the right of Britain to legislate for Ireland and the limitations imposed upon the indigenous parliament as a result. In the past these complaints were not of great significance due to the power of British rule. However, by 1780 this power was much reduced due to the American war and also the fact that in Ireland there was now a well-organised and a well-armed militia to support any new demands.

The principal advocate for greater legislative independence was Henry Grattan, an Irish lawyer who became MP for Charlemont in the Dublin parliament in 1775. His speeches demanded that Ireland be granted its rightful status as an independent nation under the same crown as Britain. Inside parliament, these proposals were always blocked by judicious use of **patronage** that secured British majorities when it came to a vote. Outside parliament, the presence of the Volunteers in conjunction with the poor performance of Britain's forces in America – Lord Cornwallis had surrendered in 1781 after being surrounded by American and French troops at Yorktown – meant that Britain was in a more vulnerable position. Taking advantage of this change in circumstance, in February 1782 a number of Volunteers in Ulster held a meeting at Dungannon's parish church where they passed resolutions demanding legislative independence for the Irish parliament.

EXTEND YOUR KNOWLEDGE

Henry Grattan (1746–1820)
Born in Dublin, Grattan was a lawyer and MP to the Dublin parliament, first for the borough of Charlemont and then Dublin city. He was an outspoken supporter of greater Irish rights and, although a Protestant himself, he supported both Catholic emancipation and legislative independence during the latter 18th century. He welcomed the rise of the Irish Volunteers as a means to achieve these ends but did not seek a complete break with Great Britain. The more independent Irish parliament between 1782 and 1800 is often dubbed 'Grattan's parliament' due to his efforts in securing greater autonomy for it. In 1804, he became a Westminster MP in order to continue his defence of Catholic emancipation, although his more conservative stance on the issue put him at odds with the radical Catholic spokesman Daniel O'Connell.

SOURCE

From the principal resolution passed at the Volunteers' meeting held at Dungannon parish church on 15 February 1782. The meeting became known as the Dungannon Convention.

The claim of any body of men, other than the King, Lords, and Commons of Ireland, to make laws to bind that kingdom is unconstitutional, illegal, and a grievance.

The demands of the Volunteers very much reflected the growing assurance that the Protestant middle and upper class had obtained after slightly less than one hundred years of dominance. During this time they had enriched themselves and now sought greater political freedoms that they believed their status deserved. Faced with such determination and in the aftermath of the humiliating loss of their American colonies, Britain, under the leadership of a new Whig government, was eager to conciliate Ireland and therefore conceded greater autonomy to the Irish parliament. Known generically as the Constitution of 1782, these concessions repealed the 1720 Act and also reduced Britain's control over legislation in Ireland to a simple right of **veto**. In addition, the new government granted an annual **Mutiny Act** and declared that Irish judges were to be irremovable, except by parliamentary action. By agreeing these terms Ireland became a technically independent nation which shared a monarch with its neighbouring island.

KEY TERMS

Veto
A mechanism that allows the holder to block legislation it does not agree with.

Mutiny Act
These were Acts passed which governed the actions of the army. By granting Ireland this power it gave the Irish parliament authority to punish soldiers who refused orders.

In achieving this advance, the Irish Volunteers and their parliamentary supporters secured greater legal political influence for Irishmen. However, the realities of this agreement bore little resemblance to what was discussed. While the Irish parliament had greater legislative powers, the Irish government was still under the control of the lord lieutenant. He was therefore able to exercise considerable influence over the Irish MPs because the government that controlled the patronage – peerages, appointments and political pensions – which they could benefit from. Given this ability, the British administration was still able to wield significant power over Irish affairs.

To address this situation, the Volunteers held a second convention in Dublin on 10 November 1783. The dominant figure was Henry Flood, whose powerful oratorical style demanded attention. His desire for a more representative parliament which better reflected public opinion, so that the influence of the Lord Lieutenant might be mitigated, was consequently taken up and later presented to parliament. Despite the Volunteers' military organisation, parliament refused their reform plans and, unwilling to use force, the Volunteers simply went home. In the wake of this failure the Volunteers as a movement for political reform gradually diminished. In 1784, a third convention was attempted. However, this drew only a handful of delegates and very little public interest.

The French Revolution and the rise of the United Irishmen

Following the reforms within the constitution of 1782, Irish politics settled into middle-class respectability. The Volunteers had achieved some changes and were not prepared to actually attack the parliament to secure further reform as this might affect their own standing within the political arena. As well-to-do gentlemen, such action exceeded their own comfort and they accepted what they had already achieved.

By the end of the 1780s, however, this placidity was shaken by

revolution in France. The promotion of republican values in such a violent and public manner sent shockwaves through the Irish nation. First there was a conservative reaction to the excesses of the revolutionaries from the gentry of Ireland. Then sympathy for the principles espoused by them came from a more radical quarter of younger individuals who had increasingly grown disillusioned by the continued dominance of British influence over Irish affairs. These younger men marked a growing radicalism within Ireland – a new attitude that demanded greater political autonomy. They also felt that such a goal could only be won with a union between Catholics and Protestant radicals to challenge the dominant conservativism that governed the Irish political landscape.

These views were articulated by a young Protestant barrister called Theobald Wolfe Tone whose pamphlet entitled *An argument on behalf of the Catholics of Ireland* was published in 1791. He made a persuasive argument in favour of a substantially reformed Irish parliament that was directly elected by the people of Ireland without influence by the British Crown. Following its publication, a series of clubs dedicated to such a political agenda were quickly established amongst liberal thinkers. The first Society of United Irishmen was founded in Belfast on 14 October 1791. Its Dublin equivalent emerged the following month, and collectively they undertook to reshape public opinion.

SOURCE

3 From *An argument on behalf of the Catholics of Ireland* by Theobald Wolfe Tone written in 1791. Tone was a Protestant lawyer and founder of the Society of United Irishmen which sought to overthrow British rule in Ireland.

The misfortune of Ireland is, that we have no National Government, in which we differ from England, and from all Europe. In England the King is resident, and his presence begets infinite advantages; the Government is English, with English views and interests only; the people are very powerful, though they have not their due power; whoever is, or would be Minister, can secure or arrive at office only by studying and following their will, their passions, and their very prejudices: hence the interests of king, ministers, and people, move forward in one and the same direction, advanced or retarded by the same means, and cannot even in idea be separated.

But is it so in Ireland?

What is our Government? it is a phenomenon in politics, contravening all received and established opinions: it is a Government derived from another country, whose interest, so far from being the same with that of the people, directly crosses it at right angles: does any man think that our rulers here recommend themselves to their creators in England, by promoting the interest of Ireland, when it can in the most remote degree interfere with the commerce of Great Britain?

The demands of the United Irishmen were set out in their manifesto in 1794 wherein they outlined the following.

- Ireland would be divided into 300 parliamentary constituencies equal in population.

- Every man should have a vote.

In addition to these aims it was understood that further Catholic emancipation would be necessary since Catholics were not allowed to stand for parliament. Therefore, additional reform would be required to provide better representation for the Irish population which was predominantly of that faith. This reformed parliamentary system was to be achieved using public opinion to persuade the authorities to institute change. However, following the outbreak of war with France in 1793, Britain was much more resistant to extending further powers and therefore did not countenance any such changes in neighbouring Ireland. The reluctance of the British forced the United Irishmen to adopt more aggressive tactics encouraged by the American and French examples. In 1796, under the influence of Tone who had negotiated a deal with the French, an invasion force of 14,000 men attempted to land in Bantry Bay in the south of Ireland to eject the continuing British occupation while they were distracted by the war. Only poor weather prevented any landing from taking place and the ships were scattered into the Atlantic before returning to Brest.

The 1798 uprising

The attempted invasion marked a more radical approach to Irish politics. The continuation of British domination, despite agreeing the celebrated 'constitution of 1782' (see page 14), had forced a more determined spirit which was further reinforced by a growing demand for Catholic rights. In taking up this additional cause, the United Irishmen were able to attract strong numbers – by 1797 there were more than 200,000 of them. Emboldened by these numbers together with a French alliance, Tone co-ordinated a new uprising in May 1798 in which he hoped to sever Ireland's connection with Britain and achieve an independent state.

The uprising of 1798 was not well executed. Despite having approximately 15,000 fighting men, the rebellion was poorly co-ordinated and they could not take important towns such as Belfast or Dublin. Therefore, the rising was largely confined to the countryside. With more than 20,000 soldiers, British forces were able to secure a decisive victory at Vinegar Hill outside Enniscorthy in June. This success was partly down to the disorganisation of the United Irishmen but also the failure of immediate French support. This was not quick to arrive since the French regime had targeted Egypt as their main overseas priority and therefore did not send troops immediately. When these did arrive in late August they were few in number, amounting to only 1,100 men, and the rebellion did not really reignite. For his troubles, Tone was held in custody where he chose to commit suicide rather than face British justice.

The significance of the 1798 uprising cannot be overlooked. Certainly it was a failed rebellion, but it nonetheless transformed the future of Ireland. It attempted to secure greater independence, but instead it drew the country closer to Britain. Armed conflict in Ireland, at a time when Britain was vulnerable, made it clear to the British government that the Irish parliament was not strong enough to be relied upon. Ireland was at their 'back door', and therefore, in the interests of strategic security, Britain needed the country to be properly administered. Following the rising it was evident to the prime minister, William Pitt, that direct administration was necessary, and in 1801 an Act of Union was formally passed with the support of the Irish parliament, making Ireland a more integral part of the British state.

ACTIVITY
KNOWLEDGE CHECK

Irish fortunes between 1774 and 1801

Having read about the fortunes of Ireland before 1801, produce a timeline depicting the main political events that took place. Circle the three that you feel are most significant in terms of promoting Irish fortunes and briefly explain why.

The Tithe Wars

The union with Britain brought with it new challenges for the Irish people – not least a lingering resentment that their political autonomy had been removed by a 'foreign power'. Also there was greater sensitivity towards existing laws that became substantially modified by the new authority. The best example of this is the campaign against **tithes** during the early 1830s.

KEY TERM

Tithes
A tax of ten percent on produce or earning that was given to the Church.

Tithes were a form of goods-based tax raised to support the Church and they had been present in Ireland since the 12th century. Prior to the **Reformation** in the 16th century, they had been payable to the Catholic Church. Paying any form of tax has always been resented, but the tithe was particularly resented because it was intended foremost as a means of funding Churches and their clergy. Following the establishment of the Church of Ireland in 1536, this meant that Catholics were also required to pay for the new Protestant Church despite not having anything to do with it. Although their Church did not suffer financially, this requirement fostered a deep antipathy by Catholics towards the tithe on religious and economic grounds – they now had to pay two amounts of this tax. This was subsequently added to when new legislation was passed by the British in 1823 extending tithe assessment to pastureland as well as tillage land. Prior to 1823, pastureland for grazing cattle had been exempt. However, the Tithe Composition (Ireland) Act made the tax a general land-based monetary charge that consequently became payable twice-yearly by larger numbers of Irish farmers. This had originally been intended to make the system more uniform. However, in reality it antagonised even more farmers, some with significant political influence, at a time when political agitation was already growing over Catholic emancipation and many Irishmen and women were beginning to see the value of collective organisation.

KEY TERM

Reformation
A split within Christianity dividing Catholicism and Protestantism.

The resentment that the new Act generated was primarily a reaction to the requirement to pay the tithe generally, but it was also seen as an example of British oppression – particularly given that the tithe had now been extended to include pasture farmers also, upon what many Irish felt was the whim of the British authorities. This belief encouraged a desire to resist the payment among many farmers, which marked the start of a period of direct action in Ireland.

The Tithe Wars begin

The campaign against the tithe system is more accurately a boycott of payment rather than a 'war'. It began in October 1830 in the county of Kilkenny, in the south of the country. It followed a period of agricultural depression that saw reduced prices and therefore less money coming to the farmers themselves. Due to this economic difficulty, the additional requirement of paying the controversial tithe became a focus of discontent which, against the backdrop of recent political success with Catholic emancipation, ignited a wave of protest towards the tax. Throughout Ireland, farmers refused to pay the tithe, and by 1833 there were 22 counties in which the tithe was not paid. The arrears amounted to more than one million pounds.

The quick spread of this protest is evidence of the level of antipathy towards the tax, and also the extent of support for such a challenge. It was openly supported by the Catholic Church, and in particular Archbishop MacHale, who was one of the most senior priests in Ireland. Such support was the result of the manner in which the protest took place. It was passive protest that simply required the participants to refuse payment rather than to march or commit more aggressive acts. This method was employed because it encouraged the greatest number of participants which in turn amplified the impact of the action by greatly reducing the revenue generated and sending a clear, majority-backed message to the British authorities.

Despite beginning as passive resistance, however, the boycott did see some violence as police and local yeomanry were used to seize property in the absence of payment. This heavy-handed approach resulted in several violent outbursts – notably at Newtownbarry in County Wexford on 18 June 1831 where 14 resisting farmers were killed by local yeomanry and in Carrickshock, County Kilkenny, on 14 December 1831 where protestors killed a bailiff and 12 police officers trying to enforce the tithe demands.

Ending the Tithe Wars

After June 1833 the government abandoned the use of force to extract tithe payments because this practice had destabilised the countryside and significantly alienated the rural Irish population. It had also given the Irish a means of directly challenging British rule and had brought the two sides into open conflict. For the British this was also an awkward battle to win as the passive resistance employed by Ireland's farmers was able to make a mockery of the situation, even before events turned more violent, and it went even further to undermine the British position. For example, when seized stock was publicly sold to raise the arrears, the sales would have to be abandoned because they were turned in to a public spectacle with absurdly large prices being bid for that stock by those attending the auction. This action in its own right humiliated the government agents employed to conduct the sales since it was clear that the majority of participants could not pay the amounts they offered and therefore the auctions failed. At a higher, political, level it also was seen as damaging to British prestige. Combined with the increasing level of violence that had developed after 1831, it was therefore felt to be more politically expedient to replace the tithe system altogether before further damage was done to Anglo-Irish relations.

SOURCE

From an affidavit written by a Church of Ireland minister as part of a claim for relief under the Clergy Relief Fund, and submitted to British government representatives in Dublin Castle in 1832.

> a large mob assembled and the sale was prevented by strangers in the crowd bidding extravagant sums, the horse not being worth above three or four pounds and people unknown calling up forty, fifty and a hundred pounds and by this means making the sale a farce and the horse was obliged to be discharged upon which, one of the priests who attended gave the signal for a cheer and the tumult continued for some time to the great terror of His Majesty's subjects.

Not only was there political gain in ending the tithe war, there was also economic benefit. Given that the purpose of the tithe was to support the Church in Ireland, the refusal to pay resulted in many ministers seeking relief from the government so as to maintain themselves. This relief was supplied in the form of the Clergy Relief Fund which was set up in 1832 and provided loans from public money that were eventually written off by the government. By providing for this relief the British authorities were actually spending out more than the tithe might have brought into the Church, and so it also made economic sense to seek a better relationship with the farmers so that the cost could be passed on.

The eventual settlement of the tithe issue saw its replacement with the Tithe Rentcharge Act in 1838, which made the tithe payable only by landlords rather than by all occupiers. This reduced the agitation among the majority of tenant farmers and restored order in the countryside.

Daniel O'Connell and the Repeal Association

The Tithe Wars were primarily a protest brought about because of economic difficulty. However, they arguably took on a political dimension by presenting Ireland with further cause to challenge British authority. This was significant because it kept alive a general awareness of Britain's role in Ireland and how, for nationalists, this 'foreign power' could impact upon Irish people's lives. By drawing further attention to this situation, the issue of Ireland's union with Britain remained at the forefront of many minds and increasingly demanded further consideration.

The establishment of a more formal union put an end to legislative independence for Ireland as the country became part of the United Kingdom. The absorption of the island reduced fears among British MPs of growing nationalist sentiment as the Irish were now formally part of the richest country in the world and therefore had a lot to benefit from. Despite the possible riches that union offered, it also brought challenges to the relationship throughout the 19th century. The greatest constitutional challenge was that of repeal.

The idea that Ireland would meekly accept losing much more of its independence to Britain was perhaps somewhat ambitious. Certainly nationalist agitation was markedly reduced. Despite a small, failed uprising in 1803, which saw its ringleader Robert Emmet executed, the Irish remained silent on the issue of legislative independence, preferring instead to focus their energies on the successful campaign for **Catholic emancipation** in 1829. But this did not mean that they accepted the political situation. Having achieved greater independence prior to the union, nationalists did not forget what they had lost, and with the victory of the Tory party in 1841 under the premiership of Robert Peel, Irish nationalists sought to address the issue of repeal of the union – a desire which they had quietly wrestled with since its creation.

The driving force behind this new endeavour was the champion of Catholic emancipation, the Kerry barrister and MP for Clare, Daniel O'Connell. In 1840 he founded the Repeal Association with the intention of using this organisation to raise funds via a 'repeal rent' – subscriptions to the association – and to mobilise public opinion which, well financed, could then pressurise the Westminster parliament into granting repeal. He sought to achieve this pressure through the use of 'monster meetings' – huge public gatherings that had the potential to draw tens of thousands of people. In the past he had used these to great effect in the cause for Catholic emancipation, and he felt the same methods could be equally effective a decade later. In 1843 more than 40 such meetings took place and several were said, albeit from sympathetic observers, to have been attended by between 100,000 and 500,000 people.

EXTEND YOUR KNOWLEDGE

Daniel O'Connell (1775-1847)
Daniel O'Connell was born in County Kerry in the south of Ireland and was the nephew of a local Catholic landowner. He studied in France but left because of the growing extremism in the country that eventually led to revolution in 1789. In 1794, he continued his studies in London where he was called to the bar in 1796. As an educated Catholic, O'Connell was keen to see the political rights of Catholics restored after their removal during the Protestant ascendancy, and after 1805 he became a prominent figure in the movement for Catholic emancipation. In 1823, he helped to found the Catholic Association which quickly grew due to his organisational talents and skill at speech-making. Regularly drawing tens of thousands of people to his meetings, O'Connell was able to become the MP for County Clare. This forced the British government to consider restoring political rights to Catholics and led to emancipation in 1829. On the back of this success, O'Connell turned his attention to the repeal of the union, and using the same technique of 'monster meetings' he hoped to persuade the British government to restore an Irish parliament. Despite his earlier victory, O'Connell did not achieve this aim because the British authorities were prepared to use all necessary force to maintain the union, and O'Connell was not willing to use violence. He died in 1847 with the union still intact.

The numbers involved were arguably the result of the popularity of the issue, and O'Connell was of the opinion that with such numbers it would be impossible for the British to ignore their demand.

SOURCE 5

From a speech made at the Corn Exchange in Dublin by Daniel O'Connell when launching his repeal campaign on 15 April 1840. Cited in the *First Series of Reports of the Loyal National Repeal Association of Ireland* (1840).

The actual mode of carrying the repeal must be to augment the numbers of the Repeal Association, until it comprises four-fifths of the inhabitants of Ireland... when such a combination is complete, the parliament will naturally yield to the wishes and prayer of an entire nation. It is not in the nature of things that it should be otherwise.

Such a combination as I have spoken of was never yet resisted by any government, and never can. We are arrived at a stage of society, in which the peaceable combination of a people can easily render its wishes omnipotent.

The failure of the Repeal Association

The numbers generated by O'Connell's call for repeal offered great hope to the Irish. At his meeting held at Tara on 15 August 1843 it was estimated that there were 750,000 people present, and such a figure was undoubtedly noticed by the British. Despite such a presence the cause of repeal did not enjoy significant success beyond mobilising support amongst the people. Within parliament there was great reluctance to even consider the issue, and so the demands did not yield the result O'Connell expected. The reason for this was that British policy-makers believed very strongly in the union. To countenance its repeal was tantamount to agreeing the dismantling of the empire – an idea that was completely absurd in the 1840s when the country was rapidly expanding as a result of the industrial revolution, and the empire was providing a ready source for international trade.

SOURCE 6

An illustration published on 19 August 1843 in the *London Illustrated News* of a meeting of the Repeal Association at the Corn Exchange in Dublin.

WEEKLY MEETING OF THE REPEAL ASSOCIATION, CORN EXCHANGE, DUBLIN.

SOURCE 7

From a speech made by the Tory prime minister, Sir Robert Peel, on 9 May 1843. Cited in C. Gavan Duffy, *Young Ireland* (1880).

There is no influence, no power, no authority which the prerogatives of the crown and the existing law give to the government, which shall not be exercised for the purpose of maintaining the union; the dissolution of which would involve not merely the repeal of an act of parliament, but the dismemberment of this great empire... Deprecating war as I do all war, but above all, civil war, yet there is no alternative which I do not think preferable to the dismemberment of this empire.

The resolve of the British parliament therefore was absolute; they would go to all necessary lengths to prevent repeal, and on 8 October 1843 they banned a meeting of the Repeal Association to be held in Clontarf, on the outskirts of Dublin. In banning the event hours before it was due to be held, the British government forced O'Connell to make a choice: to submit to the ruling or to directly challenge the government and risk conflict should the military be deployed to enforce the ban order. The decision was not easy for O'Connell, but much of his broad appeal lay with his oft-repeated desire to operate within the law. As such, when faced with this legal decision, he chose to abide by the rule of law and cancelled the gathering.

The failed meeting at Clontarf signalled the end of the repeal movement because it undermined that movement's basic principle – that the peaceful organisation of the people could force the government to change its opinion. Instead of bending to public demand, the government's resolve remained strong and suggested a willingness to resort to more forceful measures should its will be tested. Unwilling to offer an aggressive challenge, and having lost much of its credibility, O'Connell's movement began to fracture in the years after 1843. Although the Repeal Association continued to collect its annual subscription in 1844, the movement was at a loss as to how to proceed after Clontarf and slowly declined along with O'Connell's health. In 1847 he died fully aware that his effort to repeal the union had failed.

The impact of Young Ireland

The failure of the Repeal Association was certainly a blow to the hopes of Irish nationalism, and with its demise went a lot of hope for political change. The level of expectancy that O'Connell had raised drained the spirit of many nationalists when his attempts faltered, and his Association was formally wound up in 1848, a year that might have been regarded as a low point in Irish nationalist history. However, O'Connell's attempts were not a complete failure. Although he had been unable to achieve his goal of repeal, his efforts inspired a younger generation of nationalists to take up the cause and transform it into a more robust and radical movement that would have a significant impact on Ireland in the last half of the 19th century.

Young Ireland

These young nationalists were the first supporters of the repeal movement and were largely associated with it through the weekly newspaper *Nation*, which was set up in 1842 to help publicise repeal. Chief amongst its members were a Dublin protestant barrister called Thomas Davis, a Catholic journalist called Charles Gavin Duffy and a Unitarian solicitor called John Mitchel. Together these men formulated a broader set of ideas about Irish nationalism than those which O'Connell had considered, and in doing so they offered a more complete platform for opposing British rule. Whereas O'Connell had been interested only in repeal and rights for Catholics, the Young Ireland group embraced much grander ideas and was more resolved to achieving them through whatever means necessary.

Among the most fundamental ideas of Young Ireland was its concept of Irish nationality, which it maintained included all those who lived in the country regardless of religious faith. More radically, it demanded complete separation from Britain – first through political persuasion and then by physical force if necessary. The ideas of Young Ireland embraced a more romantic view of nationalism – one that drew a great deal of inspiration from the 1798 uprising and welcomed the potential for personal sacrifice to achieve its goals. With this attitude it garnered support and criticism in equal measure. For the older generation its ideas were too naive and hot-headed; it did not consider the religious dynamic sufficiently or recognise the military capability of Great Britain. For many of the younger generation its rhetoric captured the imagination and reignited a more traditional spirit of nationalism that emulated Theobald Wolf Tone and Robert Emmet – heroes who had died for their country.

The Young Ireland movement was initially created to support the Repeal Association – it worked alongside O'Connell to press for the reinstallation of an Irish parliament. However, the conservatism of the repeal leader became a source of contention between them. In 1846, the 'Young Irelanders' seceded from the association after O'Connell demanded they agree to renounce the use of force as a legitimate method of achieving their goals. Unwilling to agree to this demand, on 13 January 1847 Young Ireland established its own nationalist platform called the Irish Confederation, wherein the split from O'Connell was essentially formalised.

The emergence of Young Ireland as a competitor to the established Repeal Association can in one sense be seen as a contributing factor in the decline of O'Connell's organisation. Combined with the failed Clontarf meeting, the development of a new, more spirited organisation was certainly an attractive prospect for those who sought a more dynamic nationalist force, and Irish Confederation clubs spread across Ireland's cities – and even into some British towns. Despite this seeming popularity, however, these clubs may be seen simply as a symptom of general disaffection with the failed repeal movement rather than any real commitment to a more aggressive Irish nationalism. The ideas of Young Ireland did not enjoy much support outside Dublin, and its open-minded stance towards religion did not win it much support among the Catholic clergy.

The consequence of this lack of support – particularly among the clergy whose views greatly influenced the majority Catholic population – was that the movement could not build up a strong support base that was actually prepared to act. This inherent weakness also affected the leadership of Young Ireland who differed very significantly over how best to push for their objective of an independent Ireland. On the moderate wing of the movement was Charles Gavin Duffy and the MP for Ennis, William Smith O'Brien, who advocated parliamentary pressure by building up support amongst the liberal gentry in Ireland. These views were challenged by John Mitchel and James Fintan Lalor who favoured a more radical approach that encouraged a peasant-led rebellion to remove the British authorities. Each perspective acknowledged a shared desire for greater control of Ireland, but they undermined the viability of the organisation as an effective movement for change by encouraging deep divisions amongst the leadership.

The 1848 rebellion

The consequence of these divisions was realised in 1848 when Young Ireland attempted a rebellion following the outbreak of revolution in France at the start of the year. The uprising itself was a hasty and poorly organised affair that lacked real resources or direction. It transpired after the arrest of John Mitchel for **sedition** in May and, following his conviction, Young Ireland made arrangements for an uprising in the early summer. The intention was to copy the coup that had taken place in France and had seen the French king, Louis Phillippe, replaced by a republic. However, the British government was aware of Irish discontent and had established a wide network of spies who quickly exposed the conspiracy. The consequence was that the government poured 10,000 troops into Ireland and suspended **habeas corpus** on 21 July 1848. By taking such decisive action it was anticipated by the British authorities that the discontent and political demands would be dropped, as they had been in the past. But instead the Young Ireland movement moved from Dublin into the southern countryside in the hope of raising troops among the farming communities of Tipperary and Kilkenny. Taking this action evidenced a shift from previous nationalist activities of the recent past and, instead of being cowed by the show of British force, nationalists sought to make a stand. This was a more assertive nationalism that was prepared to push for its objectives despite the weight of British supremacy. This effort manifested itself in several minor encounters with British troops – first at Killenaule on 28 July and then on 29 July at Ballingarry where Young Ireland, under the leadership of William Smith O'Brien, was persuaded to make a stand. The 'battle of Ballingarry' was itself a stand-off between the Young Irelanders and a small detachment of police officers who had taken refuge in a farmhouse. The episode saw two rebels killed after the police refused to surrender, but then, with reinforcements arriving to support the police, the remaining rebels broke rank and disappeared. In the aftermath of the confrontation, order was restored and several of Young Ireland's leaders, including O'Brien, were arrested and sentenced to death, which was later commuted to transportation to Van Diemen's Land (Tasmania, Australia) in 1849.

Legacy of Young Ireland

The failure of the 1848 rebellion signalled the demise of Young Ireland and after less than ten years in existence the movement failed to achieve any of its tangible goals. Like the Repeal Association, it had offered a great deal of promise but then quickly succumbed to the determination of British rule without really challenging that resolve in any meaningful way. In the short term it was an abject failure. Despite the lack of objective success, Young Ireland did promote the cause of independence and rekindled a more romantic sense of Irish nationalism which reached back to the days of the United Irishmen and traditional defiance. This, more than anything else, can be seen as the potent legacy of the movement because it reconnected the Ireland of the mid-19th century with its nationalist past and conjured up images of a pre-union Irish nation, which would provide further inspiration for a new generation of men and women intent on securing independence for their country. In this sense the Young Ireland movement was a conduit that connected Irish nationalism of the past with Irish nationalism of the future and ensured that its history was not forgotten in the fast-paced world of the 19th century.

ACTIVITY
KNOWLEDGE CHECK

Growing opposition, 1801–48

1 What similarities can you see in the manner of the various Irish opposition movements?

2 Was the opposition successful according to their respective goals?

3 Why do you think some opposition was successful and other opposition was less successful?

4 Even if opposition movements failed to meet their own objectives, does that mean they were entirely ineffective?

The Irish Republican Brotherhood

The failure of the 1848 uprising did not signal the end of Irish opposition to British rule and many of those who participated in the event were able to flee abroad where they continued to develop nationalist desires for independence and keep alive the idea of freedom for Ireland. Among those who fled abroad was James Stephens who had fought alongside William Smith O'Brien at Ballingarry but who had been able to escape to Paris after the uprising's collapse. In Paris, Stephens became involved in the revolutionary underground movement that had developed and became exposed to the continental way of organising secret societies, which involved small circles of members who did not know other members outside their circle. Being involved in this movement gave Stephens new ideas about how to oppose British rule in Ireland, and upon his return to that country in 1856 he was ready to revive revolutionary activities.

On 17 March 1858, in Dublin, Stephens established the Irish Republican Brotherhood (IRB). It differed from previous nationalist organisations in as much as it was a dedicated revolutionary group that sought to create an Irish Republic rather than simply repeal the union. It was also primarily made up of working men rather than the broader membership that previous organisations had enjoyed, and this was also because of the time Stephens spent in Paris. He had become more aware of socialist ideology and the condition of the lower classes and felt this might help Ireland's cause. The Brotherhood shared some similarities with the ideas of Young Ireland, but it was more decisively in favour of aggressive, revolutionary methods. As a revolutionary organisation, the IRB employed oath-swearing to secure its secrecy, and also the continental system of 'cells', which were mutually exclusive circles of members that only knew those in their immediate group. The purpose of this structure was to prevent infiltration from spies and ensure the integrity of the group in the event of a member being captured.

The emergence of the IRB signalled a determined shift in Irish nationalism. Prior to its inception, opposition to Britain's presence in Ireland since the union had been limited to moderate demands for repeal whereby Ireland could run its own affairs, but from under the umbrella of British protection. The newly created IRB, more commonly known as **Fenians**, however, was much more radical in its demands – wanting complete independence for the island and being willing to act with violence

KEY TERM

Fenian
This was a generic name given to a member of the Irish Republican Brotherhood and anyone who supported an Irish Republic. It was also the name of the IRB's American branch, which took the name originally from third century AD Irish warriors called the *Fianna*, who were believed to be the bodyguards of a legendary Gaelic warrior called Fionn MacCumhail.

in order to achieve it. In this endeavour the Fenians shared a similar ethos to the United Irishmen of the 18th century. However, with the cell structure they employed, it had a much more secretive, revolutionary and modern feel to it that offered, at least potentially, a more viable method of challenging the might of the British Empire.

The strategy that was adopted by Stephens and the IRB was to take advantage of any foreign war or difficulty that Britain became embroiled in so that the government's attention might be directed elsewhere and any troops in Ireland might be redeployed abroad, leaving the country 'unguarded'. As a strategy this was a sensible approach given British strength and the limited resources of the IRB, but in the late 1850s there was little to distract the British. Mutiny in India, another of Britain's imperial possessions, during 1857 presented a glimmer of hope, but the Irish organisation was not big enough to take advantage of this opportunity. This decision itself suggests a maturity among Irish nationalists – to bide their time until the right opportunity emerged rather than rush in to an attempted revolution without real planning, as they had done in 1848.

During the early 1860s the IRB was able to recruit very effectively and by 1864 Stephens claimed at least 80,000 members, although a more realistic figure is perhaps 54,000 which came from Philip Coyne, a New York Fenian who was able to make a tour of the organisation in that year. In either estimate the numbers are impressive for a secret society with revolutionary intent. Many of the numbers were achieved by Stephens' own hard work and skill as an organiser, but he was also helped by the death of Terrence McManus in 1861, whose funeral generated significant interest in Ireland.

McManus had been involved in the 1848 uprising and was captured and transported to Van Dieman's Land. He escaped and found his way to America. Following his death in January 1861 and subsequent burial, the American branch of the IRB wanted to ship his remains back to Ireland for burial, which in October of that year they were able to do following exhumation. The public procession of McManus's remains was opposed by the Catholic Church and also the older conservative participants in the 1848 uprising, such as William Smith O'Brien, who had embraced constitutional means to achieve their goals following the failure of the rising. This opposition was due to fear that publicly burying a noted republican escapee might generate British hostility. Also, the Church could not be seen to endorse revolutionary organisations. Despite this opposition more than 50,000 people followed the coffin through Dublin, and in December the Bishop of Cloyne allowed the body to be buried in a church in Queenstown against the instruction of Cardinal Cullen, the most senior priest in Ireland.

The McManus episode was a significant victory for the IRB because not only did it see its numbers rise dramatically during those weeks – more people joined the movement in the three weeks that the body was in Ireland than in the previous two years – but it also allowed Stephens to outmanoeuvre the more conservative elements of Irish nationalism in terms of public support for their respective ideas. More than any other event in the early 1860s, this victory gave the IRB more confidence in its position and the possibilities open to it.

EXTRACT

From Brian Griffin, 'Social Aspects of Fenianism in Connacht and Leinster', *Eire-Ireland*, vol. xxi, no. 1 (Spring 1986).

they [the Fenians] were losing the '**tug-of-the-forelock**' mentality that traditionally pervaded Irish society. The Fenians came mainly from the lower classes – artisans, town and country labourers, small farmers. Some of them, at least instinctively, resented the place delegated to them in Irish society by their social betters... Lack of deference became almost a physical characteristic in the eyes of the authorities.

1867 Fenian Rising and aftermath

The growth in support by the mid-1860s offered the IRB a better opportunity for success against the British and this was further improved by the conclusion of the American Civil War. The end of this conflict allowed many American soldiers claiming Irish heritage to travel to Ireland in order to support a planned uprising in 1865. This event was postponed because of the failure to acquire sufficient weapons for a viable attempt – only 6,000 firearms for 50,000 people willing to fight. But in March 1867 a rising was staged after James Stephens was arrested during a government clampdown of suspected conspirators. Although he managed to escape he was compelled to leave the country and therefore was not part of the attempt.

Without the organisational skills of Stephens the 1867 rising was not well managed and, like the 1848 rising, it petered out into a series of small skirmishes rather than a co-ordinated revolution. In part this was the result of division within the leadership in Stephens' absence and the poor management of the meagre resources they actually had. In Dublin there were only 1,500 weapons, including pikes, for the IRB 'soldiers', and this was not sufficient to offer strong enough resistance. Stephens' replacement – General Francis Millen, a former officer in the Mexican Army – was very aware of this shortcoming and therefore proposed a guerrilla-style attack whereby they could 'hit and run' rather than participate in a pitched, open battle. But he was ignored by several IRB commanders who preferred an open engagement which ultimately did not work to the few strengths of the IRB and resulted in the quick defeat of the attempted rising. This was also undermined by the fact that some leaders, such as the American officer Godfrey Massey, turned themselves in as government informants when it became clear they were not going to be successful. By April 1867 more than 200 IRB prisoners were taken and order began to be restored.

SOURCE 8

The Manchester Martyrs. A poster produced by Irish nationalists, c1893, commemorating the three Fenian men executed by the British on 23 November 1867: William Philip Allen (top), Michael Larkin (left), Michael O'Brien (right).

ALLEN.

LARKIN.

O'BRIEN.

THE THREE MARTYRS EXECUTED AT MANCHESTER, ENGLAND.

NOVEMBER 23RD 1867.

GOD SAVE IRELAND.

The days after the failed rising saw the IRB in a vulnerable state and with many of its personnel trying to evade arrest. Among the fugitives were two of the rising's principal leaders – Thomas Kelly and Timothy Deasy – who travelled to Britain with the hope of reviving the movement once more among sympathisers in that country. On 11 September these men were arrested for vagrancy after being found asleep in a Manchester park and on 18 September they were transferred to prison. During this trip the IRB effected a rescue attempt in which one policeman was shot – Sergeant Brett, who would become the first Manchester police officer to be killed on duty.

The resultant investigation found many Irishmen in Manchester targeted and more than 26 arrested during a flurry of anti-Irish sentiment, but only five were charged and put on trial. Of these, three were found guilty and sentenced to death by hanging: William Allen, Michael Larkin and Michael O'Brien. These men were executed on 23 November 1867 before a crowd of more than 8,000 who had gathered to witness the event. To prevent a rescue attempt 2,500 police officers were drafted in to surround the prison.

The executions were a product of public demand for justice combined with a desire to stamp out any challenge to British authority by underground organisations. By taking such a hard line the government was arguably sending out a warning to those who might seek to oppose it in the future and dissuade them from further action. In the event the executions only created martyrs to the Irish cause, which offered propaganda value but also encouraged a harder attitude towards Britain whose government was felt to have acted so oppressively.

HOW DID THE CAMPAIGN FOR HOME RULE CHANGE IRISH NATIONALISM BETWEEN 1870 AND 1910?

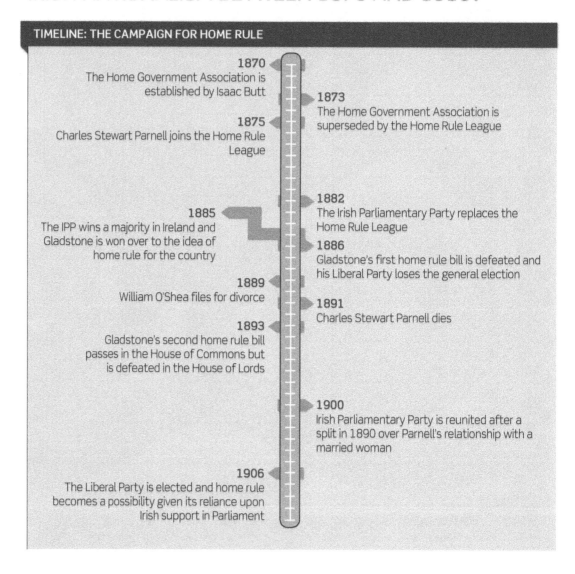

TIMELINE: THE CAMPAIGN FOR HOME RULE

1870
The Home Government Association is established by Isaac Butt

1873
The Home Government Association is superseded by the Home Rule League

1875
Charles Stewart Parnell joins the Home Rule League

1882
The Irish Parliamentary Party replaces the Home Rule League

1885
The IPP wins a majority in Ireland and Gladstone is won over to the idea of home rule for the country

1886
Gladstone's first home rule bill is defeated and his Liberal Party loses the general election

1889
William O'Shea files for divorce

1891
Charles Stewart Parnell dies

1893
Gladstone's second home rule bill passes in the House of Commons but is defeated in the House of Lords

1900
Irish Parliamentary Party is reunited after a split in 1890 over Parnell's relationship with a married woman

1906
The Liberal Party is elected and home rule becomes a possibility given its reliance upon Irish support in Parliament

Isaac Butt and the Home Rule League

The failure of the Fenian rising quieted radical nationalism but did not end the growing demand for greater Irish autonomy. With the IRB regrouping and rebuilding in the years after 1867, the brief vacuum that was created provided an opportunity for more moderate nationalists to step into the political arena once more. This is not to suggest, however, that the line of Irish opposition was entirely unbroken, and the moderate nationalism that emerged after the 1867 rising was entirely motivated by the same objectives as the more radical nationalists before it. Certainly there was a shared desire for Irish autonomy, but beyond that aim they were very different. The failure of Stephens' radical approach encouraged moderates to push for change using constitutional means, and also to reduce their demands. Rather than seek total independence, the new movement, headed by a Protestant barrister called Isaac Butt, sought home rule – a subordinate Irish parliament that governed domestic affairs only. This objective was at once a more conservative goal, but one that potentially offered a greater chance of success following the failure of Irish extremism. In this manner the adoption of new tactics was a pragmatic acceptance that force was no longer viable and that to achieve its aims, nationalism should adjust its operations. This would suggest that politically minded Irish leaders were aware of their own limitations and that they saw nationalism as more than a romantic gesture which the ill-planned uprisings of 1798 and 1867 may have implied. It also evidenced a more complex relationship between Irish nationalists themselves that challenged the idea that Irish opposition was entirely consistent.

As a Protestant barrister, Butt's own nationalism was very different from the Catholic-dominated ideas of the IRB which portrayed Britain as an oppressor, and instead placed greater value upon the benefits that a positive relationship with Britain could bring. He recognised the growing disaffection among Irish men and women and accepted that political change was necessary, but only so far as to diffuse the militant separatist tendencies that the IRB had espoused. In this sense the moderate nationalism that emerged after 1867 was not simply a different means to achieve independence, but rather an effort to gain greater autonomy within a reformed union that promoted Irish interests.

The vehicle with which Butt sought to achieve his objectives was the Home Government Association which he established in 1870. This organisation, known as the Home Rule League after 1873, contested the General Election in 1874 and won more than half of the Irish seats – 60 out of 101 – giving them a useful degree of influence in the British parliament where they continually pressed for home rule at every opportunity that they were given. Despite a reasonable number of MPs, Butt's request for a separate parliament for Ireland was not taken seriously by either of the main parties in Britain and consequently his efforts met with no tangible success. The continued failure of Butt's attempt at persuading parliament to grant home rule caused growing opposition within his own party who felt his approach was not the right policy to adopt and that deliberate obstruction would be more effective. This method was practised by Joseph Gillis Biggar and John O'Connor Power and worked on the principle that by obstructing the daily business of law-making through not ending debates in the house or making long speeches on minor issues, parliament would be slowed down and forced to grant the League what it wanted in order to conduct their activities effectively. Butt himself saw these tactics as ungentlemanly, but the repeated failure of his own methods weakened his credibility within his own party. He steadily became marginalised as the obstructionist policy gathered greater momentum among the younger members of the party for whom clear action offered a more attractive opportunity.

The shift towards more assertive action underlines the continued desires that many Irish citizens – especially Catholic nationalists – retained, despite the reduced demands of the Home Rule League. By the 1870s these nationalists, notably Joseph Biggar, were increasingly more demanding of political change than their more conservative Protestant supporters because it was Roman Catholics who had been most affected by British rule. For these Catholics the Home Rule League was an initial means to achieve reform that had lost impetus under the leadership of the moderate Isaac Butt. In this regard it is reasonable to suggest that although it would seem that the radicalism of the IRB had been diluted, the continued existence of a nationalist agenda through the League kept alive the prospect of a more autonomous Ireland. This maintained and renewed interest in the wake of the failed uprising, and ensured its ideas would not be forgotten. In this sense, although Isaac Butt himself was not successful, his movement acted as a lifeline for nationalist sentiment which, by the early 1870s, was beginning to strengthen once more as momentum gathered around the obstructionists. This energy was given significant direction after the emergence of Charles Stewart Parnell, MP for County Meath, in 1875.

Charles Stewart Parnell and the Irish Parliamentary Party

Under the leadership of Isaac Butt, the Home Rule League became divided and its potency as a medium for effective change was reduced. This was arguably the result of Butt's own leadership style and his unwillingness to countenance any alternative methods that younger members of his party, frustrated by continual failure, increasingly sought. The arrival of Parnell gave the obstructionists the upper hand as the young MP had a strong family name and a great deal of personal charisma that won him many friends in parliament. Born to a nationalist-sympathising father and Irish-American mother, Parnell was strongly motivated towards giving his home country greater legislative powers. He actively supported the policy of obstruction, becoming the principal speaker of the group. Although the policy was unpopular among Butt and his followers, obstructionism was hugely popular in Ireland and amongst the more radical Fenians who, in 1877, elected Parnell as the president of the League's sister organisation – the Home Rule Confederation of Great Britain – and cemented his growing reputation as a nationalist leader.

Parnell gave the League greater dynamism, which was in stark contrast to Isaac Butt's timid approach, and when the old leader died in 1879 it was Parnell who eventually assumed the leadership in 1880. Under his control the League adopted a more strident approach to home rule and was renamed the Irish Parliamentary Party (IPP) in 1882.

The Irish Parliamentary Party

The renaming of the League did not diminish the organisation's agenda and it remained committed to securing home rule for Ireland using parliamentary means. What the new name did represent, however, was the party's more tightly structured organisation and direction that Parnell enforced. Under his leadership, members of the party were required to uphold a promise, known as 'the pledge', to vote and act as they were told by Parnell and the party hierarchy. This level of control ensured that Parnell knew the full extent of his party's influence and could guarantee effective opposition through unanimous support of his agenda. Such comprehensive marshalling of his party's votes gave Parnell substantial influence in parliament – particularly after 1884 and 1885 when changes to the **franchise** and distribution of parliamentary seats gave more representation to Ireland and more seats to the Irish Parliamentary Party.

> **KEY TERM**
>
> Franchise
> The right to vote in public elections.

After 1885, 86 of the 103 parliamentary seats reserved for Ireland went regularly to the IPP and this gave it significant leverage within parliament. It was often courted for its support on difficult bills that the main parties could not pass on their own. Such influence gave Parnell considerable opportunity to press for the IPP's demands, and when forming his third administration in 1886, the prime minister William Gladstone was motivated towards introducing a home rule bill for Ireland. Gladstone's personal motivations for supporting home rule are discussed further in Chapter 2, but the balance of power that Parnell's party commanded was undoubtedly a contributing factor. Party majorities were diminishing and politics itself was becoming more competitive, with parties seeking to gain advantages wherever they could. The Liberal victory gave Gladstone 335 seats, the Conservatives under Lord Salisbury achieved 249, and Parnell's Irish Party had 86. With this distribution the Liberal government had no outright majority and therefore Parnell's party held the balance of power. Arguably it was this political motive that helped to encourage Gladstone's endorsement of home rule as a means of securing the Irish vote which Parnell controlled. In this sense, the direction that the Irish leader gave to his party was crucial in bringing about proposed legislation for creating a new Dublin parliament.

The first home rule bill

SOURCE 9

From William Gladstone's speech about home rule for Ireland after his introduction of a home rule bill into parliament in April 1886. Gladstone was the prime minister of the Liberal government in Britain and he had been won over to the idea of home rule following the 1885 election which saw the majority of Irish seats being won by Parnell's Irish Parliamentary Party.

Something must be done, something is imperatively demanded from us to restore to Ireland the first conditions of civil life – the free course of law, the liberty of every individual in the exercise of every legal right, the confidence of the people in the law, apart from which no country can be called, in the full sense of the word, a civilised country. [The Government must decide] how to reconcile Imperial unity with diversity of legislation. Mr. Grattan not only held these purposes to be reconcilable, but he did not scruple to go the length of saying this

'I demand the continued severance of the Parliaments with a view to the continued and everlasting unity of the Empire.'

Was that a flight of rhetoric, an audacious paradox? No; it was the statement of a problem which other countries have solved; and under circumstances much more difficult than ours. We ourselves may be said to have solved it, for I do not think that anyone will question the fact that, out of the last six centuries, for five centuries at least Ireland has had a Parliament separate from ours. That is a fact undeniable. Did that separation of Parliament destroy the unity of the British Empire? Did it destroy it in the 18th century? Do not suppose that I mean that harmony always prevailed between Ireland and England. We know very well there were causes quite sufficient to account for a recurrence of discord. But I take the 18th century alone. Can I be told that there was no unity of Empire in the 18th century? Why, Sir, it was the century which witnessed the foundation of that great, gigantic manufacturing industry which now overshadows the whole world. It was, in a pre-eminent sense, the century of Empire, and it was in a sense, but too conspicuous, the century of wars. Those wars were carried on, that Empire was maintained and enormously enlarged, that trade was established, that Navy was brought to supremacy when England and Ireland had separate Parliaments. Am I to be told that there was no unity of empire in that state of things?

Introduced in April 1886, Gladstone's home rule bill proposed to grant a new parliament to Ireland that would take responsibility for all domestic affairs in that country while also retaining Ireland as a member of the British Empire. The proposal was felt to be historic – the union had been in place for 85 years and now there was the possibility of its repeal. However, for many nationalists the offer was far short of what they demanded. Despite granting a new parliament, to be called an Assembly so as not to stir up ideas of the old Irish parliament of the 18th century, Britain retained significant powers including control of defence, foreign affairs and coinage. As such it still left Ireland tied to the British Empire, and for more radically-minded nationalists this was not the independence they desired. Even Parnell recognised the limitations of the proposal. However, he was aware that the bill was an opportunity to secure a significant improvement of the current situation and encouraged his party to vote in favour of it.

Despite the moderate nature of the bill, it was vigorously opposed by the Conservative Party and also Irish **unionists** in the north of Ireland who openly sided with Conservative and disapproving Liberal MPs to block the bill when it was voted on in June 1886. This blanket of resistance was motivated by the perception that the bill would see the beginning of the dismantling of the Empire and, therefore, should be opposed at all costs. The result of the vote was 311 in favour and 341 opposed – including 93 Liberals who opposed their leader on the issue and voted with the Conservatives. In the short term, defeat of the bill was a disappointment to Parnell, but the fierce debate it encouraged captured Irish imaginations and raised the prospect of future success. The result had only been achieved because of Liberal opposition, but the 93 who challenged were a minority within the party and in fact the introduction of the bill actually saw 225 Liberals commit to the proposition. In this light, the Irish had won significant support from one of Britain's largest political parties. So, rather than failure, 1886 can be regarded more positively as an important achievement that bode well for future aspirations.

KEY TERM

Unionist
A general term applied to supporters of the union between Britain and Ireland and opposed to home rule. Those Irish who held this view were to be found largely within Protestant communities in the province of Ulster where British identity was much more clearly felt.

The revival of the Orange Order

Supporting the opposition of the Irish unionists was the Protestant-dominated Orange Order – a political club that had formally been established in 1795 (see page 43), and which was committed to the memory of William III and his Protestant victory over the Catholic King James II in 1688. This organisation celebrated Protestantism and particularly its ascendancy over Catholics during the 18th and 19th centuries, organising triumphalist annual parades to commemorate the victory, which often resulted in sectarian violence. During the mid-19th century, the organisation waned as it was increasingly subjected to government scrutiny because of its perceived threat to public order, and in 1836 the Grand Lodge of Ireland had voluntarily been disbanded.

The threat of home rule, however, saw a resurgence of Orange activity and quickly local branches were well populated once more, providing a strong network of grass-root support that proved instrumental in the growth of the Ulster Unionist Party. Furthermore, as a political club with local branches – or 'lodges' – throughout Ulster and a tradition of marching, it could easily be organised to register public opposition to any proposed legislation. Having successfully supported unionist opposition to home rule in 1886, the Order maintained a presence in the province and was equally involved in subsequent attempts to introduce further bills.

The decline of Parnell

The failure of the home rule bill marked a turning point in Parnell's fortunes. As a politician his power was at its height following the publicity surrounding the bill. However, after 1886 personal events and a growing number of opponents combined to bring him down. The power he had achieved in Ireland worried conservatives who felt his position might promote another bill and, therefore, they conspired to discredit the Irish politician. In April 1887, *The Times* newspaper published letters incriminating Parnell in the murder of Lord Frederick Cavendish (then the new Chief Secretary of Ireland) and his Permanent Under-Secretary Thomas Henry Burke, on 6 May 1882. These had been particularly brutal murders that took place in Dublin's Phoenix Park. The letters were later exposed as forgeries created by an Irish opponent of Parnell called Richard Piggott, and upon his re-entry to parliament in 1890 after the investigation, Parnell was given a standing ovation.

SOURCE 10

From Richard Piggott's forged letter published in *The Times* and reputedly from Parnell, dated 15 May 1882. It was intended to undermine the Irish Parliamentary Party leader. Piggott was an Irish journalist who disliked Parnell despite being a nationalist in his early life.

Dear Sir, – I am not surprised at your friend's anger, but he and you should know that to denounce the murders was the only course open to us. To do that promptly was plainly our best policy. But you can tell him, and all others concerned, that, though I regret the accident of Lord Frederick Cavendish's death, I cannot refuse to admit that Burke got no more than his deserts. You are at liberty to show him this, and others whom you can trust also, but let not my address be known. He can write to House of Commons.

Yours very truly, Chas S. Parnell.

The 'Phoenix Park Letters' suggested that Parnell had attracted significant opposition and that people were actively seeking to undermine his political position. This was eventually achieved not by his opponents, but by his own actions. In December 1889, William O'Shea, previously one of Parnell's loyal supporters, filed for divorce from his wife Katherine citing her adultery with Parnell. This relationship had existed for a number of years and in fact Parnell was the father of three of her four children. The resultant scandal split the Irish Parliamentary Party as its members' various religious sentiments and personal morality were brought to bear on the issue of adultery. Here the Catholic Church was especially influential, since it upheld the sanctity of marriage and placed blame on the cause of divorce – in this case Parnell himself.

A Level Exam-Style Question Section C

How far do you agree that the Irish nationalist movement was successful in achieving its aims between 1774 and 1891? (20 marks)

Tip

When answering this question try to think about the different types of nationalism – militant and constitutional: was either of these more effective than the other?

Having received the condemnation of the Church, Parnell also lost a lot of support in Ireland's rural areas where the Church's guidance was particularly followed. This divide was further deepened when Parnell refused to give up his leadership and the bitterness that crept into the party remained there until Parnell died on 6 October 1891. The party would only be reunited in 1900 under the leadership of John Redmond.

Parnell's contribution to Irish nationalism was tremendous. He brought about the first home rule bill to be debated in parliament and, in doing so, stirred the interest of the whole nation. Although his final years were tarred by scandal the progress he helped to bring about – particularly liberal support for home rule and his creation of an influential Irish parliamentary party, ensured that the desires of Ireland's nationalists could not be ignored for too much longer.

EXTEND YOUR KNOWLEDGE

John Redmond (1856–1918)

Redmond was first elected to parliament in 1881 as MP for New Ross in County Wexford and after 1891 he was MP for Waterford. He was a strong supporter of Parnell and after the divorce scandal he led the Parnellite faction until the party was reunited in 1900. As the leader of the Irish Party he used his position and natural eloquence to win support in England for home rule. After 1910 he effectively used his party's influence over the Liberal government to encourage a home rule bill to be presented to parliament in 1912. Although the bill seemed likely to pass, by 1914 the Ulster Unionists had threatened armed resistance and Redmond, pragmatically, accepted an 'opt out' for the Ulster counties. When war broke out he pledged Irish support for Britain and was surprised when the Easter Rising took place in 1916. He died in 1918 following an operation for gallstones.

ACTIVITY
KNOWLEDGE CHECK

Getting home rule considered

1 How important were individuals in promoting home rule?

2 How did Parnell in particular encourage the introduction of a home rule bill?

3 Why do you think Parnell enjoyed greater success than Isaac Butt and previous nationalists?

THINKING HISTORICALLY Change (7a)

Convergence and divergence

Political change in Ireland 1774–1890				
1798 Failed uprising by the United Irishmen	1801 Union with Great Britain	1843 Failure of the Repeal Association	1882 The Home Rule League is renamed the Irish Parliament Party	1886 First home rule bill is introduced

Religious change in Ireland 1774–1890				
1791 Theobald Wolfe Tone establishes the United Irishmen, which embraced both Catholics and Protestants	1823 Daniel O'Connell organises the Catholic Association to mobilise Catholic support for emancipation	1829 Catholic Emancipation is achieved	1842 Thomas Clarke and Young Ireland embrace a religion-neutral Irish identity	1889 William O'Shea files for divorce and divides nonconformists on the issue of adultery

1 Draw a timeline across the middle of a landscape piece of A3 paper. Cut out ten small rectangular cards and write the above changes on them. Then place them on the timeline with political events above the line and religious below. Make sure there is a lot of space between the changes and the line.

2 Draw a line and write a link between each change within each strand, so that you have four links that join up the changes in the *political* part of the timeline and four that join the religious changes. You will then have two strands of change: *political and religious*.

3 Now make as many links as possible across the timeline between political change and religious change. Think about how they are affected by one another and think about how things can link across long periods of time.

You should end up with something like this:

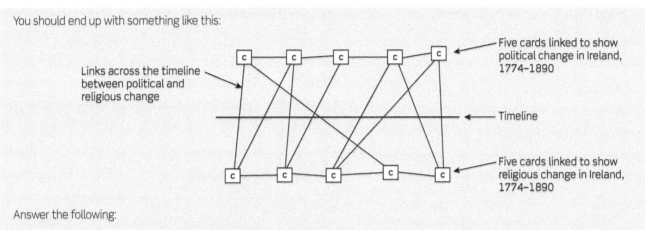

Links across the timeline between political and religious change

Five cards linked to show political change in Ireland, 1774–1890

Timeline

Five cards linked to show religious change in Ireland, 1774–1890

Answer the following:

4 How far do different strands of history interact with one another? Illustrate your answer with two well-explained examples.

5 At what point do the two strands of development converge (i.e. when do the changes have the biggest impact on one another)?

6 How useful are the strands in understanding the growth of Irish nationalism during the 19th century?

WHY DID THE TENSIONS IN THE YEARS 1910–23 RESULT IN CIVIL WAR?

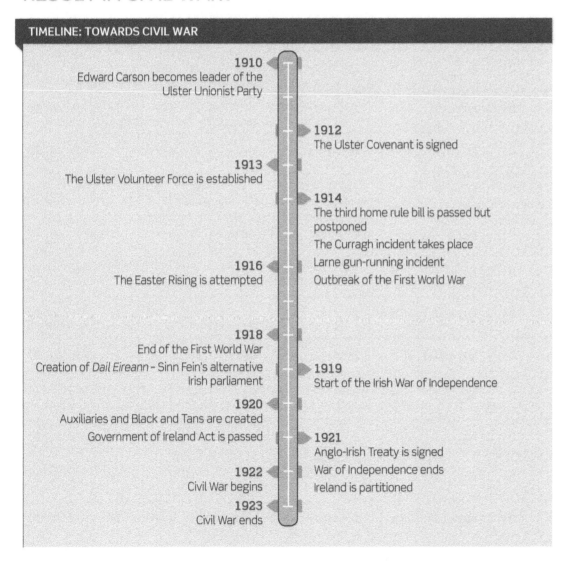

TIMELINE: TOWARDS CIVIL WAR

1910 Edward Carson becomes leader of the Ulster Unionist Party

1912 The Ulster Covenant is signed

1913 The Ulster Volunteer Force is established

1914 The third home rule bill is passed but postponed
The Curragh incident takes place
Larne gun-running incident
Outbreak of the First World War

1916 The Easter Rising is attempted

1918 End of the First World War
Creation of *Dail Eireann* – Sinn Fein's alternative Irish parliament

1919 Start of the Irish War of Independence

1920 Auxiliaries and Black and Tans are created
Government of Ireland Act is passed

1921 Anglo-Irish Treaty is signed
War of Independence ends
Ireland is partitioned

1922 Civil War begins

1923 Civil War ends

Following the death of Parnell, moderate Irish Nationalism lost a significant amount of potency as the Irish Parliamentary Party continued to be divided until the turn of the 20th century. Filling the space left behind by Parnell was a slew of cultural and political groups that in combination began to fire the imaginations of a new generation of Irish nationalists who sought not simply home rule but separation from Britain entirely. In 1884, the Gaelic Athletic Association had been founded, which had endeavoured to restore Irish pride in traditional sports such as hurling. Nine years later the Gaelic League was established with the intention of restoring the cultural traditions of Ireland – including Gaelic as a native language, which by 1903 was being taught in 1,300 national schools. The institution of these bodies collectively inspired a more assertive nationalism that increasingly became less content with the moderate aims for home rule – especially following the failure of two such bills in 1886 and 1893 after conservative unionist opposition had been successfully mobilised. The new demand was for complete independence, and in the pursuit of this goal nationalists began to turn towards more radical politics, such as those promoted by separatist parties, for instance Sinn Fein, which had emerged by 1905 (see page 32). By drifting towards such ideas, nationalists increasingly began to upset unionist supporters in the north of the country, and by 1910 there was a well-organised opposition established there.

Edward Carson and the UVF

The growth of Irish nationalism was not met with unanimous approval in Ireland. In the north of the country – notably the province of Ulster, where there was greater British support – the prospect of home rule was viewed with significant distaste. The basis for this lay in religious fears among Ulster's majority Protestant community that home rule would equal 'Rome rule', implying that under a Dublin parliament Catholicism would be forced upon the country. This fear resulted in the creation of Ulster's own political organisation to safeguard the interests of Irish people whose allegiance lay with Britain and the Protestant faith. This organisation was established in 1886 and became known as the Ulster Unionist Party. After 1910 its leader was Sir Edward Carson, a Dublin-born barrister and Unionist MP for Trinity College. As a respected barrister who had successfully defended the Marquis of Queensberry against Oscar Wilde's libel action in 1895, Carson was also MP for Trinity College from 1892 and was, therefore, a well-known public figure who gave significant gravitas to the party.

Given Ulster's historical ties to mainland Britain, Carson and the Ulster Unionist Party, together with the support of the Orange Order, were able to tap into a large reservoir of Protestant fears over home rule for Ireland. In Ulster the population was 1,581,969, and of this number, 890,880 were Protestant. So unionists were confident of their chances of blocking any future proposal to offer home rule. The Ulster Unionists had already defeated a second home rule bill in 1893 by siding with Conservatives. However, in April 1912 a third bill was proposed by the Liberal Party. This was brought to parliament in payment for the Irish Parliamentary Party's support for the Liberals once they lost their majority after

1910, and became reliant upon Irish support – the cost of which was a home rule bill. Despite the Unionists' strength in Ulster, the Irish Parliamentary Party held the balance of power in the Westminster parliament and as such there was a genuine fear that, together with Liberal support, the bill might pass.

Edward Carson (1854-1935)

Born in Dublin and educated at Trinity College, Edward Carson started his legal career as a Crown prosecutor and achieved success during the 'Plan of Campaign', which was an attempt by Irish politicians to help tenant farmers in Ireland by forcing absentee landlords to reduce rents during times of poor harvests. As reward for his service Carson was appointed solicitor-general for Ireland and also elected MP for Trinity College in 1892. An outspoken critic of home rule, he was celebrated for his impassioned speech against the measure in 1886. As a barrister, Carson successfully defended the Marquis of Queensbury against Oscar Wilde's libel action in 1895 and established himself as a one of Ireland's best legal figures. In 1910 he became leader of the Ulster Unionist Council and promoted the defence of unionism during the third home rule debate which began in 1912. As a unionist, Carson was the first signatory to the Ulster Covenant - a document which emphasised unionists' commitment to the existing union, and also sought to force the end of home rule by threatening military action in 1914. Following the War of Independence and eventual partition of Ireland in 1921, Carson declined the role of first Northern Irish prime minister and accepted a life peerage as an appeals judge in the House of Lords. He retired in 1929 and died six years later.

The Ulster Covenant

The union was a crucial feature of Unionist identity – they viewed themselves as 'British' rather than 'Irish' and feared that any devolved power would lead, ultimately, to an Irish republic that would promote Catholicism and marginalise their own faith. Given these fears Carson sought to stir up public sentiment against home rule by arranging for the organisation of what became known as the Ulster Covenant on 28 September 1912. This was a document that declared its signatories' opposition to home rule and, more threateningly, their willingness to use all means necessary to prevent the bill's passage. It was signed by 471,414 Ulster men and women amidst great ceremony – the day on which they signed the Covenant became known as Ulster Day and it clearly reflected the extent of opposition in that province to the proposed legislation.

The signing of the Ulster Covenant was a public gesture designed to highlight the scale of discontent and also mobilise public opinion against home rule. On the day itself factories in Belfast closed and special church services were conducted prior to the signing of the document. Throughout the day batches of 500 people were then admitted to the City Hall so that they could sign their names, and the hall itself was not closed until 11.00pm. The hope underlying this event was to dissuade parliament from considering the bill by declaring the mind of the Ulster population – it was an appeal to the Conservative Party and other potential opponents of home rule to consider the wishes of those loyal citizens in Ireland who did not want to be cut adrift from the mainland and left upon the mercy of an Irish Catholic parliament.

SOURCE
11

The Ulster Covenant that was signed by around 500,000 people on 28 September 1912. The covenant was intended as a declaration of Ulster men and women's determination to oppose home rule in Ireland, and it was signed amidst great ceremony on what became known as 'Ulster Day'.

Being convinced in our consciences that Home Rule would be disastrous to the material well-being of Ulster as well as of the whole of Ireland, subversive of our civil and religious freedom, destructive of our citizenship and perilous to the unity of the Empire, we, whose names are underwritten, men of Ulster, loyal subjects of his Gracious Majesty King George V, humbly relying on the God whom our fathers in days of stress and trial confidently trusted, do hereby pledge ourselves in solemn Covenant throughout this our time of threatened calamity to stand by one another in defending for ourselves and our children our cherished position of equal citizenship in the United Kingdom and in using all means which may be found necessary to defeat the present conspiracy to set up a Home Rule Parliament in Ireland. And in the event of such a Parliament being forced upon us we further solemnly and mutually pledge ourselves to refuse to recognise its authority. In sure confidence that God will defend the right we hereto subscribe our names. And further, we individually declare that we have not already signed this Covenant.

The above was signed by me at _____

Ulster Day, Saturday 28th, September, 1912.

God Save the King

The Ulster Volunteer Force and the 'Curragh incident'

In support of the Covenant and to emphasise the determination of the Unionists to prevent home rule, in January 1913 a militia was formed to defend the province. This body of men were formally known as the Ulster Volunteer Force and quickly amassed a membership of more than 90,000 – many of whom were retired British army officers who were able to make the UVF a potent political tool for the unionist leadership in Ulster.

The organisation of a **paramilitary** group to defend the interests of Ulster's Protestant unionist population had echoes of the nationalist Irish Volunteers that had paraded in the 18th century, except this group was set up to prevent home rule rather than demand it. Although the motivation was different, the British authorities was just as determined to prevent a locally organised private army from forcing them into any particular decision and, therefore, took steps to minimise any threat that the volunteers might have posed.

KEY TERM

Paramilitary
A military force organised in the same way as an army, but which does not belong to any nation state.

The first of steps these occurred in March 1914 after the third home rule bill looked set to pass the House of Commons and almost certainly to become law. Anticipating trouble from the unionists, and particularly its Ulster Volunteer Force, the British government contemplated their military options in Ireland should trouble break out. Such was the level of feeling against home rule in Ulster that the prospect of an armed confrontation seemed likely and, in taking steps to organise themselves so vehemently against the measure, it was the unionists who were viewed as the antagonists. The traditional response to any threat within the British Empire was usually to deploy troops. However, before any direct order to that effect could be made, the British army officers garrisoned at Curragh in County Kildare threatened to resign their commissions rather than be used to coerce the unionists to accept home rule. The majority of these officers were themselves of Protestant descent or had Irish family connections, such as General Hugh Gough – the commander of the mutinous garrison, whose mother was from Waterford in the south of the country.

The 'Curragh incident' is significant for several reasons. The first is that it highlighted the depth of feeling that existed towards the unionists' plight – even among the loyal soldiers of the British army. Secondly it gave the unionists greater confidence to challenge the proposed legislation. In the first instance the threat of resignation was brushed over by the war office who issued a document saying that British troops would not be used against the men of Ulster. Although later repudiated by the government, the content of the document was in effect the truth: Britain could not use British troops to subdue the unionists because of the evident sympathies that existed amongst the army on the issue of home rule.

In addition to the clear sympathy that existed for unionism, the confidence that Carson and his Party gained following the incident was fundamental to the growing division that began to develop within Ireland itself. Nationalists had eagerly sought home rule since the union was first established, and now it was a possibility, those opposed to such unity in Ulster threatened to undermine all that they had gained. Buoyed by the support of the army, unionists were able to strengthen their position in April 1914 by taking possession of a cache of firearms shipped in from Germany to a small stretch of coastline at Larne. Known as the Larne gun-running incident, the episode saw the UVF acquire more than 25,000 rifles and three million rounds of ammunition which, although still not enough to arm the entire force, was a significant political victory for the unionists and also reintroduced the gun to Irish politics after years of parliamentary action. Following this event Irish nationalists sought to reinforce their own paramilitary organisation – the Irish Volunteers – and just as war broke out in Europe in July 1914, Ireland looked set for its own armed conflict.

Against this backdrop the third home rule bill was finally passed, receiving royal assent in September 1914. However, it was immediately postponed because of the war. This decision gave Ulster Unionists some comfort but it antagonised many nationalists who felt its postponement was proof positive that Britain never intended to grant home rule.

ACTIVITY
KNOWLEDGE CHECK

Unionist fears

1 Write down a list of reasons why unionists were so afraid of home rule.

2 From this list, decide which reason is most important and explain why you have made this choice.

3 Based on the reasons you have come up with, do you think the methods that unionists employed to prevent home rule were justified?

Changing attitudes and nationalist responses

The sudden shift towards arming men was nothing new in the long course of Irish history. Since the land began to be settled by the English in the 16th century, there had often been violent clashes between the native Irish and the English settlers. This continued as religion grew to be a divisive influence, and it was only in the 18th century that relations began to improve. However, uprisings in 1798, 1803 and 1867 maintained the principles of traditional aggression. Recourse to violent action was, therefore, not a new departure for Ireland. However, given the successes that more peaceful action had won for the country – Catholic emancipation in 1829, the introduction of three home rule bills in 1886, 1893 and 1914 – it is significant that it was re-adopted after 1914.

The unionist motives for the adoption of force have already been considered above (the spectre of home rule encouraged their action), but the nationalist drift to arms was not just mirroring unionist actions and had its origins in a more assertive nationalism that grew after the death of Charles Stewart Parnell.

The emergence of the Sinn Fein Party and growing militancy

In the years after Parnell, nationalist politics drifted as his party struggled with the legacy of his affair with Katherine O'Shea. The split that had ensued did not heal with his death and it was only in 1900 that the party was able to formally unite once more. By this time, however, there had emerged a new political force in Ireland which renounced the idea of home rule in favour of a more radical programme that demanded greater independence. This policy was given a political voice in 1905 by the creation of a new party called Sinn Fein – a Gaelic phrase meaning 'ourselves alone'. The party was organised by a journalist called Arthur Griffith who had the idea that Ireland could be independent of British rule but share the monarch as a figurehead. The manner in which he envisaged this could be achieved was through a more radical policy of obstructionism that the old Irish Parliamentary Party had previously adopted. This involved removing all Irish MPs from Westminster and relocating them to a new parliament in Ireland where they would effectively then carry out a policy of self-sufficiency until Britain conceded defeat.

This separatist approach held a great deal of attraction for younger nationalists who had grown frustrated by the failures of the Irish Parliamentary Party, because it offered a more direct approach that they felt would yield greater reward.

The Easter Rising

The frustration of these individuals meant they increasingly looked to the militancy of earlier nationalist politics. Through the IRB, which had largely recovered following its ill-fated 1867 rising, they sought to capitalise on the growing threat of unionism and use the opportunity to create their own armed force that could further their own agenda. Just as the unionists sought to use the threat of violence to retain the union, the nationalists sought to use force to end it entirely.

During the home rule crisis that emerged in the north of the country between 1912 and 1914, separatist nationalists in the south used the opportunity to strengthen their own paramilitary organisation – the Irish Volunteers – and prepare for a rising themselves. In September 1914, following the postponement of the home rule legislation, the IRB leadership met and agreed that such a rising should take place before the war ended so that they might be able to take advantage of help from Germany and also Britain's more vulnerable position. Responsibility for the preparations was given to a small military council in May 1915, which included Patrick Pearse, Joseph Plunkett,

Sean MacDermott, Eoin Ceannt and Thomas Clarke. Over the course of that year they began planning for an armed insurrection, eventually settling on Easter week 1916 as the best opportunity.

Preparations for the rising did not go smoothly and the British government was aware of a planned uprising after intercepting radio communications between the IRB and Germany. However, it decided not to arrest the suspected leaders until after Easter Monday – by which time the rising had already begun.

SOURCE 12

The Sinn Fein rising as it affected property. A montage of images showing the impact of the Easter Rising in Dublin. It was produced by the British weekly illustrated newspaper, *The Graphic*, on 13 May 1916. *The Graphic* was a supplier of illustrated news items and intended to rival the more famous *Illustrated London News*. It sought to use images in a more vivid manner than its rival and hence this striking montage of Easter week.

THE SINN FEIN RISING AS IT AFFECTED PROPERTY

The damage to property is estimated at £2,000,000. One hundred and seventy-nine buildings were destroyed by flame and shell, the area that suffered most being Lower Sackville Street, where the General Post Office stood. It was the rebels' central stronghold, and was entirely burnt out.

A BARRICADE AT THE FOUR COURTS RESCUING VALUABLES FROM THE SMOKING RUINS A BARRICADE MADE OF MOTORS

FROM THE TOP OF THE NELSON COLUMN: BOTH SIDES OF SACKVILLE STREET, SHOWING THE BURNT-OUT IMPERIAL HOTEL AND POST OFFICE

THE CENTRE OF THE DEVASTATED AREA: A CORNER OF SACKVILLE STREET AND EDEN QUAY, VIEWED FROM O'CONNELL BRIDGE

KEY TERM

Irish Citizen Army
This was a private army organised in 1913 by the Irish Transport and General Workers Union to protect workers who were on strike from the Dublin police force who were quite heavy-handed with them.

The rising took place on 24 April 1916 and involved 1,000 armed Volunteers and around 200 **Irish Citizen Army** personnel who seized prominent buildings around the city of Dublin, including the General Post Office. They then issued a proclamation of independence (see Source 13) that declared Ireland to be a republic under the administration of a nationalist provisional government. Despite the determination of the insurgents Britain was quick to respond to the threat and by 29 April the rising was over. Sixty-four rebels and 132 British personnel had been killed, along with 200 civilians, and there was immense damage to property following the British government's use of artillery to subdue the rising.

SOURCE

13 From the Irish Republican Brotherhood's 'Proclamation of Independence' issued 24 April 1916 in Dublin during the Easter Rising.

IRISHMEN AND IRISHWOMEN: In the name of God and of the dead generations from which she receives her old tradition of nationhood, Ireland, through us, summons her children to her flag and strikes for her freedom.

Having organised and trained her manhood through her secret revolutionary organisation, the Irish Republican Brotherhood, and through her open military organisations, the Irish Volunteers and the Irish Citizen Army, having patiently perfected her discipline, having resolutely waited for the right moment to reveal itself, she now seizes that moment, and, supported by her exiled children in America and by gallant allies in Europe, but relying in the first on her own strength, she strikes in full confidence of victory.

We declare the right of the people of Ireland to the ownership of Ireland, and to the unfettered control of Irish destinies, to be sovereign and indefeasible. The long usurpation of that right by a foreign people and government has not extinguished the right, nor can it ever be extinguished except by the destruction of the Irish people. In every generation the Irish people have asserted their right to national freedom and sovereignty; six times during the last three hundred years they have asserted it to arms. Standing on that fundamental right and again asserting it in arms in the face of the world, we hereby proclaim the Irish Republic as a Sovereign Independent State, and we pledge our lives and the lives of our comrades-in-arms to the cause of its freedom, of its welfare, and of its exaltation among the nations.

The Irish Republic is entitled to, and hereby claims, the allegiance of every Irishman and Irishwoman. The Republic guarantees religious and civil liberty, equal rights and equal opportunities to all its citizens, and declares its resolve to pursue the happiness and prosperity of the whole nation and all of its parts, cherishing all of the children of the nation equally and oblivious of the differences carefully fostered by an alien government, which have divided a minority from the majority in the past...

Although the rising was short-lived, its impact would be felt for years to come – not so much for the event itself but rather the consequences that followed. In the aftermath of the rising the British government sought to make examples of the rebel leaders so as to underline their authority and dissuade further attempts. However, the extent of the brutality which Britain exercised had the opposite effect. Of the 90 men condemned to death only 15 were actually executed. Amongst this number was the IRB's military council, which had orchestrated the rising: Patrick Pearse, Thomas Clarke, Eoin Ceannt, Sean MacDermott and Joseph Plunkett, together with the leader of the Irish Citizen Army, James Connolly. These executions hardened Irish hearts to the British authorities and perhaps did more to alienate Irish minds than anything before it.

The War of Independence/Anglo-Irish War

The legacy of the 1916 rising was that many people in Ireland increasingly became embittered towards British rule. This manifested itself in the 1918 General Election when out of the 105 seats available to Ireland, the Irish Parliamentary Party obtained six, the Unionists 26 and Sinn Fein the majority with 73 seats. This result characterised the elevated desires for separation from Britain among the Irish population, and following its success the Sinn Fein Party organised itself into a new parliament for Ireland called *Dail Eireann* (Gaelic for 'parliament of Ireland'), which then undertook to carry out the policies of obstructionism that Griffith had spoken of years before. This involved essentially ignoring the Westminster parliament and acting as though they were an independent state by bypassing British institutions and listening only to the instruction of the *Dail*. This action was met with anger by unionists in the north and Britain responded by sending troops into the country in 1919 to break up the parliament and assert British authority there. The ensuing conflict became known by Irish nationalists as the War of Independence.

The war is formally acknowledged as beginning when nine Irish Volunteers – since 1918 increasingly referred to as the Irish Republican Army – killed two police officers in Soloheadbeg, County Tipperary on 21 January 1919. This encouraged the deployment of British troops to support the police force in subduing the illegal nationalist parliament and its affiliates. Having become aware of the futility of trying to fight the British conventionally in open battle, the IRA employed **guerrilla warfare**, which played to their strengths, such as local knowledge and significant popular support. In Dublin a special squad was created by Michael Collins (an IRB military leader and elected member of Dail), to deliberately target and kill detectives in the city's police force. This particular strategy drew considerable controversy due to its cold-bloodedness and it led to a protracted war which encouraged the British to use increasingly aggressive tactics, including house searches that left property damaged and also interrogation of Irish citizens, in an attempt to defeat the nationalists.

KEY TERM

Guerrilla warfare
This is a form of military warfare in which private armies or civilian troops employ hit-and-run tactics and ambushes against a larger traditional force.

EXTEND YOUR KNOWLEDGE

Michael Collins (1890–1922)
Born in Clonakilty in County Cork, Michael Collins moved to London in 1906 where he joined the IRB. In 1915, he returned to Ireland and took part in the Easter Rising the following year. He escaped execution and quickly became a leading figure in the nationalist movement in subsequent years, being elected as a Sinn Fein candidate for the Irish parliament, *Dail Eireann*, in 1918. When the War of Independence broke out, he was a military commander in the Irish Volunteers – increasingly called the Irish Republican Army – and organised its intelligence network. Using spies and informants he was able to co-ordinate the assassination of undercover agents in Ireland using a special 'squad' deliberately selected for that purpose. When the truce was signed in July 1921, Collins was one of the negotiators sent to talk with the British government and he was one of the signatories to the Anglo-Irish Treaty. In the ensuing civil war, Collins sided with the newly created Free State against his friend Eamon de Valera who led the anti-treaty forces. He was killed on 20 August 1922 in County Cork during an inspection tour of the southern counties.

Eamon de Valera (1882–1975)
Born in New York but raised in Limerick, de Valera was one of the most pre-eminent Irish nationalist leaders during the fight for, and after, Ireland's independence. He joined the Gaelic League (a cultural group dedicated to the Irish language) in 1908 and the Irish Volunteers in 1913. He played a role in the Easter Rising but was saved from execution because of his American roots. In 1917, he stood as a Sinn Fein candidate in East Clare and won the seat but chose to abstain from sitting in the British parliament as a means of protest. In 1919, he became the first president of *Dail Eireann* (Irish parliament). He refused to attend the Anglo-Irish Treaty negotiations, and later rejected the terms his negotiators Michael Collins and Arthur Griffith had agreed. In the resulting civil war he supported the anti-treaty forces but was arrested in 1923. In 1926, he founded a new political party called *Fianna Fail*. It was with this party that he became prime minister of the new Free State and engineered a new constitution for Ireland in 1937, which saw the country become a republic. In 1959, he became president of Ireland, a job he held until 1973.

The thrust of British power came initially from the police force – the Royal Irish Constabulary. But very quickly it was apparent this force could not contain the IRA attacks and, therefore, the army and two new auxiliary forces were sent to Ireland in 1920. These two new regiments – the Auxiliaries and Black and Tans as they came to be known – operated independently and were intended to reinforce British control; the Auxiliaries as a counter-insurgency unit attached to the RIC, and the Black and Tans as additional military support. However, they were poorly disciplined and their officers allowed them to commit acts of violence against the Irish population in response to IRA attacks. Perhaps the best known of these reprisals was the Croke Park stadium massacre on 21 November 1920, when a detachment of Black and Tans drove an armoured car into the sports field during a football match and fired their weapons into the crowd, killing 14 people. The motivation for this attack had been Michael Collins and his squad's assassination of 14 undercover British army officers (known as the Cairo gang) the same day. Collectively 28 people died, and the day became known as Bloody Sunday.

This approach had a very negative effect upon the country and actually gave the IRA more supporters as the war continued, while at the same time reducing any authority that Britain retained there. In this sense the policy of the Irish nationalists was very effective because it forced the British to realise that their own position in Ireland was increasingly untenable. By the summer of 1921, 405 policemen, 150 military and 750 IRA and civilians had lost their lives in the conflict.

With the casualty rate escalating, public opinion demanded a truce, which was agreed in July 1921. Then, in December, after months of negotiations, a treaty was agreed by both sides.

The Government of Ireland Act 1920 and Partition

After 1918 the postponed Home Rule Act was reconsidered since the war had ended. The Liberal prime minister David Lloyd George was committed to the principle and in 1919 his government sought to carry through the measure which had been passed five years earlier. During this period of postponement, however, the political landscape had changed significantly and the Irish Parliamentary Party, with whom the Liberals had agreed home rule, was now a small minority with most Irish votes going either to the Unionist Party or Sinn Fein. This development created a difficult situation since unionists were against home rule, and Sinn Fein had abandoned Westminster and established its own parliament in Dublin.

The principal outcome of this new situation was that the unionists were the largest Irish representative body in Westminster and, therefore, would need to be carefully considered in any decision that was to be taken. Responsibility for arranging the basis of home rule was given to Walter Long, an ex-Ulster Unionist Party leader, who recommended that if home rule had to be granted then it should be on the basis of two separate parliaments: one for the south and one for the north, so as to reflect and consider the wishes of each region. The suggestion was adopted as a workable solution to an otherwise difficult question that had been unanswered since 1886, and on 23 December 1920 it passed a vote in parliament and subsequently became law as the Government of Ireland Act.

Unionists all voted against the bill because they preferred Ulster to remain part of Britain and felt the measure was a poor alternative. As a compromise, it perhaps offered the best opportunity for settling the issue of Ireland. However, it arguably came too late as events in Ireland had overtaken the issue of home rule: Irish nationalists in the 26 counties in the south now sought independence and, when the Act came into force, they were waging a war against the British government such that home rule could not be implemented there. In Ulster, a northern Irish parliament was convened after elections in 1921, and a strong unionist government was installed led by James Craig (the new Unionist Party leader after Edward Carson stepped down following the passage of the Act).

Anglo-Irish Treaty, 1921

With Ulster settling into a new political future under a Unionist government, the south of Ireland was still trying to find a solution to the conflict it had been engaged in. The agreement that was reached on 6 December 1921 was a compromise. It did not grant Irish nationalists the independence they sought but rather, as Michael Collins put it, 'the freedom to achieve freedom'. Britain conceded **dominion status** to the 26 counties in the south and this meant that they could act with greater autonomy that would pave the way for independence in the future. In agreeing these terms, the Irish negotiators were aware that many of their colleagues would baulk at the limitations of the offer, particularly the continued link with Britain and, more significantly, the partition of the island. After unionists refused to agree to the terms, Ulster was allowed its own governing institutions rather than being forced to be part of a new Irish state.

KEY TERM

Dominion status
This is recognition as an autonomous community within the British Empire of equal status to Britain itself.

Although falling far short of what nationalists had hoped to achieve, the nationalist negotiators, who included both Arthur Griffith and Michael Collins, felt the terms offered the means to achieve independence. Once the British prime minister, David Lloyd George, also conceded fiscal autonomy (control over their own money) the Irish negotiators felt the deal was a good one.

Despite the possibilities the treaty offered, it was rejected by the other Sinn Fein leaders, including Eamon de Valera, the president of *Dail Eireann*, because it contained an oath of allegiance that they felt continued to subordinate Ireland to Britain. Following intense debate in the Dail, the treaty was ratified by a slender majority of 64 to 57 and on 7 January 1922 it was formally accepted.

Civil War

SOURCE 14
The bombardment of the Four Courts in Dublin by the Free State forces, which marked the start of the civil war on 28 June 1922. The shelling was an attempt to remove Irish Republican Army personnel who had occupied the building.

The outcome of the vote was met with public acclaim in the south of Ireland, but it did nothing to reduce the opposition of those Sinn Fein and IRA nationalists who felt the treaty was inadequate. Unable to reconcile themselves to the legislation, within six months of its passage, these men – under the command of Liam Lynch, a local IRA commander from County Cork – organised themselves into an anti-treaty armed force that planned to overthrow the new Irish government which had been elected. In arming and placing themselves against the treaty these hard-line nationalists forced Ireland into civil war. Over the next year the country witnessed further bloodshed as the infant Irish government tried to assert its authority over this new threat it faced.

Civil war officially began on 28 June 1922 when government troops attacked the anti-treaty force's headquarters in Dublin. Such was the disorganisation of the anti-treaty Irregulars, as they became known, that they did not perform effectively in open battle and, therefore, they were easily subdued in the city by the better-trained government troops. Reverting to the same guerrilla tactics as they used in the War of Independence, the Irregulars were more effective in the countryside. However, by December they were all but defeated after the government introduced

internment and the death penalty for anyone found with weapons. This authoritative approach quickly reduced any support that still existed for the Irregulars When Liam Lynch died in April 1923, his replacement, Frank Aiken, called a ceasefire at the end of that month and then ordered the IRA to lay down its arms on 24 May 1923. The civil war was over.

In 1920, home rule was granted and Irish nationalists finally achieved the autonomy that they had desired since the union began in 1801. After more than 100 years of parliamentary and military pressure they were able to distance themselves from Britain – a country that had been such a prominent feature in the history of their nation. However, this achievement was very different from that which they had anticipated. Rather than a united nation, Ireland was divided, regionally and, for a time, also by civil war. The cause of this development was not simply religion since, periodically throughout 1774–1923, it was clear that Protestants and Catholics could work together. The United Irishmen and Young Ireland movements each exemplified this possibility. Compounding the religious differences was also a growing sense of different identities. The majority Protestant population in the north, notably the province of Ulster, positioned itself very definitely with Britain, while the southern provinces maintained a greater sense of Irish identity. With the growing success of nationalism and the prospect of greater Irish power, these differences began to become more apparent. As a minority within the country of Ireland, Protestant unionists feared that their religion and identity would be overwhelmed by a Catholic Irish government. For their part, Irish nationalists became discontented with the idea of home rule and sought independence – a desire that brought them into direct conflict with their own movement. After 1923 peace was finally achieved, bringing an end to a politically volatile period in Irish history.

> **KEY TERM**
>
> **Internment**
> Detaining people who are perceived to be a threat during wartime.

ACTIVITY
KNOWLEDGE CHECK

The road to civil war

Using the material you have read and your own knowledge, explain why you think civil war took place after the acceptance of the Anglo-Irish Treaty in 1922.

ACTIVITY
SUMMARY

Growing Irish radicalism

1 Write down a list of Irish nationalist actions that took place over the period 1774–1923.

2 Create a line graph where the x axis represents the time frame 1774–1923 and the y axis is a scale of radicalism from 1 to 10.

3 Plot each event you have listed according to how radical you feel it was.

4 Look at your graph and explain any observations you have about the nature of Irish action over the course of the period.

 WIDER READING

Collier, M. *Britain and Ireland, 1867–1922*, Pearson (2008)

Harkness, D. *Ireland in the Twentieth Century: Divided Island*, Macmillan (1996)

Laffan, M. *The Resurrection of Ireland: The Sinn Fein Party 1916–1923*, Cambridge University Press (1999)

Moody, T.W. and Martin, F.X. (eds), *The Course of Irish History*, Mercier Press (1994)

Newsinger, J. *Fenianism in Mid-Victorian Britain*, Pluto Press (1994)

Pearce, R. and Adelman, P. *Great Britain and the Irish Question c1774–1922*, Hodder Education (2016)

Pelling, N. *Anglo-Irish Relations 1798–1922*, Routledge (2003)

3.2 British reaction: from resistance to acceptance

KEY QUESTIONS

- How successful were Britain's efforts to maintain control of Ireland before 1885?
- What motivated the decision to consider home rule between 1885 and 1922?
- How important were the attitudes of Britain's prime ministers and politicians to the question of increasing Irish independence?

INTRODUCTION

The growing demand in Ireland for greater autonomy was an issue that the British government was initially very reluctant to even consider. The country was seen as a crucial part of Britain's imperial identity, and to even think about extending greater power to the island was generally felt amongst the political classes, especially in the 18th century, as tantamount to dismantling the empire. Amongst Conservatives especially, the idea was distasteful and not even to be given any thought. More liberal politicians recognised the need to be more accommodating in order to prevent any potential aggression that might threaten British interests in Ireland. In terms of policy, therefore, there was an attempt at moderate change both with regard to promoting reform and also to avoid encouraging greater discontent.

Over the course of the late 18th and the 19th centuries, new politicians had new solutions to what they often referred to as the 'Irish question'. In part, this was a natural development of modern thought, but it also reflected the growing determination of the Irish people and the impact that this determination might have upon Britain itself. This attitude was enhanced in 1801 when Ireland was bound more tightly to Britain through the Act of Union. This raised opposition amongst the indigenous Irish and forced Britain's politicians to consider reform. The notable reforms were the passage of Catholic emancipation in 1829 and then after 1884, when the right to vote was extended to more of the working classes, and in 1885, when parliamentary seats were redistributed. Following these changes, there was a greater political imperative to reconsider Ireland's position as more Irishmen could vote and gain influential seats in the Westminster parliament. This political motivation, along with periodic bouts of aggressive nationalist fever, was an important consideration for later politicians – especially those such as William Gladstone and David Lloyd George who recognised the importance of the changed political landscape.

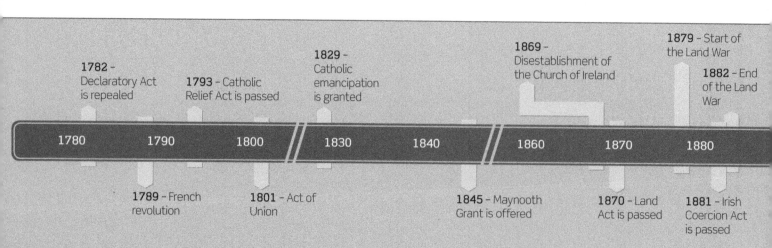

1782 – Declaratory Act is repealed

1793 – Catholic Relief Act is passed

1829 – Catholic emancipation is granted

1869 – Disestablishment of the Church of Ireland

1879 – Start of the Land War

1882 – End of the Land War

1780 1790 1800 1830 1840 1860 1870 1880

1789 – French revolution

1801 – Act of Union

1845 – Maynooth Grant is offered

1870 – Land Act is passed

1881 – Irish Coercion Act is passed

HOW SUCCESSFUL WERE BRITAIN'S EFFORTS TO MAINTAIN CONTROL OF IRELAND BEFORE 1885?

Reasons for changing approaches to the government of Ireland

Ireland had always raised difficult questions for British politicians. This was partly because the land had been settled through conflict and such methods often produce friction, but also because the majority of the population followed a different Church to that of Britain. In Ireland 80 percent of the population was Catholic, while in Britain the majority was Protestant. This in itself was not necessarily problematic. However, over the course of Britain's relationship with Ireland before 1774, religious attitudes and official policies encouraged a divide that fostered a lingering sense of injustice amongst the Irish, especially Catholics, which successive governments would have to contend with.

Not least among the sources of discontent was the established Church of Ireland, which was Anglican and the official Church rather than the majority Catholic one. The promotion of this Church was part of the broader Protestant ascendancy which gave that faith and its membership more favourable opportunities than the majority Catholic population – for example, Catholics were not able to stand for seats in the Irish parliament. This Church reflected the reality that many Catholics felt to be true – that they were outsiders within their own country. Discrimination and alienation were feelings that promoted ongoing discontent among the wider Irish community. After 1774, this became a significant feature of Anglo-Irish relations – not least because of the aggressive methods that Irish nationalists, and later unionists, adopted to achieve their goals.

The Irish parliament gains greater legislative powers

The manner of British response to Irish disaffection varied throughout the period and often reflected other considerations at the time. In the late 18th century, the greatest direct threat to Britain was the American war, which began in 1776 and was fought to gain American independence from British rule. The significance of the conflict with regard to Ireland lies in the sympathies that Irish people, specifically Protestant Irish MPs desirous of greater political power for the Dublin parliament, had for the American patriots – these men were effectively fighting for the same principles that the Irish harboured. Given the parallels between the American and Irish positions, the British government was keenly aware of the potential for further trouble in Ireland. The subsequent defeat of British forces in America in 1783 only sharpened this awareness and left Britain seeking a way to mitigate the loss of one of its most important colonies and prevent further imperial losses.

It is from this position of damage limitation that Britain's policy in Ireland in the 1780s can be considered. The replacement of the Tory administration under Lord North in 1782 saw a replacement Whig government that was anxious to soothe Irish opinion. During the war this opinion had started to demand the removal of legislative restrictions upon the Irish parliament that had been imposed by **Poynings' Law**. This had encouraged an Act of Parliament declaring all Irish parliamentary decisions to be subject to the approval of the British parliament. The result was effectively British control of Irish legislation, a fact that was formalised in 1720 by the Declaratory Act which gave Britain direct legislative powers. The initial cause of this demand had been the reduction in trade because of war and the clear preference that British policy gave to British businessmen at the expense of the Irish.

> **KEY TERM**
>
> **Poynings' Law**
> An Act of Parliament passed in 1494 and encouraged by the Lord Deputy of Ireland Sir Edward Poynings. It declared all of the Irish parliament's legislation to require the approval of the British parliament.

Although the immediate issue of trade was resolved in favour Ireland in 1779, when restrictions on Irish traders were abolished, the episode had encouraged a broader demand for political freedom for the Irish parliament. It was this demand that the new Whig government was keen to address in the wake of the American defeat.

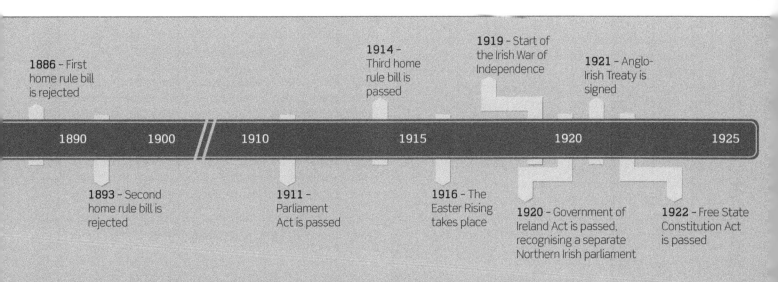

1886 – First home rule bill is rejected

1893 – Second home rule bill is rejected

1911 – Parliament Act is passed

1914 – Third home rule bill is passed

1916 – The Easter Rising takes place

1919 – Start of the Irish War of Independence

1920 – Government of Ireland Act is passed, recognising a separate Northern Irish parliament

1921 – Anglo-Irish Treaty is signed

1922 – Free State Constitution Act is passed

1890   1900   1910   1915   1920   1925

The solution was to repeal the Declaratory Act and significantly modify Poynings law in 1782 so as to leave Britain with only the power of veto. In addition, Ireland was granted its own Mutiny Act, which gave it greater control over the armed forces in the country. By granting these powers the Whigs were hopeful of diffusing the growing demand for reform so that Britain could still retain Ireland within the empire. The immediate consequence of the action was to reduce Irish demands and restore a sense of order to the country.

The Catholic Relief Act 1793

The reforms made in the early 1780s were concessions from the British government to a country that had begun to demand changes. They were made at a time when Britain was vulnerable – the loss of America was a blow to both confidence and pride and, as a result, there was a strong degree of willingness among British politicians to concede reform rather than risk losing another colony. In this sense, British policy was often directed by fears of greater consequences rather than a principled wish to improve the experiences of those in Ireland.

This was particularly apparent less than ten years later when Ireland once more sought greater powers after finding new inspiration in the French revolution, which began in 1789. The growth of the subsequent United Irishmen organisation and the efforts of the **Catholic Committee** in seeking redress of the **Penal Laws** raised the issue of reform again, and on this occasion the British government was willing to conciliate.

KEY TERMS

Catholic Committee
An organisation of Catholic gentry created in 1756. These men want to raise their standing in Ireland by supporting the Hanoverian British monarchy despite originally supporting a Stuart succession.

Penal Laws
These were a series of laws passed in 1695 against Catholics. They included measures such as a ban on holding public office and inheriting Protestant lands, and were designed to promote the Church of Ireland.

The Catholic Committee sent a delegation to London in 1793 to speak directly to the prime minister, William Pitt the Younger, about reforming the anti-Catholic Penal Laws. The Committee's requests had been opposed by the Lord Chancellor of Ireland, John Fitzgibbon, who felt that any changes to the Protestant Ascendancy would ultimately result in Britain's relationship with Ireland being severed. Despite this opposition, however, Pitt and his administration were once again content to calm Irish sentiment. They encouraged the Irish parliament – technically autonomous but in reality under British influence – to pass the Relief Act in 1793, removing the majority of barriers to Catholics except the right to hold public office. The motivation behind this action was arguably inspired by an impending war with the new French Republic and the wish to first call upon Irish troops to support this campaign, and second to avoid making Irish Catholics a potential ally for France. Given these considerations it is reasonable to suggest that British policy towards Ireland was dictated largely by external circumstances rather than popular sympathy. Whether the same

decisions would have been made had the British been victorious in America and war with France did not take place is only open to speculation. Certainly there was sufficient doubt amongst British politicians towards granting reforms to suggest that when Britain felt in a stronger position it would not concede powers so readily.

The Act of Union, 1801

The Catholic Relief Act was not intended to further the political fortunes of Ireland, and British sympathy towards such an idea was quickly dispelled by the end of the century. The growth of the United Irishmen movement after 1791 resulted in an attempted uprising in 1798 in the hope that while Britain was engaged in war with France, Ireland might be able to secure its independence using French support against Britain. The attempt emerged after Irish nationalists grew more impatient and sought to break Britain's grip on Ireland by force of arms. The attempt was a failure and the outcome was devastating for Irish nationalists. Rather than independence Ireland was bound even more tightly to Britain through an Act of Union which came into effect in 1801. Under this legislation the Irish parliament was removed and the British parliament took direct control of Irish affairs, although Irish representatives were permitted 100 seats in that legislative body.

In one sense the Act of Union can be seen as a response to the manner in which demands were made to the British government. The actions of the Volunteers and Catholic Committee were reasonably moderate. However, the United Irishmen's attempted uprising was an attempt to encourage revolution. In this sense it is possible to suggest that British politicians were reacting to a direct threat using more determined action. This idea has merit and is also supported by the strengthened position that Britain found itself in after 1798. War with France was temporarily coming to an end. Just as the union was receiving the royal assent, Cornwallis was negotiating a peace in France, which eventually became the Treaty of Amiens in 1802, and Britain was consequently better placed to take a stronger stand. Implicit within this line of argument is the idea that the empire remained fundamental to British identity and that, when faced with a direct challenge, the British government would respond in a decisive way to maintain the existing order of things.

As part of this analysis, the union also evidences Britain's determination to maintain a strong Anglo-Irish relationship despite growing opposition in Ireland itself. In this sense the uprising by the United Irishmen can be seen as a jolt to the British system. It was an event that forced Britain to consider the place Ireland occupied within the empire, and also to accept that the issues present there needed addressing in a more permanent manner; minor reforms would not be enough. In this vein, such was the level of Catholic expectation that William Pitt had also been willing to amend the oath of supremacy (see page 76), which precluded Catholics holding public office. His intention was to bridge enmity within Ireland. However, George III felt this was a step too far and objected to the measure. Pitt resigned his office in March 1801, having been unable to fulfil his pledge to the Irish people.

Within the arguments surrounding the passage of the Act of Union there runs a clear theme of conservative, imperialist, thought.

Despite evident growing opposition (i.e. the rebellion and also the Irish Volunteers' earlier efforts (Chapter 1) that highlighted desires for changes even from Protestant landowners) Ireland was not to be lost and all measures necessary were to be taken to secure it. In this sense British opinion reflected a reasonably short-sighted way of thinking, and certainly a belief that Ireland was better off under British rule. Despite expectations among the political establishment that bringing them under direct rule might calm Irish spirits, the Act of Union actually encouraged further discontent. In binding them more closely to Britain, the extent of this discontent was more starkly highlighted.

SOURCE

1 From the Act of Union between Britain and Ireland, passed 1 January 1801. This Act was passed because of the 1798 rebellion and recognition by William Pitt that Ireland needed to be managed more effectively. By uniting the two countries, he anticipated that greater investment and mutual opportunity would placate the Irish and improve relations.

Article First

That Great Britain and Ireland shall upon Jan. 1, 1801, be united into one kingdom; and that the titles appertaining to the crown, &c. shall be such as his Majesty shall be pleased to appoint.

Article Second

That the succession to the crown shall continue limited and settled as at present.

Article Third

That the United Kingdom be represented in one Parliament.

Article Fourth

†That such Act as shall be passed in Ireland to regulate the mode of summoning and returning the lords and commoners to serve in the united Parliament of the United Kingdom, shall be considered as part of the treaty of union.

†That any peer of Ireland may be elected to serve in the House of Commons of the United Kingdom, unless previously elected to sit in the House of Lords, but shall not be entitled to the privilege of peerage, etc.

His Majesty may create peers, and make promotions in the peerage of Ireland after the union, under certain regulations. Peerages in abeyance to be deemed existing peerages, and no peerage to be deemed extinct but on default of claim for a year after the death of the late possessor. If a claim be after that period made and allowed, and a new creation shall have taken place in the interval, no new right of creation shall accrue to his Majesty on the next extinction of a peerage.

Questions touching the election of members to sit in the House of Commons of the United Kingdom on the part of Ireland shall be decided as questions touching such elections in Great Britain.

When his Majesty shall declare his pleasure for holding a Parliament of the United Kingdom, a proclamation shall issue to cause the lords and commons, who are to serve on the part of Ireland to be returned as shall be provided by any Act of the present session in Ireland.

†The lords of Parliament on the part of Ireland shall have the same privileges as the lords on the part of Great Britain, and all lords spiritual of Ireland shall have rank next after the lords spiritual of the same rank of Great Britain, and shall enjoy the same privileges (except those depending upon sitting in the House of Lords)

ACTIVITY
KNOWLEDGE CHECK

Union with Ireland

1 What do you feel was the main motivation governing the reforms Britain offered to Ireland before 1801?

2 In your opinion, why did Britain pass the Act of Union in 1801?

The Maynooth Grant, 1845

The Act of Union was intended to subdue Irish discontent by bringing them more formally into a union with Britain, whereby they would enjoy the same privileges as British citizens. Additionally it was expected that the position of the Protestant minority in Ireland would be strengthened as part of a Protestant majority in the United Kingdom. By taking these steps the governing classes in Ireland would be better placed to maintain order and therefore be able to promote greater stability. Despite these intentions, however, the union actually generated greater discontent on both sides of the Irish Sea. The growth of nationalism has been considered earlier, but in Britain there was also ill-feeling towards the legislation. In particular, anti-Catholic sentiment was common in the country, and this blended with broader, negative, racial attitudes towards the Irish generally. In 1780, London had been the scene of the Gordon Riots – violent anti-Catholic protests following the proposal to reduce Catholic discrimination laws – and by forging a formal union with Ireland, the Act had pricked anti-Catholic sentiment once more by bringing them more closely into the British fold. Although no protest took place, this sentiment remained a source of resentment among many of the English, and it was unintentionally stirred in the mid-century by the prime minister Robert Peel.

Following his government's opposition to the repeal movement of Daniel O'Connell, Peel sought to improve the relationship between Protestants and Catholics in Britain and Ireland by making concessions that might reduce the simmering tensions that the Repeal Association had generated. The manner of these concessions included what became known as the Maynooth Grant, which proposed to increase government spending on a Catholic **seminary** that had been created in 1795. It was called the Royal College of St Patrick and was established at Maynooth in Ireland, funded by a grant paid for, first, by the Irish parliament and, after the Act of Union, by Britain. This sum was initially £8,000, but in 1845 Robert Peel proposed to increase this figure to £26,000 together with a £30,000 sum to help pay for repairs to the building. By increasing government funding, Peel hoped to extend a goodwill gesture to Ireland following his government's recent opposition regarding repeal of the union (banning a meeting to be held at Clontarf in 1843). In doing so, he also hoped to detach moderate Catholics from the repeal movement itself.

KEY TERM

Seminary
A training college for priests.

Although intended to promote relations and diffuse a political challenge, the issue of the grant actually generated considerable ill-feeling within Britain and amongst the Protestant communities.

SOURCE 2

Great Meeting at the London Tavern to oppose the increased grant to Maynooth. An engraving from the *Illustrated London News,* 19 April 1845.

The basis for the ill-feeling was a general anti-Catholic attitude that existed within Britain and among Conservatives especially. Indeed, within his own party Peel faced considerable opposition to his measure, with critics citing the dangers that existed for Britain, a Protestant state, financing a Catholic school. Among the most vocal of his critics was the Conservative MP for East Kent,

John Plumptre, who felt that extending the grant would encourage greater demands from Catholics, and even threaten the security of the state.

SOURCE
3
From an address given by John Plumptre MP, 10 March 1845 to a public meeting in London encouraging Protestant opposition to the Maynooth Grant.

The step was taken, and other privileges have since been granted; and now the Established Church is the "monster evil" of Ireland, which must be removed; and it is too plain that no arrangements will be satisfactory which do not leave the Church of Rome supreme and dominant. The power and influence, which by various provisions have been conferred on the Roman Catholics, instead of making them tranquil and grateful subjects of the United Empire, have been, and still are, employed for the advancement of their further objects; — and, being emboldened by what they have already obtained, they tell you plainly, they will not be satisfied, if this and that object of their desires be withheld from them.

Brother Protestants, — Are you acquainted with the character of the books which are used at the College of Maynooth?... I am acquainted with the contents of some of these books; and I declare to you, that many of the doctrines inculcated from them into the minds of the students for the Roman Catholic priesthood, whom you are liberally to support, are such as all honest and sincere Christians would shudder at. I affirm to you, that, under the direction of such doctrines, if circumstances might allow a practical appeal to them, our Protestant monarch would not be safe upon her throne; the liberty, the property, the lives of our Protestant fellow-countrymen would not be secure.

And you are to contribute to the training up of priests, who are to be taught out of these books, and who will disseminate what they learn through the length and breadth of the sister island!... I ask you, will you yield to this, without the energetic and uncompromising use of all legitimate and constitutional means to avert the disgrace; the danger, the sin, that are threatening to befall your Country? Will you not pour your Petitions into Parliament from every city and borough, from every village and hamlet, from every congregation loving Protestant truth?

In England, the opposition was led by Conservatives such as Plumptre and also 'Voluntaryists', who were individuals who opposed any form of government grant-giving to private institutions. In Ireland, the opposition was led by the **Orange Order** and together they raised significant protest against the bill. However, when parliament came to vote on it, the measure passed 323 to 176.

KEY TERM

Orange Order
A Protestant political organisation set up in 1795 to maintain the memory of William III's victory at the Battle of the Boyne in 1691 which saw the beginning of the 'Protestant ascendancy'. As an institution it promotes and guards the interests of Protestants in Ireland.

That the measure was so controversial among certain quarters, even of Peel's own party, and yet was passed by a reasonable majority suggests that his motives and methods were ultimately accepted. Given that the motivation came almost immediately after a growth in Irish demands for repeal, the offer of the grant can be seen as a concession designed to calm Irish spirits that appeared to be encouraging greater agitation. In this manner, the grant was perhaps recognised as an easy way to rehabilitate

Anglo-Irish relations following the Repeal Association's activities and the consequent government opposition, which had been evidenced by the banning of the Clontarf meeting in 1843. By taking quick steps to reduce the impact of this opposition, Peel sought to demonstrate his government's benevolence in the hope that perhaps moderate Catholics would recognise these qualities and choose to work with the government rather than against it. In this sense, the grant was less about funding a Catholic seminary and more about securing a better reputation with the moderate Irish classes, winning influential friends in Ireland who might therefore promote support for the British parliament rather than push for the return of a Dublin-based one.

British attempts to maintain control over Ireland after 1840 met with very challenging events. Most notable was the onset of famine in the mid-1840s (see page 108 onwards) and then the growth of a more organised radical and aggressive nationalism in the form of the Irish Republican Brotherhood (IRB), or 'Fenians' as they became more commonly known (see page 21). These events presented very significant difficulties for Britain in terms of its management of Ireland – especially the famine. They gave nationalists the opportunity to construct effective rhetoric with which to attack the British state and win popular appeal amongst Irish men and women in the pursuit of their intended goal of political freedom. Indeed, the perceived failures of Britain to adequately provide for Ireland during the famine years directly inspired nationalist action in the form of the Young Ireland uprising in 1848 (see page 20). This itself inspired the creation of the IRB ten years later, when supporters from the Young Ireland movement were able to return to Ireland, bringing with them new ideas for revolutionary organisation from abroad, where they had endured self-induced exile. During their hiatus, Ireland's relationship with Britain had quietened down following mutual prosperity in the 1850s and 1860s. This saw the income of farmers rise by two-thirds that of 1854, as high food prices and a reduced population promoted individual economic benefits. Upon the formation of the IRB, however, nationalism was pushed to the forefront once more. Following a series of attacks – most famously the Fenian rising in 1867 (see page 22) – the British government, particularly under the administration of William Gladstone after 1868, became more determined to seek a solution to the ongoing 'Irish question' that would bring about a more lasting and positive relationship between the two countries (see page 45).

The Irish Coercion Act 1881

Since Ireland came into the union, there had grown a greater political awareness amongst MPs of the issues that affected the people who lived there. Principally, the union had been about maintaining control over the country, but with a much closer connection, Britain became more responsible for the problems that developed there. Towards the end of the 1870s, a sense of this responsibility became more obvious as Irish people raised resistance to a long-rooted problem that had existed in Ireland but which had never been appreciably dealt with – the system of landownership and rents. In seeking to address this problem, the British government showed a greater awareness of Irish needs but also a continued determination to maintain order and control over the country.

With the exception of Belfast and Dublin, the majority of Ireland's income came from farming the land, and a significant proportion of the country's population were either **tenant farmers** or labourers on other people's farms. In part, the reason for this was the high percentage of Catholics who did not own their own land as a result of the Penal Laws that denied them the same opportunities as Irish Protestants. The consequence was that most Catholic farmers simply rented their land from larger, usually Protestant, landowners.

> **KEY TERM**
>
> Tenant farmer
> A person who rents the land that they farm.

In 1879, protests began to take place amongst tenant farmers in opposition to the cost of rents, and there was a demand for their reduction following a particularly poor winter and general decline in agricultural income as a result. Protest began in County Mayo and quickly spread throughout the southern provinces and into Ulster by 1880. The extent of discontent was the result of economic distress coupled with a general feeling of resentment among Catholic farmers towards the system of landownership that allowed Protestants greater control over the land and also the right to set their own rent prices, which they felt was at their expense. Between 1879 and 1882, this agitation was known as the Land War and was co-ordinated by the Land League – an organisation that was deliberately created to give direction to what became one of the largest mass-movements in Irish history.

Given the extent of the Land War, the 1880 General Election was fought in Ireland on the land issue. As a result, the Irish Parliamentary Party won 63 of the 100 seats available to the country. This gave the Irish an influential voice in the new British parliament which saw a Liberal government formed under William Gladstone. The victory Parnell and his party achieved encouraged Gladstone's government to consider the land question since it was clearly an issue of significant importance to the Irish and also to the political and economic stability of the country.

The solution that Gladstone sought was, like Peel and the Maynooth Grant, an act of conciliation designed to reduce the immediate dangers perceived in Ireland. Privately he worked on a new Land Bill that would address the inequalities that Irish people experienced. In part, his motivation was moral as he felt it was right to address the question of inequality in Ireland. But also it could be suggested that growing parliamentary influence for the Irish Party encouraged a softer approach than simply using force against the protests. In the immediate term, however, the actions of the Land League in encouraging the **ostracism** of rent collection agents raised the level of tension in Ireland. Despite reluctance, the prime minister was forced to support a measure that increased the powers of coercion so as to bring order to the

> **KEY TERM**
>
> Ostracism
> The act of deliberately isolating and ignoring.

situation. Many of his own Cabinet – including the Secretary for Ireland, William Edward Forster, who had attempted to introduce temporary legislation to support Ireland while the Land Bill was being prepared – believed this was getting out of control.

The measure that was introduced in January 1881 was officially titled the Protection of Person and Property Act. However, it is often referred to as simply the Coercion Act. It allowed the authorities in Ireland to arrest and detain, without the need for evidence or a trial, anyone they felt was committing an offence. Under this legislation hundreds of people were charged – including the leader of the Land League, Michael Davitt.

The introduction of this legislation was not entirely new. Coercion Acts had been passed before, but the legislation of 1881 was introduced reluctantly. Rather than use force, the British government was looking at conciliation measures. But it was driven to passing coercive measures because of Irish action and also the failure of the House of Lords to pass the compensations for disturbance bill – a temporary measure intended to reduce suffering in Ireland, but rejected because of its potential impact for landlords. In this sense the Coercion Act can be seen as a reluctant last resort rather than a first response, a shift which marked a more sympathetic attitude from Britain towards problems in Ireland.

SOURCE 4

From the *South Australian Register* in Adelaide, 14 March 1881, reporting on the passage of the Irish Coercion Act.

The number of offenses committed last year was enormously greater than in any previous year since the great famine, – and two thirds of the whole were perpetrated during the last three months of it. The rapid growth thus made evident furnishes a strong appeal for instant and vigorous action, and the further fact that redress is unattainable in the ordinary way renders it still more emphatic. During the three months ending with last January there were 2,590 agrarian offences...

By the substitution of the unwritten law of the League for the law of the land, and by the agencies employed to enforce the dictates of illegal authority, an absolute reign of terror had been introduced. Every interest in the country was affected and endangered. Shopkeepers were unable to issue processes against their debtors, and in all ways the law-abiding inhabitants were made to suffer. As Sir. Forster put it, those who defied the law were safe, while those who kept it were in danger...

The Chief Secretary for Ireland himself manifested the utmost repugnance to the duty he felt himself compelled to discharge, and the House was as sad as it was stern in dealing with the measure. Delay is more excusable than precipitancy. The Government had reason to hope that the announcement of their determination, which was made with all gravity last November, would have produced a salutary effect, and there is some justification for their waiting until all ordinary means of treating the cancer were exhausted before resorting to special legislation. The other objection is that remedial measures ought to have priority over those of coercion, but this view is clearly untenable. A Land Reform Bill is promised, but while there is incipient Fenian rebellion and pronounced agrarian revolt to be dealt with [and] they must first be disposed of...

WHAT MOTIVATED THE DECISION TO CONSIDER HOME RULE BETWEEN 1885 AND 1922?

Gladstone's conversion to home rule, 1885

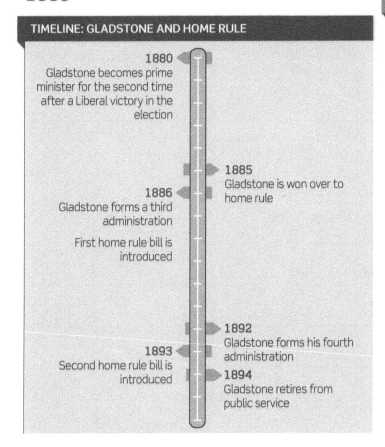

TIMELINE: GLADSTONE AND HOME RULE

1880
Gladstone becomes prime minister for the second time after a Liberal victory in the election

1885
Gladstone is won over to home rule

1886
Gladstone forms a third administration

First home rule bill is introduced

1892
Gladstone forms his fourth administration

1893
Second home rule bill is introduced

1894
Gladstone retires from public service

The attempts by Gladstone to address the issue of land reform in Ireland were the start of his final effort to settle the Irish question. After 1885 he adopted the cause of home rule for Ireland and this objective remained his primary focus for the duration of his political life.

Since his first administration in 1868, Gladstone had been interested in the Irish question and had determined to improve the relationship between the two nations following the Clerkenwell bombing in that year. His interest in home rule particularly grew in 1885 when he came to believe that it was a just and fair way to address the issue of political power in Ireland after the increasing demands made by the nationalists. His belief was cemented later that year following the electoral success of the Irish Parliamentary Party which had, since 1870, been seeking to achieve that policy. The victory enjoyed by Parnell and his party reinforced Gladstone's own belief in the morality of pursuing home rule on the grounds that clearly the nation had spoken in that election and elected Irish nationalists wherever they were able to. On this basis Gladstone had two good reasons to support the measure. Firstly, his own sense of morality told him that the Irish people had been quite definitive with their vote, selecting 86 nationalist candidates from the 103 Irish seats available. Secondly, with the 86 Irish Parliamentary Party seats, there was also a political motivation to support home rule. In this case the Irish Parliamentary Party held the balance of power in the Westminster parliament since the Liberals failed to win an outright majority.

EXTEND YOUR KNOWLEDGE

Clerkenwell Prison bombing, December 1867
To support the Fenian uprising, Richard Burke had been employed in November 1867 to acquire weapons from Birmingham, but he had been arrested while trying to do so and imprisoned in Clerkenwell. In December his Fenian colleagues, including Michael Barrett, who would later be the last person publicly hanged in Britain for his part in the attempt, sought to rescue him by blowing down the prison door using gunpowder hidden in a wheelbarrow. The explosion killed 12 people and injured 120 others.

Consequently, it is fair to suggest that despite Gladstone's personal belief that home rule was right, it is reasonable to suggest that it was also necessary for the Liberal government to operate effectively. In this analysis, it is worth noting that British politicians had begun to accept that further reforms to Ireland would be necessary. The union of 1801, by granting Irish seats in Westminster, had presented Ireland with a way to influence British politics as much as it allowed Britain to influence Irish affairs.

The first and second home rule bills

The first attempt at legislation came in 1886 and offered a **devolved** Irish parliament which would recognise Ireland's claim to nationhood and also renounce Britain's right to legislate for Irish affairs, with the exception of defence, trade, coinage and foreign treaties. Under this proposal the daily business of administration would be conducted by a Lord Lieutenant of Ireland who would be the monarch's representative and not accountable to the Irish parliament. In this sense it was effectively a return to the same political arrangement that existed before the Act of Union in 1801.

KEY TERM

Devolved
To have transferred power to a lower level.

The Irish Parliamentary Party agreed to the proposal in principle and, although it wanted more from the bill, saw it as a starting point for negotiation. The Conservative Party, however, saw the bill as a betrayal of the empire and resolutely opposed it in its entirety. Although it could not defeat the bill on its own, it was supported by a split among the Liberals. Under the direction of the former party leader, Lord Hartington, many Whig Liberals opposed the measure on similar grounds as the Conservatives. On the left of the party, Joseph Chamberlain (who also opposed the bill on the grounds of imperial unity) wished to be the one to institute reform as a means of becoming party leader after Gladstone and felt this particular change was too much. The bill was defeated by 30 votes.

SOURCE 5

An illustration created by the engraver and news illustrator Walter Wilson in 1886 showing William Gladstone introducing the first home rule bill in April of that year.

INTRODUCTION OF THE HOME RULE BILL: MR. GLADSTONE DELIVERING HIS PERORATION.

Seven years later, a second bill was introduced which differed from the first only in that it allowed Irish MPs to continue to vote in the Westminster parliament on issues of Irish taxation. It was passed in the House of Commons but was defeated by an overwhelming majority in the House of Lords, 419 votes to 41, and at 84 years old Gladstone did not have the strength for a third attempt.

THINKING HISTORICALLY Interpretations (6a)

Ever-changing history

Our interpretations of the past change as we change. This may be because our social attitudes have changed over time, or perhaps a historian has constructed a new theory, or perhaps technology has allowed archaeologists to discover something new.

Work in pairs.

Make a timeline that starts with *Introduction of the first home rule bill* and ends 50 years in the future. Construct reactions that illustrate the point that time changes history. In the future box you can speculate how people might react to the event in 50 years' time. Below is an example using a different event:

1867	1868	1886	1973	2066
Event: The Fenian uprising	Fenian sympathiser: 'a disaster' British official: 'a betrayal of our trust'	Irish home rule MP: 'a vindication of moderate methods' A British Conservative MP: 'the start of the current betrayal'	Marxist historian: 'a significant step in Ireland's revolution' Northern Irish citizen: 'a cause of the problems we have today' American student: 'a really interesting episode in Irish history'	?

Answer the following questions.

1 Identify three factors that have affected how the introduction of the first home rule bill is interpreted over time, or might affect it in the future.

2 If a historian was to write a book proposing a radically new interpretation of the introduction of the first home rule bill, how might other historians react? What would affect their reaction?

3 How will the future change the past?

The home rule bill of 1914

The defeat of the second home rule bill saw the issue fade from the political limelight as the Conservatives achieved office in 1895 and other problems took hold – such as the deepening split within the Irish Party over Parnell's affair with a married woman. As a consequence the political affairs of Ireland on a national level were largely left as they were and it was not until 1906, when a new Liberal government was formed, that the prospects for further discussion about Ireland's future brightened.

Principally the opportunity for home rule emerged with the eventual re-election of the Liberal Party in 1910 after two elections in that year had resulted in hung parliaments. Since that election the returning government's majority had declined significantly. The consequence of this was that in order to form an effective government that could pass legislation in parliament, the Liberals needed the support of John Redmond and his reunited Irish Parliamentary Party. Holding the balance of power in the British parliament gave Redmond a distinct advantage for achieving home rule as it made the Liberal government beholden to him. This was a fact that was not lost on the Liberal prime minister Herbert Asquith, who was therefore prepared to take up the cause of home rule once more.

SOURCE 6 The election results of 1910 in terms of seats won.

January election		December election	
Conservative Party	**Number of seats** 273	Conservative Party	**Number of seats** 272
Liberal Party	**Number of seats** 275	Liberal Party	**Number of seats** 272
Labour Party	**Number of seats** 40	Labour Party	**Number of seats** 42
Irish Parliamentary Party	**Number of seats** 82	Irish Parliamentary Party	**Number of seats** 84

A bill proposing home rule was introduced in the Commons on 11 April 1912. It was endorsed by Redmond despite the bill's retention of the position of lord lieutenant and evident shortcomings for the separatist Irish nationalists who wanted a complete break with Britain. Opposition from conservatives was overcome in the Commons with the support of the Irish Parliamentary Party, which gave the Liberals the necessary majority. However, the conservative unionists in Ulster adopted a more aggressive stance and threatened violence to protect their Protestant interests (see page 30). Faced with this opposition the prime minister was able to secure Redmond's agreement to allow the northern opponents to home rule to be excluded from the legislation in an attempt to reduce their threats. Though in effect this would split Ireland, Redmond reluctantly took a pragmatic view and accepted, reasoning that it was only by one step at a time that Ireland would find its own feet. With the support of the Irish Parliamentary Party the bill was passed in the House of Commons by ten votes but was heavily defeated in the House of Lords, where Conservatives retained a majority. The bill failed by 326 votes to 69 when it was presented in January 1913. Although rejected by the Lords, since 1911 this chamber only had the power to delay legislation for two years and therefore the bill would come into effect after that time.

The Irish people were within grasping distance of securing their first Irish parliament in more than 100 years. Unfortunately they would have to wait a little longer because, in July 1914, Europe erupted into war and home rule had to be set to one side.

ACTIVITY
KNOWLEDGE CHECK

Passing home rule
Create a summary table about the three home rule bills. You should use the following headings for your columns: 'Reform bill'; 'Motivation for introduction'; 'Factors influencing the outcome'.

The Irish Free State Constitution Act 1922

The effort of the Irish Parliamentary Party in combination with the increased influence which that party enjoyed after 1885 was fundamental in the achievement of home rule in Ireland. Over the course of 30 years the issue remained a constant feature of British politics with three bills being brought to parliament. Home rule became a central policy for the Liberal Party after Gladstone's conversion, and it was increasingly seen as a morally right principle. It was also arguably a political necessity – a bargaining counter with which to ensure the support of the Irish Party when it held the balance of power.

The passage of the home rule bill in 1914, and its subsequent manifestation as the Government of Ireland Act, was not the end of Irish problems however. Immediately following its passage another Act was passed suspending the enactment of home rule until after the end of the war, and this generated significant ill-feeling among radical Irish nationalists. These men felt vindicated by the Suspensory Act believing it was proof positive that Britain was never going to grant Ireland greater powers. These nationalists had increasingly sought independence and an Irish republic rather than home rule. After 1914 they began preparing for an armed uprising which took place in Easter week 1916. The aggressive manner in which the British government reacted to the rising was, from its perspective, a justified action given wartime pressures. However, it gave republican nationalists the opportunity to stir up public feeling against Britain and this resulted in a bitter conflict that developed after 1919, ending in 1921 with the Anglo-Irish Treaty.

The agreement reached within this treaty was the basis for the official Irish Free State Constitution Act, which offered the prospect of finally resolving the Irish question by granting sufficient changes that would be suitable to all interested parties. Within its pages it held a reasonable compromise that was expected to bring an end to the conflict in that country. As a result it was well received in parliament and received royal assent on 5 December 1922. It formally granted the following.

- Ireland would legislate for itself, but as a nation within the British Empire.

- Ireland would have fiscal autonomy.

- The country would still share the British monarch and swear an oath of allegiance.

- Northern Ireland could choose to secede and return to Britain if it wanted to.

The extent of this offer was substantially short of what republican nationalists demanded because it was not a complete break: Ireland would still be part of the British Empire, albeit with greater autonomy than ever before. They also disapproved of the oath of allegiance and the implicit acceptance that Ireland would be split in two as the unionists in the north would undoubtedly vote to stay with Britain – which they did on 7 December 1922, two days after the south of the country was granted greater legislative powers.

SOURCE

From the Irish Free State Constitution Act passed in 1922. This Act formally granted more autonomous power to Ireland, allowing it to legislate and raise taxes independent of Britain. It also granted Ulster the right to secede if it wanted to do so.

The said Constitution shall be construed with reference to the Articles of Agreement for a Treaty between Great Britain and Ireland set forth in the Second Schedule hereto annexed (hereinafter referred to as the Scheduled Treaty) which are hereby given the force of law, and if any provision of the said Constitution or of any amendment thereof or of any law made thereunder is in any respect repugnant to any of the provisions of the Scheduled Treaty, it shall, to the extent only of such repugnancy, be absolutely void and inoperative and the Parliament and the Executive Council of the Irish Free State shall respectively pass such further legislation and do all such other things as may be necessary to implement the Scheduled Treaty.

The limitations of the document evidence the continued British wish to retain some connection with Ireland despite the conflict that developed between them. In this sense the Act was a recognition that Ireland must have greater autonomy as that was clearly the wish of the majority population. In the increasingly more democratic world of the early 20th century this principle was generally accepted. It was also an acceptance in itself that the country had grown more independent and should therefore be allowed to stand on its own two feet despite British reluctance. In this sense what emerged after 1922 was a structured separation that eased both sides into new roles.

HOW IMPORTANT WERE THE ATTITUDES OF BRITAIN'S PRIME MINISTERS AND POLITICIANS TO THE QUESTION OF INCREASING IRISH INDEPENDENCE?

The changing relationship enjoyed between Ireland and Britain was shaped first by Irish demands, but also the attitudes of Britain's politicians – especially its prime ministers. These men were central to the events that transpired throughout the period between the late 18th and early 20th centuries, and the gradual shift from determined control to acceptance of greater autonomy owes much to the changing attitudes of these figures. Certainly influenced by Irish action and political motivations, Britain's political establishment was increasingly realistic about the changing nature of Anglo-Irish relations. It sought to address these changes as effectively as it could in the interests of Great Britain.

Changing attitudes of British politicians to agitation and rebellion, c1774–1922

Until the late 18th century, British politicians had always maintained a consistent policy towards Ireland – to ensure order and stability in that country for the benefit of the wider Empire. Despite episodes of Irish opposition such as the Williamite Wars in the late 1600s, this policy had generally been successful and Britain, throughout the ensuing century, retained a firmness of action with regard to Ireland that left little opportunity for dissent. After 1774, however, the British political establishment was forced to adjust its attitude because of external demands that ignited internal problems. A long process of political antagonism began that eventually saw Ireland become a free nation.

Integral to this achievement were the changing attitudes of Britain's politicians, which evolved from a traditional conservative–imperialist mindset into a more liberal one. This transformation was the product of several important factors, not least agitation and open rebellion from the Irish themselves. Each of these individually affected British political opinion and collectively invited progressive change in Ireland.

Early agitation and rebellion in Ireland

As part of an empire that spanned the globe, Ireland was susceptible to global influences, and this largely manifested itself through the manner in which British politicians reacted to these influences. Perhaps the most significant of these during the late 18th century was revolution – first in America after 1775, and then in France in 1789. These events were fundamental in changing British political opinion towards Ireland because they first encouraged a greater and more aggressive demand for extended political rights among Irish citizens, and secondly they forced British parliamentarians to consider the dangers of the growing agitation in Ireland.

Perhaps most formative was the loss of Britain's American colonies in 1783. They had been prominent possessions and the gaining of their independence following a successful war with Britain brought to attention what could be achieved if a nation was prepared to act decisively. The aftermath of the war saw the collapse of Lord North's Tory government and its replacement by a Whig administration under William Pitt the Younger, who was anxious to conciliate Irish opinion which had been stirred up by the events abroad (see page 14). The emergence of the Irish Volunteers and their demand for enhanced legislative powers for the Dublin parliament was especially threatening to politicians who valued the continuation of empire and feared that with America's loss, Ireland might be the next casualty. It was this reactionary thinking that stimulated a more open-minded approach to Ireland and saw legislative reform offered. This took two forms. First there was the Constitution of 1782 (page 14) which was negotiated by William Cavendish-Bentinck, the 3rd Duke of Portland. Then there was a Catholic Relief Act in 1793 when war with the new French revolutionary government raised the spectre of an Irish Catholic uprising in support of their co-religionists in France.

EXTEND YOUR KNOWLEDGE

Lord North (1732–92)

Frederick North was the 2nd Earl of Guilford and was known as Lord North after 1752. Elected Tory MP for Banbury at 22, North served that constituency for the duration of his political career. He served in many political roles, including Chancellor of the Exchequer, before becoming prime minister in 1770. His administration had generally been regarded as having helped stir up trouble in America by responding to the American patriots' Boston Tea Party raid in 1773 with coercive measures that eventually saw the creation of the Declaration of Independence in 1776 and the start of the American War of Independence. His government collapsed after defeat in America. Despite a brief coalition with Charles Fox, leader of the Whigs, North fell from power in 1782.

These reforms were intended to placate growing Irish calls for political change at a time when Britain was vulnerable – first having lost America, and then facing war with a revolutionary government that had spurned monarchical government and executed their king, Louis XVI, in 1793. In this sense, the progressive attitudes that were seemingly exhibited through the extension of greater rights in Ireland were in reality borne from a stronger desire to protect British interests. The aim was to grant a little to secure the whole. Early reform was a pragmatic decision rather than a moral imperative.

1801–68

By undertaking pragmatic reforms, British politicians initially hoped to preserve the empire and Ireland's place in it. Despite this intention they actually raised Irish expectations and fostered further opposition that demanded attention. This was even more significant following the Act of Union in 1801, which placed Irish Protestant MPs in the Westminster parliament. This was arguably the single most important factor in changing the opinions that British politicians held towards Ireland because it placed Irish political figures amongst them and therefore gave them a direct means to effect change. It also presented the

potential opportunity for Irish MPs to hold the balance of power at the heart of the British political system in the event of an indecisive election. This last point was instrumental in achieving independence in the 20th century.

After the union with Britain, therefore, Irish affairs became more widely known within British political circles, and this elicited a mixed response – sympathy from some and hard-headedness from others as the century wore on. One of the most emotive issues that informed British political thought was religion and particularly the groundswell of Irish Catholic support for emancipation, which dominated Irish affairs until the late 1820s. As a Protestant nation, British public opinion, and therefore noticeable political opinion, was generally anti-Catholic. In the 1780s there had been violent riots against the reduction of official discrimination against them, which had been echoed by the king, George III, in his unwillingness to support an Irish Catholic relief bill in 1791. This general antipathy towards Catholicism was maintained primarily within the House of Lords throughout the early 19th century. This was particularly evident following Daniel O'Connell's emergence at the head of a large Catholic Association in 1823, which determined to achieve Catholic emancipation, allowing people of that religion the opportunity of sitting in the Westminster parliament (see page 73).

The threat posed by O'Connell and his followers exposed the degree of mixed feeling towards Ireland: anti-Catholicism had been a particularly strong opinion in Britain. However, since the Act of Union, a growing number of politicians, Whig and Tory, began to promote more inclusive policies. From the Whig party Lord John Russell was a notable supporter. Among the prominent Tory supporters in the 1820s was George Canning the Foreign Secretary. Upon briefly becoming prime minister in 1827 before his untimely death, Canning actually proposed a bill of emancipation with the support of the Whigs. These individuals had circumspect support from more pragmatic thinkers such as Robert Peel and the new prime minister Arthur Wellesley, the Duke of Wellington, who saw the massive demonstrations from O'Connell as damaging to Anglo-Irish relations and therefore a necessary issue to address. These figures were challenged by strident anti-Catholic figures such as Sir Edward Knatchbull and Sir Richard Vyvan. They bitterly opposed the measure and actually split the party on the issue, resulting in the eventual collapse of the Wellington administration after emancipation was passed in 1829.

The question of emancipation divided the Tory Party, but it was able to become law because a majority in parliament were sympathetic to the issue. This was a result of the Catholic Association's agitation. Though unable to sit in parliament, Catholics could vote for MPs to it and successfully did so in the 1826 general election, which saw four counties' MPs replaced by supporters of emancipation. This influence presented a political interest to being open to the idea. However, there also existed a broader wish to maintain stability in Ireland, and increasingly MPs felt the continuation of such outward discrimination towards the largest section of the country's population was not the best way to achieve this.

Once again, however, it is reasonable to suggest that these MPs were only willing to concede on selected issues. When O'Connell began to agitate for the repeal of the union after 1840, British political opinion remained opposed to the idea, believing it to be the beginning of the dismemberment of their empire. In the face of O'Connell's Repeal Association (modelled on his earlier Catholic organisation), the British political establishment stood firm. It chose to ban meetings such as that planned to be held at Clontarf in October 1843 and was prepared to back this decision with force.

On this point, the repeal movement of the 1840s was arguably a watershed moment in 19th-century Irish history because it drew the line beyond which British politicians would not cross: giving Ireland greater legislative powers. This reluctance would characterise Anglo-Irish relations for the next 80 years and encourage such growth in agitation that once more political realism would be demanded.

Growing sympathy for Ireland and Unionism, 1868–1922

The emergence of home rule as a political issue after 1843 placed nationalist aspirations at the centre of Irish policy, and so British politicians were mindful of stirring discontent to a level that would force open rebellion and destabilise the union. Such rebellious discontent had become evident as early as 1848 with the Young Ireland uprising (see page 20) and then again in 1867 with the Fenian rising (see page 22) and these events initially met with strong opposition from the British establishment. Following these episodes came a more thoughtful response aimed at ensuring an improved relationship between Britain and Ireland. This was initiated by William Gladstone when he became prime minister after 1868, and throughout his, and subsequent, administrations, a more conciliatory line was adopted.

SOURCE 8

From Liberal MP Evelyn Ashley's recollection of Gladstone upon hearing that he was to become prime minister, 1 December 1868. © H.C.G. Matthew 1997.

I was standing by Mr. Gladstone holding his coat on my arm while he, in his shirt sleeves, was wielding an axe to cut down a tree. Up came a telegraph messenger. He took the telegram, opened it and read it, then handed it to me, speaking only two words, namely, 'Very significant', and at once resumed his work. The message merely stated that General Grey would arrive that evening from Windsor. This, of course, implied that a mandate was coming from the Queen charging Mr. Gladstone with the formation of his first Government. I said nothing, but waited while the well directed blows resounded in regular cadence. After a few minutes the blows ceased and Mr. Gladstone, resting on the handle of his axe, looked up, and with deep earnestness in his voice, and great intensity in his face, exclaimed: 'My mission is to pacify Ireland.' He then resumed his task, and never said another word till the tree was down...

Conciliation had always been present in British political thinking. However, in the second half of the 19th century the situation was more complex. The Irish Parliamentary Party had become a significant force in the Westminster parliament and a more radical Irish nationalism had developed through the revived Irish Republican Brotherhood that demanded complete separation from Britain rather than just home rule. The development of these features greatly informed political attitudes because each

made some devolution of power to Ireland very likely. Though undesirable for many politicians, and particularly unionists such as Joseph Chamberlain and Lord Hartington, this prospect needed to be addressed – especially after 1885 when the Irish Parliamentary Party won 85 seats at the expense of the Liberals and Conservatives, strengthening the case for home rule.

The issue of home rule became a divisive one in British politics. Liberal politicians broadly accepted the need for such devolution in the interests of better relations and, in 1910, the political support of the Irish Parliamentary Party. However, the Conservative Party, together with more hard-line Liberals, sought to retain Ireland under the existing system. It was from the Liberal opponents of home rule that the Liberal Unionist Party was formed in 1886 under the leadership of Lord Hartington and with 77 MPs in that year. This party aligned itself with Conservative opposition and formally merged with them in May 1912 to create the Conservative and Unionist Party (referred to simply as the Conservative Party). Collectively they formed a unionist opposition to home rule, which complemented the Unionist Party in Ulster and presented a determined defence of the existing relationship between the two countries.

Unionism in Britain reflected a reactionary attitude to Irish affairs, refusing to accept the growing need to offer concessions to the country whose majority population demanded change. Certainly it considered the interests of the Ulster Protestant population, but in doing so it denied the interests of the minority Catholic community in Ulster and also Catholic interests throughout the rest of Ireland where it was in the majority. It also denied the constitutional influence of the Irish Parliamentary Party which had helped to foster a more conciliatory approach in the first instance. Here the moderate demands of this party were at once more preferable to the separatist demands of the IRB and later, Sinn Fein, such that more progressive politicians recognised the need to appeal to this group. This sentiment was undoubtedly enhanced by the decisive position that the Irish Parliamentary Party obtained by 1910, holding the balance of power after an indecisive election, and demanding home rule as the price for their support of the Liberal Party after that election. Unionism did not accept these forces and continued to oppose Irish demands even after the passage of home rule in 1914.

With home rule on the statute books, British politicians, with the exception of unionists, had accepted the idea of greater legislative powers for Ireland as the best possible outcome given the growing discontent and constitutional power of the Irish nationalist movement. In this sense they had once more adopted pragmatic solutions in order to retain Ireland within the empire. This was noticeably evident when conflict broke out in 1919 and, though willing to support devolved power, politicians employed military force to avoid complete separation. This pragmatic approach was not substantially different from that of earlier statesmen. However, it differed in that, when decisions were reached, they were taken collectively by involving the Irish rather than handing them a decree. This greater acceptance of equal standing amidst pragmatic action is perhaps the lasting change that affected British political attitudes.

William Pitt the Younger, 1759–1806

TIMELINE: CHANGING BRITISH ATTITUDES

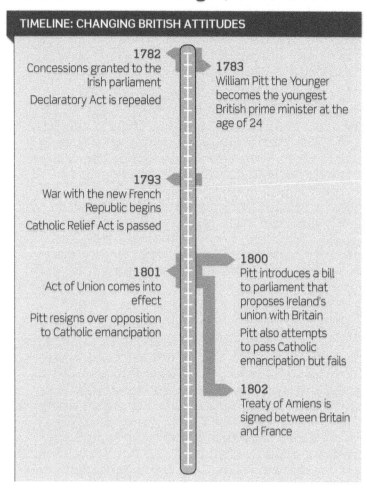

1782
Concessions granted to the Irish parliament
Declaratory Act is repealed

1783
William Pitt the Younger becomes the youngest British prime minister at the age of 24

1793
War with the new French Republic begins
Catholic Relief Act is passed

1801
Act of Union comes into effect
Pitt resigns over opposition to Catholic emancipation

1800
Pitt introduces a bill to parliament that proposes Ireland's union with Britain
Pitt also attempts to pass Catholic emancipation but fails

1802
Treaty of Amiens is signed between Britain and France

Pitt the Younger was of particular significance to Ireland during this period because he was the politician who introduced the idea of a closer union with Britain and even considered Catholic emancipation. This was following the concessions that had already been granted before his term of office, notably the Constitution of 1782. In promoting further reforms, Pitt arguably opened the door to possibility and sent a message to Irish nationalists that change was obtainable if sought in a determined manner.

By opening a door, Pitt was not, however, hoping that nationalists would step through it. Though aware that reform was always necessary to promote effective government, his intention in Ireland was to prevent further losses to the empire in the wake of the American defeat, and he saw offering limited reform as a means to achieve this. In the context of the American victory, the demands of the Irish Volunteers and the threat they posed was amplified because the British establishment was vulnerable and still coming to terms with its loss. In this interpretation, Pitt's actions are better understood as damage limitation and attempting to reinforce a position before it became any weaker.

The prime minister had made an astute political calculation. Following the reforms, many of Ireland's moderate nationalists were significantly more amenable to British control, which was exercised through the lord lieutenant – a position appointed by Britain to control the Irish government. Indeed, in 1790, nationalist politicians such as Henry Grattan and the Ponsonbys,

who had argued for greater Irish parliamentary power in the early 1780s, even publicly supported Ireland's link with Britain when it was challenged once more following the French revolution the previous year. Consequently, by securing the interests of Irish nationalism's more respectable elements, Pitt had arguably strengthened Britain's connection with Ireland.

The Catholic Relief Act 1793

Pitt further attempted to redress Irish difficulties by seeking to reduce the controversial discrimination towards Irish Catholics. Having won over many of the Protestant Irish nationalists through the reforms to the Irish parliament in the 1780s, Pitt looked to the Irish Catholic experiences in the early 1790s following the threat posed by the French revolution in 1789. This event saw the death of Louis XVI and the installation of a republic similar to that in America the previous decade. The revolution stirred up notions of liberty and equality and encouraged more radical elements of Irish nationalism to seek further improvements to their parliament's authority and for greater equality for Catholics in particular. In this matter the British and Irish parliaments were not initially won over to the idea because of the threat that greater Catholic rights might pose to the position of the Protestants in Ireland. Despite misgivings, however, Pitt, along with conservative thinkers such as Edmund Burke, reasoned that to deny Irish Catholics greater rights might motivate them to support the new French republic – a country with which Britain was soon to be at war.

On the grounds of British strategic interest – Ireland was a possible staging post for a French invasion of England because of the large, disaffected Catholic population – a Catholic Relief Act was passed. This granted rights that had previously been denied to that faith, and included:

- the right to vote
- the right to hold civil and military positions.

This Act was an important step closer to greater equality in Ireland. However, it did not allow Catholics to sit in parliament, and therefore discrimination had been reduced rather than ended.

Pitt and the Act of Union

The extent of Pitt's desire to maintain Ireland within the empire is best exemplified by the legislation he passed following the United Irishmen uprising in 1798. Having defeated this attempted revolution, Pitt recognised the need to look more carefully at British policy in Ireland. In the 1780s he had attempted to improve economic relations between the two countries by making the pairing a **free trade** area. But his ambitions had been blocked by less progressive interests within his own party and the Tories, who preferred to maintain British economic dominance. The re-emergence of Irish discontent, however, gave him a new opportunity to address the relationship.

KEY TERM

Free trade
An economic principle that suggests international trade improves when left alone by governments and in the absence of regulations, tariffs and quotas.

The solution that Pitt arrived at was a union between the two countries where Ireland would come into the fold of the United Kingdom under a British parliament, to which they would also send representatives. The rationale for this reflected Pitt's belief that the problems in Ireland could be overcome if the Irish were given a better opportunity to improve themselves, whereby they would then be able to recognise the benefits of membership in the empire. A closer union between the two countries would, on an economic level, encourage investment into the country by British capitalists. That would consequently help to raise the living standards there, while also providing Pitt with an opportunity to improve the position of Irish Catholics – a continual source of nationalist distress. He reasoned that the religious fears of the Protestant community would be reduced as they would no longer be a minority in Ireland but a majority in the United Kingdom – itself a Protestant state. By overcoming this fear, Pitt then felt it would be possible to address the issue of religious inequality and particularly Catholic emancipation, which he felt was an especially significant factor behind Irish discontent. As a result of addressing this and extending greater equality, he anticipated that Irish critics would be silenced.

A successful union bill was introduced into parliament in 1800 after judicious use of patronage had won over the Irish parliament, and the legislation came into effect in January 1801. Despite this success, Pitt's attempt to include Catholic emancipation was refused by the king, George III, and failing to change his opinion, Pitt resigned in February 1801.

William Gladstone, 1809-98

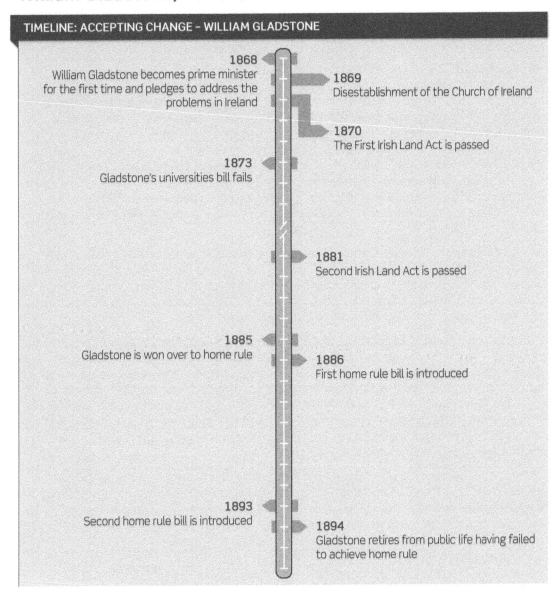

TIMELINE: ACCEPTING CHANGE – WILLIAM GLADSTONE

1868
William Gladstone becomes prime minister for the first time and pledges to address the problems in Ireland

1869
Disestablishment of the Church of Ireland

1870
The First Irish Land Act is passed

1873
Gladstone's universities bill fails

1881
Second Irish Land Act is passed

1885
Gladstone is won over to home rule

1886
First home rule bill is introduced

1893
Second home rule bill is introduced

1894
Gladstone retires from public life having failed to achieve home rule

Even before his conversion to, and energetic prosecution of, home rule after 1885 (see page 51), Gladstone had been a sympathetic supporter of Irish affairs, having been won over to the plight of that country in 1868. From this time onwards he grappled with the problems there and went further than any British politician to promote a lasting settlement that he felt would finally solve the Irish question.

The Irish Church Act 1869

His first attempt concerned the ongoing issue of religion, and in particular the contentious Church of Ireland. This Church had, since the 17th century, been recognised as the official church in Ireland despite the country's overwhelmingly Catholic leaning and Protestants making up less than one-eighth of the population. The most notable problem with the church and its position was that it required both Protestant and Catholic Irish men and women to pay a tithe for the Church's upkeep. This requirement was acceptable to most Protestants (although many in Ulster did not support this Anglican Church and were therefore aggrieved at having to pay a contribution), but it was completely resented by Catholics, whose own church was ignored. Religion had been a source of contention in Ireland since Protestants first settled there, and government policies had often discriminated against the Catholic communities ever since. For Gladstone, the Church of Ireland's special position was a glaring representation of these inequalities. So, if progress was to be made and Irish opposition quieted, this public example of injustice needed to be remedied.

The manner in which Gladstone sought to address the religious issue was to disestablish the Church and give it the same standing as the Catholic Church so that no preference existed. It was his intention that by taking this action Ireland and Britain might start to find an easier relationship once more. On 26 July 1869, Gladstone saw his Irish Church Act become law despite opposition from the Conservative Party and even objections from the queen.

The Land Act 1870

Reforming the Church was a first step in Gladstone's general policy towards Ireland. Such was the embedded nature of the problem that he also sought to address other fundamental issues such as the system of landownership and also education. With changes in these areas Gladstone hoped to improve the Irish people's experiences and thereby promote a more harmonious union. In 1870, Gladstone therefore sought to attempt land reform. Just as the Protestant Church, had been preferred, landownership was primarily the preserve of the Protestant community, and the majority of Catholics were usually tenant farmers on their lands. By 1870 there were approximately 500,000 tenant farmers in the country. The issue of renting, and particularly **absentee landlordism**, was a source of significant discontent in the rural areas, and this had led to periodic outbreaks of protest and occasional violence.

The basis for this often lay in the few rights that tenants enjoyed under the existing system. The Protestant ascendancy, though much reduced by 1870, still favoured the dominant Protestant landowners, who could evict tenants from their land without much legal recourse for the evictee. In effect, the 'system' was on their side. Under these circumstances, tenants enjoyed few rights or protections and were essentially at the mercy of the landowner.

In 1870, Gladstone introduced legislation that granted legal rights to tenants, including compensation in the event of wrongful eviction and the right to buy the land they worked using government loans. It also stated that rents should not be 'excessive' so as to avoid the practice of **rack-renting** which had become popular among absentee landlords who had debts of their own to pay. The Act itself was written by Gladstone, Chichester Fortescue and John Bright – liberal-minded politicians who felt that extending more legal rights to tenants was morally just and also good for economic development. It was John Bright who pushed for the inclusion of the government loans clause, believing that this would empower tenant farmers and encourage greater productivity.

Subsequent Land Acts would later be passed by Gladstone and other ministers, but the 1870 Act was the first occasion that demonstrated a British government's commitment to the rights of tenants rather than landowners. It marks an important shift in attitude amongst British politicians to the question of land ownership in Ireland.

Universities bill, 1873

The final piece of legislation Gladstone sought to enact during his first administration was his universities bill, which was designed to reform the state of higher education in Ireland. As with his previous legislation, Gladstone wanted to reduce the injustices prevalent in the country because he felt it was both morally right and might resolve the ongoing discord that existed there.

Higher education in Ireland was facilitated by Dublin University and its single college – Trinity College – which had been founded in 1592. This was originally a Protestant institution, and although Catholics were admitted after 1793 following the Catholic Relief Act (see page 40), it retained a strong Protestant ethos and its teaching staff were themselves Protestant. Catholic education was undertaken at the Catholic University of Ireland and also the secular institution of Queen's University which had colleges in Belfast, Galway and Cork. The bill that Gladstone introduced to parliament proposed to abolish all the colleges and unite them within an expanded Dublin University, which would become a secular institution. His intention was designed to try to reduce religious division by removing the means by which that division was tangibly maintained. Individual institutions teaching their own religiously inspired syllabuses did little to reduce simmering religious tensions. Therefore, to promote a better relationship, Gladstone reasoned that these institutions should be merged.

In proposing this legislation Gladstone intended to promote a better religious relationship within Ireland, which he anticipated would help reduce the discontent within that country. However, his intentions were undermined by the Churches themselves. Together with Conservative misgivings about the proposed syllabus for the enlarged university, these Churches openly criticised the bill and when it was introduced to parliament in 1873 it failed to pass by three votes.

The failure of Gladstone's university bill was mitigated to an extent by his earlier successes with regard to the Church of Ireland and the Land Act that his government had introduced in 1870 (see pages 54 and 132). With these reforms Gladstone had successfully presented himself as a figure determined to secure a better deal for Ireland and thereby effect a more positive relationship between that country and Britain. This was further reinforced during his second term in office after 1880, when his government was successful in passing a second Land Act (see page 147) and effectively bringing an end to three years of rural discontent. Having achieved these progressive reforms his commitment to the political future of Ireland became the next great hurdle.

Gladstone and home rule

The success Gladstone enjoyed did not completely solve the Irish question, but it had remedied substantial injustices within the country. In tackling some fundamental areas of discrimination, his actions demonstrated that a British government was not anti-Irish and had the capacity for progressive policy-making. The greatest legacy that Gladstone left, however, was the Liberal Party's commitment to home rule. Having been won over to the issue in 1885, Gladstone sought to introduce legislation to this effect in both 1886 and 1893 following the first bill's failure (see page 45). Although the second bill also failed, the policy had become a distinctive feature of the Liberal Party. By giving the issue a place within a British party **manifesto**, Gladstone had arguably strengthened the Irish cause by giving it a more mainstream outlet beyond the Irish Party itself – he had made home rule a British party cause also.

SOURCE 9

Cartoon published in the Dublin newspaper *The Weekly Freeman* in 1886. It depicts Gladstone trampling his unionist opponents. This newspaper was the weekend edition of the popular nationalist newspaper the *Freeman's Journal*.

ACTIVITY
KNOWLEDGE CHECK

Pitt, Gladstone and Ireland
Write out separate lists of the reforms made by both William Pitt the Younger and William Gladstone, and then answer the following questions.

a) Which reforms do you think are most important in terms of promoting a better relationship between Britain and Ireland?

b) What factors influenced the creation of these reforms?

c) How significant do you think the time period in which each prime minister operated was in terms of the reforms they made?

KEY TERM

Manifesto
A political party's collection of policies, usually presented during an election.

Herbert Asquith, 1852–1928

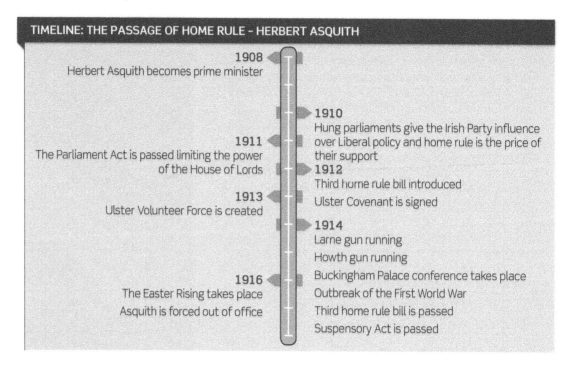

TIMELINE: THE PASSAGE OF HOME RULE – HERBERT ASQUITH

1908
Herbert Asquith becomes prime minister

1910
Hung parliaments give the Irish Party influence over Liberal policy and home rule is the price of their support

1911
The Parliament Act is passed limiting the power of the House of Lords

1912
Third home rule bill introduced
Ulster Covenant is signed

1913
Ulster Volunteer Force is created

1914
Larne gun running
Howth gun running
Buckingham Palace conference takes place
Outbreak of the First World War
Third home rule bill is passed
Suspensory Act is passed

1916
The Easter Rising takes place
Asquith is forced out of office

The premiership of Herbert Asquith played a central role in the developments in Ireland and in particular the fortunes of the Irish Party's home rule policy. Although he was a less than enthusiastic supporter of the measure, it was Asquith's administration that introduced a third, successful, home rule bill in 1912. In bringing about this change, Asquith is of great significance to Britain's growing acceptance of Irish nationalist demands, and he reflects the complicated relationship that many British politicians had with Ireland. His personal reluctance, out of necessity, gave way to political acceptance, mitigating his own private concerns about granting more autonomy to a country that had been bound to Britain since the end of the 18th century.

Accepting home rule and introducing a bill

Asquith became prime minister of a Liberal government following the resignation of Henry Campbell Bannerman in 1908. As an individual, Asquith was not an immediate supporter of home rule, but out of political necessity rather than any moral principle he was obliged to present a home rule bill for Ireland in April 1912. This was on a similar basis to the previous bills in 1886 and 1893, and it granted a separate Irish parliament for most domestic affairs, with Irish representatives still attending Westminster for financial and foreign policy decisions. This action itself evidences the power that Irish politicians had been able to win through parliamentary methods, and also the shifting attitude among British politicians that acknowledged the fact that Irish demands could not be ignored. In this sense, it suggests a realistic awareness about the new relationship that the two countries might enjoy in the 20th century. The bill was hugely significant not just because it offered home rule, but because it was sure to become law since the House of Lords' blocking power had been severely restricted in the 1911 Parliament Act of the previous year. With only the power of delay, the Conservative-dominated Lords would not be able to defeat the bill if it was passed in the House of Commons but only postpone it for two years. With the Commons finely balanced and Redmond's Irish Party holding the balance of power, passage was effectively assured.

Asquith and the Unionists

In bringing forward a home rule bill, Asquith was evidently aware of the Irish Parliamentary Party and its demands. However, he failed to completely understand the depth of feeling towards the issue by the Unionists in Ulster, and his initial bill did not address this feature, offering only a single parliament for Ireland. By ignoring the anti-home rule sentiment in the north, the prime minister arguably failed to ensure that what was already a controversial bill did not provoke undue political unrest.

The introduction of the bill was met with significant protest in Ulster, and in 1913 they organised a paramilitary group called the Ulster Volunteer Force, notionally to defend the province against the prospect of Catholic rule. It was also an attempt to reinforce their political power by trying to intimidate the British government with the possibility of force if the bill was allowed to proceed. The creation of this body gave the Unionists a position of strength which, had Asquith been more sympathetic towards their concerns, may not have been so commanding. In this sense his significance is both that he introduced legislation, but also allowed for the re-introduction of arms into Irish politics – a feature that would become quite prominent in the immediate and longer-term future of the country.

During 1912–14, what became known as the Home Rule Crisis developed as both the Unionists, supported by the Conservative Party, and more radical nationalists created paramilitary groups in an attempt to ensure their goals were achieved. Having allowed for the escalation of tensions by not considering them clearly in the proposed bill, Asquith found himself in the position of trying to mediate between two increasingly fractious groups. His solution was to consider some devolved power to the north that would be separate from the rest of Ireland. However, the Irish Party, in its position of power, also remained wedded to its demands that the country, in its entirety, be given home rule. It would not consider any compromise that offered the possibility that Ulster could remain part of the Britain.

Given this unyielding position, the prime minister, in need of support from the Irish Party, stood firm against the Unionist attempts to extract the right of exclusion from the proposed home rule bill which, after Conservatives had accepted the measure in June 1912, they had recognised as a realistic possibility. In January 1913, the leader of the Unionists, Edward Carson, proposed that a nine-county Ulster be able to remain part of Britain, but this was refused by Asquith.

After its defeat in the Lords in 1913, the bill was due to become law in 1914 (after a year's delay that the Lords' defeat had instituted ran out). As such, 1914 saw considerable political activity on behalf of the Unionists to secure some kind of deal before it was formally enacted. In the years after 1912, tensions had risen in the north and this had resulted in the creation of a paramilitary force that quickly armed itself in 1914 by smuggling weapons from Germany to the northern port of Larne in the hope of defending their right to remain part of Britain. As a countermeasure radical Irish nationalists also brought in 25,000 rifles through the port of Howth, and civil war seemed a possibility.

In an attempt to prevent such a conflict and negotiate a compromise, George V and Asquith arranged a conference between the British government, Unionists and Irish nationalists to be held at Buckingham Palace. Despite good intentions the conference lasted for three days and achieved nothing since the Irish Party was unprepared to compromise on the issue of division. The failure of this attempt threatened potential civil war in Ireland. However, on 4 August 1914 war with Germany broke out and the issue of home rule was overshadowed. The home rule bill was made law on 18 September but was postponed from coming into effect by a Suspensory Act which Asquith pushed through on the grounds of the existing conflict. This Act stated that home rule would not be enacted for at least 12 months or until the end of the war with Germany. When introducing it, Asquith also stated that a separate provision for Ulster would be considered at that time. Therefore, Ireland would have to wait even longer for its final outcome.

The difficulties Asquith had with the issue of home rule were perhaps born from his own concerns about the idea and the unfavourable position his government found itself in after 1910. Being so dependent on the Irish Party meant he was operating from a position of weakness with regard to the Unionists and, therefore, could not effectively deal with the situation. By failing to do so, his actions saw the introduction of greater intimidation techniques, particularly by the Ulster Unionists, which only made the difficult situation even worse. In this regard it would be reasonable to say that the outbreak of war in Europe was perhaps a stay of execution in terms of causing civil war in Ireland. Just as for the rest of Europe, however, the war would only create further damage in Ireland, which would have far-reaching consequences.

David Lloyd George, 1863–1945

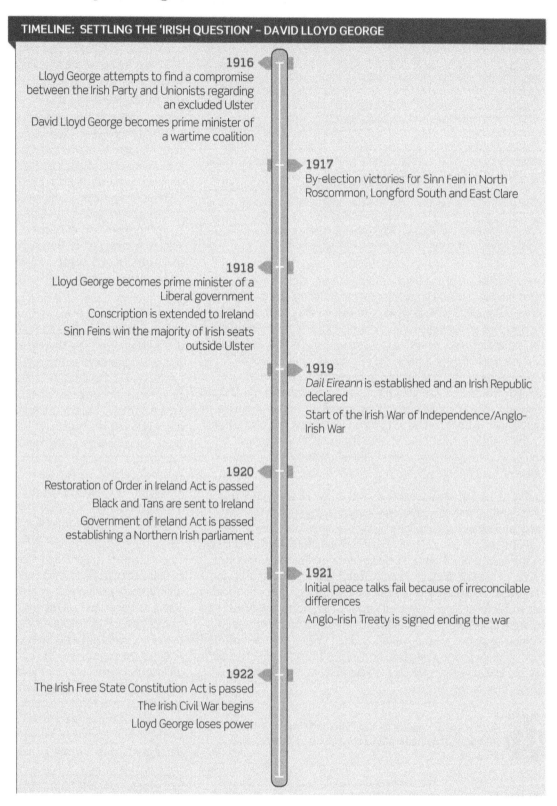

TIMELINE: SETTLING THE 'IRISH QUESTION' – DAVID LLOYD GEORGE

1916
Lloyd George attempts to find a compromise between the Irish Party and Unionists regarding an excluded Ulster
David Lloyd George becomes prime minister of a wartime coalition

1917
By-election victories for Sinn Fein in North Roscommon, Longford South and East Clare

1918
Lloyd George becomes prime minister of a Liberal government
Conscription is extended to Ireland
Sinn Feins win the majority of Irish seats outside Ulster

1919
Dail Eireann is established and an Irish Republic declared
Start of the Irish War of Independence/Anglo-Irish War

1920
Restoration of Order in Ireland Act is passed
Black and Tans are sent to Ireland
Government of Ireland Act is passed establishing a Northern Irish parliament

1921
Initial peace talks fail because of irreconcilable differences
Anglo-Irish Treaty is signed ending the war

1922
The Irish Free State Constitution Act is passed
The Irish Civil War begins
Lloyd George loses power

In December 1916, Asquith's coalition government collapsed and a new coalition of Liberal and Conservative ministers under the premiership of David Lloyd George was formed. Lloyd George had served in Asquith's administration as Chancellor of the Exchequer but, in 1916, he had sided with the Conservative Party and Labour Party in order to replace Asquith, whom he had criticised for his administration's prosecution of the war.

Lloyd George was already acquainted with Irish affairs even before taking office. Under Asquith he had been asked to resolve the differences between the Unionists and the Irish Party following the Easter Rising, when the situation became more pressing. The growth of radical, separatist nationalism had raised the political stakes, and Asquith had hoped that Lloyd George might find a way of forcing a compromise given the threat that had been posed. His attempts were made between May and June 1916 when he was able to persuade Redmond to agree to a temporary exclusion of Ulster. However, the Unionists were not prepared to accept what Edward Carson described as 'a stay of execution' and so this early attempt failed in July.

SOURCE

From a report on an Irish nationalist debate on home rule and the possible exclusion of Ulster held in June 1916 in Belfast. The debate was organised by the Irish Parliamentary Party and northern nationalists. The report was written by Captain W.H. Owen for Lloyd George.

On entering the hall I found the Very Rev. Canon Keown of Inniskilling speaking against the proposals... The speaker followed the common lines:

1 Laying stress on the doubt as to the temporary nature of the scheme

2 Suggesting that a separate executive was to be set up in Belfast, and

3 That an exhibition of courage and determination in opposing the present scheme, would result in other and more acceptable terms being offered by the Government.

Mr Joseph Devlin [leader of the northern nationalists] rose to speak... he firmly believed that if the proposals were adopted and an Irish Parliament set up in Dublin, the benefits attendant upon a scheme of that nature would soon become evident to the excluded counties and they would of their own accord very soon seek to be included under the jurisdiction of and Irish Parliament... it is not too much to say that Mr Devlin's words turned the tide in favour of the proposals

By the time Lloyd George first assumed the role of prime minister in December 1916, the political environment in Ireland was already changing, and when he was re-elected in 1918 the landscape was very different. Even before 1918 the Irish Party was losing support to the more separatist nationalist party Sinn Fein, and in three separate by-elections in early 1917 its candidates or sympathisers won seats: Count George Plunkett in North Roscommon, Joe MacGuinness in Longford South and Eamon de Valera in East Clare. These had each stood on a platform of Irish independence alongside **abstentionism** and consequently did not take their seats in the Westminster parliament. What these by-elections demonstrated was a sharp shift to greater radicalism. This was further evidenced in the 1918 General Election when Sinn Fein won 73 out of the 105 seats available to the Irish, completely undermining the political authority of Redmond's moderate Irish Party. When Lloyd George himself was returned in that same election, the pressures to address Ireland were mounting.

KEY TERM

Abstentionism
A method of political pressure employed by Irish nationalists which involved them deliberately not taking their seats in the British parliament when they had been elected to do so.

The Government of Ireland Act
Just as in 1916, Lloyd George's intention was to resolve the Irish problem, and in October 1919 he set up a committee under the chairmanship of Walter Long, First Lord of the Admiralty, to consider the best way to do this. Long was himself a unionist and favoured exclusion from any potential home rule bill, and this formed the basis of his committee's recommendations. Lloyd George subsequently put these to parliament in December 1919. The main features of these proposals were:

- the creation of a six-county Northern Ireland which would have its own government, including a separate parliament (see Figure 2.1)

- the creation of a 26-county Southern Ireland which, like the north, would also have a separate government and its own parliament.

These proposals were formally introduced to the British parliament in February 1920 and became law by the end of the year. The decision to partition the country was based upon the belief that it would be a temporary measure and that in the future the country would be reunited when political and religious tensions relaxed. The compromise reflected Lloyd George's realistic perspective about Irish politics. In taking this route he thought that it was the best hope for a solution: it served to sooth both unionist fears of domination by a Catholic parliament in Dublin, and also nationalist demands for more freedom (although the latter had desired a united Ireland and, therefore, Lloyd George had further bridges to mend with them).

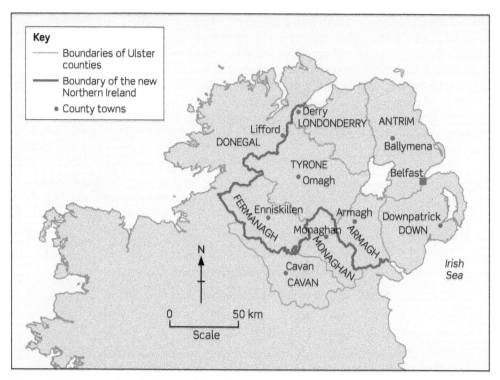

Figure 2.1 The counties of Ulster and those included within the new Northern Ireland as proposed by the Government of Ireland Act 1920. M. Collier, *Edexcel GCE History AS Unit 2 D1 Britain and Ireland 1867-1922* (2008).

Lloyd George and the War of Independence/Anglo-Irish War

The Government of Ireland Act was introduced amidst conflict in Ireland. The pressures that had mounted after the 1916 rising had seen the growth of Sinn Fein and a more militant Irish nationalism. Following the election victory of this party in 1918, its members abstained from attending the British parliament and instead established their own body, *Dail Eireann*, in January 1919. *Dail Eireann* which proclaimed the birth of an Irish Republic – a completely independent state that went far beyond the concept of home rule. The result of this action was the outbreak of war between Britain and Ireland which became known to nationalists as the Irish War of Independence and to Britain as the Anglo-Irish War.

The war itself was primarily fought using guerrilla tactics, and the Irish Volunteers, now known as the Irish Republican Army (IRA), targeted members of the police force, the Royal Irish Constabulary (RIC). By the end of 1919, 18 policemen had been killed. In response to this violence, parliament passed the Restoration of Order in Ireland Act in 1920, which replaced trial by jury with court-martial. The intention was to speed up the conviction rate of suspected IRA members. The Act also allowed for the imposition of martial law in those counties where violence was exceptional – notably Cork and Kerry in the west of the country. This action was also complemented by the prime minister's decision to recruit ex-soldiers to serve in the RIC. They were skilled at imposing these military measures and conducting aggressive tactics such as search and seizure and interrogation. These men became known as the Black and Tans because they wore a combination of dark green RIC jackets with khaki trousers due to a shortage of uniforms, and they gained a reputation for violence and indiscriminate attacks.

At first Lloyd George was supported in his attempts to restore order to Ireland. However, by 1921 public opinion began to turn because of the atrocities committed by the Black and Tans. Bloody Sunday (see page 35) and the burning of Cork city centre in late 1920 were two of many they undertook. With this turn against his policy Lloyd George was aware that a new approach was needed. Having settled the Unionist fears with the Government of Ireland Act, he felt in a stronger position to compromise with the Irish nationalists, and in June 1921 he invited their leader Eamon de Valera to peace talks in London.

The Anglo-Irish Treaty, 1921

SOURCE

12
Letter from Lloyd George to Eamon de Valera, 24 June 1921, following the creation of the Northern Irish parliament earlier that year. His intention was to encourage a meeting with the Sinn Fein leader to discuss an end to the existing conflict.

> Sir,
>
> The British Government are deeply anxious that, so far as they can assure it, the King's appeal for reconciliation in Ireland shall not have been made in vain. Rather than allow yet another opportunity of settlement in Ireland to be cast aside, they felt it incumbent upon them to make a final appeal, in the spirit of the King's words, for a conference between themselves and the representatives of Southern and Northern Ireland, I write, therefore, to convey the following invitation to you as the chosen leader of the great majority in Southern Ireland, and to Sir James Craig, the Premier of Northern Ireland:
>
> (1) That you should attend a conference here in London, in company with Sir James Craig, to explore to the utmost the possibility of a settlement.
>
> (2) That you should bring with you for the purpose any colleagues whom you may select. The Government will, of course, give a safe conduct to all who may be chosen to participate in the conference.
>
> We make this invitation with a fervent desire to end the ruinous conflict which has for centuries divided Ireland and embittered the relations of the peoples of these two islands, who ought to live in neighbourly harmony with each other, and whose co-operation would mean so much not only to the Empire but to humanity.
>
> We wish that no endeavour should be lacking on our part to realise the King's prayer, and we ask you to meet us, as we will meet you, in the spirit of conciliation for which His Majesty appealed.
>
> I am, Sir, Your obedient servant, D. Lloyd George

An initial meeting between Lloyd George and Irish nationalists, including Eamon de Valera and Arthur Griffiths, failed in July 1921 because of the irreconcilable difference between the two parties – Lloyd George was only willing to consider dominion status, while de Valera insisted on an independent Irish Republic. By the autumn of that year, however, de Valera was willing to talk once more. A new conference was arranged at which terms would be discussed and, eventually, the Anglo-Irish Treaty would be signed.

The conference was always going to be a challenging event as both sides had very different views on Ireland's future. Lloyd George and his negotiating team, which included political heavyweights such as Winston Churchill and Austin Chamberlain, were determined to give Ireland no more than dominion status, which would keep Ireland part of the British Empire and also subjects of the British monarch. Although de Valera did not attend the conference, his **plenipotentiaries** shared his views that Ireland should either be an independent republic or within the British Empire but with republican status.

The negotiations were hard fought, but the British were firmly against de Valera's proposals for republican status and they would not be moved from their position. Gradually they were able to wear down the Irish negotiators, who included Arthur Griffith and Michael Collins, and they eventually accepted the idea of an Irish Free State within the British Empire, which they felt would be a springboard to independence.

On the question of Ulster, the Irish representatives had been tasked with pushing for an all-Ireland parliament and they required Lloyd George to put pressure on the Northern Irish government under James Craig to agree to these terms. Britain was reluctant to concede on this issue, but the prime minister did agree to a boundary commission to reconsider the borders. On this basis he then pushed for an agreement on the grounds that failure to do so would result in the recommencement of hostilities. After granting further financial powers to the proposed new Irish parliament, a treaty was signed on 6 December 1921.

The final terms of the treaty included the following.

- Ireland was given dominion status – complete domestic independence with limited foreign policy powers.

- The British monarch would be head of state.

KEY TERM

Plenipotentiary
Negotiator who has been given complete power to take independent action as they feel is in the best interest of their state.

- An oath of loyalty would be required.

- A boundary commission would be appointed to reconsider the borders of Northern Ireland.

The deal was certainly a victory for the British, since they were able to retain Ireland within the Empire and with the king as head of state. The Irish saw this as a step closer to the united republic they desired. They anticipated that the issue of Ulster would be resolved by the boundary commission which, they hoped, would make the northern government so small as to be unworkable and, therefore, allow it to be absorbed into a reunited state.

Michael Collins and Arthur Griffiths felt the deal was a good one under the circumstances – they were well placed to know that the IRA could not sustain a war much longer due to low ammunition and resources. But despite their realistic efforts, it was not well received in Ireland. Irish nationalists split over the treaty and the country descended into civil war just as the Irish Free State Constitution Act was passed in 1922, formally granting power to a new Irish parliament.

ACTIVITY
KNOWLEDGE CHECK

Asquith and Lloyd George

1 Make a list of each prime minister's actions with regard to Ireland.

2 Now answer the following questions.

   a) How different were Asquith and Lloyd George's approaches to the Irish question?

   b) What do you think motivated each prime minister's approach?

The creation of the Irish Free State and a Northern Ireland parliament in the early 1920s was the culmination of a slow evolution in British political thought which began in the 18th century. Between 1774 and 1922, successive British governments struggled with the growing demands for greater Irish powers, and when it became clear that simple coercion would never be enough to subdue a nation's aspirations, they sought to adopt more conciliatory methods. This shift reflects a pragmatic attitude that sought to achieve the best possible outcome for Britain while recognising that the Irish people would not accept their existing circumstances. Throughout this period, successive prime ministers and politicians acknowledged this position and undertook to resolve the increasingly challenging Irish question in a mutually beneficial manner. In doing so, pragmatism transformed resistance into acceptance.

A Level Exam-Style Question Section C

How far do you agree that British policy in Ireland between 1774 and 1922 was largely unsuccessful? (20 marks)

Tip

When answering this question give particular attention to the term 'unsuccessful' – what was Britain trying to achieve and did they do so?

ACTIVITY
SUMMARY

Change over time

Between 1774 and 1922 the British attitude towards Ireland changed. Using the material you have read in this chapter together with your own knowledge, address the following tasks.

1 Describe what the situation was in 1774 and 1922.

2 In terms of the loss of British influence, how much change had taken place during this period?

3 What influenced the changes you have identified?

4 Are there any major turning points (events that had a particularly important impact on the course of future events) that you can identify?

 WIDER READING

Bartlett, T. *Ireland: A History*, Cambridge University Press (2011)

Boyce, D.G. (ed.), *The Revolution in Ireland*, Palgrave (1987)

Connolly, S.J. (ed.), *The Oxford Companion to Irish History*, Oxford University Press (1998)

Foster, R. *Modern Ireland 1600–1972*, Penguin (1990)

Harkness, D. *Ireland in the Twentieth Century: Divided Ireland*, Macmillan (1996)

Moody, T.W. and Martin, F.X. (eds), *The Course of Irish History*, Mercier Press (1994)

Pelling, N. *Anglo-Irish Relations 1798–1922*, Routledge (2003)

Townshend, C. *Ireland: the 20th century*, Arnold (1998)

3.3 | Towards emancipation, 1774–1830

KEY QUESTIONS

- What was the significance of the Penal Laws before 1793?
- How influential was the role of Daniel O'Connell in the years 1811–29?
- How important was the campaign to remove trade restrictions in the years 1778–82?

INTRODUCTION

The political struggle in Ireland was one of the longest-running challenges for the people of that nation. It was a broad issue that absorbed, and was sustained by, a variety of other concerns throughout the country's history which each contributed to the struggle in fundamental ways. During the early 19th century, perhaps the most profound of these additional concerns was the campaign for Catholic emancipation, which sought to give members of that faith the same rights as their Protestant neighbours. This was an especially significant movement because it was able to mobilise great numbers of Irish men and women and this offered a cohesive opposition that could not be ignored by Britain.

Religion had been a significant divide in Ireland since the first English and Scots settlers were planted in the country in an attempt to strengthen English control from the early 17th century. Coming from Protestant nations, these settlers were themselves Protestant and the lands they were given in Ireland were mostly taken from dispossessed Catholic Irish, who were the indigenous population in Ireland. Losing lands and being forced to declare their allegiance to an English monarch created deep-seated resentment among Catholics. Over the course of the next hundred years this was enhanced by religious persecution – especially under Oliver Cromwell in the middle of the 1600s when his **puritan** forces committed massacres against the Irish at Drogheda and Wexford. These events were motivated by military pressures rather than specific religious persecution, but nonetheless encouraged religious tensions in Ireland. When the Protestant William of Orange defeated the Catholic king, James II, at the Battle of the Boyne in 1690, his Irish Catholic supporters were subjected to greater discrimination. This was achieved through a series of anti-Catholic laws which established Protestant dominance in the country despite their faith being an overwhelming minority there. These laws became a considerable source of discontent and, therefore, between the years 1774 and 1830 there emerged a strong movement to restore Catholic rights.

KEY TERM

Puritan
A member of a Protestant group that wanted to simplify worship and regulate it more than the English Reformation had done.

1778 – Opposition to trade restrictions begins
First Catholic Relief Act allowing Catholics to lease land is passed

1782 – Catholic Relief Act is passed allowing Catholics to buy land
Poor harvests in Ireland

1792 – Catholic Relief Act is passed allowing Catholics to practise law

1775	1780	1785	1790	1795

1774 – Oath of Allegiance is issued

1779 – The Wool Act is repealed
Boycott of British goods is started

1781 – Bank of Ireland Act is passed

1793 – Catholic Relief Act is passed allowing Catholics to hold military and civil positions

WHAT WAS THE SIGNIFICANCE OF THE PENAL LAWS BEFORE 1793?

Penal Laws in Ireland

William III and the Penal Laws after 1691

The nature of William's measures against Catholics involved the creation of new Penal Laws (see Chapter 2). Following the English Civil War, the restoration of the English monarchy under Charles II saw the Declaration of Breda issued, which had offered religious toleration and pardons to all those who had been involved in the civil war – including Catholics. The Penal Laws were deliberate pieces of legislation designed to discriminate against Catholics so that they instead might choose to recognise the established Protestant Church of Ireland. The first of these laws was introduced into Ireland in 1695, and in the early 18th century they were reinforced with additional legislation. Collectively these laws included the following.

- No intermarriage with Protestants was allowed; children of any existing marriages had to be brought up Protestant.

- No religious education in Catholic theology was allowed; nor could children be sent abroad for such education.

- No Catholic could hold public office or military rank.

- No Catholic was allowed to vote.

- Any Catholic found to have converted a Protestant to their religion could be executed.

- No Catholic was allowed to buy or inherit land from a Protestant.

- The system of **gavelkind** applied to Catholic inheritance.

The extent of these laws was wide-ranging and they had a tremendous impact on Ireland, where 80 percent of the population was Catholic.

The creation of a Protestant ascendancy

The passage of the Penal Laws created a broad, two-tiered, social system wherein the Catholics were at the bottom and Protestants were at the top. This system was known as the Protestant ascendancy and it clearly exhibited the favourable circumstances that Protestants now found themselves in. As the preferred religion, they were given greater legal rights and were able to dominate Irish affairs. Within the Irish parliament, for example, they were able to conduct policy without giving any thought to Catholic interests since the Catholics could not sit in public offices or even vote others into them. This advantage was used to great effect with regard to property ownership, and in 1704 laws were passed that disallowed Catholics from buying land or renting it for more than 31 years.

> **KEY TERM**
>
> **Gavelkind**
> A legal term describing the system of inheritance whereby land was divided equally between all male heirs.

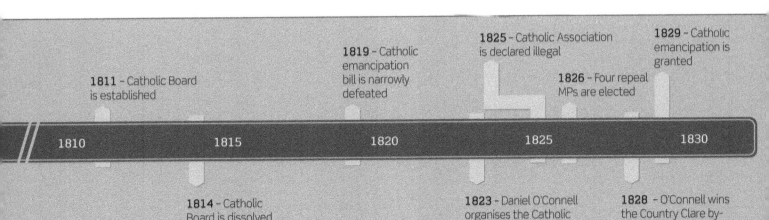

Timeline:

- **1811** – Catholic Board is established
- **1814** – Catholic Board is dissolved
- **1819** – Catholic emancipation bill is narrowly defeated
- **1823** – Daniel O'Connell organises the Catholic Association
- **1825** – Catholic Association is declared illegal
- **1826** – Four repeal MPs are elected
- **1828** – O'Connell wins the Country Clare by-election
- **1829** – Catholic emancipation is granted

1810 · 1815 · 1820 · 1825 · 1830

This ensured that Protestants retained the majority of land holdings, approximately 95 percent, and many Catholics consequently became tenants upon the land that 150 years before had been their own. By controlling landownership in particular, the Penal Laws were singly important in promoting a widening gulf between the religions in Ireland because land was the main source of power and prosperity. By handing that over to one community, it ensured the opportunity for exploitation and long-term resentment amongst the haves and have-nots.

The Protestant ascendancy grew steadily over the course of the 18th century as the **Anglo-Irish** controlled both houses of the Irish parliament and were unrivalled in their power. The position they enjoyed gave them strength but also the awareness that they were a small minority with tremendous privilege over a resentful majority. Therefore, many of the Anglo-Irish were sensitive to encouraging Catholic reforms on the grounds that it would encourage much wider demands from Catholics, which would then undermine their own position. This self-interested feeling was especially apparent with regard to the question of Catholics owning land. In 1761, and again in 1773 with Sir Hercules Langrishe, John Monck Mason (Protestant MP for County Wicklow) introduced a bill to the Irish parliament proposing to allow Catholics, to rent land for more than 31 years, but this was overwhelmingly defeated. The issue was taken up again in 1778 by Luke Gardiner who proposed allowing Catholics to take out leases of 999 years, but his bill also received significant criticism from his fellow members. Such was the fear of loss of control that the majority of Protestant politicians took a strident opposition stance by default.

KEY TERM

Anglo-Irish
A term that is used to describe the descendants of the Protestant English soldiers and traders who were given land in Ireland by the English Crown as part of the settlement of that country. These people became the rich Protestant minority that enjoyed the privileges of the Protestant ascendancy.

The 1774 Oath of Allegiance

Despite continued opposition to granting Catholics the right to lease property for extended periods, towards the end of the 18th century there were some small improvements for the Catholics. In part, this was the result of Britain's growing awareness of Irish Protestant nationalism, which had begun to seek greater powers for the Irish parliament and for Britain to reduce their interference in Irish affairs. This nationalistic sentiment was stirred up by Henry Flood and the Earl of Charlemont towards the end of the 1760s. The British authorities developed a more sympathetic attitude towards Catholics as a counterbalance to the developing Protestant nationalist demands.

Perhaps the most prominent example of this growing sympathy was the passage of the oath of allegiance in 1774 which allowed Catholics, and Protestant sects outside the Established Church, to declare their loyalty to the king, George III. Although this did not entail any specific benefits for them, it did offer the chance to start breaking down anti-Catholic sentiments that revolved around perceptions about their trustworthiness and loyalty. In the longer term this oath of allegiance would become a requirement for further Catholic reform, and after 1774 it helped to facilitate such reform because of the more positive light it positioned Catholics under.

SOURCE 1

Text of the oath of allegiance to George III which Irish Catholics were permitted to take after 1774. This was in lieu of the emancipation that William Pitt sought and it offered the chance for Catholics in particular to declare their loyalty to the British monarch.

I, A.B. do Take Almighty God and his only Son Jesus Christ my Redeemer to Witness that I will be Faithful and Bear True Allegiance to our most Gracious Sovereign Lord King George the Third and him will Defend to the utmost of my power against all Conspiracies and attempts whatever that shall be made against his Person Crown & Dignity and I will to my utmost Endeavours to disclose and make Known to his Majesty & his Heirs all Treasons and Traitorous Conspiracies which may formed against him or Them and I do Faithfully promise to Maintain Support and Defend to the Utmost of my power the Succession of the Crown in his Majesty's family against any person or Persons Whatsoever. So help me God.

The Catholic Relief Acts, 1774–93

TIMELINE: CATHOLIC RELIEF LEGISLATION

1774
Bishop Hervey introduces the oath of allegiance which Catholics are allowed to declare

1778
The first Catholic Relief Act is passed allowing Catholics to lease property for periods up to 999 years

1782
A second Catholic Relief Act is passed allowing Catholics to buy land and pass land on to their heirs

1792
A third Catholic Relief Act is passed allowing Catholics to practise law

1793
A further Catholic Relief Act is forced through parliament allowing Catholics the right to vote and hold military and civil posts with the exception of public offices

The first Catholic Relief Act 1778

EXTRACT

1 From Robert E. Burns, 'The Catholic Relief Act in Ireland, 1778' in *Church History*, Vol. 32, no. 2 (June 1963).

The Catholic relief act passed by the Irish parliament in 1778 was the first significant breach of that comprehensive system of legal discrimination against Irish Catholics known in the 18th century as the Popery laws.

The threat posed by the American War of Independence after 1775 encouraged British politicians to have a more conciliatory attitude towards Catholics. Not only were they afraid that Ireland might support the American war as a fellow colony with similar problems, but France declared war on Britain in 1778 and, because France was a Catholic nation, the British authorities anticipated that Irish Catholics might rally to the side of their co-religionists. In the spirit of self-interest and especially the preservation of order in Ireland, the British government recognised the importance of promoting a good relationship with the Irish Catholic majority. Therefore it pledged its support for the Irish MP Luke Gardiner's Catholic Relief bill, which proposed allowing Catholics who had taken the oath to bequeath landholdings to their heirs and buy land. Gardiner's bill, with British support, was forced through an unreceptive Irish parliament after compromising on allowing long leases rather than outright land purchase. The resulting legislation became the first **Catholic Relief** Act in June 1778. In addition to being able to acquire long leases, up to 999 years, this Act allowed Catholics to pass land on to their heirs, which meant that Catholic holdings did not reduce in size. This Act was a significantly progressive step for Catholics and it began the process of slowly dismantling the Penal Laws in Ireland.

KEY TERM

Catholic relief
A term describing legislation that repealed Penal Laws discriminating against Catholics.

The intention of the Act was to encourage positive feeling towards the British government during a time when that government felt threatened. It was also hoped that by granting more rights to Irish Catholics they would support Britain in the war against France and America – and even enlist in the army. In this sense, the motivation for the passage of the first Relief Act was less a principled determination to improve the conditions of Irish Catholics, and more about securing Ireland for the empire and expanding the size of the British army during a time of war. With regard to the latter motivation, it was intended that 10,000 Irish Catholics would be enlisted for the defence of their country.

SOURCE

2 From the opening article of the Catholic Relief Act of 1778. This was introduced by Luke Gardiner and it allowed Irish Catholics who had taken the oath of allegiance to pass land on to a single heir and also to take out long leases on land.

Whereas by an Act made in this kingdom in the second year of her late Majesty Queen Anne, entitled, *An Act to prevent the further growth of popery*, and also by another Act made in the eighth year of her said reign for explaining and amending the said Act, the Roman Catholics of Ireland are made subject to several disabilities and incapacities therein particularly mentioned; and whereas for their uniform peaceful behaviour for a long series of years it appears reasonable and expedient to relax the same, and it must tend not only to the cultivation and improvement of this kingdom, but to the prosperity and strength of all his Majesty's dominions, that his subjects of all denominations should enjoy the blessings of our free constitution, and should be bound to each other by mutual interest and mutual affection, therefore be it enacted... that from and after the first day of August 1778 it shall and may be lawful to and for any papist, or person professing the popish religion, subject to the proviso hereinafter contained as to the taking and subscribing the oath and declaration therein mentioned, to take, hold, enjoy any lease or leases for any term or term of years, not exceeding nine hundred and ninety-nine years certain, or for any term of years determinable upon any number of lives, not exceeding five, provided always, that upon every such lease a rent *bona fide* to be paid in money shall be reserved and made payable during such terms with or without the liberty of committing waste, as fully and beneficially to all intents and purposes, as any other his majesty's subjects in this kingdom, and the same to dispose of by will or otherwise as he shall think fit; and all lands tenements, hereditaments, whereof any papist or person professing the popish religion is now seized or shall be seized by virtue of a title legally derived by, from, or under such person or persons, *now* seized in fee simple or fee tail, whether at law or in equity, shall from and after the time aforesaid be descendable, deviseable, [sic] and transferable, as fully, beneficially, and effectually, as if the same were in the seizing of any other of his Majesty's subjects in this kingdom

EXTRACT

2 From Karen Stanbridge, 'Quebec and the Irish Catholic Relief Act of 1778: An institutional approach' in *Journal of Historical Sociology*, Vol. 16, no. 3 (September 2003).

In 1778, a Catholic Relief Act was passed in Ireland. The concessions granted to Irish Catholics were limited in comparison with those extended to Quebec Catholics: the Act eased certain restrictions pertaining to Catholic land holding and inheritance. Nevertheless, the legislation represented the first in a series of measures that eventually saw Catholics acquire citizenship rights commensurate with their Irish Protestant counterparts.

EXTRACT

3 From Thomas Bartlett, 'The Catholic Question in the Eighteenth Century', *History Ireland*, Vol. 1, Issue 1, (Spring 2003).

Protestants began to suspect that the British government in its eternal quest for troops was not above offering Catholic relief in return for Catholic recruits. Nor were their suspicions groundless, for there was in fact a plan to offer concessions to the Catholics of England, Scotland and Ireland, and this scheme formed the background to the Catholic Relief Act of 1778, the first major breach in the Penal code. This act repealed some of the Penal Laws concerning ownership of land by Catholics but its main aim was to encourage the Catholic gentry to beat the recruiting drum and enlist their co-religionists into the British army. It was Luke Gardiner, long on record as a supporter of Catholic recruitment into the army, who introduced the Relief Bill and it was put through the Irish parliament in June 1778. This Act set the seal on Irish Catholic support for the war... [and]... It firmly established the principle of Catholic relief as a key element of war-time strategy. Towards the end of the American war, another major Catholic Relief Act was passed and this 1782 Act effectively repealed those Penal Laws directed specifically at the practice of the Catholic religion. This time, however, the concession was not granted with an eye to recruits but with an intention of keeping Irish Catholics detached from the Volunteers.

Catholic relief, 1782

The passage of the first Relief Act began to open the door to further reforms of the Penal Laws – particularly for those Catholics who had taken the oath of allegiance. In 1782, a second relief bill was introduced by Gardiner and duly passed through the Irish parliament in March, again, with the support of the British government. This second Catholic Relief Act granted the right to buy land so long as it was not in parliamentary boroughs. It also removed the restrictions against Catholic education and the Catholic clergy. These reforms were especially progressive as they created the opportunity for Catholics to become more independent through landownership and the chance to improve their education. Just like the first Act, it was motivated by British security and sought to retain the support of Irish Catholics – this time to gain support in Ireland and to therefore isolate the newly created Irish Volunteers, who were calling for enhanced legislative powers for the Dublin parliament.

This military organisation had been established in 1778 to defend Ireland against possible invasion by French forces in support of the American war. It was organised by Protestants from the urban and rural middle class and gentry and was intended as a safeguard for the Irish nation. Originally able to raise 12,000 men, the Volunteers quickly became a useful tool for Protestant nationalists to seek further powers for their Irish parliament, and the movement became an effective means to threaten the British authorities. By May 1782, the Volunteers had 60,000 men and the British government was aware of the potential danger the organisation posed, especially with the American war going badly – in 1781 Lord Cornwallis had surrendered 8,000 British troops at Yorktown in Virginia. Faced with the possibility of Protestant Irish nationalist aggression therefore, a second Catholic Relief Act was thought to be an effective way to strengthen Britain's position in Ireland by once again appealing to its majority population.

The strength of argument

Use Extracts 1–3 to complete this activity.

Answer the following.

1 Read Extract 1.

  a) What is weak about this claim?

  b) What could be added to it to make it stronger?

2 Read Extract 2.

  a) Is this an argument? If yes, what makes it one?

  b) How might this argument be strengthened?

3 Read Extract 3.

  a) How have they expanded their explanation to make the claim stronger?

  b) Can you explain why this is the strongest claim of the three extracts?

  c) What elements make an historian's claims strong?

The French Revolution and Catholic Relief, 1792–93

The pattern that seems to emerge when considering the timing of Britain's attempts to restore Catholic rights is very stark: relief is offered only when there is a perception of a wider threat. Although the passage of two Acts already could suggest that further reforms were more acceptable, given that Irish Catholics had not presented any significant danger in the wake of reform, in actual fact the strength of anti-Catholicism remained very high. For example, two years after the 1778 Catholic Relief Act was passed, the violent anti-Catholic Gordon riots took place in London which saw 700 people killed. Given this level of antipathy among the general British population, it is perhaps more reasonable to suggest that their elected representatives were more compelled to introduce relief legislation for other motives.

EXTEND YOUR KNOWLEDGE

Gordon riots (1780)

These were anti-Catholic riots that took place in 1780 in England after the passage of the 1778 Catholic Relief Act, which intended to reduce Catholic discrimination. As a Protestant, Lord George Gordon had called for the repeal of the Papist Act, believing that toleration of the Catholic Church was unnecessary, and his violent speech encouraged rioting against this faith. In the course of the violent protest 700 people were killed and Newgate prison was set on fire along with other symbols of the British state.

SOURCE
3

The burning and plundering of Newgate prison and setting the felons at liberty by the mob.
A print by an unnamed artist depicting the Gordon riots of June 1780 in response to Catholic relief. It was published by Fielding and Walker in London on 1 July 1780.

The Burning & Plundering of NEWGATE & Setting the Felons at Liberty by the Mob.
Published 1st July 1780 by Fielding & Walker, Pater Noster Row.

Indeed, in support of the original idea that relief was passed out of perceived threat, two further Acts were passed during the 1790s when European nations were reeling from the French revolution which began in 1789 and saw the execution of the French king, Louis XVI, in 1793. This event, in the wake of Britain's loss of America in 1783, was fundamental to the repeal of additional anti-Catholic legislation because it openly threatened the very concept of British governance and its treatment of Irish Catholics in particular.

EXTEND YOUR KNOWLEDGE

The French revolution (1789–99)

This was a popular revolution inspired by ideas about equality and freedom. After initial political changes were forced onto the king and aristocracy in May 1789, mass protest erupted in July of that year, symbolised by the storming of the Bastille, a royal fortress in Paris and symbol of royal power. The subsequent passage of the *Declaration of the Rights of Man and the Citizen* in August embodied the fundamental principles of the revolution and emphasised the equality of men and the right of freedom for all. In 1792, a French Republic was declared after the revolutionary army defeated a Prussian force at Valmy. In January 1793, the revolutionary government executed Louis XVI and began what became known as the 'reign of terror', which saw at least 16,000 people killed. In 1799, the revolution came to an end after revolutionary army general Napoleon Bonaparte seized power and, in 1804, established himself as emperor of France.

The threat posed by the events in France echoed the vulnerability of Ireland when the French had supported America 14 years earlier. In 1792, however, this threat seemed more direct since Catholics themselves were now seeking additional reforms through their Catholic Committee which, in 1791, had begun to petition the Irish parliament for additional Catholic rights. The result of these petitions was a limited Act that granted Catholics the right to practise law in 1792. During its meetings with the Irish parliament, the credibility of the committee's claim to represent all Irish Catholics was called into question, and therefore it arranged an all-Ireland Catholic convention in Dublin in December 1792. This convention selected a delegation to travel to London and speak with the prime minister, William Pitt the Younger, about the abolition of the remaining Penal Laws. The decision to approach the British parliament was based upon the dominant position that it retained over its Irish counterpart despite the Constitution of 1872. Prior to this reform the Irish parliament had only been able to take legislative decisions with the approval of Britain, which had assumed control of the country in the 16th century. Even after 1782 when more legislative powers were granted to the Irish, its executive power (government) was still appointed by the British and served under a lord lieutenant who was chosen by the prime minister. The Catholic Committee recognised the dominant position of Britain and therefore sought its support in confronting the Protestant-dominated Irish parliament.

In taking this step the Catholic Committee was arguably taking advantage of the changing situation in Ireland. The growth of the Society of United Irishmen (see page 14) had raised the prospect of Catholic unity with Irish Protestant nationalists which, in view of the revolution in France, was especially troubling to Britain. It was with this concern in mind that Pitt was very receptive to the delegation and felt that further reforms were necessary. The outcome of these talks saw his government apply pressure to the Irish parliament to pass another Relief Act. A bill was introduced by the Irish Chief Secretary Robert Hobart and it was passed in 1793. The contents of this Act stated the following.

- Catholics were able to hold most military and civil posts.
- Catholics could vote in local and general elections.

This was a very important step for Irish Catholics since they could now vote on the same terms as their Protestant neighbours, and it suggests a growing acceptance of Catholic rights. Interestingly, however, the provision allowing them to hold military posts also reflects the trend of British reforms only when under threat. Just as the bill was being debated, another piece of legislation was being considered – a militia bill which proposed enlisting 20,000 Irishmen for defence of that country in the event of war. Just as these bills were passed, war with the new French Republic broke out and once more Britain required soldiers and a stable Ireland. In this sense the 1793 Act can be suggested to have served a particularly strategic role for Britain.

SOURCE 4

From the Catholic Relief Act passed in 1793. This allowed Catholics to hold military positions and also vote in elections. It was passed amidst fears of potential Catholic unity with Protestant nationalists following the revolution in, and subsequent war with, France.

Whereas various acts of parliament have been passed, imposing on his Majesty's subjects professing the popish or Roman Catholic religion many restraints and disabilities, to which other subjects of this realm are not liable, and from the peaceful and loyal demeanour of his Majesty's popish or Roman Catholic subjects, it is fit that such restraints and disabilities shall be discontinued; be it therefore enacted... that his Majesty's subjects being papists, or persons professing the popish or Roman Catholic religion, or married to papists, or persons professing the popish or Roman Catholic religion, or educating any of their children in that religion, shall not be liable or subject to any penalties, forfeitures, disabilities, or incapacities, or to any laws for the limitation, charging, or discovering of their estates and property, real or personal, or touching the acquiring of property, or securities affecting property, save such as his Majesty's subjects of the Protestant religion are liable and subject to; and that such parts of all oaths as are required to be taken by persons in order to qualify themselves for voting at elections for members to serve in parliament, as import to deny that the person taking the same is a papist or married to a papist, or educates his children in the popish religion, shall not hereafter be required to be taken by any voter, but shall be omitted by the person administering the same; and that is shall not be necessary, in order to entitle a papist, or person professing the popish or Roman Catholic religion to vote at an election of members to serve in parliament, that he should at, or previous to his voting, take the oaths of allegiance and abjuration...

VI. Provided also, that nothing herein contained, shall extend to authorize any papist, or person professing the popish or Roman Catholic religion, to have or keep in his hands or possession any arms... or to exempt such person from any forfeiture, or penalty inflicted by any act respecting arms, armour, or ammunition

---

ACTIVITY
KNOWLEDGE CHECK

Motivations

Think about the motivations that encouraged the extension of Catholic relief in Ireland and answer the questions below as fully as you can.

1 What was the purpose of the Penal Laws?

2 How were Catholics treated in Ireland before 1793?

3 What do you think was the overriding motivation for extending Catholic relief?

A Level Exam-Style Question Section B

How accurate is it to say that Catholic relief between 1778 and 1793 was largely motivated by the British government's improving attitude towards Irish Catholics? (20 marks)

Tip

When answering this question you should consider the context in which Catholic relief was passed – is there any significance in the dates provided?

HOW INFLUENTIAL WAS THE ROLE OF DANIEL O'CONNELL IN THE YEARS 1811–29?

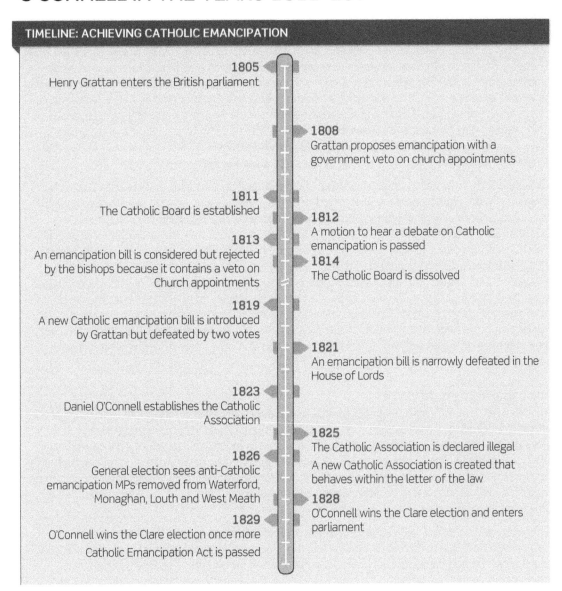

TIMELINE: ACHIEVING CATHOLIC EMANCIPATION

1805
Henry Grattan enters the British parliament

1808
Grattan proposes emancipation with a government veto on church appointments

1811
The Catholic Board is established

1812
A motion to hear a debate on Catholic emancipation is passed

1813
An emancipation bill is considered but rejected by the bishops because it contains a veto on Church appointments

1814
The Catholic Board is dissolved

1819
A new Catholic emancipation bill is introduced by Grattan but defeated by two votes

1821
An emancipation bill is narrowly defeated in the House of Lords

1823
Daniel O'Connell establishes the Catholic Association

1825
The Catholic Association is declared illegal
A new Catholic Association is created that behaves within the letter of the law

1826
General election sees anti-Catholic emancipation MPs removed from Waterford, Monaghan, Louth and West Meath

1828
O'Connell wins the Clare election and enters parliament

1829
O'Connell wins the Clare election once more
Catholic Emancipation Act is passed

Daniel O'Connell and the impact of the Catholic Board in 1811 and Catholic Association in 1823

The gains Catholics had made by 1800 were substantial given the position they had been in the previous century and this success only emboldened demands for further reform. Most of the inequalities of the penal laws had been repealed by 1793. However, there remained the ban on Catholics holding public office and, in particular, being able to stand for election to the Irish and then, following the Act of Union (see Chapter 2), the British parliament. The demand for Catholic emancipation became the dominant issue in Ireland during the early decades of the union and it was taken up consistently by prominent individuals – first Henry Grattan, and then more successfully by a young barrister from Country Kerry named Daniel O'Connell.

Henry Grattan and Catholic emancipation

The union with Britain in 1801 transformed the issue of extending Catholics the right to stand for public election. Prior to the merging of Ireland's parliament with that of Britain's, the main Protestant criticism of further emancipation was the belief that with political power the Catholics would destroy the Church of Ireland and overthrow the existing land settlement that still favoured the Anglo-Irish.

With Ireland's political future now decided in Westminster, these arguments were less persuasive as there would still be an overwhelmingly Protestant majority in Britain that would counter the perceived threat. Following this change, Irish supporters of further emancipation found sympathetic friends within the British parliament, which offered a more optimistic chance of success.

The push for emancipation was begun once more in 1805 when Henry Grattan entered the British parliament as the representative for Malton, an English constituency, and then Dublin City after 1806. Though a Protestant, Grattan had been won over to emancipation and sought to introduce a bill proposing such at the first opportunity. Despite his motivation, however, Irish Catholics were not well organised and the few political activists that existed were mostly aristocratic and very conservative. They shrank from any kind of action that might aggravate the British government and jeopardise what position they had achieved. They even baulked at the creation of a petition to parliament that was suggested by some of the younger, middle-class activists in 1805. It was this timidity that weighed down Grattan's efforts when the opportunity arose in 1808.

Unlike the Irish Protestants, English anti-Catholicism hinged on the belief that, as Catholics with allegiance to the papacy in Rome, they could never be loyal subjects. Grattan proposed to counter this fear by introducing a bill granting emancipation, but with a government veto on Church appointments – therefore the Crown could block any nominations they felt were politically unreliable. This bill was introduced in May 1808. However, it did not enjoy popular support in Ireland. Many of the aristocratic Catholics accepted the terms, but the middle classes very much saw them as a betrayal of their Church and also Irish national interests. The level of discontent that the veto raised upset the Catholic bishops who then, in September 1808, decided to reject it. The bill had already been rejected in the House of Commons by a vote of 281–128 so the issue became academic. However, it undermined the position of the Catholic aristocratic activists, and after the bill's defeat their influence dwindled as it was apparent they did not share the interests of the wider Catholic community.

The Catholic Board, 1811–14

The failure of Grattan's bill precipitated a shift within the emancipation movement. The established aristocratic leaders such as Grattan were increasingly marginalised by a more progressive groundswell among the emergent Catholic middle class. In Ireland this transition was embodied in the creation of the Catholic Board in 1811 which was intended to co-ordinate the growing Catholic demand for themselves. This organisation had a much wider representative base: several aristocratic members, clerical supporters, but overwhelmingly middle-class Catholics who were committed to emancipation without any veto.

The leader of this Board was Daniel O'Connell, an Irish barrister who had been one of the first Catholics to be called to the bar in 1798. O'Connell enjoyed a successful career but had ambitions to enter politics and therefore sought to win emancipation for his faith. The Board maintained its opposition to any qualification for emancipation on the grounds that it was an affront to their rights and that no Protestant qualification existed. After 1808 the political landscape was more accommodating to the idea of emancipation, and in June 1812 a motion was passed by 225–106 for the issue to be considered once more. The new prime minister, Lord Liverpool, also decided that the question should be a free discussion without the interference of government, and in February the following year, a bill was reintroduced.

The circumstances surrounding this bill were particularly controversial for the Board's membership, and they would ultimately see the demise of O'Connell's organisation in 1814 because of internal disputes that emerged. The bill itself was very similar to that of 1808 and like its predecessor it contained a veto on Church appointments. This was a particularly contentious inclusion and, although the bill was defeated within committee at an early stage, it had already upset the Catholic Board which had therefore rejected the proposal out of hand. It was this resolute and determined stance that caused a split within the Board as its aristocratic members supported the veto and thought O'Connell's rejection was too aggressive.

The development of internal discord over the rejection significantly undermined the harmony of the Catholic Board which, given its broad base of support, depended on this for unity. The resulting arguments among those in favour of the veto and those against it spilled over into the public domain spoiling the organisation's prestige, and it caused its dissolution in June 1814 after it was deemed that the peace had been broken.

Despite its demise, a further bill was introduced by the redoubtable Grattan in 1819 – one year before his death. This proposal retained the veto and was only narrowly defeated by two votes in the British parliament. Inspired by this marginal defeat, Grattan's successor as champion for Catholic emancipation, William Plunket (the MP for Dublin University), introduced two further bills – one for emancipation and the other a separate bill for retaining the veto. Both passed the House of Commons but were defeated in the upper chamber, the House of Lords. Clearly, in the absence of the Catholic Board the issue of emancipation had not lost much momentum. However, it remained an elusive goal.

EXTRACT

From J.C. Beckett, *The Making of Modern Ireland, 1603–1923*, Faber and Faber (1981). Beckett was Professor of Irish History at Queens University in Belfast – an institution in which he spent the majority of his career.

Between 1801 and 1829 the only issue that gave any measure of unity or continuity to Irish political life was that of Catholic Emancipation. But it was not until the 1820s that the demand for Emancipation was widely organized or vigorously pressed in Ireland. For two decades after the union the struggle was concentrated in Westminster and carried by protestant champions, who received but feeble and divided support from the Irish Roman Catholics. Grattan made the cause peculiarly his own. After a temporary withdrawal from politics he was returned to parliament for an English constituency (Malton) in 1805 and his first speech was on the political difficulties of Roman Catholics. From 1806 until his death, in 1820, he sat as one of the members for the city of Dublin, devoting himself tirelessly to the cause of Emancipation; he found increasing support among both Irish and English members, so that it seemed only a matter of time until the house of commons should be converted; and even in the house of lords the hostile majority was shrinking. But British opinion was deeply divided on the subject; George III remained inflexibly opposed to Roman Catholic claims, and his son, on assuming the regency, maintained the same attitude. It required the pressure of a popular Irish movement to break down the barrier, and until the 1820s such a movement was lacking.

When Grattan entered parliament in 1805, organized political activity among the Irish Roman Catholics was confined within the narrow circle of the aristocracy and landed gentry, together with a few lawyers and wealthy merchants, mainly resident in Dublin. The great majority of them shrank from anything approaching popular agitation

The Catholic Association, 1823

The failure of the Catholic Board saw the creation of a new movement to press for the cause of emancipation in 1823. This new organisation was called the Catholic Association. Like the earlier Board, the Catholic Association was made up from a wide social base and it aimed to recruit as many people as possible. Members were asked to pay a subscription of one penny a month; which was known as 'Catholic rent' and was collected when they attended mass on Sundays. The purpose of this money was to sponsor the organisation's activities and promote the cause of emancipation. In its first year, the Association raised £1,000 a week – 960,000 pennies each month – and by the end of 1823 had been able to invest £10,000. The financial success of this organisation was testament to its popularity, and with secure finances it quickly became a significant body that began to push more firmly for Catholic emancipation.

This was achieved through the publication of pamphlets and funding public meetings on the issue of further reforms. These methods were intended to publicise the issue as much as possible and also attract additional members so that the group became very difficult for politicians to ignore. They were effective methods and as the agitation became more vocal, membership increased, reaching six figures by the end of 1823. Given the rapid growth of this organisation, the British government became quite concerned about the potential threat to stability that it presented. In June 1825, the government chose to ban the Association.

Such was the groundswell of support for the movement, however, that the ban did not stop O'Connell, and in 1826 a new Catholic Association was established. This organisation was careful to avoid fiery rhetoric so as to not give the government an excuse to ban it a second time. The re-establishment of the movement coincided with a general election, which presented a good opportunity for the well-organised Association to use its vast support base to promote its cause. Throughout the election, it campaigned for sympathetic emancipation candidates and actively against those who opposed that. The outcome of the election saw the Irish counties of Roscommon, Louth, Longford and West Meath reject their existing candidates in favour of emancipation supporters, and this gave the cause a louder voice in the new parliament.

The County Clare elections, 1828 and 1829

SOURCE 5

Daniel O'Connell addressing a crowd in County Clare in 1828. An illustration published in the artist, J. Haverty's, book *The Monster Meeting in the Irish Highlands* (1843). The illustrations were made on the spot in Cliften with members of the meeting sitting for Haverty.

KEY TERMS

By-election
An election to fill vacancies that arise between general elections.

Reshuffle
A right of the prime minister to reorganise the personnel within his government.

The significance of the Catholic Association and the popularity of the emancipation issue was further evidenced in a **by-election** held in County Clare in 1828. At this time it was customary that when the prime minister undertook a **reshuffle** of his ministers any new candidate who was given a government position had to stand for re-election. In June 1828, the sitting MP for Clare, William Vesey Fitzgerald, had been selected as President of the Board of Trade – a position he accepted – and therefore he had to participate in a by-election.

Another election offered the opportunity for the Catholic Association to promote another emancipation candidate and potentially cause the government public embarrassment if Fitzgerald was defeated. Fitzgerald had a strong position – he had been the MP for ten years, was a resident landlord with a good reputation, and he was also sympathetic to Catholic emancipation. Despite these qualities, however, he was joining a government that opposed further Catholic reforms, and therefore the Association was keen to challenge him. They first sought a Protestant to stand against him, and the best candidate was Captain William Nugent McNamara. However, he was unwilling to stand, as Fitzgerald was a close friend. Upon failing to find a Protestant willing to stand, Daniel O'Connell, a Catholic, announced his candidacy on 24 June 1828. There was no law forbidding Catholics standing for election, but they could not sit in parliament because of the requirement to swear an oath of supremacy (see page 76) to the British monarch above all others, which was incompatible with their religion since it effectively forbade their allegiance to the See of Rome. Therefore, O'Connell's decision to stand was essentially to embarrass the government and, if he won, highlight the gross unfairness of the remaining Penal Laws.

SOURCE
6

From the election manifesto of Daniel O'Connell written in June 1828 to support his candidacy as MP for County Clare in the July 1828 by-election. O'Connell was standing as a Catholic candidate against the incumbent Protestant, William Vesey Fitzgerald, who had just been appointed as President of the Board of Trade.

Dublin, June 1828

Fellow Countrymen,

Your county wants a representative. I respectfully solicit your suffrages, to raise me to that station.

Of my qualification to fill that station, I leave you to judge. The habits of public speaking, and many, many years of public business, render me, perhaps equally suited with most men to attend to the interests of Ireland in Parliament.

You will be told I am not qualified to be elected: the assertion, my friends, is untrue. I am qualified to be elected, and to be your representative. It is true that as a Catholic, I cannot, and of course never will, take the oaths at present prescribed to members of Parliament; but the authority which created these oaths (the Parliament), can abrogate them: and I entertain a confident hope that, if you elect me, the most bigoted [sic] of our enemies will see the necessity of removing from the chosen representative of the people, an obstacle which would prevent him from doing his duty to his King and to his country.

... Electors of the county of Clare! Mr Vesey Fitzgerald claims as his only merit, that he is a friend to the Catholics – why, I am a Catholic myself; and if he be sincerely our friend, let him vote for me, and raise before the British Empire the Catholic question in my humble person, in the way most propitious to my final success. But no, fellow countrymen, no; he will make no sacrifice to that cause, he will call himself your friend, and act the part of your worst and most unrelenting enemy...

Electors of the county of Clare! choose between me and Mr Vesey Fitzgerald; choose between him who has so long cultivated his own interest, and one who seeks only to advance yours; choose between the sworn libeller of the Catholic faith, and one who has devoted his early life to your cause; who has consumed his manhood in a struggle for your liberties, and who has ever lived, and is ready to die for the integrity, the honour, the purity, of the Catholic faith, and the promotion of Irish freedom and happiness.

Your faithful servant,

DANIEL O'CONNELL

A Level Exam-Style Question Section A

Study Source 6 before you answer this question.

Assess the value of the source for revealing the motivations behind Daniel O'Connell's activism on behalf of the campaign for Catholic emancipation.

Explain your answer, using the source, the information given about its origin and your own knowledge about the historical context. (20 marks)

Tip
When addressing this question you should consider the implications that O'Connell's victory might have for Britain's parliament – would he be able to sit?

The advantage that O'Connell enjoyed was the well-organised machine of the Catholic Association, and once he had announced his candidacy it began canvassing the voters in Clare. Among the most active of these canvassers were O'Gorman Mahon and Thomas Steele, who even went so far as to be willing to duel with any landowner who objected to his tenants being approached. On the day of the election itself, the Association and its clerical supporters in particular even conveyed voters to the polling booths to ensure as many people as possible cast their vote for O'Connell.

SOURCE 7

From the *Dublin Evening Post*, 3 July 1828. This newspaper appeared three times a week at a cost of 5*d* (5 pence) and was therefore generally only read by the wealthy members of Dublin city.

Eight o'clock. Between 300 and 400 of John Ormsby Vandeleur's freeholders are now passing up the street to the Court House, preceded by colours, every man with a green leaf in his hand, and amidst the loudest cheering from the townspeople. They are western men from Kilrush, and brought in by their clergy to vote for O'Connell. Along the road the general cry of these men was – 'Here's Kilrush, high for O'Connell, high for our priest'. Mr O'Leary the priest of Kilrush, came with them and the town is full of Catholic clergy. There are fifteen booths opened for the polling.

Ten o'clock. Mr M'Inerney, the priest of Feakle, is just passed in at the head of a number of freeholders from that parish, carrying green boughs, and music before them.

Eleven o'clock. Another large body of men has passed in, preceded by a green silk flag, Shamrocks wreathed in gold – 'Scariff, and civil and religious liberty' in gold colours.

Mr O'Connell has been chaired to the Court House, and at the door implored the people to be true to their religion and their country.

Mr Maguire is moving about the streets and addressing every group of freeholders. The qualification oath is require, and magistrates are now administering it at the office of Mr Henry the sub-sheriff. This will retard the election if preserved in.

Twelve o'clock. Rev. Mr Murphy of Corofin, is come in with Mr Staunton Cahill, at the head of at least 500 men decorated with green branches and walking in ranks. Mr Murphy stood up in his gig, and was hailed with the loudest cheering.

On the strength of the Association's efforts at marshalling the Catholic voters, O'Connell won the seat comfortably: 2,057 to 982 votes. On the day, the gentry and well-to-do farmers supported Fitzgerald, but the small farmers, who were predominantly Catholic, were swayed by the issues, the cajoling of the Association and also the moral weight offered by the Catholic clergy. The extent of the result was impressive. However, the implications of it were profound – the Duke of Wellington's Tory government could not ignore the issue of emancipation and the excitement that O'Connell's victory had generated among Catholics potentially threatened the peace in Ireland should nothing happen in its wake.

Country Clare election, 1829

O'Connell's success had placed emancipation squarely upon the political agenda once more because of the public interest that the Clare election had stimulated. Faced with the prospect of upsetting the Catholic majority, now about 85 percent of the population, Wellington and Robert Peel, his home secretary, sought to pass a bill allowing Catholics to sit in parliament. When the bill passed, in 1829, for the first time Catholics were granted the same political opportunities as their Protestant neighbours. The final bill that passed, however, was not made retrospective and therefore O'Connell could not take his seat without standing in an election once more or taking the **oath of supremacy**, which was incompatible with Catholicism. When O'Connell tried to take his seat in May it was declared vacant by the solicitor-

general Nicholas Conyngham Tindal, who demanded a new election. Arguably this move was a last-ditch and stubborn attempt by anti-Catholic elements within parliament to delay his sitting considering the overwhelming number of votes O'Connell had won only the previous year. In the duly organised second election O'Connell stood unopposed and was re-elected on 30 July 1829. Without any further means of prevention, he became the first Irish Catholic to sit in the House of Commons.

ACTIVITY
KNOWLEDGE CHECK

Growing Catholic activism

1 Write down the gains that Catholics made between 1801 and 1829.

2 Briefly outline the reasons why the Catholic Board did not enjoy as much success as the Catholic Association.

3 What do you think changed to make the Catholic Association more successful?

The passage of the Roman Catholic Relief Act 1829 through parliament and its impact

The victory of O'Connell had brought the issue of emancipation to the top of the political agenda for the Tory administration in Britain. The Duke of Wellington had become prime minister after a year-long period of Tory instability. The party, which had been in power since 1809, lost the strong leadership of Lord Liverpool who died in 1827 and found it difficult to replace him. During the next nine months, the Tories saw three different leaders and consequently became quite vulnerable; factions had emerged and the confidence that strong leadership encouraged had disappeared. Against this background, the escalating events in Ireland presented a considerable challenge to the weakened government, and therefore both the Duke of Wellington and his home secretary, Robert Peel, undertook to address the threat quickly.

Given the extent of interest that had been generated by the County Clare by-election, and in combination with the government's sense of vulnerability, both men were aware that to openly deny the issue of emancipation would potentially create unrest in Ireland that might ferment rebellion. In this sense, the decision to consider further emancipation was therefore born from self-interest on the part of the Wellington administration, and the perceived position of strength that the Catholics now enjoyed in Ireland given the organisation that the Catholic Association had managed to instil.

In attempting to pass new legislation the government needed to win over the king, George IV, and also many Conservative critics in the House of Lords who remained quite opposed to further Catholic reform. Wellington and Peel were helped in their attempt by the Whig party whose sympathies lay with Catholic emancipation. It was this bi-partisan support, in addition to that of liberal Tories who were also sympathetic, which was enough to push the bill through the upper house in 1829. To encourage the king to sign the bill into law, Wellington threatened to resign and, reluctant to see the collapse of another Tory government, George IV grudgingly consented. In April 1829, the Roman Catholic Relief Act was therefore passed.

The provisions of the new Act included the following.

- Catholics could sit as MPs in Westminster.

- Catholics were able to stand for all public offices except those of lord chancellor, monarch, regent, lord lieutenant of Ireland and judicial appointments.

SOURCE 8

Cartoon showing the Duke of Wellington and Robert Peel murdering John Bull while the pope and satan look on. Published c1829 and probably created by the Northumbrian political satirist William Heath.

The Roman Catholic Relief Act removed the majority of the remaining disqualifications faced by Catholics, and for this reason it was a great step forward – however, it came at a price. To ease the bill through parliament Peel accepted a more restricted franchise so as to pacify the most critical opposition led by Sir Edward Knatchbull and Sir Richard Vyvyan. This involved the passage of the second bill: the Parliamentary Elections (Ireland) Act 1829, which increased the qualification for voting from the traditional **40-shilling freehold** to a £10 householder. This effectively reduced the number of poorer Irish voters who did not reside in property worth £10, and saw the number of Irish voters fall from 215,901 to 39,872.

KEY TERM

40-shilling freehold
A qualification allowing people who owned property worth 40 shillings a year the vote.

The Act was accepted by Daniel O'Connell and he took his seat in July 1829. In doing so, however, he became a figure of some resentment among the poorer Irish Catholics, who were now disenfranchised, and once the excitement over its passage had died down the realities of the legislation began to be seen.

Despite the reduction of Irish voters, the passage of the Roman Catholic Relief Act was a significant improvement for Catholic rights. It removed the majority of the remaining Penal Laws and gave Catholics the opportunity to take greater control of their futures by taking the decision-making out of Protestant hands and giving it to Catholic representatives if they were successfully elected. Certainly the franchise was significantly restricted but, with the opportunity to elect Catholic MPs, there was at least the chance to address that issue in parliament.

SOURCE

William Cobbett, an English radical reform supporter, writing in the weekly newspaper *The Political Register* on 29 August 1829. This paper had been established by Cobbett in 1802 and had an average weekly circulation of 6,000.

The measure of *Catholic Emancipation*, as it has been ridiculously, and still is ridiculously, called, has really made the state of the county worse than it was before, and worse than it would now have been, had not that measure been adopted... Every man of sense will ask, how several millions of wretched people, several millions of creatures half-naked and half-starved, should be raised into comfort and content by a mere sharing of the lay, legislative and executive powers between Protestants and Catholics, without any change whatsoever in the principles upon which those powers are executed, or in the manner or price of the execution?

HOW IMPORTANT WAS THE CAMPAIGN TO REMOVE TRADE RESTRICTIONS IN THE YEARS 1778–82?

The significance of the campaign in the Irish parliament to remove restrictions on Irish trade, 1778–82

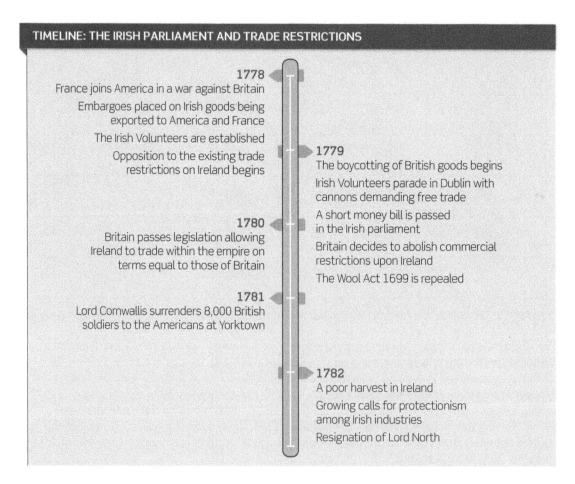

TIMELINE: THE IRISH PARLIAMENT AND TRADE RESTRICTIONS

1778
France joins America in a war against Britain
Embargoes placed on Irish goods being exported to America and France
The Irish Volunteers are established
Opposition to the existing trade restrictions on Ireland begins

1779
The boycotting of British goods begins
Irish Volunteers parade in Dublin with cannons demanding free trade
A short money bill is passed in the Irish parliament
Britain decides to abolish commercial restrictions upon Ireland
The Wool Act 1699 is repealed

1780
Britain passes legislation allowing Ireland to trade within the empire on terms equal to those of Britain

1781
Lord Cornwallis surrenders 8,000 British soldiers to the Americans at Yorktown

1782
A poor harvest in Ireland
Growing calls for protectionism among Irish industries
Resignation of Lord North

Since Ireland had become a colony of Britain, its economic position was placed as a secondary concern below the economic interests of Britain itself. Various Acts of Parliament such as the **Navigation Act** 1651 and **Wool Act** 1699 deliberately subordinated Irish financial opportunities to the benefit of England. Such was the impact of this policy that by the late 18th century Ireland was not financially stable and was particularly reliant upon British support. Under the administration of Lord North, however, such support for Ireland was slow in coming, and after 1778 an armed Irish militia sought to force economic reform from Britain. The outcome of this episode saw the British government offer concessions which, in the immediate term, addressed the economic situation but, in the long term, gave the inhabitants of Ireland a clear process by which to seek further reforms from that country.

The demand for free trade

The economic frailty of Ireland was brought to the forefront of Irish minds during the American War of Independence. The development of this conflict disrupted trade routes and consequently had a damaging effect upon the Irish economy, which had traditionally relied upon exportation of textiles and beef to the USA and Britain in order to support itself. As the country's trade opportunities declined, attention became focused upon the reasons for such decline, and within the Irish parliament that attention was levelled at the preferential trade agreements that British merchants had at Ireland's expense. The outbreak of war had seen **embargoes** placed upon Irish goods being exported to America and France in 1778. This had a severe impact on the Irish economy. For example, one-third of all beef exports went to France in 1764, but by 1780 this had fallen to zero. Overall, between 1772 and 1780, the market for Irish beef declined by 40 percent and never really picked up again until much later.

The economic position that Ireland found itself in during the early years of the American war stimulated growing demands from many within the Irish parliament for a reconsideration of the existing economic agreements between Britain and Ireland, which had always favoured the British. To redress this imbalance the Irish parliament sought to push the issue of lifting trade restrictions. In 1779, it began to consider the idea to only pass a short money bill which granted the Irish government funds for six months rather than the annual provision it usually voted. This was an attempt to force Britain to consider the Irish request for the lifting of restrictions by exploiting the poor financial position that the Irish government was in. It could not meet all of its expenses and had to borrow £30,000 in 1778 from a private banking firm called La Touche. In addition, the cost of maintaining the Irish regiments serving abroad had to be met by the Bank of England after April 1779 as there was not enough money in the Irish exchequer.

The prominent figures pushing for the lifting of trade restrictions were Henry Grattan, Hussey Burgh and Henry Flood. These three were Protestant landowners and prominent members of the Irish parliament, who had loosely bound themselves into a **patriot** group that desired greater controls for the Irish legislature – of which economic freedom was a particularly important step. It was these men who drove the debate for free trade (see Chapter 2) and successfully passed a resolution in the Dublin parliament in October 1779 to formally demand unlimited trade rights from the British government.

KEY TERMS

Navigation Act
An Act of Parliament passed in 1651 which forbade the use of foreign ships by colonies for trade with one another.

Wool Act
An Act of Parliament passed in 1699 which limited the amount of wool Ireland could produce, thereby giving British wool merchants better trade opportunities.

Embargo
This is an official ban on trade with another country.

Patriot
In 18th-century Ireland this was a term used to describe Protestant individuals in Ireland who became more aware of their Irishness and therefore sought to promote that country's interests rather than British ones.

EXTEND YOUR KNOWLEDGE

Henry Flood (1732–91)
Henry Flood was the illegitimate son of Warden Flood, Chief Justice in Ireland. As a member of the Anglo-Irish community, Flood, like many fellow Protestants, entered politics in 1759 and became a prominent figure in the move to grant Ireland's parliament greater powers after 1779. As a key member of the growing patriot faction in Dublin, Flood, along with Henry Grattan, helped to exploit the increasing calls for trade restrictions on Ireland to be removed as a means to achieve greater freedoms for his country. After 1782, he grew disenchanted with the limited reforms that were granted to Ireland and he sought further reforms from Britain. Having failed to extract further concessions he eventually retired from politics in 1790 and died the following year.

The demand for an improvement to the existing trade restrictions was not confined to Irish politicians and, during the discussions taking place in Dublin, within the wider city a general boycott of British goods was started. This was a public agreement between citizens and it was policed by the Irish Volunteers, who would publish transgressors' names in local newspapers. In addition to the public pressure being brought to bear, the Volunteers also contributed in a more direct manner that used intimidation to achieve the ends they sought.

On 4 November 1779, after the king had made a polite but non-committal reply to the Irish parliament's resolution, the Irish Volunteers paraded in full military regalia outside the parliament house with signs demanding 'a short money bill' and, more threateningly, pulling cannons adorned with the slogan 'free trade or this'. This was an especially effective method given the circumstances of the late 1770s: Britain was at war with both America and France, and Ireland was vulnerable to attack as Irish troops were serving abroad and the country had limited defences. It was clear that the aim of the carefully orchestrated parade was to secure the demands of the Irish Volunteers by exploiting the current position of weakness that Britain felt itself to be in.

Immediately following the parade, the Irish parliament passed the short money bill that it had been considering, and the lord lieutenant John Hobart, the Earl of Buckinghamshire, had to accept it because of his administration's need for money. In the short term, these funds would help with general running costs, but the limited period they were granted for impressed upon him the need to convince the British government to address the issue of free trade.

The repeal of trade restrictions

The Lord North administration in London was slow to consider the threat, but in December 1779 it introduced proposals to the House of Commons to repeal all of the commercial restrictions that currently caused Irish discontent (notably the Wool Act), and this was achieved before the end of the year. In January 1780, Ireland was permitted to trade directly with other parts of the empire on the condition that they set duties equal to those in force in Britain. This was to ensure fair competition between Irish and British merchants. A further Act in March allowed Ireland to import gold and silver from England, and effectively by the end of 1780 the Irish were in the same commercial position as Britain with the exception of Britain's **East India Company monopoly**, which remained exclusively British.

KEY TERMS

East India Company
This was a trading company established in 1600 which imported goods from India in return for British exports to that country. It was one of the biggest companies of its kind throughout the 17th and 18th centuries and was influential in the development of Britain's empire during this time.

Monopoly
The exclusive right to trade.

SOURCE 10

Resolution of the British prime minister Lord North's government of 20 December 1779 to extend free trade to Ireland following pressure from the Irish Volunteers and Dublin politicians. Cited in A. Kippis, *The New Annual Register*, Volume 6 (1786), Government Resolution.

Resolved, Nem. Con. that a liberty to trade with the British colonies in America and the West Indies, and the British colonies on the coast of Africa, in like manner as the trade is carried on with Great Britain and the said colonies and settlements, will be productive of very great commercial benefits, and will be a most affectionate mark on the regard and attention of Great Britain to our distresses, and will give new vigour to the zeal of his Majesty's brave and loyal people of Ireland, to stand forward in support of his Majesty's person and government, and the interest, the honour, and the dignity of the British empire.

The repeal of trade restrictions was a significant progression for Ireland and it promoted a broader campaign for greater legislative power so that these new economic rights would be protected in the future. Spearheading this campaign was Henry Grattan as the prominent member of the patriot group within the Irish parliament. On 19 April 1780, he made a formal declaration of independence in the Irish House of Commons, which had the backing of Catholics and Protestants following their economic gains. It was also given more weight having the Volunteers in support as this organisation was well armed and the only real source of defence in Ireland given the continuation of the American war. Although the debate was adjourned by a vote of 136 to 97 with many supporters feeling that the time was not quite right to assert Irish rights in such a way, the question had been raised and under the existing circumstances the patriots were in a position of relative strength.

The Constitution of 1782

Continuing economic depression and threat of invasion reinforced this position and, in December 1781, patriots within the Volunteer regiments in Armagh arranged for an all Ulster Volunteers' convention to be held in Dungannon in February the following year. Two hundred and fifty delegates attended this meeting on 15 February and they represented 25,000 armed men in the north of the country. The agenda of the meeting had been drawn up by Grattan and Flood and it emphasised the desire for greater legislative powers – the basis of which the convention agreed unanimously. In parliament Grattan raised the question once more, but again it was felt by more cautious members of the House to be too soon and the motion was postponed 137 to 68. The new lord lieutenant Frederick Howard, the Earl of Carlisle, who had taken office in 1780, was aware that this issue was not going away and if no attempt was made to conciliate this growing patriot opinion then Ireland might become impossible to govern.

In March 1782, the british prime Minister, Lord North, resigned his position after British troops surrendered at Yorktown, Virginia, and he was replaced by a Whig administration under the Marquess of Rockingham – Charles Watson-Wentworth. Anxious to prevent further discontent in Ireland, especially as the American war was going so badly for them, and having received news of the extent of feeling from the new lord lieutenant, the new British government was quick to offer concessions. In April 1782, it adjusted Poynings' Law and repealed the Declaratory Act (see page 39) which had each given Britain the power to legislate for Ireland. By removing these political restrictions, the Irish parliament was granted effective autonomy over its domestic legislation and, although the executive was still controlled by a British lord lieutenant, this achievement became known as the Constitution of 1782.

SOURCE 11

From a letter by the Duke of Portland – the new lord lieutenant of Ireland after 1782. It was written to the prime minister, the Marquess of Rockingham, in April 1782.

It is no longer the parliament of Ireland that is to be managed or amended to. It is the whole country. It is the church, the law, the army (I fear, when I consider how it is composed), the merchant, the tradesman, the manufacturer, the farmer, the labourer, the catholic, the dissenter, the protestant, all sects, all sorts and descriptions of men, who... unanimously and most audibly, call upon Great Britain for a full and unequivocal satisfaction.

This Constitution signalled a political victory for Irish politicians, but the authority they had won had only been possible because of the circumstances in which Britain found itself in the late 1770s. War with America and France had weakened Britain's ability to control Ireland, and this opportunity had been skilfully exploited by the growing number of Irish patriots. In creating their own military force to defend Ireland in the event of invasion, the Irish Volunteers became a useful tool with which to build their case for more autonomy. It could effectively be used to intimidate the British government – or at least be seen as a source of threat that could promote their chances of extracting concessions from Britain. This was further enhanced by the economic condition in which Ireland found itself. War had restricted international trade by shrinking markets, and this led to decline in the already fragile Irish economy, which then stirred up popular discontent as living standards dropped. The resulting campaign for the repeal of trade restrictions gave the nation a common goal around which to gather, and this in turn strengthened the demand for political change. Its victory in 1779–1780 with the repeal of the commercial restrictions therefore became a springboard for future political activity. In the short term, however, their benefits to the Irish economy were mixed and the anticipated economic prosperity was not immediate.

ACTIVITY
KNOWLEDGE CHECK

The trade restriction campaign
1 What motivated the start of the opposition to the trade restrictions?
2 Why was the campaign successful?
3 What political significance do you think the campaign had for Ireland?
4 If you were to think of one or two words to describe the significance of the campaign upon Ireland's political ambitions what would they be and why?

The impact of the removal of the restrictions on the Irish economy

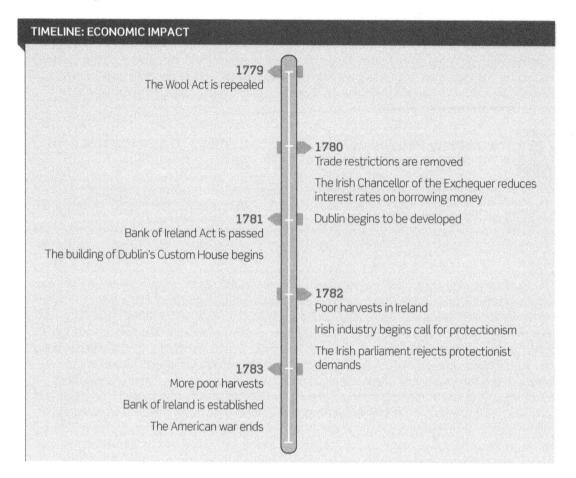

TIMELINE: ECONOMIC IMPACT

1779
The Wool Act is repealed

1780
Trade restrictions are removed

The Irish Chancellor of the Exchequer reduces interest rates on borrowing money

Dublin begins to be developed

1781
Bank of Ireland Act is passed

The building of Dublin's Custom House begins

1782
Poor harvests in Ireland

Irish industry begins call for protectionism

The Irish parliament rejects protectionist demands

1783
More poor harvests

Bank of Ireland is established

The American war ends

Limited impact?

By removing the trade restrictions, the British government anticipated that Ireland's economy would improve. In the months and years following repeal, however, very little actually changed. This was largely because of the continuation of the American war, which had depressed markets and interrupted trade. While the war continued, it was difficult for any improvements to take effect. This position was further hampered by bad harvests in 1782 and 1783, which added to the existing discomfort felt in Ireland.

One of the most depressed markets was that of the woollen industry which, since the 17th century, had been restricted by the cap placed on the export of woollen goods. This restriction had been to the benefit of Britain's textile producers who therefore had less competition for their own product. Although this cap was removed in 1779, the industry did not significantly improve and the common argument for this failure was the continued domination of Ireland's domestic market by British goods. In the years after the removal of the trade restrictions, therefore, the Irish parliament was **lobbied** to pass protectionist legislation that raised tariffs on British imports so that they became more expensive, and therefore promoted the sale of Irish products. This proved to be an abortive attempt to promote Irish industry as Ireland could not afford to compete with Britain whose demand for textiles accounted for nine-tenths of Ireland's exports in that material. Given this reality, the Irish parliament rejected the proposals. They were afraid that Britain might first look to trade elsewhere, and then impose tariffs on Irish goods as a counter-measure.

KEY TERM

Lobby
An action that is taken by groups who want to influence the government. It involves trying to win support by persuasion.

The attempt to address the lingering economic distress in the country, however, is evidence that the concessions made in 1779 and 1780 did not dramatically affect the Irish economy. In part this was because of the ongoing war, but it was also because the reforms to trade did little to actually improve the lives of the majority of those living in Ireland. The real economic problem as far as Irish Catholics were concerned was the unanswered question of land distribution and absentee landlordism, which withdrew approximately £800,000 from an economy that produced only £4 million annually. In this sense, the opening up of trade opportunities was a welcome improvement which, in the post war world, could yield a better return for industry. However, the real issue was the significant amounts of money, around one-quarter of the nation's earnings, leaving the country to be spent in Britain.

General prosperity

Despite individual industries continuing to struggle, there was some evidence that the economy slowly improved after 1780. The Chancellor of the Exchequer, William Hamilton, reduced the interest rate on borrowing from six percent to five percent in 1780. This encouraged greater borrowing for public works in Ireland, including the building of a **Custom House** on the River Liffey which began in 1781. This commitment was also underlined by the passage of a Bank of Ireland Act the following year which signalled the Irish parliament's intention to promote financial development in the country. The reduction of the interest rate in particular stimulated local growth by providing employment opportunities, but in the medium and longer term it also encouraged absentee landlords to return to the country as Dublin was gradually transformed, becoming a vibrant centre for high society. Returning with these landlords was their spending power, and consequently this injection also helped to promote further prosperity, which only increased after the conclusion of the American war in 1783.

Despite some small improvement, the changes to the trade regulations did not immediately transform Irish fortunes. The American war kept economic growth fairly confined for the next couple of years after the restrictions were repealed, and therefore general growth was quite slow. However, what the reforms did achieve by allowing Ireland effective trade parity with Britain, was the creation of a more independent platform from which the country could build a more prosperous nation when trade picked up once more.

Between the years 1774 and 1830, the fortunes of Irish Catholics changed dramatically. Before 1774, they were subject to punitive laws that restricted their rights and prevented them from living on an equal footing with their Protestant neighbours. In part, this was a deliberate attempt by the British state to control the Irish nation, whose population was 80 percent Catholic and significantly outnumbered the small Protestant community there. By trying to strengthen this minority, however, the Penal Laws actually undermined their position in the long term because the privileges that they enjoyed became a source of great resentment among the wider population. Although not immediately, this resentment was acknowledged by the British authorities in the late 18th century as war with America raised the prospect of potential rebellion in Ireland if nothing was done to improve the Catholic position there. The reforms made at this time opened the door to further reforms after 1801 when Ireland was formally bound to Britain in union. By combining the Irish and British parliament, there was the chance to sway British opinion and use the electoral process to further Catholic rights. These opportunities were not necessarily anticipated, but prominent individuals such as Daniel O'Connell were able to exploit them to the best advantage of Irish Catholics.

KEY TERM

Custom House
This is an office that receives the custom duties – taxes – on imports into the country.

A Level Exam-Style Question Section B

'The British government response to Irish demands for the repeal of trade restrictions between the years 1778–1782 was mainly the result of the presence of the Irish Volunteers.'

How far do you agree with this statement? (20 marks)

Tip
When answering this question you should consider how important the Volunteers were compared with other reasons – why was there a demand for the removal of trade restrictions in the first place?

The Custom House in Dublin, which was built in the 18th century. This drawing was created by T. Hart, c19th century.

ACTIVITY
SUMMARY

Emancipation

1 Create a graph that represents how the fortunes of Catholics improved between 1774 and 1830.

2 Label the key events on your graph.

3 Study the graph you have created and note down any significant observations about the progression of Catholic relief. Is there a pattern or anything significant about the timing of reforms?

4 Write a paragraph explaining why you think emancipation was able to be successful between 1774 and 1830. You should consider the nature of change over time when writing this.

WIDER READING

Beckett, J.C. *The Making of Modern Ireland, 1603–1923*, Faber and Faber (1981)

Connolly, S.J. (ed.), *The Oxford Companion to Irish History*, OUP (1998)

Foster, R. *Modern Ireland 1600–1972*, Penguin (1988)

Moody, T.W. and Martin, F.X. (eds), *The Course of Irish History*, Mercier Press (1994)

O'Corrain, D. and O'Riordan, T. (eds), *Ireland 1815–1870: Emancipation, Famine and Religion*, Four Courts Press (2010)

Pelling, N. *Anglo-Irish Relations 1798–1922*, Routledge (2003)

3.4 Industrialisation in Ulster, 1825-55

KEY QUESTIONS

- How important were the textile industries in Ulster before 1855?
- What impact did the development of shipbuilding have upon Ulster?
- What was the impact of industrialisation upon the people of Ulster?

KEY TERM

Planter
A member of a group of English or Scottish people who were deliberately given land in Ireland as part of England's attempt to colonise the country and anglicise the Irish. The main bulk of these settlers arrived in Ireland in the early 17th century.

INTRODUCTION

The traditional view of Ireland is that it maintains a primarily rural economy with few cities and a population very much tied to the land. During the 18th century this was perhaps a reasonably accurate impression, but only in as much as it had not really embarked upon serious industrialisation as England had done. When technology began to be developed, Ireland was equally quick to identify the possibilities it offered and, given its close union with Britain, it was in a strong position to benefit from the industrialisation that Britain underwent. This was perhaps most evident in the north of the country and in the province of Ulster especially. As a heartland for Protestantism since the arrival of the first English and Scottish **planters**, Ulster had always enjoyed a close relationship with Britain and the people there very much felt themselves to be Anglo-Irish rather than simply Irish. The ties that many of the people of Ulster enjoyed with Britain subsequently translated into a close commercial partnership with that nation in addition to that which it enjoyed with Dublin and the south.

The basis of this close commercial relationship lay in the industries that grew up in Ulster. Before the 1820s, this was primarily textiles, particularly linen, cotton and wool, which relied heavily upon Britain as the province's prime market for export. Here Ulster goods were sold on within the country and also re-exported further afield. Such was the nature of this close relationship that when industrialisation took hold in Britain, Ulster also derived some benefit from the technological changes being undertaken – for example, shipbuilding became one of Belfast's greatest assets in the 19th century. This was at a cost, however. Just as new innovations encouraged industrial growth, they also threatened some of the more traditional industries, which could no longer compete with the new machines. They also encouraged a growing population, which brought with it additional problems that come with rapid urbanisation. Industrialisation was both a blessing and a curse, helping to shape the identity of modern Ulster.

1824 - Steam power is introduced to Belfast shipbuilding

1826 - Belfast's first steamship is built by Ritchie and MacLaine

1829 - Andrew Mulholland opens his York Street spinning mill

1837 - Work on widening Belfast docks' approach channel is begun

1839 - The first railways line in Ulster is opened between Belfast and Lisburn

| 1825 | 1830 | 1835 | 1840 |

1825 - James Kay creates the wet-spinning process

1828 - James and William Murland establish Ulster's first wet-spinning mill

1832 - William Murtagh becomes Ireland's first recorded cholera death

1838 - Belfast's first iron steamship is built by Victor Coates and Company

1841 - William Dargan completes the first cut to Belfast docks' approach channel

HOW IMPORTANT WERE THE TEXTILE INDUSTRIES IN ULSTER BEFORE 1855?

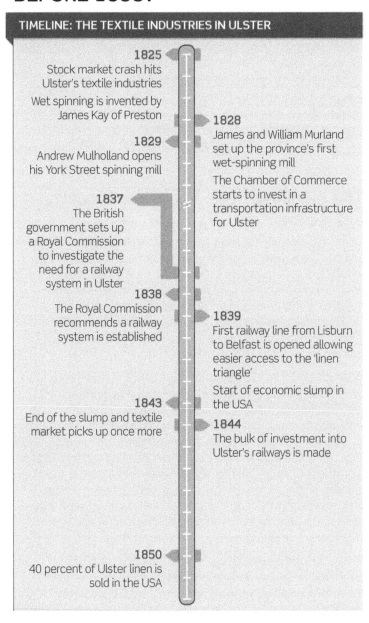

TIMELINE: THE TEXTILE INDUSTRIES IN ULSTER

1825
Stock market crash hits Ulster's textile industries

Wet spinning is invented by James Kay of Preston

1829
Andrew Mulholland opens his York Street spinning mill

1837
The British government sets up a Royal Commission to investigate the need for a railway system in Ulster

1838
The Royal Commission recommends a railway system is established

1843
End of the slump and textile market picks up once more

1850
40 percent of Ulster linen is sold in the USA

1828
James and William Murland set up the province's first wet-spinning mill

The Chamber of Commerce starts to invest in a transportation infrastructure for Ulster

1839
First railway line from Lisburn to Belfast is opened allowing easier access to the 'linen triangle'

Start of economic slump in the USA

1844
The bulk of investment into Ulster's railways is made

The importance of the textile industry in Ulster

Manufacturing has been the bedrock of many countries' prosperity and Ireland was no different. Despite having a significant agricultural economy in the south and west, during the early 18th century the north-east of Ireland was a growing heartland for textile production, of which linen was the most prominent. In 1715, the province of Ulster produced two million yards of linen cloth, yet by the 1790s this had risen to over 40 million yards and accounted for one-third of the country's exports to Britain. Complementing this success were the equally prosperous wool and cotton industries. These also developed in Ulster and enjoyed particular growth after the 1770s when they were protected by tariffs imposed by the Irish parliament so as to ensure stable growth for the country's economy. One motivation for this preferential treatment was the number of people it employed – by 1811, 50,000 people were engaged in the manufacture of cotton. By 1821 more than 40 percent of the Irish population worked in manufacturing of some kind and in Ulster this was textiles in the main. As an employer, therefore, the textile industry was a significant contributor to the nation's prosperity. Combined with the income it brought in through exportation to Britain and the rest of the empire, it was among the most important sectors of the Irish economy.

What the textile industry did in particular for Ulster was to help develop a distinct merchant class who were quick to establish trade routes with Britain during the 18th century. By the 1820s these routes had become very well established – particularly those running from Belfast to Liverpool. While these ships carried an array of Irish produce, including livestock and agricultural produce, the biggest export was textiles and especially linen cloth. Such was the importance of this particular trade route that by 1826 it was conducted principally by steamships rather than the more established tall ships which traditionally relied on good winds to speed their journey. This was an expensive means of transportation because of the high coal consumption of the early vessels. However, they were also much quicker and this enabled a more efficient trade system that was to the benefit of both Ulster and Britain. For Ulster it highlighted the internal weaknesses of the province's transportation system, which sometimes held up the steamships because of cargo arriving late to the ports.

1845 - Dargan's island is renamed Queen's Island

1849 - William Dargan completes the second cut to the approach channel

1853 - Robert Hickson opens a shipyard on Queen's Island

1845 | 1850 | 1855 | 1860

1847 - Passage of the Belfast Harbour Act and the creation of Belfast Harbour Commissioners

1851 - Thompson and Kirwan establish a dock on Queen's Island

1854 - Hickson employs Edward Harland as his yard manager

That cargo often included necessary supplies of coal that the steamships needed to burn. The awareness of this limitation resulted in growing demand for investment in the province's transportation network, and after 1828 the Belfast **Chamber of Commerce** devoted a significant portion of its time to raise money for investment into the roads, canals and especially the rail network in Ulster. The long-term benefits of this investment would improve communication within the province and notably promote industrialisation there. By aiming to create strong internal trade links, Ulster would become a desirable place for new businesses to locate and for more established ones to grow. In terms of this aim, undertaking such moves in the 1820s was effective timing. It took full advantage of the rapidly expanding industrial economy of Britain and also the benefits of technological innovation which were developing as part of the wider industrial revolution.

KEY TERM

Chamber of Commerce
This is a local association created to promote the interests of businesses in a given area.

The linen industry and the expansion of Belfast

The linen industry was particularly important to the Irish economy as a whole in addition to Ulster as a single province. On a national scale it added considerably to the general prosperity of the country through the export of its goods to Britain. In the late 18th and early 19th centuries there was a great demand for Irish cloth as it was recognised as amongst the best quality available. During this period, there was a burgeoning trade that significantly contributed to the developing Irish economy.

In terms of individual prosperity, this industry also offered small farmers the chance to supplement their agricultural income. Such was the demand for linen, particularly during the Napoleonic wars when the need for sail cloth was high, that the few mills that existed during the 18th century could not keep up with demand even though 13 new mills had been built between 1805 and 1809. Therefore, farmers were encouraged to take up weaving during the fallow months as a means of enhancing production. In addition, it also had the positive by-product of improving their own personal incomes.

What this practice created was a **cottage industry** based upon the manufacture of linen, which by the 1820s had grown into a much broader commercial enterprise within Ulster. This province produced the majority of the country's 50 million yards of linen by that time. Much of this was done in Belfast – a town that had quickly grown into an industrial heartland for linen production and which in 1820 employed more than 2,000 people within its 15 mills. After 1825 Belfast grew at an even greater rate, and so tightly bound was its success to the linen industry that it became known as 'linenopolis'. The reason for this development was the River Lagan which ran through the city and provided the opportunity to exploit the development of **wet spinning**, which created a much finer yarn for cloth-making. The benefits of this method were that yarns could also be spun in much larger quantities and returned better profit margins than cotton; during the 1820s cotton could fetch 10 pence a pound while linen could make 4 shillings. The prospect of these better margins encouraged substantial growth within Belfast and in turn the population increased as more people moved to the town for work in the new mills that were quickly being established.

KEY TERMS

Cottage industry
A business that is operated inside people's homes.

Wet spinning
A method of spinning invented by James Kay of Preston in 1825. It involved soaking the linen flax in warm water for about 14 hours in order to soften the fibres so that it could be spun much tighter.

The decline of the woollen and cotton industries

Linen was certainly the most prominent textile industry in Ulster and it had a notable influence upon the development of Belfast, which quickly transformed from a small market town into the country's most industrialised centre during the 19th century. Supporting this development, however, were the cotton and woollen industries, which had also enjoyed a strong position in Ulster and had contributed very effectively to the prosperity of that province before 1825.

Between 1770 and 1824 the cotton industry had been protected by the Irish parliament, and the agreements it had reached with Britain gave it a great advantage over its competitors. Imported cotton goods were subject to a ten percent charge so as to encourage the growth of an Irish domestic market. This protection afforded the Irish cotton spinning and weaving industries to flourish, and for a brief while the success of the industry eclipsed even that of linen. By 1824, however, this pre-eminence began to falter, and after 1825 the industry went into decline. By 1850, of the 19 cotton spinning mills in operation in Ulster, only four remained.

The cause of this reversal has traditionally been ascribed to a shortage of capital and the expense of coal, which made production so costly, resulting in a commercial crisis in 1825 and ultimately a failure to complete with cheaper producers in Britain. This conventional wisdom has been challenged recently – firstly, on the issue of expensive coal, which in reality only accounted for two percent of the total cost of production and could be offset by the relatively cheap labour costs prevalent in Ireland. Furthermore, rather than lacking capital for investment, actually cotton mill owners took the deliberate decision to transfer their operation from cotton spinning to flax spinning for the creation of linen after 1825. The motivation for this switch was threefold.

- Firstly, there was increased competition from British producers.

- Secondly, the invention of wet spinning made linen production more attractive.

- Thirdly, a stock market crash in 1825 drastically affected the cotton industry in such a way that it never really recovered.

SOURCE 1

From a Belfast banker speaking to a House of Lords committee convened in 1848 to investigate the commercial distress of 1825. Here he is commenting on the state of Ulster's cotton industry.

We were not able to compete with Manchester and Glasgow in the spinning of cotton... our cotton mills have been converted in to linen mills, there are some remaining but they are not doing much; we have a good deal of weaving and bleaching and things of that sort connected with the cotton manufacture but yarn for that purpose is all imported and a good deal is done on Scotch account.

The development of a strong cotton spinning industry in Britain, which was able to produce cotton at a lower cost because of the increased use of the machinery, it employed was certainly a challenge for the Ulster industry. This test was felt more acutely after 1824 when the protective tariffs were removed, leaving Irish yarn to compete on an equal footing with other suppliers. The motivation behind the removal of this advantage for Ulster was the growing number of British politicians who sought to promote free trade as a means of advancing Britain's own prosperity and taking full advantage of its growing industrial capacity. Given this challenge, the opportunity to convert their mills to linen production was an attractive proposition. The process was quite similar following the timely invention of wet spinning in 1825, and this meant the cost and inconvenience of the shift would be marginal. Consolidating the decision to transfer was also the awareness that production of linen offered a greater profit margin. Raw cotton cost 10 pence per pound and could be sold for 18 pence when spun, compared to flax which cost 6 pence per pound but could be sold for 4 shillings.

Dovetailing with the removal of protection for the industry was also a commercial crisis which emerged in 1825–26 following a decline in the value of the British stock market. This led to investors trying to take their money out of the businesses in which they had invested in order to minimise their losses. This hit the cotton industry in particular because of the growth it had enjoyed during the previous 50 years. The knock-on effect for Ulster, like the British cotton industry, was high unemployment. In Belfast alone, in 1830 there were 700 heads of household and their 3,000 dependents bordering on the verge of starvation as a result of their inability to find work as cotton weavers.

The woollen industry

Just like the cotton industry, Ulster's small woollen industry also suffered because of the growing competition from Britain. This was not only because that country was the main importer of Ulster wool, but also Britain's domestic woollen industry was developing. Therefore, it made more sense during the commercial crisis for Britain to safeguard its own industry rather than support Ulster's. In addition to this loss, prior to the 1830s Ulster had also supplied Ireland's domestic market with the majority of wool that it demanded. However, by 1838 this supply had been reduced to only 14 percent due to the competition from other countries. Furthermore, this competition made great use of new technologies such as steam-powered looms, which meant that wool could be produced in much greater quantities at lower prices than the more traditional methods of hand-loom weaving that existed in Ulster. The decline of this industry in the wake of the stock market crash and subsequent commercial crisis meant that Ulster became dependent upon the linen industry which had successfully made the transition to steam power and was, therefore, able to withstand the depressed textile markets of the mid-1820s.

ACTIVITY
KNOWLEDGE CHECK

The importance of the textile industry
1 What were the main textile industries in Ulster?
2 How did these industries affect the province?
3 How secure were these industries?
4 Which industry was most important and in what way?

The impact of railways and mechanisation upon the linen industry

Ulster's textile industry began to become concentrated upon linen, and its production became more industrialised with the adoption of steam-powered wet-spinning techniques after 1825. This transition was most marked in the growing town of Belfast (it formally became a city in 1888) which not only became a significant linen producer itself, but also became the main port from which that material could be exported to Britain (its main buyer) and the rest of the world. Between 1831 and 1851 the population of this town doubled as people came looking for work, and it quickly became the province's biggest urban and commercial centre.

A significant implication of Belfast's rapid growth as a major hub for commerce was the need to link other parts of Ulster to that town. Before the 1820s a significant portion of the linen industry had developed in the homes of private individuals as a supplement to their farming incomes which declined during the winter months. To ensure the success of these smaller industries, therefore, access to Belfast became a very important issue in the next decade.

The railways

By 1825, outside of Belfast, linen production was mostly centred in what historian W.H. Crawford has termed the 'linen triangle' – the area between Lisburn, Dungannon and Armagh (see Figure 4.1). Therefore, it was important for this area to have good access to the ports and, by extension, foreign markets. Each of these areas was landlocked and required an effective means for transporting their goods to the **entrepôts**.

KEY TERM

Entrepôt
A port or trading post.

Ulster had a canal system on which construction had begun in 1733 and was centred around Lough Neagh, but this was slow and cumbersome. The industrial age manufacturers required a more flexible and efficient system. The realisation that Ulster's internal transport networks were neither quick nor efficient enough to maximise the commercial potential of Ulster's linen industry was quickly acknowledged, and in the late 1820s investment in creating a substantial railway network began.

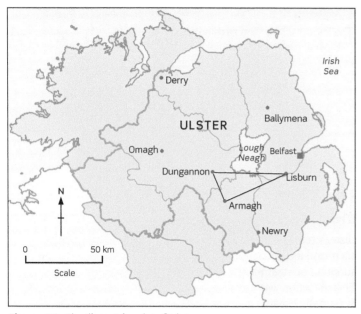

Figure 4.1 The 'linen triangle' of Ulster.

Supporting this development was a government-sponsored **Royal Commission** which was convened to investigate the development of a broader railway network in Ireland. In 1837, it produced a general report about the need for investment. Then, in a larger second report published in 1838, it made the recommendation that the British government fund a national Irish railway so as to create a uniform service for the benefit of the whole nation. This was challenged by those who felt the railway should be entirely managed and funded through private enterprise on the grounds that the recommendations would simply allow government officials to grant contracts to their own supporters rather than those with the best plans. Eventually the recommendations were dropped in 1842 after failure to agree any compromise and a growing reluctance in Britain to spend public money on a railway for Ireland. In the meantime, however, private work had already begun on establishing a rail service. It was accepted that in order for industry to progress, particularly in Ulster, an effective communications network had to be created to link the outlying mills and small factories to the industrial hub that was growing in Belfast.

KEY TERM

Royal Commission
An executive appointed panel created to investigate, and make recommendations for, a particular aspect of government policy.

The first line created was from Belfast to Lisburn, which opened in 1839 at a cost of £107,000. It served as an important means of opening up the interior and promoting easier access for these outlying areas to send their goods to foreign markets. Further lines were established in the following years and this reached a climax in 1844–45 when more than 80 percent of the total investment on the railways for the years between 1835 and 1850 was made. The outcome of this rapid investment by private companies was that by the end of the century more than 1,000 miles of line had been laid, linking 90 percent of the population.

The significance of this investment for linen was that it helped to consolidate the industry at a time when industrialisation had undermined other textile interests. Since linen had begun as a cottage industry, the trend towards industrial development around Belfast threatened the medium- and long-term future of the province's smaller producers in more isolated areas. The creation of good rail links, however, gave them a lifeline with which to attach themselves to this centre and make an essential contribution to the ongoing success of their industry. This had a twofold effect.

- Firstly, it allowed the province as a whole to prosper from the continued demand for Ulster linen.

- Secondly, it made the overall industry much more stable by the provision of a continuous supply of goods that consequently helped to ensure confidence among purchasers abroad.

EXTRACT

1 From Jamie Johnston, *Victorian Belfast*, Ulster Historical Foundation (1993).

During the 19th century Belfast continued to serve as the market town for the farmers of the Lagan valley and surrounding countryside. The improvements in the port and harbour facilities in the early 19th century increased the importance of Belfast to this local area as a link with the markets of mainland Britain.

However, farmers in the rest of the province initially had difficulty in taking advantage of these improvements as it was so difficult to transport their goods to Belfast. This was because not many roads of good quality led to Belfast in the early 19th century. For example, the main road between Belfast and Antrim, which was Belfast's main link to the north of the province, was only built in the 1830s. Large areas of the countryside were left untouched by canals.

The introduction of the railway to the province completely changed this picture. Railways could carry linens and agricultural goods from all parts of the Ulster countryside to Belfast where they could be processed and shipped to mainland Britain and around the world.

Mechanisation

In addition to the development of the railway system, which helped to improve communication and trade opportunities for the broader provincial community, the mechanisation of the linen-making process also ensured greater prosperity. In part the reason for this can be seen by looking at the manner in which Ulster's other textile interests declined – essentially being out-produced and out-priced by the larger and more efficient mills of Lancashire and Glasgow. These centres were quick to see the advantages of mechanisation and, therefore, were able to harness the new technologies early into the 19th century, developing large industrial mills across Ulster that consequently placed themselves in a dominant position for the growing markets. Ulster's own cotton and woollen industries, by contrast, were primarily based upon smaller, private enterprises that were spread throughout the province and employed hand-loom weaving. This could not compete as effectively with the steam-powered mills of England and Scotland.

In order to be able to compete effectively in the industrialising age it was necessary to mechanise, and there was a conscious effort to do so within the linen industry after 1825 and with the adoption of wet spinning. This allowed the Ulster businesses to take advantage of the local availability of flax which was relatively inexpensive compared to the cost of imported cotton. By producing their own yarns, the cost of making linen was reduced and this offered the opportunity for greater stability in terms of both a regular supply of raw materials and the ability to offer competitive prices. The first wet spinning mill was established in 1828 by James and William Murland in Annsborough, a small town near Castlewellan in County Down, and further mills emerged during the next decade as more manufacturers acknowledged the benefits of adopting the new process. In 1834, there were 12 dedicated flax spinning mills in Ulster, and by the end of the 1830s this had risen to 35, which suggests the confidence that manufacturers such as the Murlands, Hugh MacCall and Andrew Mulholland had in the new process. These individuals became large employers in Belfast – by the end of the century Mulholland employed 5,000 people at his firm and was believed to be the largest spinning company in the world at that time. The fact that others quickly followed in this enterprise points towards the success that the first mills of this kind, such as Murland's, were having. With more firms switching to mechanisation, the spinning industry in Ulster was rapidly transformed into a major industrial force.

While Ulster's spinning industry was transformed, weaving the linen remained a traditional, hand-loom affair. The reason for this was that early power looms could only weave coarse linens, which were inappropriate in Ulster since this region specialised in finer linens. Given this technological difficulty, Ulster retained hand-loom production for another 20 years after switching to wet spinning after 1825. Only when the price of hand-loom weaving became more expensive did manufacturers then invest in the new power looms that were capable of weaving finer cloth. But this did not happen until weavers' wages rose significantly after the 1840s when famine and emigration saw a decline in the number of weavers available and a subsequent increase in demand for this skill.

SOURCE 2

From the *Irish Linen Trade Handbook and Directory* published in 1876.

> The rapid improvement in linen manufacturing which followed the introduction of the wet spinning system, and the cheapness with which yarns were produced, and the great regularity in regard to weights, counts, etc., as compared with the hand spun material, enabled manufacturers to considerably reduce the price of cloth. Irish cloth rapidly displaced German cloth abroad, and some of the South American markets, which formerly took the manufactures of Silesia and Brabant etc., were now supplied with Irish Sileasians and Brabants etc.

The demand for wet-spun yarn increased throughout the mid-century, causing a slump in the earnings of hand spinners in Ulster and effectively precipitating a rapid decline in their enterprise. Although this traditional process went into decline, the advent of mechanised spinning – and then, in the late 1840s, mechanised weaving – allowed the linen industry in Ulster to grow and be successful in the mid-19th century at a time of significant competition from other producers such as England's Lancashire mills.

Competition certainly made things more difficult. However, Ulster businesses had successfully developed new markets of their own. Prominent amongst these was the USA, which developed a growing demand for the finer-quality linen cloth that Ulster produced. This country became a keen importer of Irish cloth in the mid-century and it accounted for 40 percent of the province's linen cloth exports by 1850. This market was, therefore, very profitable and linen manufacturers were able to take advantage of this large and expanding market because of the mechanisation of the industry. Not only did this allow firms to meet the great demand in the USA, but also, with the lower production costs that mechanisation afforded, mills had a better chance of weathering any economic difficulties that occurred – notably a slump between 1839 and 1842 when the USA suffered depression and the market consequently contracted as trade declined. Additionally, when the market picked up once more after 1842, mechanisation enabled Ulster's mills to quickly make up their profits and even expand as the markets developed in the ensuing years.

> **A Level Exam Style Question Section B**
>
> How significant was the introduction of mechanisation to the demise of Ulster's cotton industry between 1825 and 1855? (20 marks)
>
> **Tip**
>
> *When answering this question you should consider additional reasons for the decline of the cotton industry after 1825 and evaluate these against the impact of mechanisation mentioned in the question.*

WHAT IMPACT DID THE DEVELOPMENT OF SHIPBUILDING HAVE UPON ULSTER?

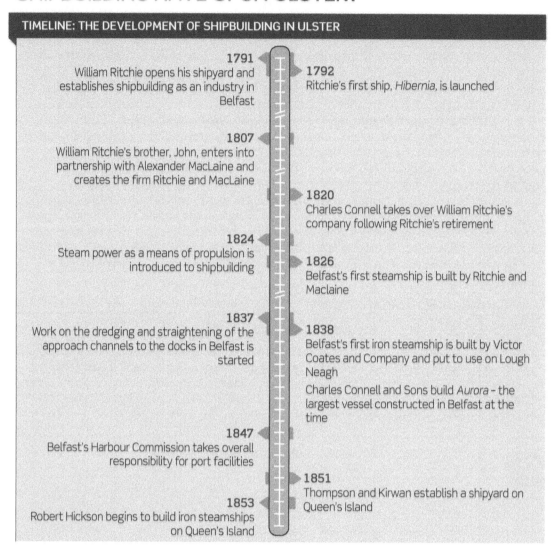

TIMELINE: THE DEVELOPMENT OF SHIPBUILDING IN ULSTER

1791
William Ritchie opens his shipyard and establishes shipbuilding as an industry in Belfast

1792
Ritchie's first ship, *Hibernia*, is launched

1807
William Ritchie's brother, John, enters into partnership with Alexander MacLaine and creates the firm Ritchie and MacLaine

1820
Charles Connell takes over William Ritchie's company following Ritchie's retirement

1824
Steam power as a means of propulsion is introduced to shipbuilding

1826
Belfast's first steamship is built by Ritchie and Maclaine

1837
Work on the dredging and straightening of the approach channels to the docks in Belfast is started

1838
Belfast's first iron steamship is built by Victor Coates and Company and put to use on Lough Neagh

Charles Connell and Sons build *Aurora* – the largest vessel constructed in Belfast at the time

1847
Belfast's Harbour Commission takes overall responsibility for port facilities

1851
Thompson and Kirwan establish a shipyard on Queen's Island

1853
Robert Hickson begins to build iron steamships on Queen's Island

The development of shipbuilding

Linen was without doubt a very prominent industry for the north-east of Ireland and it would be easy to suggest that this area was totally reliant upon its success. However, Ulster was a rapidly developing area and it was able to attract a range of new industries which, in turn, promoted industrial diversification. This was especially important for the region's future prosperity because it strengthened the overall security of the province's economy by spreading the risk so that it was not so reliant upon one industry. In tandem, it also encouraged more people to Ulster, which naturally fed into the general economy and further enhanced its ongoing progress.

The industry of note that really shaped the future of Ulster, and in particular Belfast, was shipbuilding. This had developed quite late in Belfast – during the last decade of the 18th century. However, by 1825 it had three established shipbuilding yards: Ritchie and MacLaine; Charles Connell and Sons; and Thompson and Kirwan. Between 1820 and 1850, these yards built more than 50 ships between them and, although this was small in comparison to the larger yards in Glasgow and Liverpool, they helped to establish Belfast as the single most prominent centre for shipbuilding in Ulster. Upon their foundation, the famous yards of Harland and Wolff, builders of *Titanic*, and Workman Clark and Company were established in the later 19th century – cementing Belfast as a shipbuilding centre of international repute.

In the 1820s, however, it was far from clear that Belfast would enjoy such a prosperous future in shipbuilding since the city was not well adapted for large-scale building and lacked the space for such an enterprise. In particular, the River Lagan, which provided Belfast with its access to the sea, had significant bends in it, which produced narrow channels that only small ships could pass through. Consequently, the industry remained relatively small until significant modernisation took place in the late 1830s to open up the Lagan and allow the industry the increased space it needed in order to flourish. Even with these changes, however, Belfast remained a difficult place to establish such an industry. Its eventual success after 1850 benefited from adopting and mastering the new techniques of shipbuilding and, more importantly, attracting orders from other ports such as Liverpool, where shipbuilders were increasingly finding it difficult to fulfil contracts. This was because the docks there were always being expanded due to increasing traffic and, therefore, firms were continually having to be relocated as this work was undertaken. In this sense, therefore, Belfast's own shipbuilding industry owed as much to factors outside its control as to the steps it deliberately undertook.

EXTRACT

2 From the historian John Lynch, *An Unlikely Success Story: The Belfast Shipbuilding Industry 1880–1935*, Ulster Historical Foundation (2001).

The success of the industry is a matter of historical fact but in the 1830s, when factory-based linen was beginning to transform Belfast from a commercial centre into an industrial town, the location offered little to attract a shipbuilder. Unlike Cork or Dublin, there was only a very limited tradition of wooden shipbuilding, from which modern iron or steel construction might have developed. The Lagan, upon which Belfast stands, was totally unsuited for large scale shipbuilding until massive improvements were undertaken in the 1840s. The city could offer a reservoir of cheap unskilled labour, which, in the view of Pollard and Robertson, was of great importance. However, shipbuilding depended upon skilled labour, a commodity which was not available in Belfast, or even in Ireland, and which therefore had to be recruited from other areas.

Even after the Lagan was dredged and straightened to form the Victoria channel in the 1840s, it was far from ideal a site for the construction of large vessels, being more congested than the Thames, where such constraints are frequently blamed for the decline of shipbuilding on that river

Early shipbuilding in Belfast

In 1826, the first steamship, called the *Chieftain*, was built in Belfast by Ritchie and MacLaine after the introduction of steam propulsion into that city two years earlier. This was a significant step in the development for shipbuilding in Ulster as it signalled the modernisation of this industry in the province and showed Irish shipbuilders as being equal to the task of building modern vessels for the industrial age. Despite this development, the ships that these firms produced were still made of wood as this was the traditional means of construction. However, in 1838 the first Belfast-built iron ship was sailed upon Lough Neagh, which precipitated a transformation in Irish shipbuilding. This vessel, called the *Countess of Caledon*, was a lake steamer and it was built by an engineering and boiler-making firm Victor Coates and Company. The reason for this was that the technical requirements

for constructing iron ships were closer to engineering than the more traditional wood-based shipbuilding techniques. As a result the original shipyards were slow to adapt to the new methods, instead continuing to produce wooden vessels using their established practices. As the century continued, however, these traditional methods were quickly eclipsed as increasingly iron ships became the preferred means of construction. This transition, combined with the use of steam power, marked Belfast out as a prominent centre for modern shipbuilding after 1850.

The growth of shipbuilding in Ulster added to the rapid expansion of Belfast and it quickly became the industrial centre of the province. As this industry grew, it also benefited international trade as the docks were expanded to help accommodate the development of the shipbuilding yards. This resulted in an increased capacity to manage a larger volume of seaborne traffic from around the world. In 1815, the Belfast ports cleared 91,000 tonnes of shipping – usually exporting domestically produced goods and livestock and importing raw materials such as coal, which was not readily available in Ireland. By 1835, however, it was able to clear 291,000 tonnes, and the town's increasing ability to manage this level of shipping made it internationally recognised in addition to becoming Ulster's busiest port.

The development of shipbuilding was consequently very important to Ulster's growing positon as Ireland's most industrialised province. Outside of Ulster, the area around Dublin was well developed while Cork, in terms of shipbuilding, even surpassed Belfast. In 1826, the **ship tonnage** built in Cork amounted to 1,094 tonnes, while Belfast was a distant second with its output of 364 tonnes. However, the northern town was a fast-developing area that after 1850 would become the epicentre of Irish shipbuilding. The opportunities that Belfast and its growing shipbuilding industry created were fundamental to the prosperity of Ulster because they helped to breathe new life into the province by promoting diversification. That had the twin benefits of offering the economy greater security, and also enhancing employment prospects for the region. This last feature was especially important since the population in Belfast had grown from 37,000 in 1821 to 75,000 by 1841, and Ulster itself had seen a population increase of 18.8 percent during the same period. The shipbuilding yards of Belfast were in one sense a motivating factor for this increase because people naturally chose to move into the town for work, which the growing yards could offer. However, they also served as a welcome source of regular, long-term employment as shipbuilding was a skilled trade requiring dedication and experience. By offering this type of employment, the yards were also providing a strongly anticipated sense of job security for those taken on, and this had its own benefits in terms of families being able to establish themselves more easily and think about the future.

KEY TERM

Ship tonnage
This is a measurement of the cargo-carrying capacity of ships. The higher the tonnage, then the bigger the ship is.

The importance of the Charles Connell and Sons and the Thompson and Kirwan yards

Charles Connell and Sons

The first shipyard of note to be built in Belfast was William Ritchie's yard. However, this was taken over in 1820 by Charles Connell following Ritchie's retirement, although his name continued in the shipbuilding industry after his brother John entered into partnership with Alexander MacLaine in 1807. As Ritchie and MacLaine, this company prospered and even produced the city's first steamship in 1826. However, the original firm, now under the control of Charles Connell and Sons, remained the dominant shipbuilder in Belfast.

Charles Connell was a Scottish shipbuilder who operated out of a yard in Scotstoun on the River Clyde but, after the retirement of William Ritchie, the business moved to Ireland. In 1832, it built a 310 tonne ship called *Fanny* which was designed to service trade in the Far East and which made history by being the first ship to bring tea to Belfast directly from its origin in Canton. This 'first' was subsequently capitalised on when, in 1838, the company built the *Aurora* which was the largest vessel then produced in Belfast. The company continued to produce well-built ships. In 1841 the *James Duncan* made the quickest passage to Constantinople (Istanbul) of that year, and then in 1842 it made the passage to Leghorn (in Italy) in only 22 days.

These ships not only exhibited the building prowess of the Belfast yards, but they also promoted Ulster's, and Ireland's, economic development by transporting home-produced goods such as linens to foreign markets. Traditionally, Ireland relied upon Britain and the USA for trade but, as more ships were produced, trade was enhanced with emerging new markets, such as Italy and Turkey. In this regard, Connell and Sons was integral to this success since the company had a prolific record for shipbuilding and by 1842 had produced 32 vessels, averaging approximately two every year.

The consistent success of Charles Connell and Sons helped to develop Belfast's reputation as a shipbuilding centre and this was critical for the development of not only the city itself, but the province's broader economy, which was heavily based on manufacturing and, therefore, relied on these ships to access new markets abroad. By the mid-19th century, Ulster was very quickly becoming the industrial heartland of Ireland and the success of large companies, such as Charles Connell and Sons, only hastened that progression.

Thompson and Kirwan

Another contributor to the growing success of Belfast shipbuilding was the firm Thompson and Kirwan, who established a shipyard on Queen's Island in the mouth of the River Lagan in 1851. This was a small company started by William Thompson, who would later serve as secretary to the Harbour Commissioners between 1857 and 1883. Like Charles Connell and Sons, Thompson primarily built wooden vessels in the traditional manner at his dry dock near Corporation Street, but later the company moved to new premises. In moving their operation from the west bank of the Lagan onto the south-east side of Queen's Island, the company hoped to expand its business and take advantage of the growing demand for ships. Despite these intentions, however, in 1853 the yard on Queen's Island was taken over by Robert Hickson, who had been a successful proprietor of an ironworks factory and who wanted to extend his existing shipyard on the island. His yard was adjacent to the Thompson and Kirwan yard and so it suited his operation to buy the extra space.

The decline of Thompson and Kirwan was essentially the result of the increasing demand for iron ships rather than the traditional wooden vessels it was used to building. The additional costs involved in using iron, and the different techniques it demanded, made it quite prohibitive for the small firm to realistically adopt and, therefore, when the chance to sell the ailing business appeared the firm was quite eager to take the opportunity. Hickson's acquisition of Thompson and Kirwan signalled an intention to build bigger iron ships and although his firm, Hickson and Company, was later sold in 1858, it had set the precedent for Belfast's future in shipbuilding.

Shipyards and expanding industry

Collectively, these shipyards helped to advance the industry in Belfast. As successful businesses themselves, they added to the economic development of Ulster by offering employment opportunities to the local population as well as encouraging more people to Belfast and making it the country's largest town. More important than just their individual success was the wider impact they had for existing industries and also the growth of new ones. In terms of the established industries in Ulster, linen especially, the growth of Belfast as an international port expanded the opportunity for trade, and in the 1840s the USA overtook Britain as the biggest importer of Irish cloth. By 1851, the combined value of exports leaving Belfast alone was £2,667,100 and this added substantially to the prosperity of both the town and Ulster.

The physical requirements of shipbuilding also gave birth to associated industries such as rope manufacturing and machine engineering for the creation of engines and boilers for the new steamships. Here, engineering firms such as Victor Coates and Company were able to expand and even develop their own line in shipbuilding right up until the 1860s. Shipbuilding, therefore, offered a profound opportunity for Ulster to develop, and throughout the mid-century it helped transform the region into an undeniably industrial centre capable to exporting across the world.

EXTEND YOUR KNOWLEDGE

Robert Hickson (1815-unknown)

Born in Tralee in County Kerry, Robert Hickson became a timber merchant at the age of 15 and after a few years moved to Liverpool in order to broaden his prospects. He established a partnership with a local businessman named James Spence, who is believed to have been his father-in-law. Together their firm, called Robert Hickson and Company, bought out Gladstone and Pace Iron Works on Eliza Street in Belfast in 1853. Having acquired this foundry Hickson then took a 21-year lease on a plot of land on Queen's Island and began to build iron ships. During the next year, he repeatedly wrote to Belfast's Harbour Commissioners to ensure they continued to modify the docks (slipways, sheds) and also that they made sure there was sufficient depth in the river to allow for the launching of his ships. In 1854, he launched his first ship, the *Silistria*, which was a wooden sailing ship. In the same year he obtained an order for an iron vessel – the *Khersonese* – which was to be 1,273 tonnes. In 1854, Hickson took on a new manager to assist him with the increasing workload. This was Edward Harland, the man who would later buy the company from Hickson in 1858 for £5,000 and in 1861 create perhaps Belfast's most famous shipbuilding firm: Harland and Wolff.

ACTIVITY
KNOWLEDGE CHECK

Shipbuilding in Belfast

1 Why did shipbuilding develop in Belfast?

2 What impact did the shipyards have on the city of Belfast?

3 How significant do you think shipbuilding was to the industrialisation of Ulster?

The work of the Belfast Harbour Commissioners

The development of shipbuilding and the early growth of international trade in the 18th century necessitated a body to manage and develop the port facilities in Belfast which were not well adapted to large-scale use. Natural restrictions, such as shallow water and bends in the river approach, made it very difficult for larger ships to dock, and in order for the city to exploit its growing industry this needed to be addressed. In 1785, the Irish parliament established the Corporation for Preserving and Improving the Port and Harbour of Belfast, more commonly known as the 'Ballast Board', and this body was intended to take responsibility for the facilities in Belfast's harbour.

By 1830 the problems of Belfast's sea access were becoming acute as the shallow waters meant that fully laden ships needed to wait for high tides in order to either access or leave the port, and these delays affected merchant's profit margins as well as causing general frustration. To address this issue, in 1830, the Ballast Board commissioned the engineering firm Walker and Burgess to find a solution to these access problems. Two solutions were presented, which each had a projected cost of between £180,000 and £200,000. They involved making two straight cuts at the bends of the river to create a single straight channel, and then deepening the river by dredging it to at least 12 feet. This was a well-received solution and the Board was very enthusiastic about it. However, several local interests opposed the idea, seeing it as an opportunity to extract advantageous concessions. Lord Donegall in particular was keen to only support the idea if MPs for Down, Antrim and the towns of Carrickfergus and Belfast were given seats on the Ballast Board.

SOURCE

3

From the Belfast newspaper the *Northern Whig*, June 1831. This paper had been established in 1823 by John Arnott who also owned a department store in the city.

Reformers of Belfast, Lord Belfast has refused to present your petition for reform; merchants and freeholders of Belfast, his papa [Lord Donegall] has ordered him to oppose the very first Bill you apply for, to mend your quays and improve your harbour... However, the whole procedure admirably illustrates the base and villainous corruption on which our representative system is founded; and ought to urge us all the more strenuously to procure such a Reform as will extricate the people out of the hands of the Aristocracy.

In August 1831, a compromise was reached allowing the MPs to sit on the Board and also for 16 further members to sit on a four-year rotational basis – to be elected by the local owners of registered shipping in the port. The subsequent Act for the further improvement of the Port and Harbour of Belfast in Ireland and other purposes was passed, and it allowed the Ballast Board to purchase land for the purpose of creating the proposed channel. Following the Act, the Board applied for £60,000 from the Board of Public Works to begin the operation, and over the next few years they bought up approximately 900 acres around the mouth of the River Lagan. In 1837, work was finally able to begin when a new Act was passed which allowed for the river improvements to be made, and a new 18-member board, still called the Ballast Board, was constituted to oversee these improvements.

William Dargan and the creation of Queen's Island

EXTEND YOUR KNOWLEDGE

William Dargan (1799–1867)
Dargan was born in Carlow where he attended school and excelled in mathematics and accounting. After 1819, he worked for the Scottish engineer Thomas Telford who specialised in tunnelling and bridge building. In 1824, he was sent to Dublin to build a road from that city to Raheny for which he was paid £300. In 1831, he became the contractor for the Dublin to Kingstown railway, and then in the same year he started work on the 46-mile long Ulster Canal. The completion of this project came in 1841 after which he continued to build many of Ireland's railways. By 1853, he had been responsible for building more than 600 miles of railroad. For his services he was offered a knighthood by the British viceroy, but he declined this offer because of his great sense of patriotism. For the same reasons, he later declined the offer of a baronetcy by Queen Victoria after she visited him at his home in Dublin in August 1853. In 1866, Dargan was seriously injured in a horse riding accident and he died on 7 February 1867.

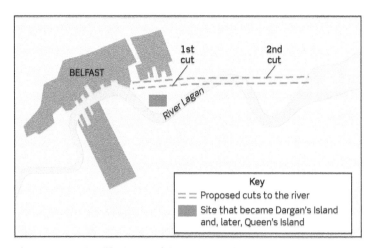

Figure 4.2 A simplified map of the proposed improvement to Belfast Harbour in 1847.

The person employed to carry out the work was a civil engineer called William Dargan, whose firm had previously built the Ulster Canal and Newry Canal, and who was well-renowned in the country. Dargan began the first cut to the river in 1840 (see Figure 4.2) and it took a year to complete, costing £42,000 in total. The material that was dug out and dredged from the river was deposited on the County Down side of the river and over the next eight years the mud that was dredged up as part of the deepening of the river was also deposited there, creating an area of approximately 59 acres in size. Dargan then cut a channel at the front of this spoil to allow for the natural flow of the Lagan, effectively creating an island in the river. In honour of the completion of the first cut, in 1841 this island was named Dargan's Island and 17 acres of it was to be used as a public park for the residents of Belfast. Following a visit by Queen Victoria in 1845, the island was renamed Queen's Island and, in addition to providing a public park, the remaining space was given over to the development of shipbuilding, providing welcome space for the burgeoning industry. The first shipyard to take up residence in 1851 was the small shipbuilding firm of Thompson and Kirwan, which built wooden ships. Two years later this was replaced by Robert Hickson and Company, who began to build iron ships. Finally it became the base for the city's most famous company, Harland and Wolff, after 1861.

The second cut was begun in 1846, and once more William Dargan was employed to undertake this work. It was completed by July 1849 and the resultant channel that was created, known as the Victoria Channel, was both wider and deeper, allowing for larger vessels to access the docks more easily. This modification significantly improved Belfast's appeal for large-scale shipping, and it opened up the city for enhanced trading opportunities as well as giving the previously cramped shipbuilding industry greater space in which to expand.

The Belfast Harbour Act 1847

In 1847, the Belfast Harbour Act saw the Ballast Board replaced by a new body called the Belfast Harbour Commissioners, which was given greater powers to manage and improve the facilities in Belfast harbour. This body worked very closely with the shipbuilders of the town to improve the harbour in a manner that best served that industry. This resulted in more land being purchased for the creation of more quays and sheds that would facilitate the desired expansion.

In addition to building further quays, the Harbour Commissioners were also motivated towards developing more industries on the harbour, and in 1853 they allowed ironworks owners Gladstone and Pace to open an iron shipyard on Queen's Island. Originally, that company had been smelters, but the business ran up debts due to the costs of smelting. Before taking up the lease on Queen's Island, Gladstone and Pace were bought out by Robert Hickson in 1853 whose company took advantage of the lease, producing its first iron ship in 1854. The Commissioners' decision to allow an iron shipyard on Queen's Island provided an opportunity to modernise shipbuilding in Belfast, and this set the foundation for that industry's future success in the latter half of the 19th century.

SOURCE 4 The opening up of Belfast harbour in 1849. A drawing published in the *London Illustrated News* in 1849.

OPENING OF THE NEW CHANNEL, BELFAST HARBOUR.—THE PROCESSION STARTING.

SOURCE 5

From the Belfast Harbour Commissioners report published in the local daily newspaper the *Belfast Newsletter* in November 1853.

The business has been commenced in a spirit that augers well for its future success and importance, the vessels contracted for being of a very large tonnage and the proprietor already finding it necessary to ask for additional space. It is also proper to observe that the other yards for timber built ships are extending their business and laying down vessels of a much larger burthen than formerly.

WHAT WAS THE IMPACT OF INDUSTRIALISATION UPON THE PEOPLE OF ULSTER?

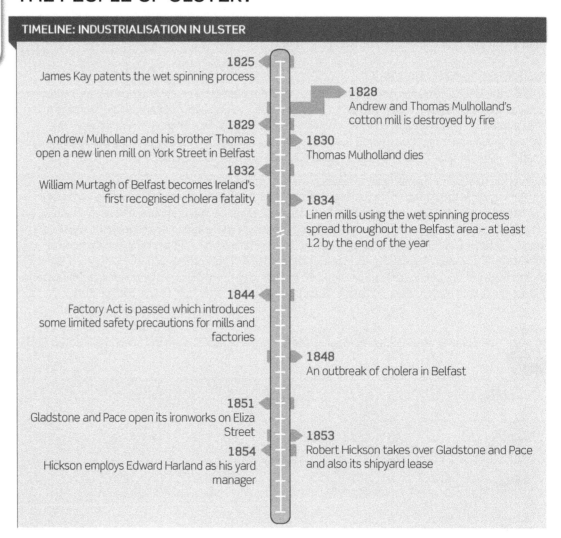

TIMELINE: INDUSTRIALISATION IN ULSTER

1825
James Kay patents the wet spinning process

1828
Andrew and Thomas Mulholland's cotton mill is destroyed by fire

1829
Andrew Mulholland and his brother Thomas open a new linen mill on York Street in Belfast

1830
Thomas Mulholland dies

1832
William Murtagh of Belfast becomes Ireland's first recognised cholera fatality

1834
Linen mills using the wet spinning process spread throughout the Belfast area – at least 12 by the end of the year

1844
Factory Act is passed which introduces some limited safety precautions for mills and factories

1848
An outbreak of cholera in Belfast

1851
Gladstone and Pace open its ironworks on Eliza Street

1853
Robert Hickson takes over Gladstone and Pace and also its shipyard lease

1854
Hickson employs Edward Harland as his yard manager

The roles of Robert Hickson and Andrew Mulholland in the industrialisation of Ulster

The industrialisation of Ulster was broadly the consequence of improved technologies and trade with Britain and the world. However, it required individuals to take advantage of these changes and make them work to the benefit of the province. There were a great number of individuals who successfully contributed to Ulster's improvement. Two that stand out in regard to the region's principal industries, linen and shipbuilding, are Andrew Mulholland and Robert Hickson respectively.

Within their specific industries, both of these men arguably led the way for progressive development – Hickson by establishing an iron shipyard upon Queen's Island and Andrew Mulholland whose company was the first to use the new wet spinning process for making linen.

Andrew Mulholland

Andrew Mulholland and his brother Thomas were originally cotton mill proprietors and their core trade was spinning. However, after a fire destroyed their mill on York Street in 1828 they turned their attention to flax spinning for the creation of linen. In part, this decision was the result of the fire that had given them a literal opportunity to start afresh, but equally influential was the declining cotton market in Ireland, which encouraged several mills to consider converting their operations. Andrew Mulholland was the first to do so, and his new mill built on the site of his original became Ulster's first steam-powered wet flax-spinning mill. His York Street Flax Spinning Company began operating in 1829 and by 1852 employed 800 people. By the end of the 19th century, it was arguably the world's largest linen company, employing more than 5,000 workers. In recognition of his contribution to Belfast's development, Mullholland was elected mayor of the city in 1845 and the following year he retired from business.

The success of this firm was a catalyst for other cotton mills in Ulster to switch their own focus and, by 1834, there were at least 12 additional flax mills in and around Belfast. They all used the new wet-spinning process invented by James Kay in 1825 and adopted on a large scale by Mulholland four years later. By 1850, this number had increased to 29 and accounted for just under half of Ulster's 62 linen mills. In only 20 years, linen production had outstripped that of cotton in the north of Ireland and this development was in no small part due to Andrew Mulholland's York Street mill. His decision to switch from cotton was pioneering and opportune in the increasingly competitive cotton market in which the smaller Irish firms could not effectively compete with the heavily industrialised Lancashire mills. Choosing to use the new technology of James Kay, he challenged traditional methods and his success promoted the advent of a more industrialised process that also made Ireland's linen spinning industry much more commercially competitive.

EXTEND YOUR KNOWLEDGE

Andrew Mulholland (1791–1866)

Andrew Mulholland was born to Thomas Mulholland and his wife Anne Doe in 1791. In 1815 his father entered the cotton manufacturing industry by purchasing a mill from McCammon, Milford and Bailey on Winetavern Street in Belfast. When old enough, Andrew and his brother Thomas joined this business and then built upon it, establishing a mill on York Street. This mill was destroyed by fire in 1828, but this proved to have a positive impact on the business. He and his brother were able to rebuild the mill, but to spin flax for linen rather than cotton. The Mulhollands were the first cotton manufacturers in Ulster to adopt the new wet spinning techniques and their mill quickly proved to be very successful in a growing linen trade. In 1845, Andrew Mulholland was elected Mayor of Belfast, and during the famine he contributed hundreds of pounds to the relief projects that were established. He retired from business in 1846.

SOURCE

From a memoir written by Hugh MacCall, a contemporary of Andrew Mulholland and fellow mill owner in Belfast. It was produced after 1828 and reflects upon the impact of Mulholland's York Street mill.

Many cautious men of that day considered the flaxen yarn project as a very hazardous undertaking, but the sturdy perseverance and mercantile energy which distinguished the house of Mulholland, while they were engaged in the cotton trace, did not wane when they set to work in the other line, and not only did flax-spinning by mechanical power succeed beyond the most sanguine expectations of the firm, but the yarn produced was so much cheaper, and so superior to the finger-spun article, that it gave a new impulse to the manufacture of linen... Belfast can never forget how much she owes to the house of Mulholland.

Robert Hickson

Hickson's contribution to the industrialisation of Ulster was twofold. First there was his imagination and ambition to establish an iron shipbuilding firm in the newly expanded Belfast harbour. Second, it was his firm that brought Edward Harland to Belfast as yard manager in 1854, precipitating the evolution of the shipyard into Ulster's most successful firm Harland and Wolff after 1861. This development ushered in a golden age for Belfast iron, and then steel, shipbuilding in the later 19th century. The success of this industry after 1854 was, therefore, directly associated with Robert Hickson's small enterprise which began only the year before.

SOURCE 7 Mulholland's York Street Mill in Belfast, c19th century.

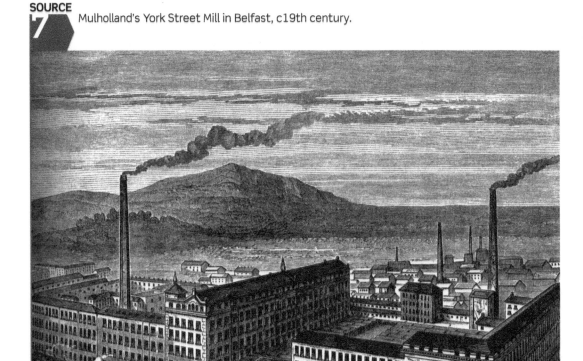

Robert Hickson began his career as a timber merchant with his brother William in Tralee, County Kerry, but after 1830 he moved to Liverpool in order to enhance his fortunes. It was while in Liverpool that Hickson entered into partnership with a local businessman named John Spence and, operating under the title Hickson and Company, they bought out a newly opened ironworks on Belfast's Eliza Street. The owners of this foundry, Thomas Nugent Gladstone and Robert Pace, had established the works in 1851, hoping to take advantage of vast coal deposits which they had mistakenly assumed existed in the Belfast area. Finding that no such reserves existed, their raw materials had to be imported, making the final iron that was produced very expensive and therefore impractical for large scale production. In an attempt to secure some profit from their venture, Thomas Gladstone sought to take a lease on Queen's Island for the establishment of an iron shipyard so that they might at least be able to make money from the iron they had already produced.

In taking on the foundry from Gladstone and Pace, Robert Hickson also acquired the lease option for Queen's Island. On 5 September 1853 he wrote to the Harbour Commissioners affirming his wish to take the lease for a plot of land approximately four acres in size, for a period of 21 years at a cost of £50 per year, rising to £200 after the fifteenth year. In return for this arrangement, he also requested that the Commissioners spend £1,500 to create new slipways and sheds for his intended shipbuilding venture – as well as ensuring they maintain the depth of the river at least 15 feet so that he could launch his ships. In making these requests, Hickson was at once giving his own company the greatest advantage for success by ensuring his venture had all the necessary resources to progress. But it also forced the improvement of Belfast's harbour and facilitated further industry there. Perhaps more importantly for Belfast's shipbuilding future, his firm was the first iron shipbuilding company to be established on Queen's Island with the intention of using modern shipbuilding techniques and materials to produce large vessels. In this regard, Hickson was building upon the earlier work of engineering firms – such as Victor Coates and Company, who had begun using iron for building ships in the 1840s – and formally establishing iron shipbuilding in Belfast.

Hickson and Company's first order came from Liverpool from Edward Bates, a ship owner, who required a 1,289 tonne wooden sailing ship, which was completed in 1854. His second order was for an iron ship called the *Khersonese*, which came in the same year from a Belfast partnership, Frederick Lewis and Edward Geoghergan, who were intent on trading in timber with the United States. Having obtained two large orders so soon into his operation, Hickson evidenced the success that shipbuilding could have in Belfast. This was further enhanced when, in 1854, the company employed the 21-year-old Edward Harland to manage the shipyard. Under his direction, the yard became more efficient as the new manager tightened up the working practices at the yard and reduced the wages of the workforce, which he found to be over the standard rate. In the immediate term this action was unpopular, but it made the firm more competitive with other yards who paid their workers less and, therefore, could produce ships at a cheaper cost.

SOURCE

8 From an editorial in the local daily newspaper the *Belfast Newsletter*, August 1854.

There are, we think, tolerably good grounds for anticipating the speedy pre-eminence of Belfast over all other Irish ports as regards the shipbuilding trade. The recent improvements in our harbour, the large accommodation about to be afforded by the reclamation of the slob between the Queen's Quay and the line of the Holywood Railway, the vastly increasing commerce of the port, and the almost unparalleled activity of our merchants, have given an impulse to the earlier efforts in this branch of trade which will not be weakened until the Lagan becomes the Clyde of Ireland.

The impact of industrialisation upon working and living conditions

Industrialisation between the years 1825 and 1855 had a profound effect upon Ulster. Economically it helped the province to become Ireland's most prosperous region after 1825 when industry around Dublin went into decline following the stock market crisis in that year. In itself, this was significant as it promoted a general improvement in people's income. For example, weavers' wages rose by 20–30 percent between 1848 and 1852 as a result of an increased demand for their skills by the linen producers in Ulster after the famine had reduced their numbers. This development also had much broader implications for Ulster society and, as industrialisation began to transform the economy, it also set in motion social change that would have a lasting impact on the province.

Living conditions

In the first instance, industrialisation had a major impact on living conditions in Ulster, largely because the growth of employment opportunities in industries such as linen and shipbuilding encouraged more people to the region. Between 1821 and 1841, the population rose from two million to 2.4 million, and the immediate impact of this change was that the urban centres in Ulster expanded quite rapidly. Rural migration increased and people followed the work, which was largely centred in Belfast and the other larger towns. With this exodus, the population living in towns increased from less than ten percent to nearly 40 percent throughout the second half of the 19th century, with an increase of 14.4 percent in the first ten years after 1821. Of these growing towns, Belfast perhaps evidences the greatest shift having had a population of 37,000 in 1821, rising to 53,000 in 1831 and then 98,000 20 years later.

The growing urban population had a substantial impact on living conditions in the towns of Ulster since the introduction of more people was not immediately prepared for and, therefore, the infrastructures in those towns remained limited. Belfast's population, for example, doubled between 1831 and 1851, and this had a severe impact on the quality of living, particularly housing. With the numbers in the town rising considerably, there was a shortage of homes. Therefore mill and factory owners, like their counterparts in Britain, found it necessary to build cheap terraced housing to accommodate their growing workforce. This was achieved as quickly and inexpensively as possible and resulted in small, poorly built houses concentrated around the industrial areas of the town near to the mills and factories. In terms of design, these properties were often **back-to-backs** and terraced so as to maximise the number of homes for the space and resources used, and this resulted in densely packed areas that offered little in terms of privacy. Such was the rapid growth of Belfast in particular that often houses were shared, accommodating several families depending on the demand. This practice was in one sense efficient, but in reality it created a very difficult existence for those who could not afford anything else. For the wealthier elements of society, it was felt that such living encouraged poor behaviour, inciting vice and other crimes.

KEY TERM

Back-to-backs
This was a cheap style of housing that sought to minimise resources by building terraced housing 'back to back' so each row shared the back wall of the other.

SOURCE 9

From Rev. W.M. O'Hanlon, *Walks among the poor of Belfast: and suggestions for their improvement* (1853). William O'Hanlon was the Protestant Minister of the Donegall Street Congregational Church in Belfast.

We entered Johnny's-entry, which lies off Talbot Street, and here we found the same degrading and demoralizing practice prevailing. In the very first house we visited in this place, the husband, wife, and six children all slept together, the eldest son being fourteen, and the eldest daughter twelve years of age. Morrow's-entry runs between Hill and Grattan Streets; and here, also, in the very first house we entered, we learned that the father (the mother is dead) and all his children occupy but one sleeping apartment, the eldest daughter being twenty-six and another daughter being seventeen years of age.

I might multiply instances of this kind *ad nauseam,* but these must for the present suffice. I should add, however, that my companion, whose work, as a town missionary, lies among people of the same social grade, informs me he often finds two, and even three, families all occupying the same room – fathers, mothers, brothers, and sisters, all sleeping indiscriminately upon the floor.

Now, Sir, let me ask what can be expected as the fruit of such domestic regimen – such total absence of all the decencies of life? Do not this, and similar foul blots upon our artificial civilisation, cause the thoughts sometimes to revert to the happier condition of the children of the wilderness? How can a particle of self-respect, or any sense of the becoming, live in such a region, and amid such circumstances? All the safeguards of morality are thrown down, and a coarse brutality produced, forming the rank and fertile seed-plot of every imaginable vice and crime. If incest, that most loathsome of all the ulcers which have ever appeared in the social body, be avoided (and who can hope that it is?) the descent from such a state of domestic life to the degradation of the street-walker and prostitute is so easy and natural, that we may cease to wonder at the number of those forlorn wretches who swarm in our alleys and lanes at night

Given the density of the population living in and around the industrial areas, sanitation was also a problem since homes were often built around a shared courtyard that accommodated a communal water pump and sewage pit. The latter was often not dug sufficiently far away from the water supply, or lined to prevent pollution of that supply, leaving the water source prone to contamination. Under these particular circumstances, there was often the risk of illness through drinking dirty water which, given the large numbers of people using the water, often led to significant outbreaks of disease – such as that of **cholera** in 1832 and 1848 (see page 104).

Working conditions

Reflecting the difficult living conditions within an industrialising Ulster, working conditions were also challenging as competition for work gave the advantage to the employers who could, therefore, place high demands on their workforce. In terms of the working day within the linen industry for example, employees were required to work between 11 and 12 hours a day, five days a week and then a six-hour day on Saturday. Much of this work was done in noisy, poorly ventilated sheds, which resulted in respiratory problems due to the continual inhalation of flax dust, known as 'pouce'. This 'pouce' filled the air and would dry up the throats of workers and cause fatal diseases such as **phthisis**. During this period, the average working life was only 16 years because of the hazardous nature of the working environment.

With the advent of a greater volume of machinery after 1825 when more mills followed Andrew Mulholland's approach and adopted steam-powered flax wet spinning, the number of accidents also increased. Until 1844, when the British parliament passed the Factory Act requiring dangerous machinery to be fenced off, mills did not follow significant safety precautions. This, in combination with long working hours, resulted in accidents such as that suffered by Sarah Jane Quinn, a linen worker in Belfast in 1854, whose head got caught in her machine, resulting in her death – see Source 10. These instances were common during the mid-century as Belfast in particular, and Ulster generally, began to develop a larger industrial foundation based upon technological improvements and the factory system.

KEY TERMS

Cholera
An infectious bacterial disease, spread through infected water supplies, that affects the small intestine. It causes severe vomiting and diarrhoea and results in significant dehydration, which is potentially fatal if left untreated.

Phthisis
This is an older term used for tuberculosis, which is a bacterial infection of the lungs.

SOURCE 10

From Belfast's daily newspaper the *Belfast Newsletter*, 1 May 1854. It details an accident in a factory which fatally injured a worker.

She was engaged at the carding part of the machinery and her head by some means got entangled in the machinery in which the greater part of the scalp was removed from the head and the skull was severely injured. She was conveyed to hospital but little hope was entertained of her survival.

Despite the dangers of working in the mills and factories, wages remained low as owners sought to maximise their profits and also, with the introduction of machinery, individual skills were not as sought after as they had been. In the early 1820s, for example, a skilled cotton worker could earn 24 shillings a week, but approximately ten years later, in 1835, this had declined to only 6–8 shillings a week. Similarly, in the shipbuilding yards during the early 19th century, when skills were scarce, workers could earn about £2 a week, but in 1836 this had fallen by 50 percent to only £1. This introduction of machinery had a twofold impact: it positively enhanced Ulster's industrial output but at the expense of reduced wages for workers, which negatively affected their overall condition.

ACTIVITY
KNOWLEDGE CHECK

Industrialisation in Ulster

1 How did Andrew Mulholland and Robert Hickson promote industrialisation in Ulster?

2 What was the significance of their contribution?

3 Was industrialisation entirely positive?

THINKING HISTORICALLY   Change (8a, b & c) (I)

Imposing realities

OPENING OF THE NEW CHANNEL, BELFAST HARBOUR.—THE PROCESSION STARTING.

Look at the picture above and answer the following question.

1 Explain why the conversation in the picture would not have happened.

The shape of history is imposed by people looking back. People who lived through the 'history' did not always perceive the patterns that later historians identify. For example, some people living through the industrial revolution may have understood that great change was taking place, but they would not have been able to understand the massive economic, social and political consequences of industrialisation.

2 Consider the beginning of industrialisation.

a) Who would have made the decision as to when industrialisation began?

b) Could anybody have challenged this decision?

c) Explain why someone living in the 19th century would have been unable to make a judgement about the beginning of a new era.

3 Who living at the present time might regard the beginning of industrialisation as an important event?

4 What does this cartoon tell us about the structure of history as we understand it?

The Belfast cholera epidemic, 1848

The growth of Ulster's urban centres, in conjunction with the generally slow development of adequate facilities to support this expansion, not only created social problems but also led to an environment that was conducive to the spread of disease. Cramped housing and poorly designed sewerage systems that allowed the local water sources to become easily polluted encouraged disease, and as early as February 1832 Belfast, and Ireland, had its first victim of cholera: Bernard Murtagh, a 34-year-old resident of Quay Lane near the River Lagan.

By the time the 1832 outbreak ended nearly a year later, it had claimed 400 lives in Belfast (0.7 percent of the city's population) and 25,000 across the country. During that outbreak, the victims' bodies were burned before burial so as to prevent the spread of infection, and the remains were interred in Friar's Bush Cemetery. To combat that outbreak, a Board of Health was convened and this instigated a rigorous policy of street cleaning, whitewashing houses and fumigation in an attempt to minimise contagion. The fever hospital also employed strict isolation for cholera cases and eventually, in 1833, the **epidemic** dissipated. Once it ended, the measures taken to address the spread were also ended and the episode quickly disappeared from the public mind as people turned their attention to ongoing industrialisation.

In 1848, a second outbreak occurred which claimed more than 35,000 lives nationwide. This second outbreak was more widespread than the first, partly because the nation had been weakened by famine (see Chapter 5), but also because industrialisation had encouraged a growing urban population which concentrated people in one area. In Belfast it was noticeably virulent because of the densely populated areas around the docks where water supplies were easily contaminated because of the volume of people using them. People also treated the River Lagan as a direct sewer and readily polluted it. They did not understand that this was the real cause of cholera rather than the popular miasma theory which suggested it was carried in the air. During this second epidemic, Belfast suffered 1,163 deaths in 3,583 cases diagnosed as cholera. This was a substantially larger number than the first outbreak. However, it was a lower mortality rate than other places in Ireland. Dublin, for example, had a mortality rate of at least 40 percent compared with Belfast's 33 percent, despite Belfast being more densely populated. The reason for this lower rate can largely be ascribed to the actions taken by the town's local authorities and prominent citizens, in particular the **Board of Guardians** (which had been set up in 1841) and Dr Andrew Malcolm (a physician and sanitation reformer). Belfast's Board of Guardians was responsible for running the local workhouse and after 1841 it installed ten beds for the sick, later extending this to 100 and, therefore, effectively supplying the town with a second hospital when the second epidemic began. Enhancing these efforts was the town's corporation (council), which gave itself greater powers to address the cholera epidemic. A feature of this was the creation of a sanitary committee headed by Dr Malcolm in 1848, the sole aim of which was to improve conditions throughout the town. This body was organised as a result of the epidemic, and although its work did not directly help that outbreak, it was empowered to order new sewage systems to be created and particularly to demand landlords improve the conditions in which their tenants lived. After 1848 this began to improve the city's health condition. More immediately, it provided the poorest families with straw bedding and also instituted a programme of house whitewashing to help improve sanitation conditions and clean up the housing generally.

In the aftermath of the epidemic in 1849, Malcolm continued to investigate the sanitation problems of Belfast and produced several reports that helped to improve the town's facilities in the 1850s. The basis of his recommendations was the overcrowding in the town's industrial areas and the need to improve these facilities in particular. These areas had grown up quickly during Belfast's rapid expansion and, because they were so inadequate, disease was a recurring theme that would continue until better housing and sewerage systems could be established.

KEY TERM

Epidemic
A widespread occurrence of an infectious disease within a particular community or place.

KEY TERMS

Board of Guardians
A body of men who were responsible for administering the **Poor Law** and taking care of the poor in their given area.

Poor Law
An Act of Parliament designed to address poverty and pauperism. Originally introduced in 1601, a new Poor Law was introduced in 1834 that provided for workhouses and a less tolerant attitude towards those who did not help themselves.

SOURCE 11

From Dr Malcolm's report, *The Sanitary State of Belfast, with suggestions for its improvement,* which was read before the British Association on 7 September 1852.

The sanitary requirements of a large city do not in reality differ from those pertaining to smaller communities, or even individuals.

1st, An abundant supply of pure, fresh air absolutely needful for the preservation of the public health. This implies the necessity for perfect ventilation, drainage, and surface-cleansing. *Parks*, therefore, and public *squares*, for the purpose of permitting free currents of air to reach every house—the proper construction and effective compulsory repair of houses, with a view to effect internal ventilation and adequate protection—the most perfect system of arterial and branch drainage, for surface-water and sewage, with the view of removing, with the least possible delay, everything that can contaminate the atmosphere, and making it available for agricultural purposes—the due and regular inspection of all public buildings and establishments where people in large numbers temporarily assemble or reside—the prohibition of all intramural burials—the due and periodical inspection of all infected houses, and all premises connected therewith—the erection of *abattoirs* far apart from habitations—the strict supervision of all offensive trades and manufactures, and, when practicable, the prohibition of smoke from large furnaces—are all matters of absolute necessity to preserve the air in a condition fit for the due maintenance of life and health, and are, therefore, indispensable a to great city.

2dly, The proper discharge of the cutaneous functions naturally demands frequent ablution and frequent change of the under garments. In like manner, the proper discharge of the digestive and assimilative functions demands a diet and regimen suitable to the condition of the individual. The means, therefore, of personal cleanliness—an abundant supply of pure water for all, and by the establishment of a suitable number of free bathing and washing places for the poor, and the strict prohibition of adulteration in food or drink, by means of a system of competent inspection—are requisite for the wants of a great city.

3dly, And, above all, it is of the utmost importance that, in every town, and in every place of education, from the princely university down to the humblest grammar-school, the great principles of ANIMAL PHYSIOLOGY, upon which the whole fabric of sanitary reform is based, should be disseminated as an *ordinary* branch of mental culture, until the great maxim of the poet, "the proper study of mankind is man," be everywhere appreciated.

A Level Exam-Style Question Section A

Read Source 11 before answering this question.

Assess the value of the source for revealing the impact of industrialisation upon Ulster's working class during the mid 19th century. (20 marks)

Tip
When answering this question you should consider how industrialisation affected different sections of Ulster's working class in addition to generally positive and negative features.

Discrepancies between Catholics and Protestants in employment

The industrialisation of Ulster after 1825 was a welcome development for local businesses, which were able to start generating significant profits for their owners who, during this period, were predominantly Protestant. The introduction of Penal Laws (see page 40) at the end of the 17th century had denied rights to the majority Catholic population and given Protestants a great political, and economic, advantage. One of the more significant laws that was passed denied Catholics the right to buy land, and so the majority of the region's wealth, which was tied to landownership until the development of industry, consequently found itself in Protestant hands. During 1820, for example, the ratio of Protestant to Catholic capital in Belfast trade and industry was 40:1 and by the end of the 19th century there were virtually no Catholic owners of large businesses.

Economically, therefore, Protestants dominated within industrial spheres and this was particularly noticeable in the Belfast Chamber of Commerce, a local institution founded in 1783 whose very existence was designed to protect businesses in the town. This organisation expanded as businesses grew in the town – in 1827 it had 76 members and by 1893 it had 260, of which only eight were Catholic. The purpose of the body was to protect local businesses and improve their standing within Belfast. In this sense, the obvious Protestant leaning presented much better opportunities for businessmen of that faith to prosper in Ireland's most industrialised town. This was a trend that extended throughout Ulster. In County Tyrone, Belfast-born Protestant George Herdman and his brother established the Sion Mills in 1835, while the Bessbrook Mills in County Armagh were built by the Quaker John Grubb Richardson in 1845. These businesses became prominent industries in Ulster and they evidence the success that many Protestant men of business enjoyed during the mid-century.

While Protestants were the owners of business, Catholics were very much the workforce – especially within the linen and shipbuilding industries. With the growth of these areas after 1820, Catholics from across Ireland migrated to Ulster in search of work and they came in great numbers. In 1821, Belfast's population was 37,000, but 20 years later in 1841 it had increased to 75,000. Certainly not all of this number is attributable to migration; some of this growth is down to families becoming larger. However, the figure offers a good perspective of the extent of Belfast's expanding population. In terms of specific Catholic growth, between 1800 and 1861 the percentage of Catholics in Belfast increased from 10 percent to 34 percent, indicating a significant expansion of that faith.

The motivation for this trend was firstly the growing linen trade which absorbed unskilled labour very effectively, particularly with the adoption of mechanisation after 1825. This work suited many Catholics since they were often the more unskilled of Ireland's labour force because of the general discrimination that they faced as a result of the penal laws. Also, many Catholic labourers had supplemented agricultural incomes by hand spinning and weaving in their homes, and this experience naturally lent itself to the industrialising textile trade in the urban centres.

The marked religious divide within Ulster's industry was widened as further industry developed, and within the emerging iron shipbuilding enterprises this was especially noticeable. This industry demanded skilled workers – such as riveters and welders – and therefore tended to employ Protestants who had greater experience in skilled trades. Many of these were attracted to Belfast from Britain's shipyards, notably those on the Tyne, Mersey and Clyde rivers where wages were not as high as in Belfast. These skilled workers formed a labour aristocracy and distinguished themselves from their unskilled colleagues through the higher wages and better working conditions they enjoyed. This hierarchy was perpetuated through the **apprentice system** which gave preference to candidates of the same religion and especially those who could pay for the five years of training required for working in the industry. The scheme of apprenticeships in Belfast's shipbuilding yards had first been pioneered by Robert Hickson after 1851 when he instituted a Premium Apprenticeship system for boys of the well-to-do over the age of 16. Under this system, a family would pay his firm to train their child on the understanding that a position in middle or senior management would follow after the five years of training. A similar system was also available to poorer individuals in order to learn their trade 'on the job', and this opportunity was often taken up by the children of existing skilled employees – usually fathers or uncles who used their position to secure their relatives a place.

At the bottom end of the employment spectrum within this industry were the simple labourers and helpers – those who fetched and carried for the skilled workers. These accounted for about half of the workforce and, as in the linen industry, they were principally made up of Catholics from the west of Ulster who moved into the towns for work as the cotton industry declined. The influx of more people to the towns made the competition for work very fierce and this occasionally spilled out into violence, notably riots in 1857. It also encouraged a greater sense of religious identification amongst the working class. In 1843, the Protestant preacher Tresham Gregg established the Belfast Protestant Operative Association (BPOA) which was intended to protect Protestant workers and their jobs from the growing number of Catholic interlopers. This membership was also intended as an organised body to help elect Conservative politicians who would ensure the maintenance of Ireland's union with Britain – a union that many Protestant workers and businessmen felt was critical for Ulster's economic development.

The Association replicated a similar organisation that Gregg had established in Dublin the year before to challenge the activities of Daniel O'Connell's Catholic Association. It adopted aggressive tactics and virulently anti-Catholic speeches to stir up the local community and press their defence of Protestantism. In July 1843, it was the cause of violent rioting with Catholic repealers in Belfast when the group interrupted a repeal meeting in the city. The group was regarded by local Protestant workers as a means of defence against the perceived gains being made by Catholics in Ireland generally, but also the gains they appeared to be making in the city specifically, as more and more Catholics moved into the area for work – seemingly swamping the workplace – throughout the mid-century. The BPOA was in this sense a grassroots organisation offering Protestant manual workers especially a means to vent their fears and frustrations at the demographic changes and political changes taking place.

ACTIVITY
KNOWLEDGE CHECK

The impact of industrialisation

1 Produce a mind map about how industrialisation affected Ulster.

2 Using your mind map answer the following questions.

   a) Did industrialisation introduce any problems for the province?

   b) What benefits did industrialisation offer?

   c) In your opinion are these problems outweighed by the benefits that it produced?

ACTIVITY
SUMMARY

The industrialisation of Ulster

1 Write a paragraph explaining the following:

   a) How the textile industry changed between 1825 and 1855, identifying any particular developments you feel are important.

   b) How shipbuilding developed, singling out the role of individuals you feel were significant.

   c) The social impact that industrialisation had on Ulster.

2 Offer a judgement as to whether you feel industrialisation was a positive development for Ulster.

WIDER READING

Bielenberg, A. *Ireland and the Industrial Revolution*, Routledge (2014)

Cameron, S. *Belfast Shipbuilders: A Titanic Tale*, Colourpoint Books (2011)

Crawford, W.H. *The Impact of the Domestic Linen Industry in Ulster*, Ulster Historical Foundation (2008)

Grada, C. *Ireland: A New Economic History*, Oxford University Press (1997)

Kennedy, L. and Ollerenshaw, P. (eds), *An Economic History of Ulster 1820-1839*, Manchester University Press (1985)

Kinealy, C. and MacAtasney, G. *The Hidden Famine: Hunger, Poverty and Sectarianism in Belfast, 1840-1850*, Pluto Press (2000)

Lynch, J. *An Unlikely Success Story: The Belfast Shipbuilders*, Ulster Historical Association (2001)

3.5 The Irish Famine, 1843–51

KEY QUESTIONS

- Why did the famine have such a devastating impact on the populace?
- What impact did the government's response to famine have on the condition of Ireland?
- How did the decline of Ireland's population affect the country?

INTRODUCTION

The history of Ireland is often associated with suffering and you do not need to delve especially deeply into the country's past to find such occasions of upheaval. Oliver Cromwell's massacres at Drogheda and Wexford and the sectarian massacres of both Catholics and Protestants during the 17th century, the Penal Laws of the 18th century, and the country's descent into civil war after 1921 are very clear examples of this. As awful as these events undoubtedly were, nothing elicits such a sense of overwhelming tragedy as the arrival of potato **blight** in Ireland during the mid-1840s. This disease rapidly spread throughout the country and devastated the potato crop, which was the staple ingredient of the majority of the population's diet. The loss of such an important food item precipitated a widespread famine, which saw the death of one million Irish men and women and the emigration of at least one million others abroad – most to America.

Famine was not uncommon in Ireland, nor indeed in other nations, and between 1300 and 1900 the country witnessed 30 episodes of this event. However, what singled out that of 1845–49 was its scale – between 1845 and 1851, the population of Ireland declined by one-fifth and it has never regained its pre-famine level. Therefore, the human impact is without question, and the effect that famine had upon Ireland was profound, not just because of the numbers involved, but because of the manner in which the tragedy occurred. It cast a glaring light upon the fragility of the Irish agricultural system – the heavy reliance upon the potato especially, but also the unequal distribution of land. Furthermore, the outbreak of famine drew a mixed response from the British government, which saw initially positive efforts to address the situation later replaced by ineffective policies that ultimately extended the suffering and caused greater harm. Though each government sought to manage the famine as well as it could, politically the events of 1845–49 did little to improve Anglo-Irish relations and left a lingering resentment among the general population.

> **KEY TERM**
>
> Blight
> A disease affecting plants that is usually spread by fungi.

1841 – Census shows only seven percent of landholdings in Ireland over 30 acres

1846 – Repeal of the Corn Laws

1841	1842	1843	1844	1845	1846

1845 – September: Blight arrives in Ireland
November: Robert Peel buys £100,000 of Indian corn for Ireland

WHY DID THE FAMINE HAVE SUCH A DEVASTATING IMPACT ON THE POPULACE?

The role of absentee landlords, middlemen, landholdings, monoculture and blight

The immediate cause of the famine was the arrival of a fungal disease, *Phytophthora infestans*, more commonly known as 'blight', in Ireland during September 1845. This disease damaged the potato crop so badly that over the next four years only one harvest would actually be successful, and as a result of the scarcity of this crop more than one million people died of starvation. In this very factual sense, the famine was a natural disaster that was simply an unfortunate, but nonetheless devastating, event. As true as this is, there are several other factors to bear in mind when considering the extent to which the famine affected Ireland. Undoubtedly it was the disease that caused the crop failure, but once this happened the condition of Ireland's agricultural system did not reduce its impact but rather enhanced it. This was due to several reasons, but chief amongst them was the system of landownership and the **monoculture** practised by Ireland's poorest farmers. These factors created a very vulnerable population without the ability to absorb any shock to its fragile existence.

> **KEY TERM**
>
> Monoculture
> The practice of growing a single crop or plant in a field at any one time.

Absentee landlords and middlemen

As a country, Ireland does not have vast amounts of natural resources, such as coal, which other nations were able to exploit during the industrial revolution. Instead, Ireland had good-quality land that lent itself to a primarily agricultural economy which, by the mid-19th century, is very much what had developed. With the exception of some industrialisation in the north-east of the country, Ireland was a farming nation, and by 1841 more than two-thirds of the population were dependent on agriculture for their livelihoods.

This was not unusual in itself, but the manner in which the land was owned in Ireland did create difficulties. As practised in several other countries, land in Ireland was owned for the most part by absentee landlords who did not live on their estates but rather employed managers to run them on their behalf while they lived elsewhere – usually in the towns or, as in the case in Ireland, in Britain. Absenteeism was a common feature of the 19th century. In Ireland this was particularly so because of the control that was exercised by Britain, and the fact that entitlement to the majority of the land in Ireland had been given to English and Scottish noble families during and after the 16th century. This had formed part of England's policy of plantation – its attempt to colonise and, therefore, pacify the country by settling loyal subjects there. This policy had seen landownership taken away from the indigenous Irish Catholics and given to English and Scottish Protestant families. These families either settled in Ireland themselves or let their new lands to others who were in the country already and then lived off the money these rents generated.

The significance of absenteeism lay in the manner by which the lands belonging to these landlords was managed. In choosing to live away from their estates, landlords required a means by which to ensure their lands efficiently generated a good income for them without them actually having to be present. The solution that many absentee landowners employed was to let their land in large parcels to local individuals who became known as middlemen. These individuals took out fixed price long leases on great quantities of land, at least 100 **acres** but usually 1,000 acres or more, and paid the landowners an agreed, regular rent. For the landowner, the system was convenient because it meant that they did not have to manage their estate since the middleman would take that responsibility, and he also provided a regular, long-term income since leases were usually for at least 21 years. In return, the middleman would effectively become a landlord himself and make his money by subdividing the land and renting it to other people. The people then became tenant farmers, paying the middleman rent for a few acres of land on which they could grow crops or keep livestock.

> **KEY TERM**
>
> Acre
> A measurement of land. One acre is equivalent to 4,046 square metres.

1848 – Young Ireland uprising

1849 – Encumbered Estates Act is passed

1851 – 245,000 Irish emigrate abroad
Famine comes to an end

1847   1848   1849   1850   1851   1852

1847 – February: Temporary Destitute Persons' Act is passed
April: Alexis Soyer sets up his model soup kitchen
April: The first 'coffin ships' sail to the United States and Canada
June: Poor Law Extension Act is passed

On the face of it, the system of using middlemen appears to be very efficient and certainly good for the absentee landlord, who was able to hand all responsibility over to someone else and simply collect an income from them, usually every six months. What this practice did in reality, however, was to institute the continual subdivision of land into smaller and smaller parcels. To maximise his income, the middleman would deliberately create small plots of land so as to foster a larger number of tenants paying him rent. Mirroring the middleman, the tenant farmers then often let sections of their plot to poorer farmers or **cottiers** in return for a portion of their crop or their labour. The result of this system was that the size of land being farmed was always being reduced, and the opportunities for farmers to extend their holdings were very expensive since it required taking on a further lease. Furthermore, with the continual subdivision of land and more people being involved in the chain, rent prices increased resulting in smaller plots being rented because of the costs associated with larger plots. In this manner Ireland remained a nation of mostly small farmers whose economic foundation was particularly fragile because the middleman system forced Irish agriculture to remain on a small scale and without an effective means to grow.

This problem was magnified by the unwillingness of the absentee landowner to make improvements to his land, such as building new homes or stables, since his income was fixed to the price agreed with the middleman. Therefore, any investment that was made would not yield a return until after the expiry of the lease. Since the landlord was reluctant to invest in his land, it could never realise its full potential, and this ensured that Irish agriculture became stagnated with little or no substantial improvement being undertaken in the pre-famine period.

KEY TERM

Cottier
A person who rented between one and three acres of land on which to grow potatoes for himself and his family. Rent was usually paid with the cottier's labour, and leases were on a year-by-year basis.

EXTRACT

From Cecil Woodham-Smith, *The Great Hunger* (1984). Woodham-Smith was a British historian and biographer. Her book on the Great Famine, first published in 1962, was highly critical of the actions of the British government and became a favoured interpretation of that event among Irish nationalists.

During the eighteenth century a new method of dealing with Irish property was adopted. Large tracts of land were let at a fixed rent to a single individual on a long lease and he sub-let as he chose. This 'middleman system' produced misery: the landlord rid himself of responsibility and assured himself of a regular income, but the tenants were handed over to exploitation. Profit was the only motive, and contemporary observers denounce middlemen as 'land sharks,' 'blood suckers,' 'the most oppressive species of tyrant that ever lent assistance to the destruction of a country'. Moreover, the middlemen degraded the land because, as the slum landlord finds it more profitable to let out a house room by room, so they split farms into smaller and smaller holdings for the sake of increased rents.

Landholdings

The system of middlemen was fundamentally problematic because it not only exploited the poorer farmers in Ireland but also prevented them from extending their landholdings and kept them tied to small plots. This became more challenging as the demand for land increased during the 18th and early 19th century because of Ireland's rapidly expanding population. With more people seeking land, plots became even smaller, and land previously considered unuseable was now being adopted. For those who could afford larger leases, there was the opportunity for some degree of commercial activity, growing produce to sell. But for the majority of farmers the land they could afford was often only several acres and if they engaged in subdivision of that land, it simply provided for their own sustenance. A census taken in 1841 found that only seven percent of landholdings in Ireland were more than 30 acres, while 45 percent were under five acres. In Connacht the number below five acres was even higher and reached 64 percent.

Those Irish renting less than five acres of land, usually between one and three, were known as cottiers and their existence was entirely subsistence-based since it was generally believed that a family needed at least one acre to sustain itself at a basic level. They were the poorest individuals who could often only afford the worst plots of land or, as was common, would work on the farmer's land in return for a patch of land on which to grow their own crops. In the early 1840s, there were more than 300,000 cottiers in Ireland and they represented the poorest of the country's population. With a population of around eight million in the early 1840s, the almost one-third of a million cottiers living hand to mouth evidences the potential vulnerability of the Irish agricultural system since the large percentage of small farms meant that every patch of available land would be farmed as much as possible so as to maximise their yield. This not only withdrew vital nutrients from the land and exhausted it, but also it did not provide any substantial surplus which could be relied upon in the event of a bad harvest. Irish farmers were effectively operating at their limit and did not necessarily have the capacity to absorb any shock that might occur.

From one of the English radical MP William Cobbett's letters from his travels in Ireland during 1834. Cobbett was interested in reform and had supported changes to the franchise only two years before. He was equally interested in social reform and travelled widely throughout Britain and Ireland to see the extent of such a need.

They [the homes of Irish cottiers] consisted of mud walls, with a covering of rafters and straw. None of them so good as the place where you keep your little horse. I took a particular account of the first place that I went into. It was twenty-one feet long and nine feet wide. The floor, the bare ground. No fireplace, no chimney, the fire (made of potato-haulm) made on one side against the wall, and the smoke going out a hole in the roof. No table, no chair; I sat to write upon a block of wood. Some stones for seats. No goods but a pot, and a shallow tub, for the pig and the family both to eat out of.

Monoculture and blight

The premium on land meant that very few of the Irish could diversify in what they grew and, therefore, they increasingly engaged in monoculture – the practice of planting only one crop at any time. In Ireland, by the 1840s, the crop of choice was the potato, which produced a high yield compared to grain crops. Such was the benefit of the potato that it accounted for more than one-fifth of the country's total agricultural output and had become the mainstay the population's diet. As a food item, the potato offered considerable benefits for the Irish, and when supplemented by milk it became almost an ideal diet because of the balance of nutrients it offered at a relatively cheap price when compared to grains. The variety that was widely grown amongst the poorer farmers and cottiers was the 'Lumper' potato because of its particularly high-yielding qualities – usually between six and eight tons per acre. As the potato became the staple diet of the poor, with families consuming between 10 and 15 pounds of them each day, Ireland's reliance on this single crop became absolute.

As good as the potato was in terms of its yields and nutritional value, it was nonetheless perishable. Unlike grain, it cannot be stored for long periods and, therefore, it is a crop for immediate use. This meant that good harvests were essential since large numbers of Irish men and women depended upon this crop as the only source of food and income. As they could not store it, there was the need to have it in regular supply – if a harvest failed then that supply would be interrupted and people would feel the effects immediately.

In July 1845, Ireland had a long spell of wet weather, although there were no undue fears for the potato harvest. However, in August there was news from England that disease had been attacking potato crops there. This disease was acknowledged as potato blight – a fungal disease that originated in South America and affected potatoes, turning them mouldy and inedible. It had been seen in American and Canada in 1842 but not in Europe until 1845. In September of that year, signs of blight were found in Waterford and Wexford and then, very quickly, across half of the country.

Given the importance of the potato to the people of Ireland, the poorest especially, the infestation of blight in their crops was catastrophic. One-third of the harvest in 1845 was destroyed and the next three successive harvests would be similarly poor: 1846 lost three-quarters of the crop, 1847 was average and 1848 was one-third deficient. Without their staple foodstuff people quickly began to starve and by the end of 1845 Ireland was in the grip of famine.

Impact of famine on the populace

Given the fragile nature of the Irish agricultural system, and particularly the over-reliance upon the potato by Ireland's poorest inhabitants, the successive decimation of the harvests between 1845 and 1848 had a catastrophic effect. The loss of one-third of the crop in 1845 was taken badly. However, there was still some hope for the next harvest. When that also failed, and more than three-quarters was destroyed, the grim realities of famine set in and in the autumn of 1846 Ireland had its first recorded deaths from starvation. These deaths were the first of more than one million Irish by 1851 – many from starvation, but also from associated diseases such as **typhus** and **relapsing fever**. These two diseases in particular were so common that they were informally known as 'famine fever' by the population. In the winter of 1847 they became an epidemic as the weather combined with the lack of good-quality food to weaken the vulnerable population. In the early months of that year alone, 250,000 people died of either starvation or fever, and it was recognised as the highpoint of famine, earning the emotive title 'black '47' amongst those who witnessed it.

KEY TERMS

Typhus
A bacterial disease transmitted by parasites such as fleas. It causes fever and a rash that if left untreated leads to delirium and then a coma. At this stage death is likely.

Relapsing fever
Another bacterial disease causing fever, rash and nausea. It is contracted from ticks and lice and usually lasts between two and nine days and then disappears. If left untreated, it returns and the cycle is repeated until treatment is given.

In addition to these diseases, many Irish men and women also suffered from scurvy having lost their vitamin C-rich potato diet. Although they tried to replace it with something significantly nutritious, often contracted other diseases that only made their lives harder – in particular xerophthalmia, which was a disease that caused blindness and was due to a lack of vitamin A in the diet.

SOURCE 2

An Irishwoman searching for potatoes during the famine. This was a first-hand drawing made for the *Illustrated London News*, 22 December 1849.

The famine was most prevalent in the rural areas, particularly Connacht in the north of the country, because of the large number of small farms. The 1841 census showed that more than 64 percent of landholdings in this province were less than five acres. This was a feature replicated across Ireland where, in fact, only seven percent of the country's landholdings were greater than 30 acres. The effects of such intense division of land were marked and the people living on these plots were vulnerable. The county of Cavan for example had a mortality rate of 42.7 percent because so much of its local population had little pockets of land which could not withstand the huge losses that blight caused.

Within this area, as in other rural areas, the worst affected were the poor cottiers for whom the potato was their only means of subsistence. They relied totally on their crop and when it failed they had nothing to fall back on. They either sought charity from others or had to wander the country looking for work and food. Of this class, as with other classes, the pressures of famine took their toll particularly upon the very young and the very old who were the most vulnerable in society. These groups found it especially difficult to survive with little to eat as they had neither the ability nor the strength to look after themselves. The social impact of their fragility was profound, and the high mortality rate among young children in particular contributed greatly to the demise of the cottier class in Ireland after 1851. This decline removed one of the country's biggest social groups and consequently affected Ireland's social structure throughout the rest of the century.

Although the cottiers undoubtedly felt the effects of famine most acutely, the suffering was not confined to this group. Better-off farmers who owned between 10 and 15 acres were also hit hard as their crops, though greater than the cottiers, were still not large enough to withstand the high level of losses that were sustained. Simply put, the potato acreage before 1845 was more than two million but in 1847 it had fallen to 250,000 acres, which effectively meant that the country saw a drop of more than three-quarters of a million acres of potatoes. Such losses were, therefore, unsustainable even for better off farmers. However, it was without question the poorest who suffered most.

The impact of the famine on the Irish overall was tremendous and this was the result of several factors. It exposed Ireland as having a dangerously vulnerable rural society in which the majority of small farmers and cottiers lived at a level of subsistence, dependent upon one crop. Such a living meant that vast numbers of Irish did not generate any surplus to see them through difficult times such as a crop failure. This position had been created by an exploitative land system that encouraged the continual subdivision of land until plots were so small that subsistence was all that could be achieved in many areas. This subdivision was good for generating rental income, but ultimately it created a fragile community of poor farmers and cottiers who were easily broken after 1842.

SOURCE 3

From a personal account of the famine made by N.M. Cummins, an absentee landlord in Cork, in a letter to the Duke of Wellington written in December 1846.

Having for many years been intimately connected with the western portion of the County of Cork, and possessing some small property there I thought it right personally to investigate the truth of the several lamentable accounts which had reached me of the appalling state of misery to which that part of the county was reduced. I accordingly went on the 15th inst. to Skibbereen, and to give the instance of one townland which I visited as an example of the state of the entire coast district, I shall state simply what I saw there. It is situated on the eastern side of Castlehaven Harbour, and is named South Reen, in the parish of Myross. Being aware that I should have to witness scenes of frightful hunger, I provided myself with as much bread as five men could carry, and on reaching the spot I was surprised to find the wretched hamlet apparently deserted. I entered some of the hovels to ascertain the cause, and the scenes that presented themselves were such as no tongue or pen can convey the slightest idea of. In the first six famished and ghastly skeletons, to all appearance dead, were huddled in a corner on some filthy straw, their sole covering what seemed a ragged horse-cloth, and their wretched legs hanging about, naked above the knees. I approached in horror, and found by a low moaning they were alive; *they were in fever*—four children, a woman, and what had once been a man. It is impossible to go through the details—suffice it to say that in a few minutes I was surrounded by a least 200 of such phantoms, such frightful spectres as no words can describe. By far the greater number were delirious, either from famine or from fever. Their demoniac yells are still ringing in my ears, and their horrible images are fixed upon my brain. My heart sickens at the recital, but I must go on. In another case—decency would forbid what follows, but it must be told—my clothes were nearly torn off in my endeavours to escape from the throng of pestilence around, when my neck-cloth was seized from behind by a grip which compelled me to turn. I found myself grasped by a woman with an infant, *just born*, in her arms, and the remains of a filthy sack across her loins—the sole covering of herself and babe. The same morning the police opened a house on the adjoining lands, which was observed shut for many days, and two frozen corpses were found lying upon the mud floor, *half devoured by rats*.

Apart from destroying the cottier class and reducing the size of the population by more than 20 percent by 1851, the famine also stimulated emigration abroad (see page 125). This practice had been underway since the previous century, but the ravages of famine had created fear among the Irish people and a desire to escape the country as quickly as possible. This encouraged a significant rise in the number of people leaving Ireland, for Britain and North America especially, and this exodus of just over one million during the famine years contributed to the reduced population by the middle of the century. It was also a reason why the country never regained its pre-famine population level once famine came to an end, since it had become a well-established practice by then. In this sense it can be said that the famine was a defining moment in Irish history. It was, first, a momentous human catastrophe which completely transformed the nature of Irish society and, second, it would create a legacy that would continue to affect the country long after the end of famine in 1851.

Why the famine happened

1 Identify at least four factors that encouraged famine in Ireland and place them under the following headings: 'Natural causes'; 'Man-made causes'.

2 Explain why you have positioned your factors where you have.

THINKING HISTORICALLY Cause and Consequence (7a & b)

Questions and answers

Questions that historians ask vary depending on what they think is important. It is the questions that interest us that define the history that is written. These questions change with time and place. Different historians will also come up with different answers to the same questions, depending on their perspectives and methods of interpretation as well as the evidence they use.

Below are three historians who had different areas of interest:

Thomas Carlyle	Karl Marx	Sir Charles Oman
A political historian who lived in the 19th century. He was interested in the idea that great men shape history.	An economic and political historian who lived in the 19th century. He was interested in the role of the lower classes and how they contributed to historical change.	A military historian who lived in the late 19th and early 20th centuries. He was very interested in the minute detail of warfare including how armies were organised and what tactics they used.

These are some key events in Irish history:

The execution of Robert Emmett	William Pitt the Younger grants Catholic relief	The Irish War of Independence 1919–21
The Act of Union with Britain	The maintenance of a Protestant ascendancy	The formation of the Irish Volunteers
The suicide of Theobald Wolfe Tone	The United Irishmen uprising	The introduction of conscription in 1918 by the British government

Work in groups of between three and six.

1 Which of these events would have been of most interest to each historian? Explain your answer.

2 Each take the role of one historian and devise a question that would interest them about each of the events.

3 Discuss each event in turn. Present the questions that have been devised for each historian and offer some ideas about how they would have answered them.

4 For each event, decide as a group which question is the most interesting and worthwhile of the three.

Answer the following questions in pairs.

5 Identify the different ways that each historian would approach writing an account of the Irish War of Independence?

6 In what ways would Carlyle and Marx differ in their explanations of the significance of the Act of Union? What would be the focus of their arguments?

Answer the following questions individually.

7 All three historians may produce very different accounts and explanations of the same piece of history. Of the three historians, whose account would you prefer to read first? Explain your answer.

8 Do the differences in these accounts mean that one is more valid than the others?

9 Explain why different historical explanations are written by different historians.

10 Explain why different explanations of the same event can be equally valid.

WHAT IMPACT DID THE GOVERNMENT'S RESPONSE TO FAMINE HAVE ON THE CONDITION OF IRELAND?

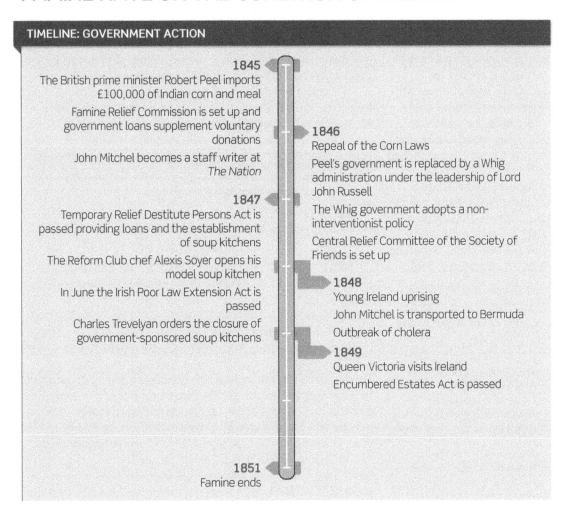

TIMELINE: GOVERNMENT ACTION

1845
The British prime minister Robert Peel imports £100,000 of Indian corn and meal

Famine Relief Commission is set up and government loans supplement voluntary donations

John Mitchel becomes a staff writer at *The Nation*

1846
Repeal of the Corn Laws

Peel's government is replaced by a Whig administration under the leadership of Lord John Russell

The Whig government adopts a non-interventionist policy

Central Relief Committee of the Society of Friends is set up

1847
Temporary Relief Destitute Persons Act is passed providing loans and the establishment of soup kitchens

The Reform Club chef Alexis Soyer opens his model soup kitchen

In June the Irish Poor Law Extension Act is passed

Charles Trevelyan orders the closure of government-sponsored soup kitchens

1848
Young Ireland uprising

John Mitchel is transported to Bermuda

Outbreak of cholera

1849
Queen Victoria visits Ireland

Encumbered Estates Act is passed

1851
Famine ends

The impact of the government response to famine

The outbreak of famine in Ireland was not a complete shock to the British government since blight had destroyed English crops in the summer of 1845 and those of Canada in 1842. These events consequently gave the authorities some idea as to the extent of potential damage the disease could cause – particularly in Ireland where the reliance upon the potato was so complete. To this end, when blight arrived in Ireland the government was quick to respond to its presence and steps were taken to address the threat. Amongst the earliest of these was the formation of a scientific commission to investigate the disease with the intention that a cure might be found to prevent its spread. Such positive action as this challenges the accepted wisdom that the British government was slow to react and indeed increased the misery of Ireland's population by refusing to supply it with effective support. One reason for this discrepancy is that people apply different interpretations to events, and such is the emotive nature of *an gorta mor* (the great hunger) that there are many contrasting opinions that lack complete objectivity. Certainly, it is reasonable to say that the government could have done a lot more than it did, but to suggest that it pursued a deliberate policy designed to enhance Irish suffering is excessive given the context of events. Another reason for the array of opinion that exists is the changing nature of Britain's response. During the years of famine, policy altered considerably and very markedly, in particular following the introduction of a new Whig administration in 1846 which replaced the outgoing Tory government under Robert Peel.

Peel's response

Under the guidance of Robert Peel, the British government response to the spread of blight in Ireland was rather sympathetic. The emergence of the disease saw the creation of a scientific commission under the direction of Dr Lyon Playfair, a chemist and good friend of Peel, which was tasked with ascertaining its nature and a subsequent means of preventing further spread. This was a proactive attempt to strike at the source of the problem rather than just deal with the symptoms of famine, which the Peel government also duly undertook. Unfortunately, the commission failed to discover that blight was a fungal disease rather than a disease of the potato itself and, therefore, the remedies it prescribed – notably sprinkling the seed potatoes with hydrochloric acid, treating the diseased crops with chloric acid, manganese oxide and salt – were entirely ineffective. Had the recommended ingredients been available they would have caused more harm than good. Five days before the Commission published its report on 15 November, Peel had initiated a relief programme to support the people affected by the blight. Here the British government can be congratulated because it took positive steps to address the problem of food supply in November 1845 by buying £100,000 worth of Indian corn and meal. It hoped to prevent soaring food prices and, therefore, allow the Irish to purchase food at a reasonable cost in lieu of being able to grow it themselves.

As decisive as Peel's action was, the Indian corn that he brought to Ireland was completely unfamiliar to the Irish. Used to eating a rich potato diet, the corn – nicknamed 'Peel's brimstone' by the peasants – was not understood and often not properly prepared, to the extent that it was often undercooked and caused diarrhoea. Out of necessity, the Irish accustomed themselves to the corn. However, it lacked many of the vitamins that their potato diet offered, vitamin C especially, and so scurvy was common. In this sense, although Peel had sought to help the Irish, his initial attempt was inappropriate and actually caused additional problems for the population. Furthermore, having purchased £100,000 worth of this corn, it was significantly inadequate compared to the loss of £3,500,000 worth of potatoes. Given this shortfall, more substantial action needed to be taken.

> **A Level Exam-Style Question Section A**
>
> ***Study Source 4 before answering this question.***
>
> Assess the value of the source for revealing the attitude of Robert Peel towards the outbreak of famine in Ireland and his efforts to address it. (20 marks)
>
> Explain your answer, using the source, the information given about its origin and your own knowledge about the historical context.
>
> **Tip**
> *When answering this question you should consider the kind of politician Robert Peel was and the political ideas that he espoused.*

SOURCE 4

From a speech made by the British Prime Minister Sir Robert Peel to parliament on 9 March 1846 about his government's efforts to assist Ireland in the wake of the potato blight. Peel's response was proactive and intended to reduce suffering initially through a programme of works and imported cornmeal.

The first act of Her Majesty's Government was to propose some measures that would be calculated to have the effect of mitigating the impending distress, by providing the best mode of relief— the supply of employment for the people. The hon. and learned Gentleman must feel that the best mode of relieving a people, with a view to their moral position, is by enabling them to supply their own wants by obtaining payment for their labour. In justice to the poorer classes—to those classes who are in a state of destitution—it would, I think, be infinitely more agreeable to their feelings, that they should be enabled to earn their subsistence by honest labour than by any other mode. The hon. and learned Gentleman is aware that the very first act of Her Majesty's Government, even preliminary to that important one which is to come under the discussion of the House this evening, was to bring in three or four measures for the relief of the poor in Ireland. We brought forward measures for the erection of piers and harbours on the southern and western coasts of Ireland, in order to enable the inhabitants with the better security to carry on their fisheries. We proposed measures to give to the grand juries of Ireland a power to raise money and to make presentments for the raising of funds for the prosecution of public works. There are other measures, also, which will involve the advance of large sums of public money. I have much satisfaction in knowing that all those measures have passed into law. The sums raised by them may possibly be inadequate for the purpose of remedying the distress. But whilst Parliament is sitting, there can be no difficulty in obtaining such further measures as may be requisite. And I must say, that if Parliament were not sitting, I should have no hesitation in taking upon myself the responsibility, as First Lord of the Treasury, of adopting such measures as I should think necessary to meet the exigencies of the case.

In addition to this action, Peel also established a relief commission in November 1845 which set up a programme of public works, and was funded by voluntary donations and often topped up by government grants – usually to the extent of two-thirds of the cost. These works not only provided food but also employment, and they gave work to about 140,000 people at one time during 1845. Such opportunity was essential since it was felt more prudent to sell food rather than give it away as this would help to maintain market prices and not cause a decline in prices which could antagonise the farming community. On the basis of this attitude, it could be suggested that Peel was more concerned with the longer-term situation rather than alleviating the immediate problem of food scarcity. But given that his government spent in excess of £365,000 in 1845–46 and offered a similar amount in loans, it is perhaps unfair to blame it so resolutely, especially since governments also need to look at the bigger picture in order to avoid any similar catastrophe in the future.

If Peel was to be blamed for looking to the long term, and perhaps his own standing with the farming community, his attempt to reduce the suffering in Ireland was certainly not a secondary concern. In 1846, he took the controversial decision to repeal the Corn Laws in Britain so as to give the Irish market in this commodity a better chance of growth. He anticipated this would bring in more income for the beleaguered nation. The Corn Laws had been in place since 1815 following the conclusion of the Napoleonic wars and the reopening of European markets, which consequently threatened the prices of English corn. The laws involved placing tariffs on foreign corn, which protected the English farmers by maintaining high prices for their own produce. By repealing these laws, Peel hoped to create a wider market in Britain for Irish corn which could help to support the relief of the country and begin the restructuring of Irish agriculture, albeit at the risk of angering English farmers.

The impact of this action was not as Peel anticipated. In terms of relieving the famine, the repeal made very little difference: Ireland had plenty of food (maize, dairy and meat), but no money with which to buy these items and, therefore, no matter how cheap grain was, the Irish could not afford it. Secondly, the political impact of his actions was that his government fell from power and gave way to a new administration in June 1846 under Lord John Russell whose approach to the famine was very different from that of his predecessor.

Russell's response

The change in government had a profound effect on Ireland. While Peel's administration took active measures to reduce distress, the new Whig authority had a completely different view of how to deal with the problem, and this alternative approach was much more abrasive than the one previously adopted. Lord John Russell, the new prime minister, was a great advocate of the economic ideas of Adam Smith and particularly the concept of *laissez-faire* or free trade, which had become an established principle among Whig politicians. This idea promoted non-intervention by government as the best means by which to deal with economic difficulties, and so the new government was disinclined to intervene in Ireland to the extent that Peel had done. In the event of another poor harvest, it was therefore decided to not buy in more grain, but rather leave the supplying of food to private enterprises.

KEY TERM

Laissez-faire
A policy that allows things to take their course naturally rather than deliberately intervening to make something happen. It is usually applied to economies where governments adopt a non-interventionist approach and allow markets to manage themselves.

SOURCE

From the Irish nationalist newspaper, *The Nation*, reporting on the attitude of the new prime minister Lord John Russell towards Ireland and its difficulties. It was published on 22 August 1846.

It appeared to the Government that, while there should be public works, and these public works should be undertaken under due control, they should not defray the cost of these works from any Parliamentary grant, but that they should be defrayed from a loan to be repaid by the counties... with reference to the supply of food, the Government did not propose to interfere with the regular trade by which Indian corn and other grain food could be brought into that country [Ireland]. He proposed to leave the trade as much at liberty as possible. He believed that the markets would be best supplied without the interference of Government... He did not propose to interfere either with the wholesale or retail trade.

Central in this decision-making process was the new Chancellor of the Exchequer, Charles Wood, and the Permanent Secretary at the Treasury, Charles Trevelyan, both of whom were keen supporters of non-intervention on the grounds of both Adam Smith's economic ideas and also the writing of the Reverend Thomas Malthus. Malthus was a population theorist and he had written extensively about Ireland – a country which he felt was vastly overpopulated and one whose population should consequently be thinned out so as to make best use of its natural resources. The ideas of Malthus lent themselves to a general sense of inevitable tragedy in Ireland: that its population was so great that eventually it would outgrow its ability to sustain itself. These beliefs were popular amongst men like Wood and Trevelyan since they complimented, and even justified, their own ideas regarding the free market and non-interventionism.

To Whigs such as these, the problems in Ireland were the consequence of poor management on the part of Irish officials and landowners since it was their deliberate exploitation of the poor farmers that had created the vulnerable agricultural system which was now exacerbating the current distress. Under this interpretation, it was meddling in the natural economy that had generated the conditions which allowed the famine to be so devastating, and therefore the most provident solution was to minimise further intervention.

EXTEND YOUR KNOWLEDGE

Adam Smith (1723-90)
An economist and moral philosopher from Scotland, Adam Smith is most remembered for his book, *An Enquiry into the Nature and Causes of the Wealth of Nations*, which was published in 1776. In this work Smith challenged the existing ideas of economic development which advocated careful protection of domestic markets via government regulation. Instead he suggested that *laissez-faire* or free trade was a more effective means to promote economic growth. Under this model, economic markets would be allowed to develop naturally without interference from government.

Thomas Robert Malthus (1766-1834)
Thomas Malthus was an English academic who is most famous for his work on population growth and establishing the 'Malthusian catastrophe'. This theory, which he outlined in his 1798 publication *An Essay on the Principle of Population Growth*, demonstrated that population grows exponentially, while food growth does so arithmetically. Eventually, therefore, populations will outstrip the supply of food. He also maintained, however, that there were natural ways to prevent such a catastrophe and that the provision of poor relief was adding an artificial barrier to prevent these remedies. His work influenced the later field of evolutionary biology and was read by Charles Darwin among others. To this day he remains a much discussed figure whose ideas prompt great controversy. The implications of this policy and the attitudes of its adherents was very noticeable in Ireland. When a second harvest failed in 1846 the government did not buy in further supplies of grain but rather simply continued with the existing policy of public works so that the Irish might earn money to buy their own food items. However, the cost was no longer borne by the administration but instead was passed on to the local Poor Rate in an attempt to force Irish landlords to manage the problem themselves. The failure of a second harvest in combination with a particularly harsh winter saw the numbers applying for relief leap from 30,000 in September to nearly 500,000 by December 1846. These numbers were increasingly difficult for the relief commission and its local committees to deal with effectively, so much so that without direct government assistance Ireland witnessed its first slew of famine deaths late in that year.

In the face of such distress and also the rising cost of public works which had reached more than £30,000 a day early in the new year, the Whig government relented from its non-

KEY TERM

Society of Friends
A nonconformist religious group
also known as Quakers, who
believe that God exists within
every person in the form of an
'inner light'.

interventionist policy. In January 1847, it passed the Temporary Relief Destitute Persons Act, which allowed for the creation of government-sponsored soup kitchens in Ireland. This practice had already been established by the private endeavours of the **Society of Friends**, who opened their first kitchen in 1846 and were now well established throughout the country, providing much needed aid. In Waterford for example, within days of opening on 21 November 1846, the Friends' kitchen provided a quart of soup and half a pound of bread each, free of charge, to more than 180 people. This quickly rose to more than 600 within a fortnight and cost the Society £6.75 per week. The money was raised through voluntary donations among the network of Friends in Ireland, and the benefits of their endeavours were conveyed to Lord John Russell by the chairman of the government's Relief Commission, Sir Randolph Routh. From the perspective of the British government, such an enterprise was acceptable because it not only offered support for the people of Ireland but it was also a cheap means of doing so that minimised intervention.

The government relief measures were only intended as a temporary solution, but they mark a significant change in the way British political minds operated during the 19th century. They also go some way to rehabilitate the actions of Russell's government which had, until this point, been very unhelpful. The passage of the Temporary Destitute Persons Act saw more soup kitchens set up throughout Ireland, and even the celebrated London Reform Club chef, Alexis Soyer, prepared a simple, cheap and easy-to-follow recipe for them to serve. His recipe was said to produce 100 gallons of soup for only £1 and yet be sufficiently nutritious to keep the Irish alive during the current circumstances. Despite these efforts, famine took a tighter hold on the population in Ireland and as the year went on the limited nature of government intervention became more obvious.

SOURCE

6 A Quaker soup kitchen at Cork in January 1847, drawn from first-hand observation by a London correspondent and published in the *Illustrated London News*.

SOURCE

7

From a letter by Alexis Soyer explaining his 'Famine Soup' recipe, which was published in *The Times* in 1847.

I first put one ounce of dripping into a saucepan (capable of holding two gallons of water), with a quarter of a pound of leg of beef without bones, cut into square pieces about half an inch, and two middling-sized onions, peeled and sliced. I then set the saucepan over a coal fire, and stirred the contents round for a few minutes with a wooden (or iron) spoon until fried lightly brown. I had then ready washed the peeling of two turnips, 15 green leaves or tops of celery, and the green parts of two leeks (the whole of which, I must observe, are always thrown away). Having cut the above vegetables into small pieces, I threw them into the saucepan with the other ingredients, stirring them occasionally over the fire for another 10 minutes; then added half a pound of common flour (any farinaceous substances would do), and half a pound of pearl barley, mixing it all well together. I then added two gallons of water, seasoned with three ounces of salt, and a quarter of an ounce of brown sugar, stirred occasionally until boiling, and allowed it to simmer very gently for three hours, and the end of which time I found the barley to be perfectly tender. The above soup has been tested by numerous noblemen, members of parliament, and several ladies, who have lately visited my kitchen department, and who have considered it very good and nourishing.

ACTIVITY
KNOWLEDGE CHECK

Britain's initial response to famine

Read Source 4 on page 116 and Source 5 on page 117. Use the material you have read and your own knowledge to answer the following questions.

1 How did the British government respond to the famine in Ireland?

2 Why did Russell's approach differ from Peel's?

3 Whose approach was more valid – Peel's or Russell's?

The Irish Poor Law Extension Act 1847

In 1847, the Whig government took further and more long-term action to address the issue of famine. Soup kitchens were only intended as a temporary measure, and a new Poor Law Extension Act that was passed in June was designed to provide a more permanent solution to the current distress. The Act was intended to amend the existing Irish Poor Law so that it could better accommodate the suffering of Ireland's poorest inhabitants during the famine and it made several important changes to the existing legislation. The most significant changes involved the nature of the provision and also, indirectly, who was to fund it. The Irish Poor Law Extension Act, together with the Irish Poor Law Amendment Act, each passed in 1847, made the following changes.

- Irish men and women had a legal right to relief – previously this had been at the discretion of the Poor Law Guardians.

- Relief could be administered outside of the workhouse if the workhouse was full or infected – previously only 'indoor relief' was permitted.

- Anyone occupying more than a quarter of an acre of land and who refused to give up their possession was not deemed destitute and, therefore, would not be eligible for relief paid for by the Poor Rate. This was known as the 'Gregory clause' after the demand for such a provision was made by the prominent landowning MP for Dublin, Sir William Gregory.

- A separate Irish **Poor Law Commission** was established distinct from the English Poor Law Commission.

The implications of these changes were quite far-reaching, particularly since by declaring relief a statutory right rather than a one-off need, it transferred the obligation of managing this effort to the existing Poor Law officials rather than the government. In addition, by establishing a separate Irish Poor Law Commission this neatly absolved government of both the burden and cost of managing famine relief. After 1847 this became the responsibility of the separated Irish commission and its own Poor Law Guardians rather than Britain's responsibility. Furthermore, the provision was to be paid for by the Poor Rate in Ireland and not the British ratepayers or the British government. This distinction placed responsibility for those affected by the famine squarely on the shoulders of Ireland's officials,

KEY TERM

Poor Law Commission
A central body created to oversee the Poor Law and administer its provisions.

and the financial demands were placed on the Irish landowning ratepayers, which in the eyes of Russell and his government was appropriate to the situation.

Although perhaps appropriate from the perspective of the Russell government, the impact of shifting responsibility entirely to the Irish Poor Rates was tremendous and it created a new set of problems that made Ireland's poor suffer even more acutely. By 1849, 932,000 people were being maintained in Ireland's workhouses for some period, with nearly twice as many on outdoor relief. This level of burden extracted a heavy cost, which was increasingly borne by Irish landowners since they were the main ratepayers. In 1847 alone, the expenditure on poor relief amounted to £1,700,000 and this money had to be found from the rates. In Kenmare, Ballinrobe, Ballina, Clifden and Westport the Poor Rate was in excess of 10 shillings in the pound, while in Scariff it was as high as 12 shillings and 6 pence. These figures were substantial and it was feared that people would be unable to maintain these levels of taxation. The consequence of this expense was that many landowners undertook with greater vigour to evict pauper tenants whose holding was more than a quarter acre since under the 'Gregory clause' these were illegible for relief. This practice had long existed in Ireland and it was the result of the poor being at the mercy of their landowner. In March 1846, 300 tenants had been forcibly evicted from their homes in Ballinlass, County Galway, despite having their rent available, because the landlord wanted to convert her land for grazing. After the passage of the Extension Act, this became a more common sight as landowners sought to reduce the number of small land-holding tenants in favour of encouraging more profitable pasture and grazing opportunities.

The problem of export of food from Ireland

Despite the tightening grip of famine in Ireland, food was still exported out of the country even at the height of the suffering in mid-1847. During that year alone, 4,000 vessels left Ireland with cargoes of foodstuffs, particularly grain, to the major ports of Britain, including Bristol, Liverpool, Glasgow and London. Between 1846 and 1850, a total of three million livestock were transported from the country – more than the number of Irish who would emigrate during the same period. This exportation of food is a prominent feature of the nationalist interpretation and, although it has validity, the volume of exports remained less than the quantities of food the British government brought into Ireland at that time. In this sense, the decision to allow exportation to continue throughout the famine period was essentially a mixture of ideology and commercialism, rather than a perceived 'anti-Irishness'. The economic principle of free trade was a dominant concept amongst British politicians during the 1840s and, therefore, they were very reluctant to close ports as was the usual practice during times of food scarcity. This was considered to be too interventionist and likely to affect the wider food markets, which could create further difficulties in subsequent years. Indeed, when Sir Robert Peel took the decision to repeal the Corn Laws he faced significant opposition from within his own party in addition to the Whigs and English merchants. This opposition was not because there was any deliberate wish to see Ireland starve, but rather that the removal of these laws would undermine both the prospects of the English corn market and the profits of English traders. On this basis, there was a strong inclination towards maintaining a commercial interest despite the humanitarian crisis unfolding in Ireland.

This commercial motivation was particularly evidenced with the new government under Lord John Russell in 1847. Encouraged by a strong belief in the free market, this administration stopped buying in Indian corn and left importation down to market forces instead of guaranteeing supply. This proved to be an unfortunate decision since the harvests were even worse in 1847 and, therefore, food was in even greater demand. Having endorsed free market principles, however, the government chose not to regulate the food market. Consequently exports from the country rose as Irish merchants sought higher profits selling abroad (especially in Europe where there were also food shortages) instead of within the home market where profit was harder to come by.

SOURCE

8 From a diary written by Lord Bessborough, Lord Lieutenant of Ireland, reflecting upon the consequences of free trade in Ireland during 1847.

I cannot make up my mind entirely about the merchants. I know all the difficulties that arise when you begin to interfere with trade, but it is difficult to persuade a starving population that one class should be permitted to make 50 per cent profit by the sale of provisions whilst they are dying in want of these.

The fact that Ireland continued to export at a time when the majority of the population was starving was the cruel reality of mid-19th century economic thinking. Although people were in distress, there was profit to be made on an individual level. On the national level there was also the bigger picture to see: markets needed to be maintained for future growth. Most politicians felt something should be done to help the Irish, but this should not be at the expense of long-term progression, and ensuring economic stability was just as important.

The roles of Charles Edward Trevelyan and John Mitchel

The famine in Ireland has elicited considerable attention from many quarters over the years, not simply because it was a great human tragedy, but because of the manner in which it was handled. For many people in Ireland, the distress suffered in the country during the 1840s was a natural disaster which could have been tempered with a more effective response from the British government. In this interpretation, which has largely become the traditional nationalist perspective, Britain could have done so much more to help the afflicted nation, but rather than take the necessary measures, it chose to protect its own commercial interests and gave only nominal support to the Irish. This view was originally developed by an Irish journalist called John Mitchel who observed the famine before becoming embroiled in the Young Ireland uprising in 1848 and subsequently being transported to Bermuda. While abroad, he collected his views and opinions of the famine, and Britain's record in Ireland generally, and wrote *The Last Conquest of Ireland (perhaps)*. This was published in 1860 and asserted a distinctly Anglo-phobic perspective that became prime rhetoric for future nationalists. With regard to the conduct of the British government during the famine, Mitchel singled out one man above all others for criticism – Charles Edward Trevelyan, the Permanent Undersecretary at the Treasury – whom he felt deliberately interfered with relief efforts because of his ideological stance and general disregard for the Irish nation. Trevelyan was intimately connected with the process of famine relief, and certainly his actions bear some responsibility. However, the extent to which he ought to be demonised remains open for debate.

Charles Trevelyan, 1807–86

Trevelyan was a key figure in Britain's efforts to bring relief to Ireland. As the Permanent Undersecretary to the Treasury, he played a direct role in the process. Consequently he has been personally associated with the response which, for many contemporary and future commentators, was felt to be woefully inadequate. Trevelyan was a keen supporter of the *laissez-faire* attitude prevailing in Britain and he applied the idea to relief efforts by making them as minimal as reasonable so as to encourage the Irish to look after themselves. Following the creation of the public works programme in 1846, he was tasked with establishing the rules by which they should operate, and those he produced were precise and lacked scope for local flexibility. Equally, they were felt to be punitive as he deliberately added stipulations that made the system very hard for those seeking assistance.

- Wage levels for public works were set below local wage levels already in existence.
- Anyone who could find agricultural work was not to be employed.
- Labourers were to be paid by the task rather than by the day.

These rulings were designed to be strict in order to deter all but the most destitute. However, they were seen as examples of British callousness – particularly only paying labourers according to their task when many were half starved. The motivation behind Trevelyan's approach was a belief in the inherent 'idleness' of the Irish and a consequent fear that if relief was excessive then they would become dependent upon it and, therefore, not be able to help themselves. This moralism was a dominant trend within British liberalism during the mid-1800s and it had been applied to the English Poor Law Amendment Act that was passed in 1834. It is reasonable to suggest that it grew in part because of the success of the early industrial revolution which had seen great wealth for those willing to work for it. In combination with the works of Thomas Malthus and Jeremy Bentham, these ideas quickly began to influence government policy.

EXTEND YOUR KNOWLEDGE

Jeremy Bentham (1748–1832)

Bentham was an English philosopher whose interest spanned law, economics and social reform. As an economist he supported the ideas of Adam Smith, although he felt Smith failed to follow his own principles at times. He is best known for his work of 1789 *An Introduction to the Principles of Morals and Legislation*, which outlined his own theory of utilitarianism. He maintains that people are motivated by pain and pleasure and, therefore, the only principles on which government should act are those that ensure the greatest pleasure for the greatest number - if this was not achievable then no action is, therefore, necessary.

SOURCE 9 From Charles Trevelyan, *The Irish Crisis*, London (1848), in which he sets out his opinion of the Irish smallholder and their general work ethic.

[The Irish smallholder] lives in a state of isolation, the type of which is to be sought for in the islands of the South Seas rather than in the great civil community of the ancient world. A fortnight for planting, a week or ten days for digging, and another fortnight for turf cutting, suffice for his subsistence, when, during the rest of the year, he is at leisure to follow his own inclinations without even the safeguard of those intellectual tastes and legitimate objects of ambition which only imperfectly obviate the evils of leisure in the highest rank of society.

Trevelyan was a keen advocate of these principles and was meticulous in his application of them in Ireland. In this endeavour, he was blamed for dragging his feet when it came to relief. Lord Bessborough, lord lieutenant of the country between 1846 and 1847, found him to have limited awareness of the conditions in Ireland and equally unprepared to adapt his moralistic principles accordingly. Even after the Irish Poor Law Extension Act passed responsibility over to Dublin and the Irish Poor Law Commission in 1847, Trevelyan retained a prominent role since it was he who ended the government soup kitchen provision following the Act's passage. Also, his orders stopped the sale of government-bought cornmeal so as to force the destitute into the workhouses. By October 1847, these activities had both ended.

As the main British political figure involved with famine relief, Trevelyan was very much the figurehead that bore the brunt of nationalist antipathy in the aftermath of the famine. However, in recent years there has been a more objective reassessment of his and Britain's actions in an attempt to offer a more rounded opinion in the face of Mitchel's rhetoric. This analysis has focused on the context of the British government's famine relief efforts and especially upon the extent of its provision. Here there is reasonable argument to suggest that the actions of Britain were not the actions of a callous government, but rather one that acted under the guidance of accepted political theories that others also supported. Furthermore, the nationalist perspective focused almost exclusively upon the limitations of relief rather than considering the benefits that it provided. In terms of the financial commitment, Britain was far from mean, providing more than £10 million in an attempt to tackle the emergency. This was a substantial sum of money at the time – equating to more than £1 billion in today's value. Additionally, the efforts to minimise suffering were undermined by a poor transport system, causing many resources not to find their way to the people in need. In this sense it is reasonable to say that perhaps the infrastructure failed the Irish people, rather than the individual actions of British politicians.

EXTEND YOUR KNOWLEDGE

John Mitchel (1815–75)
Unlike Trevelyan, John Mitchel was not a politician and had no direct role in the relief of famine. However, his contribution was to raise awareness of the situation and particularly the part played by the British. Mitchel was a staff journalist who wrote for the Irish nationalist newspaper *The Nation* after 1845. Within its pages he chronicled the extent of the potato famine in such emotive language that it stirred up broader nationalist sentiment. In articles such as 'The Potato Disease' and 'The People's Food', he offered up the origins of the current suffering, and in future articles tied the continuation of such distress to a failure in the economic system in Ireland as a result of British management and the desire of self-interest. In particular, he censured figures like Charles Trevelyan for deliberately making relief hard and also for the continued exportation of goods from the country in an effort to maintain commercial practises at the expense of starving people (Source 11).

Mitchel became increasingly hostile to British control as the famine set in, and his writing began to make greater calls for a radical solution to Ireland's problems – a possible armed insurrection to remove the oppressor nation and reorganise the system of landownership in the country. Encouraging a rebellion was a natural extension of Mitchel's growing antipathy towards British rule, particularly in the face of such distress caused, in his mind, by the exercise of British rule. On the question of land reorganisation, however, he was greatly influenced by the writings of James Fintan Lalor, a farmer's son from County Laois. Lalor, in a series of letters to *The Nation* in 1847, had called for rent strikes as part of what he felt should be an agrarian revolution to stir up Ireland's mass of small farmers. This was intended to overthrow the inequities of the existing land system, which he believed was a primary cause of the current famine. Mitchel adopted these ideas wholeheartedly as a means of encouraging greater support for his own desire for Irish independence.

SOURCE 10
Illustration drawn from life of Bridget O'Donnel and her children in West Cork, published in *The Illustrated London News*, 22 December 1849. Accompanying this illustration was an article about the experiences of Bridget and her children – evicted because of failure to pay their rent at a time when she was pregnant.

BRIDGET O'DONNEL AND CHILDREN.

SOURCE 11
From John Mitchel writing in *The Nation*, 7 March 1846. *The Nation* was a popular weekly newspaper set up by Irish nationalists to give a voice to their cause.

The Irish people, always half-starved, are expecting absolute famine day-by-day; they know they are doomed to months of a weed-diet next summer; that 'hungry ruin has them in the wind' – and they ascribe it, *unanimously*, not so much to the wrath of Heaven as to the greedy and cruel policy of England... They behold their own wretched food melting in rottenness of the face of the earth; and they see the heavy-laden hips, freighted with the yellow corn their own hands have sown and reaped, spreading all sail *for England*; they see it, and with every grain of that corn goes a heavy curse.

The rhetoric employed by Mitchel tapped into the nationalist consciousness which had been largely dormant since the Act of Union in 1801. His avid belief in the immorality and oppressive nature of British rule inspired a new generation of Irishmen to take up arms against Britain in 1848 (see Chapter 1). Though not a participant in the episode on account of his being convicted of **sedition** in the months before, Mitchel was very much the instigator of the action, and his harnessing of the famine suffering to British oppression was almost certainly a motivating factor in this attempt.

ACTIVITY
KNOWLEDGE CHECK

Ideology and the famine

1 Describe the dominant ideology behind the actions of the British government after 1845.

2 Compare this ideology with that of John Mitchel's during the same period. What differences do you observe?

3 How does ideology motivate actions?

4 In your opinion should the famine be used for ideological purposes?

HOW DID THE DECLINE OF IRELAND'S POPULATION AFFECT THE COUNTRY?

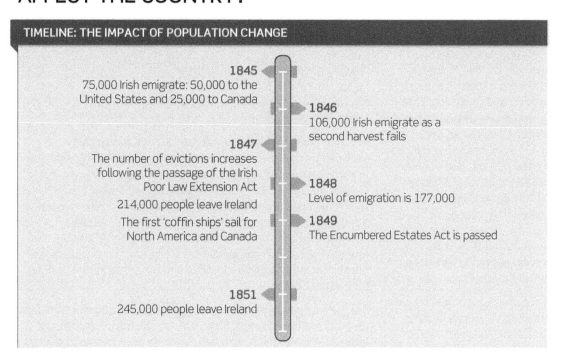

TIMELINE: THE IMPACT OF POPULATION CHANGE

1845 75,000 Irish emigrate: 50,000 to the United States and 25,000 to Canada

1846 106,000 Irish emigrate as a second harvest fails

1847 The number of evictions increases following the passage of the Irish Poor Law Extension Act

214,000 people leave Ireland

The first 'coffin ships' sail for North America and Canada

1848 Level of emigration is 177,000

1849 The Encumbered Estates Act is passed

1851 245,000 people leave Ireland

Social and economic impacts of depopulation

The rapid onset of famine after 1845 took a significant toll upon the Irish population and, including the mortality rate and emigration levels, the country lost more than 20 percent of its population during 1845–1851 – more than two million people. The cause of this loss was attributable to death and emigration in equal measure, with one million Irish dying of famine-related distress while another one million left the country. Those either choosing or being forced to emigrate for the prospect of new opportunities abroad left in their wake a nation ravaged by hunger, but also a country reeling from the loss of so many of its inhabitants. From both social and economic perspectives, the declining population had a substantial impact on Ireland which would become the legacy of those famine years.

Social impact

Perhaps one of the most significant social effects of such a decline in Ireland's population was the impact it had upon the Irish identity – and in particular the Gaelic language. Gaelic was a derivative of the Celtic language and it was native to Ireland, having been identified in the country around 400 BC. Although English quickly began to dominate the island after its colonisation in the 16th century, before 1845 the country had between three and four million Gaelic speakers. The 1851 census records only 1.8 million speakers – a decline of nearly 50 percent. While some people may have felt unwilling to admit to speaking Gaelic when the census was taken – it was not well regarded by British officials – the generally accepted reasoning for this noticeable decline was the effects of the famine. The majority of speakers lived in the rural counties in the west of Ireland and were, by and large, cottiers or small farmers whose lives depended totally upon the potato.

The decline of Gaelic speakers had begun even before the famine, but this event removed at least one million in a six-year period, which was a great loss to absorb in such a short time. As a result, the opportunity to pass on the language was markedly reduced. Thereby not only was a key signifier of Irish identity undermined, but it would also have long-term effects on the language's potential survival.

In addition to the impact on the Gaelic language, Ireland's social classes also witnessed huge changes. In 1845, there had been 300,000 cottiers. However, by 1851 this number had been reduced to 62,000, while the number of small farmers had halved. The decline of the cottier class in particular saw Ireland's rural communities transformed as the majority of these had been based upon subsistence living. However, by 1851 this had been replaced by fewer individuals holding greater tracts of land. Indeed, the number of larger farms (those over 35 acres) increased during the same period from 277,000 to 314,000, evidencing a shift away from previous subsistence practices. This change also had a knock-on effect on the social practices of Ireland's remaining population. The desire to retain larger holdings of land, for example, meant that men and women did not marry as early as they once did since that often resulted in the subdivision of land.

The concentration of larger plots also impacted upon the manner in which the Catholic religion was practised in Ireland. Cottiers and small farmers were very much traditional followers of this faith which, before the mid-19th century, was generally informal and not overly strict – mixing older pagan practices, such as wakes, with more modern concepts of Christianity. During the 1840s, however, there was a move within the Catholic Church in Ireland, promoted by Cardinal Paul Cullen, to formalise worship and strengthen the position of the clergy. This push to transform Catholic religious practices has been termed a 'devotional revolution' by the American historian Emmet Larkin and it was arguably facilitated by the impact of the Great Famine.

Efforts to reform the Catholic Church in Ireland had been underway even in the 1820s with the consecration of more churches, but it had generally been a slow process because of the extent of opposition among the Irish populace. The greatest reluctance came from the poorer classes in Ireland – those generally living in the rural areas where traditional practices were strongly held. The removal of large swathes of this class helped to promote the changes being made as not only did it reduce the extent of opposition, but the famine also encouraged a more obedient attitude towards the Church. Completing this transition was also the increased affluence of the larger landholders who were content to see the enhancement and elaboration of their Church.

Economic impact

Like society, Ireland's economy was affected by the declining population. In an obvious sense, the reduced numbers directly impacted upon the tax revenue that the country generated, but more significantly it affected the country's economic basis. Before the famine, Ireland had principally relied upon **tillage** farming and growing crops for exportation as the mainstay of its economy. The country was widely referred to as the 'breadbasket of the United Kingdom' since the majority of its foodstuffs were sold in Britain. In early 1847 for example, 34,852 **firkins** of butter were imported to Liverpool and 56,557 to Bristol.

> ### KEY TERMS
>
> **Tillage**
> Preparing the ground for growing crops.
>
> **Firkin**
> A unit of measurement equating to around 41 litres.

With the onset of famine, tillage farming was increasingly replaced by open pasture and the grazing of cattle. This shift was in part because of the desire among landowners to evict poor tenants once they became responsible for relief after 1847. In removing these people, there was a consequent desire to maintain a reduced dependency, and grazing cattle was a profitable alternative to labourer-dependent tillage farming. So what emerged after 1847 was a greater leaning towards grazing for the purpose of cash generation, with a smaller mix of tillage farming for personal usage.

The transition to pasture and grazing, and the consequent entry into livestock rearing and exportation, saw an immediate improvement after 1850 as world food markets picked up once more and farmers did not have the same labour costs as they once did. This was in part down to the effective prosecution of the 'Gregory clause' (see page 119) which had enabled landowners to reclaim more land to allow for larger-scale grazing while at the same time reducing the numbers on this land. In the quarter century after the famine, these farmers saw an increase of two-thirds in their annual income. In this strictly economic sense, therefore, it would be reasonable to suggest that the famine forced the reorganisation of Irish agriculture and that this change transformed a fragile economic system into a much stronger one. This was a system that, in the medium to long term, reaped financial benefits for Irish farmers individually and the broader national economy.

Migration and emigration

A second great tragedy of the famine was the vast number of starving and often homeless Irish who had to escape the country of their birth in the hope of finding a better future for themselves. Of the two million Irish lost during 1845–52, half migrated to Britain or emigrated abroad in what became a mass exodus from famine-plagued Ireland. Emigration had begun in the previous century but on nowhere near the scale of that undertaken during the late 1840s. This period witnessed the largest movement of Irish people and was a significant contributor to the broader **Irish diaspora** that is so prevalent in the 21st century – more than 80 million people claim Irish heritage across the world and many of these are descended from famine immigrants.

The decision to emigrate was a difficult one because of natural ties and even the financial cost of doing so – passage to North America for example cost between £2 and £5. But the failure of a second harvest in 1846, together with the rising level of evictions, left many without a choice. In the 1830s the average emigration levels in Ireland were about 5,000, but in 1845 75,000 left the country, and in 1846 this number had risen to 106,000. These figures continued to increase throughout the duration of the famine as more and more people found themselves struggling within an increasingly challenging environment where it seemed there was little chance of support.

Choosing to emigrate was by no means a guarantee of a better life, and the voyages, mostly to North America and Canada, were arduous endeavours that were themselves fraught with dangers. Such was the level of desire to leave Ireland that ships were often tightly packed so as to maximise profits for the ship owners, and this situation prompted its own raft of difficulties. Journeys to Canada took on average at least 40 days, and living in such close proximity for these extended periods often encouraged disease – especially amongst the poorer passengers who could not secure adequate berths or indeed sufficient provisions for the passage.

> **KEY TERM**
>
> Irish diaspora
> A term referring to Irish people and their descendants who do not live in Ireland.

SOURCE 12 A sketch made of the Emigration Office in Cork c1851. It was published in the *Illustrated London News*, 10 May 1851.

'Coffin ships'

Travelling with established shipping firms this was less of a problem, but many of the poorer Irish who could not easily afford the fares chose to sail in cheaper vessels that had quickly been put to sea by speculative individuals intent on making money from the rising demand. These vessels were often rotting hulks that were barely seaworthy, but for those seeking to escape Ireland they offered the only means of salvation. The first of these ships to arrive in Canada in May 1847 was called *Syria*; it carried 241 passengers of which 202 were ill with fever. Of the 100,000 who travelled this passage, one in five died on the trip – usually of typhus or malnutrition. Upon their arrival in Canada, these ships would be quarantined at Grosse Isle, a small island in the St Lawrence River outside Quebec, before being allowed to enter the city. Such were the numbers arriving that it would take five days for passengers to see a doctor and very quickly ships were queueing for 15 miles down the St Lawrence river. Unable to leave the ships, healthy individuals often succumbed to infection and bodies were, out of necessity, simply tossed into the river.

Landlord-assisted emigration

A large percentage of passengers on 'coffin ships' were Ireland's poorest inhabitants, those who had only subsisted upon the land and were consequently the worst hit by famine. These people could not afford to emigrate and, therefore, had their passages paid for by their landlords. The inclination for such charity is varied. Certainly there was a humanitarian motivation and the wish to help those less fortunate during the challenging times of famine, but equally there was also an economic benefit to assisting poor tenants to emigrate and thereby clear the land of them. An early landlord who sought to assist his tenants was Lord Palmerston, the British foreign secretary during 1846–51 and prime minister after 1855. Palmerston owned extensive lands in Sligo and Dublin and had begun helping his tenants in 1837 as a means of rationalising his estates and making them more efficient. However, once famine set in this economic motivation also belied a humanitarian instinct. In 1847, his agents, Joseph Kincaid and Robert Stewart, chartered nine ships to carry 2,000 of his tenants from Sligo to Canada and another from Liverpool that carried a further 480 tenants. This was at significant personal cost. Other landlords were less motivated by such inclinations and simply wanted to remove their poorest tenants so that they could reorganise their land in a more profitable manner. After 1847, this became even more of a priority since the changes to the Poor Law meant they had to pay for relief of their existing tenants.

Emigration took a considerable toll upon Ireland. It robbed the country of more than a million of its inhabitants and scattered them across the globe, forced to find new lives away from their homes and families. The psychological impact of this was undoubtedly substantial and the reception these migrants received was often not a welcome one, prompting further hardships. The Ireland they left behind, however, began to transform in their absence. The agricultural system in particular was gradually reorganised and Irish landlords were able to consolidate their holdings for greater effect, using the famine as the means by which to usher out the old and bring in the new.

SOURCE

13 From a land agent, Joseph Kincaid, writing to his client, Lord Palmerston, 23 March 1847. Palmerston was the British Foreign Secretary who owned extensive land in Ireland and employed Kincaid to manage his estates.

Of those who are desirous of emigrating from your Lordship's estates [in Co. Sligo after] surrendering their holdings [and] being taken out to Quebec. The list is not yet complete but I think it... 150 families comprising 900 individuals who occupy 500 Irish acres of land and the expenses of their transport would be about £2500... I have already chartered two vessells [which] will sail in less than a fortnight... and the only difficulty that now presents itself to me is... what 400 shall I take out of the 900 candidates all of whom are desirous to go. The poor creatures... see nothing but misery and starvation before them if they stay where they are.

A Level Exam-Style Question Section B

'Depopulation during the 1840s had a positive impact upon Ireland.'

How far do you agree with this statement? (20 marks)

Tip
When answering this question you should consider who benefited from depopulation and who did not.

Consolidation of landholdings and the importance of the Encumbered Estates Act 1849

The reduced population prompted the opportunity to consolidate landholdings in Ireland. Prior to the famine, land had been subdivided and subdivided once more under the middlemen system, which had provided great profits for those initial leaseholders and owners. But as the land was divided up further down the chain, holdings had become very small – often rented in less than five-acre plots with a substantial number of the poorest cottiers occupying between one and two acres. This system had made the country very fragile and its population vulnerable to natural problems such as poor harvests, and this had resulted in famine after 1845. After this year, however, the nature of land distribution changed. As the population declined, the land they had occupied was reclaimed by larger farmers and this gradually saw the transformation of landownership. Source 14 shows the extent of this change between 1845 and 1851.

SOURCE 14 Land redistribution between 1845 and 1851.

Size of landholding	Percentage change
More than 30 acres	+16.5
More than 15 acres	+5.0
Between 5 and 15 acres	−38.0
Between 1 and 5 acres	−52.0
Less than 1 acre	−48.0

The manner in which this consolidation was achieved was first the natural loss of tenants through death but then also through emigration as mentioned elsewhere, and the increased level of determination amongst landlords to evict their poorest tenants. In the case of eviction this practice has encouraged Irish nationalists to place equal blame for the famine upon both British and Irish landlords' shoulders.

Evictions

In a country where land was at a premium because of a fast-growing population, evictions in Ireland were an established practice since there was always another willing to pay a better rent. During the famine years, however, this practice took on a greater significance since it was often regarded as a callous undertaking, that was condemning those evicted for the financial benefit of the landowner. This was evident in the rigorous prosecution of the unpopular 'Gregory clause' within the 1847 Irish Poor Law Extension Act. This clause, named after the landlord who suggested its inclusion, stated that no one owning more than a quarter of an acre of land could apply for relief unless they were willing to give up ownership of their possession. In effect this was ransoming relief to the poor so that larger landowners could acquire their parcels of land and consolidate them into larger holdings – often for grazing or pasture. Under this clause, some 200,000 small plots were reclaimed during the late 1840s, and their unfortunate occupants either emigrated, entered the workhouse or simply wandered the country.

SOURCE 15 From an eyewitness account from Head Constable Dennehey of Mount Bellew in County Galway of an eviction he oversaw. Published in *The Freeman's Journal*, 28 March 1846.

The women and children... ran out of the houses half-dressed, and their frantic screams, as they gathered up some bits of clothing or furniture, was beyond all description, terrifically painful. Some were to be seen running off with the sticks that formed portions of their house roofs, and more of them, in their bare feet, were helping the men to carry off the dung in baskets on their backs and heads to the road side. Some of them clung with wild tenacity to the door-posts from whence they were dragged by the bailiffs, and those who could not be got away ran great risk of their lives by the tumbling down of the roofs and walls, and many had very narrow escapes.

The Encumbered Estates Act 1849

Supporting the consolidation of Irish landholdings, the passage of the Encumbered Estates Act in 1849 gave greater legal justification to eviction and also the sale of lands to more successful landowners. The Act itself was designed to encourage the sale of landed estates that had become insolvent and whose owner's had been bankrupted because of the famine, and thereby inject new money into Irish agriculture. To oversee the sale of these estates, the Act provided for the establishment of the Encumbered Estates Court whose three commissioners were empowered to enforce a sale, usually by auction, of any land burdened with debts exceeding its annual rental income. Any proceeds from the sale would then be distributed among creditors and a clear title of deed would be granted to the new owner under which he had legal justification to do as he wished with his purchase. By 1859, five million acres worth £21 million had been sold through the court.

The sale of so much land under this Act had significant consequences for Ireland since it became a prominent means for the ongoing process of land consolidation. This was because many of the 7,489 purchasers who bought from auctions by the court were established landowners in Ireland already, and they used their new titles to evict tenants from their acquisition and thereby increase their holding substantially. In August 1853, for example, Mr John Gerrard in County Galway was able to evict 42 families under an Encumbered Estates Court injunction so that he could use the land as he saw fit. This episode was common throughout Ireland after 1849, and it contributed substantially to the changes in landownership shown in Source 14.

Conclusion

The arrival of blight was a natural misfortune, but the manner in which it was addressed was selective by the British government, and this response has received mixed opinion. From the nationalist perspective, successive governments did not do enough to support Ireland, clinging instead to non-interventionist principles that restricted their willingness to intercede sufficiently. This view places blame with individuals such as Charles Trevelyan and John Russell, whose policies it was felt could have been more sympathetic to the Irish nation's plight. This view has become a popular one in Ireland. However, it is perhaps too emotive and fails to consider objectively the actions that were undertaken, notably the response of Robert Peel's administration to buy in Indian corn and remove the Corn Laws in 1846, the latter precipitating the fall of his government. Furthermore, the £10 million that Britain spent on famine relief was an unprecedented amount at that time and is perhaps a level of spending that suggests its governments were more predisposed to support the Irish than the nationalist view concedes. In each interpretation there is truth, and it is reasonable to suggest that governments could always do more. However, the 'Great Famine' was on a scale so large that it would be easy to see any response as not being enough.

ACTIVITY
KNOWLEDGE CHECK

Depopulation in Ireland
Using the material you have read together with your own knowledge, explain the impact of depopulation in Ireland during the period 1845-51.

ACTIVITY
SUMMARY

The Irish Famine
1 Create a table of key features relating to the Irish famine. You should use the following headings to help you: 'Causes'; 'Role of British government'; 'Role of landlords'; 'Effects upon Ireland'.

2 Using these features create an essay plan – including bullet-pointed brief explanations – for the following question:

How far would you agree that the human losses suffered in Ireland in the years 1845-51 were an inevitability?

WIDER READING

Coogan, T.P. *The Famine Plot*, Palgrave (2012)

Delaney, E. *The Great Irish Famine: A History in Four Lives*, Gill and Macmillan (2014)

Gray, P. *The Irish Famine*, Thames and Hudson (1995)

Keneally, T. *The Great Shame*, BCA (1998)

Kinealy, C. *This Great Calamity: The Irish Famine 1845-52*, Gill and Macmillan (2006)

Moody, T.W. and Martin, F.X. (eds), *The Course of Irish History*, Mercier Press (1994)

Woodham-Smith, C. *The Great Hunger*, Harper and Row (1984)

3.6 The Irish land issue, 1870–82

KEY QUESTIONS

- What was the significance of demands for land reform in 1870?
- How stable was the Irish land system during the 1870s?
- How significant were the Land Wars in addressing the Irish land issue after 1879?

INTRODUCTION

The question of land and its ownership has been a long-standing one in Irish history. As a country whose only significant natural resource is the fertile soil on which the nation exists, there has been a continual antagonism between those who own the land and those who live upon it. The basis of this resentment originated in the 17th century when much of the native Irish were dispossessed by English colonists as part of a broader attempt to enhance English control over the island. Throughout subsequent centuries, the control of this valuable resource helped to promote the dominance of an Anglo-Irish landowning class. This class were able to exert great influence over a broader Irish population, who were very dependent on the land.

> **KEY TERM**
>
> Conacre
> A system used in Ireland whereby a tenant is leased a small plot of land, usually for growing a single crop, on short-term leases.

What developed by the mid-19th century was an unequal balance wherein the majority of Ireland's rural inhabitants existed on small plots of land let to them either directly by the landowner or through a middleman. The legal foundation on which leasing was based was known as **conacre** and it provided the prospective tenant with no legal claim to the land, with rent being paid only in cash, labour or a combination of the two. The leases that were drawn up under this system usually only granted a landholding claim for 11 months of the year so that the landlord had no legal obligation to them. In this sense, it was largely a one-sided agreement since tenants could be charged excessive rates and yet not have any legal protection.

The system was arranged entirely for the benefit of the landowner at the expense of the tenants. The vulnerability of the tenants was witnessed in horrifyingly stark terms during the mid-1840s when famine hit the country and more than a million people died of hunger or related diseases. In the aftermath of this event, landholdings became increasingly more consolidated and agriculture diversified a little more, but the financial and legal arrangements still favoured the landowner and the relationship between them and their tenants continued to be strained.

Attempts to reduce this tension were made periodically after 1870. However, challenging economic conditions generated by farmers' traditional enemy poor weather, and growing markets in the USA made this increasingly difficult. Collectively, these problems weakened the position of Irish smallholders who relied on the sale of their produce to pay rents, and this hastened a deterioration in landowner–tenant relations. This decline promoted a significant period of massive protest known

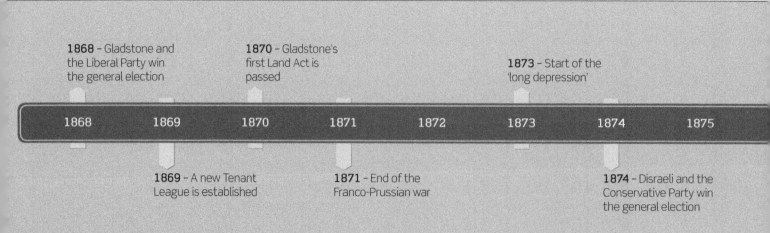

1868 – Gladstone and the Liberal Party win the general election

1870 – Gladstone's first Land Act is passed

1873 – Start of the 'long depression'

| 1868 | 1869 | 1870 | 1871 | 1872 | 1873 | 1874 | 1875 |

1869 – A new Tenant League is established

1871 – End of the Franco-Prussian war

1874 – Disraeli and the Conservative Party win the general election as the Land Wars which began in 1879 and lasted three years, only coming to an end following a deal between the leaders of the protesting farmers and the British government.

WHAT WAS THE SIGNIFICANCE OF DEMANDS FOR LAND REFORM IN 1870?

The significance of the Dublin Land Conference, 1870

The question of land was a very important one for the Irish, and following the years of famine it became closely linked to the nationalist agenda. In particular it became a symbol of British oppression since ownership lay primarily with the British or Anglo-Irish. Although the latter were also affected by the famine, it was by no means to the same extent as the poorer, Catholic Irish whose suffering was often intensified as a result of eviction from the land. Land reform was adopted by subsequent nationalist organisations – first, and most directly, with the Young Irelanders in 1848, and then in a more peripheral manner with the Irish Republican Brotherhood after 1858. The land question became vitally important for British politicians seeking to keep Ireland pacified. Indeed, following the Fenian uprising in 1867, when William Gladstone formed his first administration in 1868, he made very clear his intention to settle the broader Irish question, and one means by which he sought to achieve this was by addressing the issue of land and particularly tenants' rights.

By 1870 Ireland had 500,000 tenant farmers, 80 percent of whom held leases of not more than 12 months. Therefore, they had no legal rights or strong claim to the land they rented and were consequently reliant upon the mercy of the landowner. This sense of vulnerability combined with a more determined attitude towards securing land rights in the post-famine years had resulted in the creation of the Irish Tenant League in 1850. This was a nationwide attempt on behalf of farmers to unite in an organised manner in order to secure the 'three Fs': fair rent, fixity of **tenure** and the freedom for tenants to sell their interest in their holding subject to the landlord's approval. In setting these objectives the league felt they could empower tenant farmers and equalise the relationship that currently was so one-sided. With fixed rents for

example, landlords could not arbitrarily increase the amount they had agreed and so the opportunity to exploit their tenants would be minimised. Equally by establishing fixity of tenure, a tenant could not be evicted if he had paid his rent, which subsequently afforded a much greater degree of security. Although the league was short-lived and ended only nine years later when prosperity dampened the fires of its members, it was the first co-ordinated attempt by Ireland's agricultural community to secure enhanced rights, and it demonstrated an improved ability to mobilise as a unified front in the pursuit of their goals.

> **KEY TERM**
>
> Tenure
> The conditions under which land is held.

The collapse of the Tenant League did not see the end of the demand for land reform in Ireland and throughout the 1860s there grew ad hoc farmers' clubs which sporadically agitated for changes. In the 1868 general election, these unofficial clubs campaigned across the country in an attempt to recreate a Tenant League with Isaac Butt, a prominent lawyer and future leader of the Home Government Association, as its president. These clubs were most prominent in the south of the country since farmers in Ulster had a better relationship with their landlords by virtue of what was known as the **Ulster custom**. This involved a greater level of security which had been established in the second half of the 17th century when political and economic conditions had been particularly unstable in the province. Here tenants had asserted the right of continuous occupation of their plots by citing the stability and improvements to the land that their labours and those of their families had created during and after those difficult times. Therefore, farmers in the north already enjoyed a number of the rights being sought by farmers in the south.

> **KEY TERM**
>
> Ulster custom
> A convention primarily found in the province of Ulster whereby tenants enjoyed customary rights such as fixity of tenure because of the role they played in maintaining and improving the land during times of economic and political turmoil in the 17th century. Also referred to as tenant right.

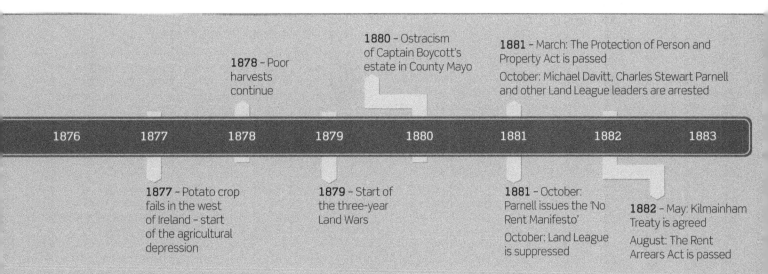

1878 – Poor harvests continue

1880 – Ostracism of Captain Boycott's estate in County Mayo

1881 – March: The Protection of Person and Property Act is passed

October: Michael Davitt, Charles Stewart Parnell and other Land League leaders are arrested

1876 1877 1878 1879 1880 1881 1882 1883

1877 – Potato crop fails in the west of Ireland – start of the agricultural depression

1879 – Start of the three-year Land Wars

1881 – October: Parnell issues the 'No Rent Manifesto'

October: Land League is suppressed

1882 – May: Kilmainham Treaty is agreed

August: The Rent Arrears Act is passed

Despite the better arrangements in Ulster, the security was based upon convention only. Therefore, the growing movement in the south, which saw a new Tenant League formally established in 1869, sought to win greater support here by pointing out the anticipated fear that any new legislation they themselves were pushing for might jeopardise the unwritten advantages that were enjoyed in that province. Though slow to commit to the new organisation, the people of Ulster did begin to call for a more formal basis for their convention and joined their southern counterparts in a broader demand for change. By 1870 the Tenant League had acquired a strong following. With some sense of this organisation and its increasing support among Irish farmers, the newly elected prime minister, William Gladstone, set about creating legislation to settle the land question and appease its supporters.

The Dublin Land Conference, 1870

With the rumours that Gladstone was preparing a bill, Irish farmers and the Tenant League were keen to influence its development so as to ensure it offered the measures they sought. To this effect, in early February 1870, a national land conference was organised in Dublin as a forum in which farmers and interested parties could openly declare their hopes. The event itself was a deliberately public affair so that it had the effect of a popular demonstration of the will of Ireland's agricultural community.

Attendees of the event came from across the country and even from Ulster farms where tenants' rights were better considered. Notable figures included the president of the Tenant League, Isaac Butt, and around 14 MPs, Lord Portsmouth and Lords Granard, Greville and Bellew, the latter presiding over the conference. Politicians who were noticeable by their absence were the vast majority of Irish Liberals. They refused to attend the event on the grounds that they were primary landowners in Ireland who, though unwilling to openly oppose land reform, were equally unwilling to endorse it through attendance at such a gathering. One of the prominent speakers at the conference was Sir John Gray, a Protestant nationalist who had been a strong supporter of Daniel O'Connell and was himself a veteran reformer. As the owner of the *Freeman's Journal*, Gray was also well placed to spread the feelings of the conference across a wider basis and it was his newspaper that recorded the proceedings with great interest. He was also a keen advocate of the 'three Fs' that the original Tenant League had pushed for and which the conference spent considerable time discussing.

The conference began on 2 February and lasted for two days in which the issue of tenant right (see Ulster custom, page 131) was the main focus. In particular there was significant opposition to the practice of eviction without real grounds for doing so. To guard against such action the conference sought assurances that eviction would only be performed if rent had not been paid, and for no other reason. The overall outcome of the gathering was a wish to extend the Ulster custom – specifically the rights of fixity of tenure and freedom to sell their interest – across the whole country, and formalise tenant rights in the hope that every tenant farmer would have strong grounds for legal protection and long-term security.

The specific impact of the Dublin Land Conference upon the land question in Ireland is hard to quantify. However, its overtly political nature, in terms of those who attended and the manner of its timing, almost certainly influenced the preparation of Gladstone's legislation which was introduced to parliament in mid-February.

The reasons for the Land Act 1870 and its significance

The passage of the Landlord and Tenant Act, informally and more widely known as the Land Act, in August 1870 was the product of William Gladstone's broader desire to promote a more harmonious relationship between Ireland and Britain. As early as 1868, he had declared his intention to pacify Ireland and by 1869 had already taken steps to address another source of that nation's discontent – religion. The passage of the Irish Church Act had disestablished the Protestant Church of Ireland and gone some way to reduce Catholic and Protestant tensions. Now the prime minister sought to tackle the equally contentious issue of land. He was not alone in believing this issue was a great source of conflict, and as early as May 1869 others within his party were voicing the same concern – notably the president of the Board of Trade, John Bright, who felt that if the issue was not adopted immediately then there was likely to be trouble in the future.

SOURCE

1

From a letter written by the President of the Board of Trade, John Bright, to Prime Minister William Gladstone outlining his concern about the need to address land reform in Ireland, dated 21 May 1869.

When the Irish church question is out of the way, we shall find all Ireland, north and south alike, united in demanding something on the land question much broader than anything hitherto offered or proposed in compensation bills. If the question is to go on without any real remedy for the grievance, the condition of Ireland in this particular will become worse, and measures far beyond anything I now contemplate will be necessary. I am most anxious to meet the evil before it is too great for control, and my plan *will meet* it without wrong to any man.

Gladstone was motivated in part by the same political need to reduce antagonism in Ireland so as to allow his country to better govern it, but he was also guided by a deep moral principle that told him Ireland deserved justice. The iniquity of that country's land system was a glaring example of the need for reform if Ireland was to receive justice. Therefore, the prime minister personally undertook to formulate a bill that would offer a greater degree of fairness. In developing his legislation, he considered proposals from within his party. This included John Bright, who wanted to give Irish tenants the opportunity to buy their own land, and also the Irish Secretary Chichester Parker-Fortescue, who suggested formalising the 'Ulster custom' and offering compensation to evicted tenants. The final bill that was introduced on 15 February 1870 comprised the following key provisions.

- The Ulster custom was recognised in law wherever it was agreed that it existed.

- Compensation was to be offered for tenants who had been evicted for anything other than non-payment of rents and for any improvements to the land that the tenants might have made.

- The protections afforded by the legislation would not apply to tenants who held leases of more than 31 years since it was assumed that sufficient protection already existed for those tenants under the terms of their leases.

- Any tenant who wished to buy their holding could do so and would be able to borrow two-thirds of the price from the government and pay this back at five percent interest over 35 years.

The final provision was known as the **Bright clause** since it was included at the request of John Bright. Gladstone was reluctant to promote owner-occupancy since he was a great believer in the system of landlordism and particularly the order it encouraged. But despite his own feelings he agreed to its inclusion so as to secure greater support for his bill from both within his own party and the Conservatives, who also endorsed tenant ownership.

KEY TERM

Bright clause
The right of tenants to buy their lease from their landlord if that landlord is amenable. Tenants would be helped to purchase by having access to government loans up to two-thirds of the cost, with a fixed interest rate of five percent over 35 years. It was known as the Bright clause after John Bright, President of the Board of Trade, who strongly advocated for its inclusion.

The bill was generally well-received in parliament and it passed its second reading by a majority of 442 to 11 in the House of Commons despite some minor criticism from figures such as Benjamin Disraeli, leader of the Conservative opposition. When it was read for a third time there was no substantial challenge at all from either house and, having been debated for three-and-a-half months, on 1 August 1870 the bill received the royal assent and was passed into law.

SOURCE 2

From the Land Act introduced by William Gladstone and passed by parliament in 1870. Upon becoming prime minister in 1868 Gladstone had resolved to address the problems in Ireland which he saw as undermining that country's relationship with Britain. He felt the land question was one of the most divisive issues between them.

1. The usages prevalent in the province of Ulster, which are known as, and in this Act intended to be included under, the denomination of the Ulster tenant-right custom, are hereby declared to be legal, and shall, in the case of any holding in the province of Ulster proved to be subject thereto, be enforced in manner provided by this Act.

Where the landlord has purchased or acquired or shall hereafter purchase or acquire from the tenant the Ulster tenant-right custom to which his holding is subject, such holding shall thenceforth cease to be subject to the Ulster tenant-right custom.

A tenant of a holding subject to the Ulster tenant-right custom, and who claims the benefit of such custom, shall not be entitled to compensation under any other section of this Act; but a tenant of a holding subject to such custom, but not claiming under the same, shall not be barred from making a claim for compensation, with the consent of the Court, under any of the other sections of this Act, except the section relating to compensation in respect of payment to incoming tenant; and where such last-mentioned claim has been made, and allowed, such holding shall not be again subject to the Ulster tenant-right custom.

2. If, in the case of any holding not situate within the province of Ulster, it shall appear that an usage prevails which in all essential particulars corresponds with the Ulster tenant-right custom, it shall in like manner, and subject to the like conditions, be deemed legal, and shall be enforced in manner provided by this Act...

A tenant of any holding subject to such usage as aforesaid, and who claims the benefit of the same, shall not be entitled to claim compensation under any other section of this Act; but a tenant of a holding not claiming the benefit of such usage shall not be barred from making a claim for compensation with the consent of the Court under any of the other sections of this Act, and where such last-mentioned claim has been made and allowed such holding shall not be again subject to such usage as aforesaid.

A Level Exam-Style Question Section A

Study Source 2 before you answer this question.

Assess the value of this source for revealing how determined the British government was to solve the land question in Ireland. (20 marks)

Explain your answer, using the source, the information given about its origin and your own knowledge about the historical context.

Tip
When answering this question you should consider the reforms the Act actually made – do you think they address the demands of Irish farmers?

Significance of the Land Act 1870

The passage of the Landlord and Tenant Act broke new ground for the British government since it was the first occasion whereby that government had sought to intervene in Irish land affairs on behalf of tenants. All previous legislation had been to the benefit of landowners. Therefore, the passage of the Act was well received by the farming community in Ireland, who anticipated that meaningful change would be forthcoming.

However, the Land Act did not immediately have a significant impact on the lives of those whom it proposed to help. This was because, as well intentioned as the Act was, it failed to substantially change anything. With regard to its first provision, that of legalising the Ulster custom for example, the decision as to where that custom currently existed was left vague. Therefore, it was incumbent upon the tenant claiming those rights to prove they applied to their tenancy. Furthermore it was also down to the tenants to prove that the rights they were claiming were in fact part of the custom in the first place. In the immediate term this undermined tenants' relationships with landlords since the existence of customary rights were now fought over in court (albeit infrequently due to cost) rather than simply being a convention that was evenly applied. Essentially, on this key issue the Act did not go far enough in terms of precise specification and, therefore, it was entirely subjective and consequently applied as such. Ultimately it made little difference to the lives of the overall tenant community save damaging landlord–tenant relations in some areas. One example of this declining relationship took place in County Donegal in 1870 when W.H.M. Style, owner of a large estate in Glenfin, was refused permission from his tenants to rent out shooting rights on their occupied holdings. This had usually been granted in the past, but increasingly tenants began to assert their rights. This was a small issue that arose from a minor dispute, but it highlights the damaging effect of the new Land Act which did little to effectively support tenant farmers and in fact encouraged a more combative attitude between them and the landowner.

SOURCE 3

Taking the (Irish) Bull by the Horns. An illustration by John Tenniel published in the satirical magazine *Punch* on 26 February 1870. John Tenniel was the principal political cartoonist for the magazine and in 1893 he was knighted for his artistic achievements which illustrated social and political life in Britain.

In addition to this shortcoming, the Bright clause did not see a sudden rise in land ownership amongst the tenant farmers. Only 877 people took advantage of this opportunity. This small uptake was because the general conditions of the clause were not particularly favourable, and nor did many farmers have the requisite one-third deposit. The poor response to this opportunity reflects Ireland's general response to the Act in practice since even the compensation provision was difficult to act upon. Indeed, in cases where a landlord wanted to evict a tenant, often the landlord would wait until the year lease had expired and then raise the rent, thereby circumventing the provisions within the Act since no rent was increased during the ownership of the lease. An alternative means by which compensation was not made was through the landlord deliberately withholding it and making tenants take legal action to claim it. In these cases tenants often could not afford to do so and, therefore, were unable to benefit from the provision granted to them within the 1870 Act.

The Act also failed to address one of the central concerns of the tenant farmers – that of high rents. On this point the Act was equally vague and initially only stated that rents should not be 'excessive'. By not quantifying what was meant by this term, there was substantial room for rent increases as it was left to local courts to decide what this actually meant. Even despite the vagary of this term, when the House of Lords came to consider the bill prior to its enactment they were able to substitute the phrase for 'exorbitant' which offered, in their eyes, even greater freedom for landowners to charge above what their tenants might be able to afford. On this point in particular, the Act can be said to have been inadequate since the main interest of Irish farmers had been the issue of rent prices, and it had been expected that the new legislation would offer some form of genuine protection against their arbitrary increase.

Despite these evident weaknesses the Act did offer the first real effort by a British government to help the Irish tenant farmers. The provision of compensation especially shows recognition that tenants must enjoy some degree of right over the land they rent such that if forced to relinquish it, some due would be owed to them. This recognition at the very least marks a more positive attitude towards the smaller tenant farmers in Ireland, even if the reality of subsequent events saw very little tangible change. On this basis, if not in practice then certainly in spirit, the Landlord and Tenant Act of 1870 can be regarded as a great step forward.

ACTIVITY
KNOWLEDGE CHECK

Early demands for land reform

1 Identify three reasons for the growing demand for land reform.

2 Briefly explain what the 'three Fs' are.

3 Outline the strengths and weaknesses of the Land Act 1870.

4 What does Source 3 suggest about the attitude of Britain towards the issue of land reform?

THINKING HISTORICALLY — Evidence (6c)

Comparing and evaluating historians' arguments

The Land Act passed in 1870 and presented in Source 2 was the first piece of British legislation that was aimed at supporting tenant rights rather than those of the landlords.

What can we say, credibly, about the Act on the basis of source materials such as these? First we need to consider the context from which the sources emerge (this is an Act of Parliament) and the wider context (there was growing demand for land reform in Ireland and an uprising three years before). A credible account also needs to avoid going beyond what the evidence allows us to claim.

Here are two historians' opinions about the Land Act of 1870 which draw upon the legislation itself.

Two historians' opinions about the Land Act 1870	
The act failed, at almost every point, to achieve the purpose for which it was intended. Even the legalisation of the Ulster custom, in appearance a very substantial concession, added little to the real security of the tenant. So far from attempting to define either the custom itself, or the areas within which it applied, the act referred in general terms to the 'usages' prevalent in the province of Ulster and elsewhere; and left it to the courts to decide each particular case on its merits. J.C. Beckett, *The Making of Modern Ireland 1603-1923*, Faber and Faber (2011).	As other historians have insisted, Gladstone's aims were essentially political: to bind Ireland to the Union and its institutions by proving that the Westminster parliament was prepared to legislate for what the mass of the Irish people considered to be their legitimate grievances. The Land Act, therefore, (in F.S.L. Lyons' phrase) 'had a symbolic significance', for, whatever its defects in strictly economic terms, it could be regarded as a further blow against the power of the Ascendancy. Paul Adelman and Robert Pearce, *Great Britain and the Irish Question, 1798-1921*, Hatchette (2005).

1 Compare the two accounts above and identify factual statements or claims that they both agree upon. Make a list of these points.

2 Look carefully at how the historians use language. Do they both use equally cautious language in making their claims, or is one more confident and assertive than the other? Is one (or both) of the historians over-claiming?

3 Look back at Source 2. Do both historians appear to have made equally effective use of the 1870 Act provisions?

4 Are both of the historical accounts equally credible or are there reasons to prefer one account more than another?

HOW STABLE WAS THE IRISH LAND SYSTEM DURING THE 1870S?

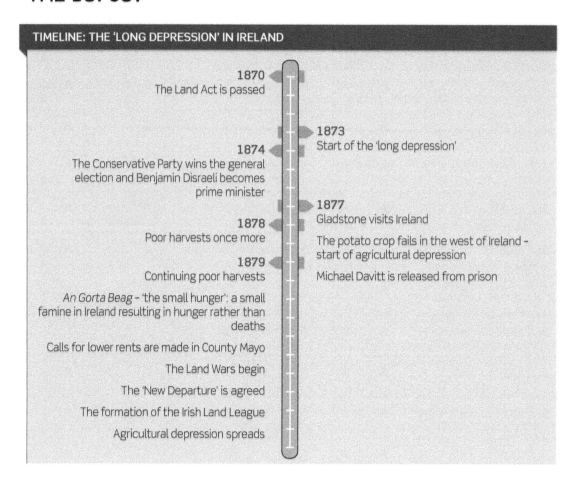

TIMELINE: THE 'LONG DEPRESSION' IN IRELAND

1870
The Land Act is passed

1873
Start of the 'long depression'

1874
The Conservative Party wins the general election and Benjamin Disraeli becomes prime minister

1877
Gladstone visits Ireland

The potato crop fails in the west of Ireland – start of agricultural depression

Michael Davitt is released from prison

1878
Poor harvests once more

1879
Continuing poor harvests

An Gorta Beag – 'the small hunger': a small famine in Ireland resulting in hunger rather than deaths

Calls for lower rents are made in County Mayo

The Land Wars begin

The 'New Departure' is agreed

The formation of the Irish Land League

Agricultural depression spreads

The impact of the 'long depression' on Irish agriculture, the problem of tenancies, evictions and rent strikes

The limited nature of Gladstone's Land Act did not immediately upset Ireland's tenant farmers. In the early 1870s they enjoyed a relative period of prosperity and evictions from the land remained relatively low. Between 1854 and 1880 for example, the eviction rate in Ireland averaged only 1.36 per 1,000 holdings per year. The value of agricultural output increased to £40.6 million in the years 1871–75 as compared to £28.8 million 20 years before in 1851–54. This improvement went a considerable way to satisfy Irish farmers and reduce their overall discontent regarding the issue of tenant right since the issue became less immediate during these buoyant times.

However, such improvement, as good as it was, also masked the limitations of the 1870 Act and left the mistaken belief among Britain's politicians that the land question had finally been answered. Upon visiting Ireland in 1877, Gladstone declared that he was quite contented that the problem was resolved. Despite such confidence, however, the problems of tenant right still remained and landlords were still able to shirk their responsibilities regarding compensation and rent capping. To this effect the 1870 Act had very little impact, and in the summer of 1877 the extent of its ineffectiveness was clearly felt when the agricultural community suffered the onset of a poor harvest, which ushered in an agricultural depression that lasted for the next four years.

The 'long depression'

Even before 1877, however, the economy was beginning to slow down as around the globe a broader financial depression was setting in after 1873 that would linger for more than two decades. This contraction was the result of an overweening confidence in the stock markets following successful speculation in the aftermath of both the American Civil War in 1865 and the Franco-Prussian War in 1871. The end of these conflicts had opened up investment opportunities and, after several years of boom, a sudden fear set in that this investment bubble might burst, leaving investors debt-ridden. As a result, the value of stock declined as investors sought to cut back on their investments, and this affected world economies. The crash of 1873 marked the beginning of slower economic growth, which has been called the 'long depression'. Although Ireland was sheltered from the effects initially by virtue of its main trade with Britain, whose economy was big enough to absorb the slowdown, by 1877 it began to feel the pinch. Irish exports to Britain began to fall after this date as that country also succumbed to depression. Having started the decade with an unemployment rate of one percent, by the end of the 1870s this had risen to 11 percent. The economic challenges that the 'long depression' created had a significant impact on the lives of Ireland's farmers and consequently added to the lingering issue of land rights in that country.

Among the first of these economic challenges was the decline in Ireland's export trade, in part the result of a sudden availability of cheap American wheat. Prices fell from $1.70 per **bushel** to only $0.66 a bushel, and this encouraged Britain to buy from the USA rather than Ireland. Historically, the sudden availability of cheap wheat from across the Atlantic has been attributed to the onset of depression in Ireland. However, the wheat market in Ireland only accounted for 10 percent of overall agricultural output in the country. So, while having a small impact, in actual fact the decline was not quite as devastating as first thought. Equally, the American provision of cheap chilled meats did not adversely affect the Irish economy immediately, since the quality of the cuts was far inferior to that offered by Ireland and therefore demand did not reduce substantially. As the depression continued, however, prices were gradually forced down, although importers did recognise the difference in quality (with the meats in particular). Despite the variance in quality, Irish farmers increasingly began to feel the pressure of the competition generated by cheaper US goods, and over subsequent years they found it harder to maintain their prices. Of greater concern was the falling price of butter, which many smallholders in Ireland, Connacht especially, sold to help pay their rents. Towards the end of the 1870s, foreign imports of this commodity began to force prices down – by at least three percent – and this gradually added to the difficulties of Ireland's smallholding farmers who relied on the income it provided. In addition to this competition there were also the perennial challenges of Ireland's inclement weather, which led to consecutive poor harvests and subsequent disease after 1877. This misfortune in particular substantially affected the country's agricultural performance.

The decline in exports was not just a problem for Ireland's merchants; competition forced prices down and this was passed on to the agricultural sector. The falling prices – such as those of wheat and butter – resulted in the value of land declining since it could no longer generate the profits it once did. The loss in value of land affected farmers substantially since it was the foundation of their livelihoods. The effect was mostly felt by small tenant farmers and crofters who worked the less-fertile marginal land and who consequently found their holdings worth almost nothing. However, such was the extent of the depression that even landowners suffered, with many losing significant rental income as increasingly tenants could not pay their dues. This problem was further compounded by low yields and bad harvests, particularly those of potatoes. Between 1876 and 1879, the value of Irish tillage fell by £14 million, and more than 60 percent of this loss was because of the failed potato crop. Without a good yield there was little chance of generating any reasonable income, especially since prices remained low because of foreign competition. In combination, the low prices and low yields created a very difficult period for Irish agriculture and these difficulties once more raised the question of tenant rights.

The problem of tenancies

When the agricultural depression set in, it was felt most severely in the west of Ireland – notably in Connacht and West Munster where farming remained a very traditional affair. The tenancies in these areas were primarily smallholdings as they had been before the famine since landowners in these areas did not convert their interests to pasture farming to the same extent as elsewhere. As an example of this variance, in the western province of Connacht 89 percent of rented smallholdings were valued at less than £15 a year compared with Leinster where only 65 percent of holdings were valued in this same category. By contrast, at the upper end of the valuations, Connacht had less than one percent of tenants on rented land worth over £100 compared with Leinster which had just over four percent. The consequence of this was that in these areas – such as Connacht, where farming remained focused on small-scale tillage – there remained a very heavy reliance upon the potato as it remained the primary source of personal sustenance, while allowing other crops such as wheat to be

Bushel
A unit of measurement for volume. One bushel is equivalent to 36.4 litres.

grown for sale. The failure of the potato crop between 1877 and 1879 highlighted the undeveloped nature of these farming areas, especially when contrasted with their more developed neighbouring areas such as Leinster and East Munster. In less-developed areas such as West Munster the spectre of famine rose once more. By 1879, in Connacht especially, there was a distinct shortage of food which resulted in a 'mini-famine' that caused extensive hunger rather than substantial fatalities. This was not on the same scale as the 'Great Famine' because of the decline of the most vulnerable cottier class. But the state of agriculture in these regions was still very challenging and the difficulties faced encouraged criticisms of the 1870 Land Act and particularly its failure to adequately address the continuing problem of tenant rights across Ireland.

EXTEND YOUR KNOWLEDGE

Mini-famine

In 1879, the decline of Ireland's agricultural performance resulted in the country's last significant famine, which became known as *an gorta beag* – the small hunger. It primarily affected the west of Ireland and, in particular, Connacht where farming did not develop significantly after the 1840s and remained reliant upon the potato. This did not see large-scale deaths because of the quick response that Britain took to address the problem – facilitated by the presence of a railway network which allowed the rapid transport of necessary food items to the areas that were most hit. Furthermore, the country's most vulnerable people, the cottiers, had effectively disappeared and as such there were few people who were living a purely subsistence existence. Given these differences, the famine of the late 1870s only saw hunger rather than the same large-scale mortality that had been generated 30 years before.

SOURCE

4 From the *Kerry Sentinel* newspaper, 2 January 1879. This newspaper became a prominent mouthpiece of the Land League, and its owner, Timothy Harington, served as president of the Kerry branch of the League.

never since the appalling misery of the Famine years commenced to subside was the condition of the Irish agricultural classes so precarious as at the present time. A wretchedly bad harvest, with an almost general failure of crops, added to a considerable reduction in the price of the chief articles of farm produce have brought our peasantry to the verge of general bankruptcy

---

The decline of agricultural prosperity after 1877 meant that these limitations were felt more acutely because those who still existed on smallholdings were immediately placed into hardship, as evidenced by the 'mini-famine' in 1879. Those who were better placed found their income reduced at a time when rents generally increased so that landlords could offset the cost of relief provided for the poorest farmers.

On this point, the 1870 Land Act was especially unhelpful. One of the key requirements of the Land Conference had been the demand for fixed rents, but Gladstone had not included such a provision because he felt it was an unnecessary interference with the property rights of landlords. So there was no attempt to control rent and tenants were still subject to arbitrary increases as the landlords saw fit. The decline in income that affected Irish farmers after 1877 was, therefore, compounded by a general increase in rents as landlords sought to recompense themselves for the money they were having to spend on poor relief. While some did reduce rents to support their tenants (in July 1879 seven landlords in County Kerry did offer abatements) the vast majority did not, and actually added to the difficulties of their tenants by offering loans instead of rent reductions. These loans were provided by government to help with relief. The landlords that accepted them often added the interest charged on them to their rent prices, or even offered these loans directly to the tenants at rates of 6.5 percent, which was often refused because of the expense.

Evictions and rent strikes

The failure of many landlords to reduce the cost of their rent at a time of economic contraction meant that hundreds of tenant farmers fell into arrears with their payments and, therefore, found themselves being evicted. In 1877, 400 families were ejected from their land and this leapt up to over 1,000 in 1878 and more than 2,000 by 1880 as the depression spread. These figures represent the whole country and, although they do not seem large, they were in fact a noticeable increase from the 1.36 evictions per 1,000 holdings per year that Ireland averaged between 1854 and 1880. That low average was the result of landowners choosing to use eviction as an inducement to pay rent rather than as a deliberate action to force tenants off their land. As a result, when eviction was threatened it was widely regarded as the final demand for payment, at which time tenants usually paid. The onset of depression, however, made paying rent more difficult and so the eviction rate started to go up as tenants increasingly defaulted or fell into excessive arrears.

The volume of evictions not only increased the level of suffering but also gave the smaller farmers a reason for their despair, and landlords increasingly became the target for farmers to vent their frustrations. Initially this took the form of rent strikes by their remaining tenants, which involved deliberately withholding rent en masse until concessions were granted. As an act of defiance, this was a desperate method since it created significant antagonism. It had the effect of increasing the volume of evictions rather than facilitating a means by which compromise could be achieved.

SOURCE

5 *Serving a process near Headford, County Galway.* Illustration by R.G. Woodville published in the *Illustrated London News*, 7 February 1880. Eviction was increasingly controversial during the Land War and it became newsworthy material as the protests developed.

The rising level of antagonism that developed in the countryside saw a widening divide between landlords and tenants which only got worse as the depression continued. The increased use of direct action, in the form of rent striking particularly, on the part of tenants signalled a greater determination to defend their rights as they saw them. The shift towards such action can be attributed to the depression specifically. Having arranged themselves into organised local farmers' groups for the express purpose of ensuring tenant rights, the Land Act that came into force was not fit for purpose – as the depression had borne out. Therefore, the move to direct action was arguably as much out of frustration as economic deprivation. Furthermore, by adopting such action, there was also the potential that further legislation might be encouraged that would remedy the shortcomings of the earlier Act.

The start of the Land Wars

The growing militancy of the tenant farmers began a brief but influential period in Irish history known as the Land Wars. This was a time of significant agrarian unrest where the farming community united in opposition to the landowning classes and became co-opted into the broader nationalist movement for home rule, thereby publicising their cause and widening the nationalist agenda, which until 1879 had largely ignored the land question. During the years 1879–82, the west of Ireland became a hotbed of discontent as farmers became more organised in their militancy. After October 1879, they were given direction by the Irish Land League, which became a nationwide body that publicised the agrarian cause and co-ordinated tenant farmers' opposition. During this period, rent striking became one of many techniques employed, and to this they added the boycotting of work and also intimidation. On several occasions, there was also the suggestion of deliberate violence such as in the murder of William Browne, Lord Mountmorres, in September 1880. In this case, Browne had served two notices to quit on tenants unable to pay their rent. On 25 September, while travelling in his carriage to a magistrates meeting, he was shot six times and died instantly. The man arrested for his murder was one of his tenants – a man called Sweeny who had been given notice to quit. Although not directly proven to have been motivated by discontent over eviction, this attack was believed to have been so motivated and, therefore, gave greater credence to the idea of a 'war' within the countryside. Despite the isolated violence, the events of 1879–82 are more accurately described as a period of communal mass protest. The aim of the discontent was to force the reduction of rents and also to encourage a new look at tenant right in Ireland.

SOURCE

6 From the *Sydney Morning Herald* dated 19 November 1880 and commenting on the murder of Lord Mountmorres. An Australian paper would have been interested in the story as Australia was used by the British government as a penal colony until 1868, and many Irish rebels were sent there during the course of the 18th and 19th centuries.

THE MURDER OF LORD MOUNTMORRES.
Lord Mountmorres was murdered at a place called Rusheen, within a mile of Clonbur, where was his residence in Galway. He had attended a meeting of the magistrates on Saturday afternoon, September 25, at the courthouse, Clonbur, at which a resolution had been passed calling upon the Government to take coercive measures, and left the town about 8 o'clock in the evening. Half-an-hour afterwards his horse and carriage arrived at Ebor Hall, a mile distant, without him. Search was made, and he was found lying at the side of the road in a pool of blood and lifeless. He had received one rifle bullet in the head, which penetrated his skull, three in the neck, and two in the body. Lord Mountmorres had most unhappy relations with his tenants, and had recently obtained ejectment decrees against two of them. As a magistrate he was also unpopular, and until quite recently he was guarded by an escort of police. A lantern was found near where the body was lying, and a bottle of whisky in the well of his carriage. The police arrested a man named Sweeney on suspicion.

The inquest on the remains of Viscount Mountmorres was held on Monday evening, September 27, by Mr C. G. Cottingham, coroner, at Ebor Hall, the residence of the de-ceased situated on the banks of Lough Corib. Sweeney, the tenant who has been arrested by the police, was not present. The inquest was held in the study. The jury having viewed the body, the face of the deceased being mangled with the wounds he had received, the following evidence was taken. Sub-Inspector Law said he saw Lord Mountmorres on Saturday last in Clonbur about 7 in the evening. He spoke to him for a quarter of an hour, and shortly afterwards saw him speaking to head-con-stable O'Callaghan. His lordship was then quite well

He did not see him afterwards until he saw his murdered body. The body was found at a place called Dooray. To the jury: The deceased had no police protection. Some time ago he had a guard of two constables, but he dispensed with it. There was a house within 300 yards of where the body was found. The body was lying on the back across the road, the feet being about four feet from the wall on one side, and the head about 4 feet from the wall on the other. His lordship had no signs of drink on him. No car could have passed near him. He was armed with a pistol...

EXTEND YOUR KNOWLEDGE

Boycotting

It was during the Land Wars that this verb, meaning to ostracise or ignore, entered the English language. An English landlord called Captain Charles Boycott ran an estate in County Mayo on behalf of its absentee owner Lord Erme. In September 1880, he served 11 notices of eviction for non-payment of rent and in response the local community persuaded all of his servants and workers to leave the estate. Without people to work his land and also without supplies being delivered to his estate, Captain Boycott and his family quickly fell into difficulties and were only saved when a gang of 50 volunteers under the protection of troops arrived in November 1880 to help bring in his crops. Once these were harvested, however, and the volunteers had returned, mostly back to Ulster where they had come from, the 'boycotting' began once more and in December 1880 the family decided to leave for England.

ACTIVITY
KNOWLEDGE CHECK

The impact of economic problems

1 Study Source 6 and assess its value for revealing the extent of feeling that existed in Ireland towards the land issue. Is there anything significant about it being published in an Australian newspaper?

2 Using the material you have read and your own knowledge, produce a detailed mind map about how the 'long depression' created a new demand for land reform in the 1870s.

HOW SIGNIFICANT WERE THE LAND WARS IN ADDRESSING THE IRISH LAND ISSUE AFTER 1879?

TIMELINE: THE LAND WARS

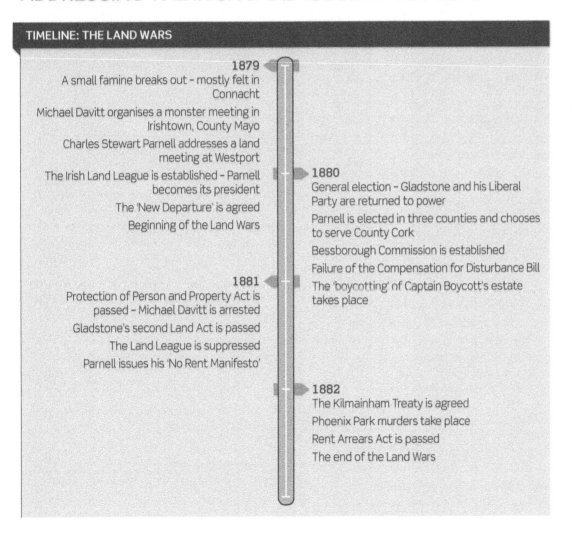

1879
A small famine breaks out – mostly felt in Connacht

Michael Davitt organises a monster meeting in Irishtown, County Mayo

Charles Stewart Parnell addresses a land meeting at Westport

The Irish Land League is established – Parnell becomes its president

The 'New Departure' is agreed

Beginning of the Land Wars

1880
General election – Gladstone and his Liberal Party are returned to power

Parnell is elected in three counties and chooses to serve County Cork

Bessborough Commission is established

Failure of the Compensation for Disturbance Bill

The 'boycotting' of Captain Boycott's estate takes place

1881
Protection of Person and Property Act is passed – Michael Davitt is arrested

Gladstone's second Land Act is passed

The Land League is suppressed

Parnell issues his 'No Rent Manifesto'

1882
The Kilmainham Treaty is agreed

Phoenix Park murders take place

Rent Arrears Act is passed

The end of the Land Wars

The roles of key individuals during the Land Wars

The Land Wars signified a period of concentrated, massive, agrarian protest that was conducted with the intention to force improvements for Irish tenant farmers. Principally they sought immediate rent reductions. However, in the longer term they also wanted more legal rights over their landholdings and dealings with the landowners. The Land Wars began in 1879 as localised opposition to evictions and the general suffering of the small farmers throughout the west of Ireland. But in October a national Irish Land League was founded that sought to co-ordinate a more organised opposition that embraced a variety of sophisticated political tactics to help the farmers in their cause. The creation of this body was the product of considerable efforts of first Michael Davitt and later Charles Stewart Parnell, who lent the land issue significant political weight. Collectively, these individuals turned the demand for land reform into a national affair, linking it with the broader nationalist agenda for home rule – greater Irish autonomy over Ireland's governance – and forcing Britain to take action.

Michael Davitt (1846–1906)

The driving force behind the co-ordination of the Land Wars was Michael Davitt, the son of an evicted tenant farmer from Straide in County Mayo. Having witnessed first-hand the pain of eviction, he became convinced of the need for land redistribution and land reform generally. After serving a prison sentence for his involvement in an IRB raid on Chester Castle, Davitt returned to Ireland where, in April 1879, he organised a meeting in Irishtown in his home county of Mayo to push for these reforms. The meeting was attended by at least 4,000 people, although some sources – notably the nationalist paper the *Freeman's Journal* – estimated the numbers to be nearer 8,000. The intention of this meeting was to present a united front and organise a co-ordinated effort to force rent reductions. The main target in that area was a Catholic priest called Geoffrey Burke, who had threatened to evict tenants on his land because of their inability to pay the rent he demanded. Using the strength of popular opinion, Davitt and the local tenant farmers marched to his estate and demanded reductions. Faced with such opposition, Canon Burke was forced to reduce his rents by 25 percent. This success, when it became public knowledge, gave heart to other farmers across the county and quickly meetings were being asked for in other districts with the intention of achieving similar results.

The success of Davitt's organised demonstration helped to spread a more focused opposition to the iniquities of the land system as the tenant farmers perceived them. He had given the farmers in Mayo direction and, more importantly, a workable means to achieve what they wanted, and this was especially significant in the development of the Land Wars and ultimately the provision of further reform. In June 1879, he organised a second mass meeting in Westport at which the new leader of the Home Rule League – Charles Stewart Parnell – addressed the crowd. This was a key moment in the development of the cause since it was at this meeting that Parnell became aware of the potential that the land issue could have for the broader nationalist demand for home rule. After this time, these two important issues were inextricably linked.

Michael Davitt (1846–1906)

Davitt was born to a tenant farmer in County Mayo. In 1852, he and his family were evicted from their farm because of the non-payment of rent, and without opportunity in Ireland they moved to Lancashire. Davitt worked in a mill there until 1857 when his right arm was severed in a machine he was operating and had to be amputated. In 1865, he joined the Irish Republican Brotherhood and was involved with a raid on Chester Castle two years later. He was arrested on suspicion of gun running and imprisoned on Dartmoor in 1870 where he remained for seven years. Upon his release in 1877, he became a more strident opponent of British rule and of the need to redistribute land in Ireland. In 1878, he travelled to America where he developed the idea of establishing a better link between the revolutionary and constitutional wings of the nationalist movement, but this was not enthusiastically received upon his return to Ireland later that year. Following the agricultural depression after 1877, he organised a Land League in County Mayo in 1879 to promote the interests of tenant farmers. After initial successes, he established with Charles Stewart Parnell a national Irish Land League, which became the main organ for conducting the Land Wars during 1879–82. Following the 1881 Land Act, he was elected as MP for Meath in 1882 and campaigned tirelessly for further justice and reform until his death in 1906.

SOURCE

7 From Michael Davitt, *The Fall of Feudalism in Ireland*, London (1904). Davitt was a prominent leader of the Land League in Ireland and this text presented his story of the Land League and the subsequent land 'revolution' that it orchestrated.

It was, in every sense, a people's meeting. No leaders, either revolutionary or constitutional, had been consulted about it, or had anything to do with its organisation or success. No priests had been invited. None could, in any case, attend as one of the purposes of the demonstration was to exert pressure upon the parish priest of Irishtown to abate the rack-rents [excessive rent] which he demanded from his tenants. In this respect the meeting scored an immediate success. Canon Burke granted an abatement of twenty-five per cent a few days after the invasion of his quiet little village by seven thousand sturdy Mayomen shouting "Down with landlordism! The land for the people!" Subsequently, it may be remarked, the same rents were reduced forty per cent more, under the provisions of the Land Act of 1881.

The Dublin press did not report the demonstration nor even allude to it in any way. It was not held under official home-rule auspices, while the fact that one of its objects was to denounce rack-renting on an estate owned by a Catholic clergyman would necessarily, at that early stage of a popular movement, frighten the timid editors of Dublin from offering it any recognition. But the local prestige won by the meeting was enormous. The speeches were fully given in the *Connaught Telegraph*. The meeting had within a few days knocked 5 shillings in the pound off the rentals of the estate which was singled out for attack. This news flew round the county, and requests for meetings reached the organisers from various districts. It was generally known that the active spirits in the organising of the meeting were members of the Fenian body, and on this account, but chiefly owing to the "attack" made upon Canon Burke, many of the alters in Mayo rang with warnings and denunciations against gatherings called by "irresponsible people," and which showed "disrespect" towards the priests. But Mayo nationalists have always had a record for courage and independence and this opposition had no effect upon the men who were resolved to push forward in the work which had scored so significantly at its initial step.

Following the meeting at Westport, Davitt founded the Irish Land League in August 1879 which became a nationwide organ for directing land agitation. Parnell agreed to be the president of this body and together the pair became instrumental in promoting the cause. By working in tandem, Davitt and Parnell embraced what became known as the **new departure** in nationalist politics. This was the recognition that the land question was one that could only be adequately answered by an Irish government. Therefore, the two issues, land and home rule, were bound together and the only way to achieve either was through collective action. It was in part a symbolic awareness, however, that the nationalists' adoption of the land issue gave greater practical support to the tenant farmers' cause. The resources of the Home Rule League were used to help promote the issues of rent reduction and tenant right across the country. Very quickly the agrarian movement came to wider public attention and it acquired both greater sympathy and support as a result.

KEY TERM

New departure
This was an agreement reached in June 1879 between Parnell, Davitt and the Fenian leader John Devoy, which acknowledged the fundamental link between the land and national questions.

Charles Stewart Parnell (1846–91)

Michael Davitt was an important organiser. His talents lay in the administration of events and co-ordinating large numbers of people into a solid and co-operative organ. By contrast, Charles Stewart Parnell's significance was in lending the movement gravitas and the voice of a nationally recognised politician. Parnell was a national figure by 1879, having becoming MP for County Meath in 1875 and then the leader of the Home Rule League in 1879 upon the death of Isaac Butt. His self-restraint and skill as an orator had given the Home Rule League a greater presence in parliament, and in his role as president of the Land League he gave the tenant farmers an inspirational figurehead who turned his own talents to securing their objectives.

This initially involved travelling to the USA in order to secure funds for the new land movement, and while there he spoke in more than 60 cities and raised £12,000 for the League and a further £60,000 for famine relief. In addition to this fundraising, he also gave speeches across Ireland in which he fired the imaginations of those to whom he spoke – demanding that the Irish should own Irish land and defend what was their property from those who would want to take it from them. His speeches encouraged defiance, but in a constitutional manner that avoided violence since that would always be to the detriment of the cause and only invite retaliation from the British. Instead, he encouraged the use of massive rent strikes which played on the numerical strength of the tenant farmers to force the necessary changes they sought.

SOURCE

8 From a speech made by the president of the Land League and Home Rule leader Charles Stewart Parnell, to a crowd of tenant farmers at Ennis on 19 September 1880.

You must show him [a farmer who takes the land of an evicted tenant] your detestation of the crime he has committed… If you do this you may depend on it there will be no man so full of avarice – so lost to shame – as to dare the public opinion of all the right thinking men in the country and transgress your unwritten code of laws… The feudal system of land tenure has been tried in almost every European country and it has been found wanting everywhere; but nowhere has it brought more exile, produced for suffering, crime and destitution than in Ireland. It was abolished in Prussia by transferring the land from the landlords to the occupying tenants. The landlords were given government paper as compensation. Let the English government give the landlords their paper to-morrow as compensation. We want no money – not a single penny of money would be necessary. Why, if they gave the Irish landlords – the bad section of them – the four or five millions a year that they spend on police and military in helping them collect their rents, that would be a solution to it, and a very cheap solution of it… In my opinion the longer the landlords wait, the worse the settlement they will get. Now is the time for them to settle before the people learn the power of combination. We have been accused of preaching communistic doctrines when we told the people not to pay an unjust rent, and the flowing out of that advice in a few of the Irish counties had shown the English government the necessity for a radical alteration in the land laws. But how would they like it if we told the people some day or other not to pay any rent until this question is settled… It shall be for the consideration of wiser heads than mine whether, if the landlords continue obdurate, and refuse all just concessions, we shall not be obliged to tell the people of Ireland to strike against rent until this question has been settled. And if the five hundred thousand tenant farmers of Ireland struck against the ten thousand landlords, I would like to see where they would get police and soldiers enough to make them pay.

This was the greatest impact of Parnell – inspiring the masses and offering a direct, legal means of achieving their aims that was able to draw support from all sections of Irish society. His speeches were reported *The Times* as well as local newspapers. This helped to give the issue a broader public awareness, while the methods he advocated – rent strikes and **moral force** direct action – were appealing to the more revolutionary sections of the nationalist movement. These included the Fenians especially, but also more moderate thinkers in the country who could sympathise with the plight of the tenant farmers. By appealing to all sections of society, Parnell was very effective at helping to mobilise thousands of Irish men and women in support of the land question and this helped to make the Land Wars one of the greatest mass movements in modern Irish history.

KEY TERM

Moral force
A way of creating an incentive to change without using physical force.

SOURCE 9 A poster demanding the non-payment of rents. These were produced by the Land League and circulated following Parnell's 'No Rent Manifesto' which he issued from Kilmainham Gaol in October 1881.

THE LAND WAR!

NO RENT!

NO LANDLORDS GRASSLAND

Tenant Farmers, now is the time. Now is the hour. You proved false to the first call made upon you. REDEEM YOUR CHARACTER NOW.

NO RENT

UNTIL THE SUSPECTS ARE RELEASED.

The man who pays Rent (whether an abatement is offered or not) while PARNELL, DILLON &c.. are in Jail, will be looked upon as a Traitor to his Country and a disgrace to his class.

No RENT, No Compromise, No Landlords' Grassland,
Under any circumstances.

Avoid the Police, and listen not to spying and deluding Bailiffs.

NO RENT! LET THE LANDTHIEVES DO THEIR WORST!

THE LAND FOR THE PEOPLE!

The impact of the Irish Land League

The growing agitation in the countryside was given a substantial boost when, in October 1879, the Irish Land League was established. This was a nationwide organisation and it was intended as the co-ordinating body for massive agitation. At its height in 1881, it had an estimated 200,000 members. It sought to achieve land reform, specifically the 'three Fs', but to generally raise awareness of and defend the tenant farmers against the excesses of landlords by giving them a clear voice and means of self-protection. Awareness came from the speechmaking and tours undertaken by Parnell, a nationally recognised figure and MP, but it also came through the reporting of Land League activities in the local and national newspapers. These activities were primarily designed to be non-violent protest actions such as:

- posters, leafleting and campaign rallies
- rent strikes
- the ostracism of 'land grabbers' (anyone who took over the land of an evicted tenant)
- local communities ignoring the landlord in their area if he had evicted tenants.

The value of rent strikes was very clear since it affected the landlord directly and also upset the local economy, but the use of ostracism was especially effective since social acceptance was an important feature of Irish society and it consequently became a powerful moral force tool. The consequence of ostracism was that the farms of evicted tenants were not inhabited by another farmer and, therefore, landlords did not get their estates worked, losing produce as well as rents, which greatly affected their own income and viability. Complementing this action was the deliberate ignoring of the landlord himself if he evicted tenants. No one in the local community would work his land or supply his estate with necessary goods – effectively cutting him out of the community and leaving him to fend for himself. This particular tactic was well documented in the case of Captain Charles Boycott and his estate in County Mayo in 1880. Having served notices of eviction to 11 tenants in September of that year, the local community, led by their priest Father O'Malley, cut him off from local supplies and also got his other workers to abandon him. Left bereft of help, he and his family tried as well as they could to manage the estate over the next month, but the undertaking was too great and crops and livestock began to suffer. Only in November when a 'relief expedition' of 50 Ulster farmers came to his aid did the estate improve. These men generally sympathised with the position of the distressed landlord and wanted to make a point about his treatment, but upon their departure the community once again boycotted his estate and by the end of the year he gave up on it and moved his family to England.

Although intending non-violent action, the Land League was happy to imply the use of violence since it was an effective way of focusing attention and encouraging landlords and politicians to consider reforms. The danger with such a tactic, however, was that sometimes people took things too far and during 1879–1882 the Land Wars were peppered with individual acts of violence. In September 1880, for example, Lord Mountmorres was murdered (see page 140). This was a high-profile death that compounded the general level of agitation in the Irish countryside during the Land Wars. Collectively, this violence drew a heavy response from the British government – first the Protection of Person and Property Act in March 1881, which saw Michael Davitt arrested, and then the suppression of the League in October 1881.

SOURCE 10

From *The New York Times*, 18 October 1879. New York had a large Irish population since thousands had travelled there during and after the Great Famine in the 1840s. As a city, therefore, there was significant interest in what was happening in Ireland.

October 18, 1879

SHOOTING AT LANDLORDS; INCIDENTS OF THE IRISH RENT AGITATION. RORY OF THE HILLS AND HIS WARNINGS – FIRING UPON THE MARQUIS OF SLIGO'S AGENT – HOW ANOTHER NOBLE LORD REPLIED TO THREATS

In "a wild district of the West" on a "lonely mountainside near Westport in the county of Mayo" shots were fired at "an aged gentleman named John Sydney Smyth", a land agent for the Marquis of Sligo and an English land lord, Mr. Cline.

A tenant on the Cline estate had recently been evicted for non-payment of rent. Another tenant had appeared to take over the land only to be threatened with the "usual" warnings in the form of sketches of skulls, cross bones, and coffins. Mr. Smyth received the following letter:

I am in this country observing the conduct and tyranny of agents and landlords. Perhaps you are not aware that there is a very large sum of money to be paid for killing you. Take heed to youself [sic] on the road between Ballycroy and Newport, for you will be killed.

RORY

Mr. Smyth dutifully notified the police. Subsequently he and his son, Sydney E Smyth, went to the Cline estate at Ballycroy to collect the rents. The Smyths were greeted by the tenants who stated they had not a penny among them and were unable to pay the rents because they had not yet sold their animals nor taken in their crops. The Smyths said they were willing to wait and parted amiably. As they traveled along the mountain road in their **jaunting car** the Smyths were fired upon by four armed men with blackened faces. No one in the jaunting car was hit. Young Smyth shot and killed one of the attackers. The other three fled. The dead man was identified as Charles Howard, who had served with the North Mayo Militia. He was said to hold no land, have no occupation, and to have been of "bad character". Sydney E. Smyth was tried and acquitted of murder in self defense.

KEY TERM

Jaunting car
A two-wheeled carriage pulled by a horse.

ACTIVITY
KNOWLEDGE CHECK

The importance of the Land League

1 What were the goals of the Land League?

2 What methods does Source 10 suggest were encouraged to try and achieve these aims?

3 How valuable a source do you think Source 10 is for assessing the importance of the Land League in Ireland?

GLADSTONE, FORSTER AND THE SECOND IRISH LAND ACT 1881

In April 1880, just as the Land Wars were becoming more widespread, a general election took place that saw the return of Gladstone and a Liberal government in Britain. For a second time Gladstone formed a government intent on addressing Irish problems. In Ireland the election had been fought on the issue of land reform, and Parnell's Home Rule League had taken 63 of the 103 seats available, while the Liberal Party only secured 15.

The implications of the growing demand for further land reform were not lost upon Gladstone. Given the poor performance of the Liberals and the ongoing agitation in the Irish countryside, Gladstone chose as his Chief Secretary for Ireland a very able and dedicated individual called William Edward Forster. Forster took the position in a spirit of goodwill towards Ireland and Gladstone to conciliate the existing discontent there, through legislation if necessary.

William Edward Forster (1818-86)

William Forster was a keen reformer, who during the Great Famine had travelled around the country and produced a report on the catastrophe, which helped to raise public awareness of the problem.

As an MP he was vice-president of the Council and a member of the Cabinet in charge of education. In 1870, he had introduced education legislation that created elected school boards and effectively established the basis of a national education system. His sense of public duty was such that he was equally motivated to look into the issue of land reform, and his initial effort was to introduce the Compensation for Disturbance bill in June 1880. This was intended as a temporary measure to alleviate the growing tensions in Ireland. It empowered courts to grant compensation to tenants evicted because of non-payment of rents, if they could prove the reason they could not pay was directly caused by the agricultural depression. It was to be applied to the west and south of Ireland, where the depression was hardest, and was not to last more than 18 months. The bill passed through the House of Commons, but in August it was heavily defeated in the House of Lords by a vote of 282 to 5 because of the potential effects it would have for Irish landlords. The failure of this bill resulted in an increase of agitation in Ireland – most famously the ostracism of Captain Boycott's estate in September 1880.

At the same time as Forster's bill was being rejected by the Lords, Gladstone created the Bessborough Commission to determine the extent of reform necessary. The commission had a specific brief to investigate the land issue in Ireland and to make recommendations for its solution. The commission heard from many interested parties in Ireland throughout 1880, including Captain Boycott, and then published their report the following year. The *Report by Her Majesty's Commissioners of Enquiry into the workings of the Landlord and Tenant (Ireland) Act 1870 and the acts mending the same* identified that the 1870 Act did not give adequate protection to tenants because compensation could only be claimed if the lease was given up, and they had to accept rent increases or sacrifice the lease and improvements they had made. Consequently, the recommendations they made were, by a majority of four to one, in favour of granting Irish tenants the 'three Fs': fair rent, fixity of tenure and freedom to sell their holding in the land.

Faced with a more hostile Irish tenant population as a result of the rejection of his Compensation for Disturbance bill, Forster was reluctantly forced to introduce new legislation to bring order to the countryside at the same time that the Bessborough Commission was underway. In January 1881, the first of the so-called Coercion Acts (see page 43), the Protection of Person and Property Act, was passed. This legislation provided for the suspension of habeas corpus and allowed the government to arrest anyone who was felt to be inciting aggression. Following the passage of the Act, 955 people were arrested under its provisions. The first person was Michael Davitt on 3 February 1881, and he was quickly followed by Parnell and other members of the League in October of that year. Forster became a much disliked figure because of this action and his life was consequently placed in danger as radical Irishmen plotted his murder. This pressure took its toll and in 1882 he resigned his position when a treaty was made between the League and the Liberal government.

Following the publishing of the Bessborough Commission's recommendations, the legislation proposed was intended as an immediate solution to reduce tensions in the countryside, primarily by reducing the level of rents that tenants had to pay. It was in one sense borne of a desire to help the country, but equally there was a political wish to subdue the Land League and promote a better Anglo-Irish relationship. The subsequent land bill was introduced into parliament in early 1881 and was passed in August the same year. The main provisions of the 1881 Land Law (Ireland) Act were:

- The creation of an Irish Land Commission to decide the levels of rent where there was dispute.

- Tenants had the right to sell their land holdings if they chose.

- Tenants were to have security of tenure as long as they were clearly abiding by established conditions that had been set out. This was known as **statutory tenure**.

Effectively the Act granted that which the Land League had demanded and, as far as the government and Gladstone understood, the provision of these greater rights to tenant farmers would deflate the burgeoning Land League and restore order to the countryside. Despite this anticipation, the Act was not as comprehensive as the Land League wanted. It did not redistribute the land as some of the more radical members of the organisation demanded. Nor did it offer any provision for the issue of rent arrears or adjustment of rent levels in the event of poor harvests or depressed economic conditions. Rent arrears affected more than 150,000 small farmers. In County Mayo alone it affected just under two-thirds of the farming population, who had been badly hit by the economic downturn and consequently could not afford to pay the cumulative rents which were growing. The absence of these requirements, especially the option of adjustment, was seen as an oversight that should be addressed since it left the legislation unresponsive to fluctuating conditions and inflexible to future changes. Given these perceived weaknesses, the reaction in Ireland to Gladstone's second Land Act was not what was anticipated by the prime minister or his government.

SOURCE 11

The Irish Devil-fish. A cartoon by John Tenniel for *Punch* magazine, 18 June 1881.

THE IRISH DEVIL-FISH.

"The creature is formidable, but there is a way of resisting it. * * * The Devil-fish, in fact, is only vulnerable through the head."
VICTOR HUGO'S *Toilers of the Sea*, Book IV., Ch. iii.

EXTRACT 1

From Michael J. Winstanley, *Ireland and the Land Question, 1800–1922* (1984).

Agrarian unrest before the famine was certainly connected with the question of access to land, but it was a product, not of an unchanging, peasant, society, but of a gradually evolving, modernising economy... Post-famine land agitation was very different and reflected the changing social structure of rural Ireland and the expectations of its inhabitants. Largely peaceful and constitutional, it was concerned with preserving recent economic gains and it was supported primarily by respectable, socially aspiring farmers.

EXTRACT 2

From T.W. Moody and F.X. Martin (eds), *The Course of Irish History* (1994).

The land war convinced British statesmen of both parties that the landlord system as it existed in Ireland was no longer defensible. Gladstone's remedy, the land act of 1881, progressively diminished the landlords' interest in the land. The fair rents fixed by the land court in the first three years showed an average reduction of nearly twenty per cent. Landlords began to feel it would be better to sell out to their tenants on favourable terms than to share ownership with them... This has been the greatest revolution in the history of modern Ireland

Reaction in Ireland and the Kilmainham Treaty, 1882

The passage of the Land Law (Ireland) Act in August 1881 was met with mixed feeling amongst the people of Ireland. For the Land League in particular, the Act presented something of a dilemma; it did grant the 'three Fs' that the organisation had been demanding, but its failure to consider arrears or adjustment still left tenants without ironclad protection against landlord exploitation. As president of the Land League, Parnell was quick to raise his concerns about the Act, and in a series of public speeches in September he demanded that its provisions be tested in the courts. He also criticised Gladstone and his Ireland secretary, William Forster, for not supporting the Irish farmers effectively. In October 1881, he was arrested on a charge of incitement and imprisoned in Kilmainham prison in Dublin.

The 'No Rent Manifesto'

Although imprisoned, Parnell continued to direct the Land League and issued a 'No Rent Manifesto' from his cell on 18 October 1881 which was published on the front page of the League's newspaper *United Ireland* four days later. With a circulation of 100,000, the manifesto was widely publicised. It called for a national rent strike to force the inclusion of a rent arrears and adjustment amendment to the Land Act. In issuing his manifesto, Parnell sought to create a nation-wide agitation against the British government's legislation – foremost for a reform of the Act, but also to help keep the movement together in the absence of its leadership.

SOURCE 12

The 'No Rent Manifesto' issued by Charles Stewart Parnell from Kilmainham Gaol in October 1881. This was intended as a way of applying peaceful pressure on landlords and, by extension, government to widen the reforms offered under the Land Act and it was signed by all the leaders of the Land League.

Fellow-countrymen! - The hour to try your souls and to redeem your pledges has arrived. The executive of the National Land League forced to abandon the policy of testing the land act, feels bound to advise the tenant-farmers of Ireland from this day forth to pay no rents under any circumstances to their landlords until the government relinquishes the existing system of terrorism and restores the constitutional rights of the people. Do not be daunted by the removal of your leaders... Do not be wheedled into compromise of any sort by the threat of eviction. If you only act together in the spirit to which, within the last two years, you have countless times solemnly pledged your vows, they can no more evict a whole nation than they can imprison them. Our exiled brothers in America may be relied upon to contribute, if necessary, as many millions of money as they have contributed thousands to starve out landlordism and bring English tyranny to its knees. No power on earth except faintheartedness on your own part can defeat you. Landlordism is already staggering under the blows which you have dealt it amid the applause of the world... One more heroic effort to destroy landlordism at the very source and fount of its existence, and the system which was and is the curse of your race and of your existence will have disappeared forever... No power of legalized violence can extort one penny from your purses against your will. If you are evicted, you shall not suffer; the landlord who evicts will be a ruined pauper, and the government which supports him with its bayonets will learn in a single winter how powerless is armed force against the will of a united, determined, and self-reliant nation.

The manifesto encouraged further violence in the countryside, and over the next seven months there were 3,498 agrarian outrages as the smallest tenant farmers vented their frustration at the limitations of the Act. These activities took the form of attacks on landlord property and persons, often at night. Intimidating letters would be sent to landlords beforehand signed by various pseudonyms of the local farmers intending to carry out the attack (see Source 10). This was not a new tactic but rather one that reconstructed the actions of agrarian groups such as the 'Whiteboys': a rural 'protest' group from the 18th century who wore white shirts over their everyday clothing when raiding an estate. Like Davitt, the British authorities saw the document as incitement and this contributed to the League's suppression in 1881.

In terms of the effectiveness of the action, although many smaller farmers were unhappy with the Land Act, there was a significant proportion – around two-thirds of the nationwide farming community – that was content with its provisions and, therefore, did not support the directed action. Given this large body, the 'No Rent Manifesto' did not enjoy the success that Parnell had anticipated and in fact it had encouraged a more violent response from quarters of the tenant farming community. This violence not only saw the Land League itself made illegal, but also brought even greater disarray to the rural areas that were already struggling because of the agricultural depression. Without effective control of the situation, both Parnell and the British government recognised that the country would only descend into further hardship and misery.

The Kilmainham Treaty, 1882

It was with this sense of deepening instability that both sides accepted the need to address the situation before things got any worse and, in April 1882, an effort was made to find some means of agreement. The main issue for Parnell and the League was that of rent arrears. Therefore, through a third party – Katherine O'Shea (with whom he was having an affair) and her husband – he proposed that if the government address this concern by passing new legislation which removed the requirement to pay these arrears, then he would use his influence to subdue the agrarian discontent and violence that was being undertaken in the country.

In return, Gladstone agreed to amend the Land Law Act to take into account the issue of rent arrears, and he also consented to the release of Parnell and the other Land League leaders. In May 1882, this arrangement was agreed in what has become known as the Kilmainham Treaty and it has generally been regarded as the end of the Land Wars in Ireland. Upon the release of Parnell and the other leaders, William Forster resigned his position as Irish Secretary in protest of the treaty and was replaced by Lord Frederick Cavendish. However, the rest of the Liberal government were content with the arrangement since it brought an end to the coercive policies of their government which had become increasingly unpopular. Further to their release, Gladstone then was able to enact the Arrears of Rent (Ireland) Act 1882, which cancelled £2 million of rent arrears built up by Ireland's farmers.

For his part, Parnell undertook to help restore order but, within days of the treaty, the new Chief Secretary for Ireland was murdered in Phoenix Park by unknown assailants. The action was strongly condemned by Parnell, but it significantly blunted much of the goodwill that the treaty had created and also showed that Parnell was not in a strong position to control the outrages as he claimed. Although the murders were undoubtedly a setback, the agreement at Kilmainham still stood, and over the forthcoming months, especially with the passage of further legislation, the agrarian discontent subsided.

Conclusion

The question of land reform in Ireland was always a challenging one since it affected the lives of so many of the country's population. For a vast majority of Irish men and women, the land was the basis of their existence and, therefore, issues such as tenant right and landownership were integral to their wellbeing. After 1870, the British government under William Gladstone had sought to adjust the inequalities within the existing land system, and the Land Act of 1870 was felt to have been a positive step forward in answering that difficult question. Far from being satisfactory, however, the limitations of this Act were brought starkly into focus during economic depression after 1873 and a deepening agricultural decline four years later. Frustrated by worsening economic conditions and a Land Act that did not effectively protect tenant farmers, tempers flared, and after 1879 a war in the countryside developed. Motivated by demands for further land reform, this aggression was harnessed by the broader nationalist movement which gave it a louder political voice – eloquently conveyed through the home rule leader, Charles Stewart Parnell. Gladstone returned to power in 1880 and new legislation was passed to pacify the growing number of outrages. But the second Land Act – although granting more security for tenants than any previous legislation – was still felt to be insufficient for a mass movement that was growing in confidence. Only with increasingly coercive measures and further compromise was the Act finally accepted, and by the end of 1882 the land issue had achieved a more comprehensive settlement that offered greater parity between landlords and their tenants. Such a change did not entirely solve the question, but it left enough clues for its eventual solution in the next century.

ACTIVITY
KNOWLEDGE CHECK

Extending land reform – the Land Act 1881

1 Outline the main provisions of Gladstone's second Land Act.

2 How did these differ from his first Act in 1870?

3 What was the Land League's problem with the second Act?

4 How did the British government address the problems raised by the Land League?

THINKING HISTORICALLY Change (8a, b & c) (II)

Judgements about change

If two professionals were asked to track a patient's health over time, one might approach this task by measuring heart rate, weight and cholesterol, while the other professional might assess the patient's mental well-being, relationships and ability to achieve their goals. Both are valid approaches, but they result in different reports. What is true in this medical case is true in historical cases. Measuring change in something requires: (a) a concept of what that something is (e.g. What is 'health'? What is an 'economy'?); (b) judgements about how this thing should be measured; and (c) judgements about what relevant 'markers of change' are (how we distinguish a change from a temporary and insignificant fluctuation).

Historians have differed in their accounts of land reform and its development in Ireland in the 19th century, and debated the significance of the Land Wars in producing this change.

Look at Extracts 1 and 2 on page 148 about the Land Wars and answer the following questions.

1 Do the accounts agree that the Land War was instrumental in achieving land reform?

2 Do the accounts agree in the chronology of change (do they see it happening in the same time period and at the same pace)?

3 Do the accounts agree in characterising change as (a) rapid, (b) dramatic and (c) impacting the economy as a whole?

4 Do the historians each think of land reform in the same way?

5 Generalising from these examples, to what extent do historians' judgements about change depend upon *what* historians decide to look at and *how* they decide to measure change?

Addressing the land issue in Ireland, 1870–82

1 Create a table using the following headings: 'Economic influences'; 'Role of individuals'; 'Popular pressure'; 'Political influences'. Under each heading write down any evidence you can about how that heading influenced the land issue in Ireland.

2 Using this evidence write a paragraph explaining how the land issue was addressed by 1882.

 WIDER READING

Bull, P. *Land, Politics and Nationalism: A Study of the Irish Land Question*, St. Martin's Press (1996)

Collier, M. *Britain and Ireland 1867–1922*, Pearson (2008)

Lee, J. *The Modernisation of Irish Society, 1848–1918*, Gill and Macmillan (1989)

Moody, T.W. and Martin, F.X. (eds), *The Course of Irish History*, Mercier Press (1994)

Winstanley, M.J. *Ireland and the Land Question 1800–1922*, Methuen (1984)

3.7 | Improving working and living conditions: trades union militancy in Ireland, 1907–14

KEY QUESTIONS

- How effective were the attempts to unionise trades and industry in the years 1907–09?
- What was the impact of the general strike in 1913–14?
- How important was the role played by British trades unions in Irish industrial affairs?

INTRODUCTION

Ireland has always been viewed as a rural economy, with pasture farming and tillage making up most of its national income and employing the majority of its population. This impression is certainly accurate. However, the country also enjoys a good degree of economic diversity – much of which developed in the mid to late 19th century. Benefitting from the industrial revolution in Britain, by 1907 Ireland had become a more industrialised nation in its own right, with significant industries in Ulster especially, but also in some of the larger southern cities of Cork, Limerick and Dublin. These were primarily based upon shipbuilding and manufacturing in the north, while Dublin had grown as a port during the previous century and now exported livestock, beer and biscuits and in return imported much of the country's coal and flour supplies. Not as densely industrial as Britain in the same period, Ireland nonetheless had achieved the basis of a modern economy and enjoyed a healthy income as a result, successfully marrying its rural and urban enterprises.

> **KEY TERM**
>
> **Urbanisation**
> An increase in the number of people living in an urban environment compared to a rural one.

Along with the economic benefits of industrialisation, Ireland also experienced the same social problems that came with it: increased **urbanisation** which saw city populations grow more quickly than their infrastructures could provide for; the creation of a vast gap between rich and poor; and a growing sense of injustice at the exploitation by employers of their growing workforce. Ireland had the additional problem of religious inequality. Catholics, especially in the north, did not enjoy the same working opportunities as their Protestant counterparts and this added to growing industrial discontent. Urbanisation problems were not unique to Ireland, but after 1907 they did affect that nation quite significantly, paving the way for greater militancy on the part of workers as they came to recognise the rights and conditions that they too deserved.

This militancy was driven by the arrival of James Larkin, a trade unionist from Liverpool, who successfully organised Ireland's workforce into unions for the purpose of improving conditions and granting it a clear forum for change. His presence threatened employers, in Dublin especially, resulting in a confrontation between them and the emerging labour movement which greatly influenced industrial relations after 1913.

1907 – January: Jim Larkin arrives in Ireland

April: Belfast dock strike

1909 – Larkin founds the Irish Transport and General Workers' Union

1911 – May: Connolly joins the Irish Transport and General Workers' Union (ITGWU) and organises the women linen workers in Belfast into the Irish Textile Workers Union

William Martin Murphy establishes the Dublin Employers' Federation

1907	1908	1909	1910	1911	1912

1908 – Larkin is suspended from the National Union of Dock Labourers (NUDL)

1910 – James Connolly returns to Ireland from America

1912 – Irish Labour Party is founded by Larkin and Connolly

HOW EFFECTIVE WERE THE ATTEMPTS TO UNIONISE TRADES AND INDUSTRY IN THE YEARS 1907-09?

Working and living conditions for unskilled urban workers

The industrialisation of Ireland brought wealth and opportunity for some, notably the owners of business. However, this was often at the expense of their workforce who were routinely exploited in the interest of profit-making – long hours for minimum pay and little chance of improving their situation because of the absence of comprehensive **unionisation** for all workers. Compounding this exploitation were equally disadvantageous living conditions brought on by the rapid growth in migration to Ireland's urban centres. Belfast had the largest population at 349,000 – an increase of 249,000 since 1850. However, Dublin's population had increased from 180,000 at the start of the 19th century to over 290,000 by 1900. Such a population shift placed great strain upon the towns in Ulster and particularly their infrastructure, which took longer to make the necessary improvements to housing and sanitation to facilitate the increased numbers; so much so, that slums quickly developed and disease was common amongst the poorer communities unable to live elsewhere.

Unskilled and casual workers in Ireland

Working conditions for the unskilled in Ireland were unforgiving. For those in permanent employ, the hours were long and wages low, with the average level for an unskilled labourer being 10 shillings and 9 pence a week. The majority of unskilled workers, however, tended to be employed in casual work, usually as **dockers** or **carters** who were taken on only when there was work available. Without any binding contracts, these individuals often had to work excessive hours. Dockers in Belfast, for example, routinely worked 75 hours a week for low wages that either did not cover, or at best barely covered, their rent and food outgoings. In 1914, the average weekly rent in Ireland was 4 shillings while a 4-pound loaf of bread, a staple in the Irish diet, cost 6 pence. Given these prices, it was estimated by historians that to keep a family at a basic standard of care it would require 22 shillings and 5 pence a week, while the average unskilled labourer only earned 10 shillings, with the deficit made up by his wife and children. Work was also often dangerous or unsanitary and there was never the security of permanent employment. When work dried up, they were the first to lose their positions in the interests of cost cutting by the employers. An early example of this was during the brief depression in 1908–09 when unemployment in Belfast's shipyards reached 20 percent. The majority of those out of work were the unskilled general workers and dockers whose positions depended on sufficient shipping and building work. In every respect, the unskilled casual worker lived a life of uncertain subsistence, without good wages or any definitive legal protection.

Such was the casual and low paid nature of many male unskilled labourers' employment that the shortfall in income often had to be made up by his wife and children working also. For women in Dublin, this was often as domestic servants, while in Belfast they were usually employed in the linen mills. In 1901, the legal age at which children were allowed to work was raised to 12. However, such was the need to earn money that the school-leaving certificates which were required as proof of

1913 – August: Murphy dismisses ITGWU members from his *Irish Independent* newspaper
August: ITGWU initiates a general strike
August: Police baton-charge strikers in O'Connell Street
August: Murphy and fellow employers lock out ITGWU employees

1913   **1914**

1913 – September: Askwith Commission is convened
November: Creation of the Irish Citizen Army
November: Larkin begins his 'fiery cross crusade' in Britain
December: Trade Union Congress holds a special conference to discuss the situation in Dublin

1914 – The general strike and lockout ends in Dublin

age were often forged and under-age children would impersonate older siblings in order to get work. The financial pressures that were placed on families made it necessary for young children to work. However, they were often unfit for the laborious tasks and long hours they had to perform. Poor diet – tea, potato bread and oats – often left them undernourished and consequently their labours made them sickly and reduced their life expectancy, which in 1900–02 was 49.3 years for males and 49.6 for females. The mortality rate was also higher amongst infants and children. In Belfast it stood at 153 per 1,000 births, while Dublin had an even higher rate of 169 per 1,000 in 1900.

Living conditions for unskilled urban workers

Reflecting the conditions of employment for Ireland's working classes, their living conditions were equally poor. This was especially evident in the city of Dublin, which had grown substantially by 1907 but did not enjoy the extent of industrial success that Belfast had. With two major businesses – the Guinness brewery and Jacob's Biscuits – together with being a significant port, Dublin had attracted large numbers of people to the city but could not easily afford to improve the facilities quickly enough to accommodate its new residents. Consequently, slum areas developed around the city. Many of its beautiful Georgian buildings became homes for multiple families, often sharing rooms. In 1914, for example, following the collapse of a slum building in Church Street which killed seven people, a survey was conducted into the housing situation. It found that 25,822 families were living in 5,322 **tenements**; of this number more than 20,000 families each lived in only one room together.

SOURCE

1

From *Dublin Made Me* – a memoir published in 1979 by Todd Andrews, a local Dublin-born republican remembering his early childhood. Andrews was born in 1901 and was a participant in the War of Independence and Civil War. He was a public servant until his death in 1985.

Even in winter the children of the poor were mainly without boots. They were ragged and frozen looking and sometimes had newspapers tied around their legs with string, in the manner of puttees. Sacking was commonly used instead of overcoats; all the coalmen wore it over their shoulders. Smells are very evocative of places and times past, and of all the unpleasant smells I recall the worst was that of a slum tenement. One of the girls who looked after me often brought me home with her. She lived with her parents in one room in Gardiner Street. The stench of the house when you entered the hall was disgusting. Urine and excrement (visible as well as smelling) mingled with all the stinks that the human body can exude. There was no indoor lavatory and only one outdoor lavatory and one outdoor tap for the whole building. The room where the girl lived with her father, mother and two sisters, had two beds with old rags for bed clothes, and no furnishings except a table, a few chairs, a china dog, and statues of the Blessed Virgin and the Sacred Heart.

Belfast also had its share of slums, but Dublin in particular did not provide well for the poorer sections of its growing population. A study conducted by T.J. Stafford, Medical Commissioner of Health for the Local Government Board, which examined 1,254 local families, concluded that half of the city's population lived in poverty and could not meet basic requirements for general good health. Malnourishment was a constant problem as diets consisted primarily of bread and tea with occasional vegetables – staple carbohydrates to fill the body, which lacked necessary additional vitamins and minerals. Conditions in the tenements were especially unpleasant since sanitation was often very poor and, with a large volume of people living in such confined spaces, it was difficult to keep the accommodation in good order.

For the unskilled labouring poor, living conditions were abject, and this was reflected in the mortality rates which were markedly above those in Britain. Dublin's rate in 1905 for example was 22.3 per 1,000 people, while Glasgow was 17 per 1,000 and London 15.6 per 1,000. The main cause of death was often pulmonary tuberculosis, a bacterial lung disease that was common amongst the poor, and which was propagated by a weakened immune system that could not fight off the resultant infection. Tuberculosis, like cholera and typhus, was a disease that thrived in poor living environments such as those described in Source 1.

The significance of the founding of the National Union of Dock Labourers 1907 and the Irish Transport and General Workers' Union 1909

The conditions in which the unskilled worked and lived in Ireland was in great part down to the inability of this section of the population to take effective action to improve their positions. Living conditions, for example, were a direct consequence of the poor wages that they could earn – for the majority of families a single room was all they could afford, and therefore without the opportunity of a wage increase, or even permanent employment, there was little chance of a better lifestyle. Changing the level of wages, however, was a difficult task since casual unskilled workers did not enjoy the same degree of protection as their skilled permanent colleagues who could rely to some extent upon their expertise when it came to negotiations. After 1907, unskilled workers were given the chance to help themselves with the organisation of Irish dockers into the National Union of Dock Labourers.

The National Union of Dock Labourers and the Belfast strike, 1907

The National Union of Dock Labourers (NUDL) had been founded in Glasgow in 1889, and then quickly relocated to Liverpool. It was a vehicle for achieving better conditions for the less-skilled workers on the docks who, until then, had no representation. In January 1907, the union began to recruit in earnest in the ports of Ireland – most notably in Belfast which had become the country's largest port, overtaking Dublin, in the previous century. The driving force behind this recruitment process, and the general organisation of the Belfast dockers, came from Jim Larkin. He was originally a Liverpool-based docker whose experiences in England had encouraged him to join the union and actively organise on its behalf. Having lost his job in England after taking part in strike action in 1905, Larkin moved to Ireland as a full-time organiser for the NUDL.

EXTEND YOUR KNOWLEDGE

Jim Larkin (1876-1947)

It is generally agreed that Jim Larkin was born to poor Irish immigrant parents in Liverpool. Growing up in Liverpool's slums he received little education and became a docker on the ports after first going to sea and losing an apprenticeship at 14. In 1892-93, he joined the Independent Labour Party for which he spent considerable time outside of his work undertaking propaganda efforts and public speaking. He advocated the overthrow of capitalism and creation of a socialist commonwealth. In 1901, he joined the NUDL and in 1903 he became a foreman. He was one of only a few foremen on the Liverpool docks to go on strike in 1905 against the firm T. and J. Harrison. Losing his positon after the strike, he became a full-time organiser for the NUDL and went to Ireland to unionise the dockers there. In 1907, he co-ordinated the Belfast dock strike and was able to get Protestant and Catholic workers united in the aim – he even managed to get the Royal Irish Constabulary to support the action. In 1909, he founded the Irish Transport and General Workers Union after falling out with the NUDL over an organised strike in Dublin that was not condoned by the union. He was accused of diverting union money for his own cause and was put on trial for embezzlement in 1910. After conviction he was imprisoned for one year. The ITGWU became the largest union in Ireland under Larkin's energetic leadership. In 1911, he created a newspaper, the *Irish Worker,* and then with the support of James Connolly he established the Irish Labour Party in 1912. In 1913 he co-ordinated one of the largest strikes in Irish history, the Dublin lockout, in an attempt to get better wages for the unskilled workers of that city. After the collapse of this strike, Larkin moved to America and became increasingly involved with the communist movement. Upon his return to Ireland in 1923, he founded the Irish Worker League - a communist organisation for which he worked until 1941.

Larkin was able to unionise Belfast's 3,100 dockers, both Protestants and Catholics, which was a considerable achievement since the two religions did not enjoy cordial relations on the waterside. In May 1907, he co-ordinated a strike against the Belfast Steamship Company to secure union recognition, shorter working hours and better wages. Specifically they wanted a minimum wage of 27 shillings for a 60-hour week. In June, these demands were presented to all the companies in Belfast and while some smaller ones agreed to the demands, the larger companies refused to even consider them. After this time, the strike became much broader and drew support from the carters after July and even some skilled workers from the shipyards who came out on **secondary strike** action. The significance of this broadening out of the strike was that the traditional means by which employers would break strike action became increasingly impractical. Usually they would import **blackleg** labour in the place of the employed workers, but even if they could replace the dockers and get the

ships emptied, there was no one willing to transport the goods elsewhere.

KEY TERMS

Secondary strike
A strike by other industries in support of the initial strike action.

Blackleg
A term used to describe a person who continues to work while others are on strike.

The strike was further escalated in mid-July when a low-ranking, sympathetic police officer named William Barrett refused to ride in a vehicle that was transporting blackleg labour to the docks. His action precipitated a mutiny in the Royal Irish Constabulary (RIC) as 300 other police constables also refused to protect the employers' blackleg workers and troops had to be drafted in to carry out protective duties. The strike came to a climax when, on 10 August, a massive meeting attended by 10,000 Protestant and Catholic workers resulted in a clash with troops and caused the deaths of two bystanders. The strike was eventually ended when the NUDL leader James Sexton and the leaders of the General Federation of Trade Unions (GFTU), Allen Gee and Isaac Mitchell, sought to find a deal for the different striking groups that was also favourable to the employers. Their motivation to bring the strike to a conclusion was based upon the positions they held. As trade union officials they had assumed personal interests as their roles offered middle-class careers that presented an opportunity for advancement. In the interests of promoting these opportunities, Sexton and the others saw themselves not as leading a militant struggle, but rather as arbitrators between employer and employee. The outcome of their dealing saw the carters persuaded back to work after promises of a wage increase but no union recognition, and this left the dockers isolated and eventually defeated by the end of August.

Significance of the Belfast strike, 1907

The dock strike in 1907 was a significant moment in Irish labour history for several reasons, notably because it was the first time that the unskilled workers were able to organise for their own benefit. Trade unionism in Ireland before the 20th century was primarily a conservative movement dominated by the skilled professions. However, 1907 was an opportunity for the broader masses of unskilled workers to assert themselves. Furthermore, the dock strike evidenced widespread worker solidarity across the employment barrier – although started by the unskilled dockers, other professions quickly joined them in support of their demands. These secondary or 'sympathy' strikes increased the potency of working-class industrial action and showed how much could be achieved if people supported one another in numbers. Although the strike itself was eventually defeated, this was only due to the efforts of the unions themselves, and it was only achieved by dividing the worker's ranks. In this sense, while the event failed to achieve exactly what they demanded, it was nonetheless a positive experience from the point of view of further action in the future.

A particular feature that the dock strike developed, which is also worthy of consideration, was that the sympathy generated among the working classes in Belfast also ignored religious backgrounds and united Protestants with Catholics against the employers. In a city, and indeed a province, where **sectarianism** was rife because of political developments and the question of home rule, such unity was marked and evidenced a deep-rooted resentment of the general conditions under which the working classes laboured. Prior to 1907, the issue of religion was generally a very effective traditional means of dividing the working population with each denomination 'keeping with their own' rather than embracing the other. In part, this was the result of historical discrimination and the dominance of the Protestant religion during the 17th century and beyond. However, it was also a feature of the growing competition for jobs, especially in skilled trades. What 1907 demonstrated was the potential to overcome this religious barrier and support one another in a new, class-based division against the employers. Like sympathy striking, this was a potentially powerful tool for the labouring classes to utilise in their campaign to improve their overall conditions.

EXTRACT

1 From Emmet Larkin, *James Larkin* (1968). Emmet Larkin (no relation) was a prominent historian of Irish history and his book about James Larkin is widely regarded as the standard text on the trade unionist.

The myth that has grown up around James Larkin claims Belfast as one of his greatest achievements. What happened in Belfast can, of course, be conceived in the most grandiose terms. It could include the destruction of religious bigotry, organising workers for the revolutionary act, and contributing to the dignity and integrity of the working classes. The rub is that Larkin did achieve these things, but only to a limited extent... In the long run Larkin achieved little of a tangible nature in Belfast, not because he was something less than he should have been, but because his enemies were too powerful and circumstances too adverse. In the short run he shook Belfast to its roots.

SOURCE

2 The 2nd Royal Sussex Regiment arriving at Belfast docks to help end the strike, July 1907.

The Irish Transport and General Workers' Union, 1909

The Belfast dock strike evidenced the growing strength of a working-class voice and also a confidence that had been instilled by organisation into a union. Despite these advances, the position of the workers did not improve substantially and this was arguably down to the backtracking by the union's leadership – especially James Sexton, General Secretary of the NUDL, who had sought to diffuse the increasingly explosive situation after the August meeting. In one sense, this was an appropriate undertaking because of the deaths of two bystanders and a consequent desire to restore some clear order to the situation. In another sense, however, securing a deal for particular sections of those on strike at the expense of others quickly led to the end of the strike, taking the workers from a position of strength to that of accepting a deal that was to the advantage of the employers. This undermined the effectiveness of the strike action and left many workers vulnerable, especially the dockers who were the last to return to work.

What it also did was to alienate Jim Larkin who felt let down by the NUDL leadership and its conservative feelings towards the August meeting. In subsequent months, Larkin organised additional branches of the NUDL in Ireland, encouraging a militant stand against the employers. This brought him into further confrontation with Sexton, who seemed more inclined towards developing good relations with the employers. In many regards, this was an appropriate objective in terms of negotiating benefits. However, it contrasted with Larkin's more socialist stance and, frustrated by the perceived softness of Sexton, in January 1909 he organised a new union to co-ordinate Ireland's workers. This was called the Irish Transport and General Workers' Union (ITGWU) and it was intended as a broad-based organisation for all trades, but specifically for the unskilled workers who otherwise had little representation in Ireland.

The significance of the ITGWU was that it was deliberately intended as a general union rather than a specific trades union, which would therefore promote a much larger membership. This method paid off. By early 1911 the membership was 5,000 and by the end of the year it was in excess of 18,000, making it the country's largest union. The size and broad base of the organisation gave unskilled workers a much better chance to promote their interests because it increased the likelihood of broader and more impactful strikes since anyone within the union, regardless of their actual job, would be required to strike if that was the overall decision. The implication behind such an organisation, therefore, was the creation of a much stronger workers' union that could more effectively push for, and protect, workers' rights. In this sense, the ITGWU signalled the birth of a more militant intention to address the issue of working conditions and also to ensure that employers began to recognise the power of those whom they employed. This was somewhat of a departure for Irish unionism since older unions were often inclined to try to negotiate with employers for better wages or shorter hours, and in these negotiations there was usually the tacit acceptance that the employers were in the dominant position. Consequently unions would only seek to extract improvements that employers were willing to grant. The suggestion with Larkin's new organisation was that, with the strength it could wield, the power balance would shift and the workers would be in a much more advantageous position to make demands of their employers.

In addition to the broad base of the ITGWU, it was also the first Irish union to outwardly embrace a more radical agenda. Unlike other unions, it adopted syndicalism as its central ideology, and this involved more than just rights for workers, being a new economic system that offered an alternative to the capitalist system that existed. In its simplest form, syndicalism is a form of socialism that encourages the organisation of syndicates – small self-organising groups – to manage and run industries. These groups would be made up of the workers themselves and therefore the differences between employers and workers would be removed. As an ideology, syndicalism was quite a radical pursuit in the early 20th century and the creation of the ITGWU was viewed with some concern by employers.

ACTIVITY
KNOWLEDGE CHECK

Growing militancy

1 Why did unionism grow in Ireland after 1907?

2 What made the Belfast strike such a challenging action for employers?

3 How did the Irish Transport and General Workers' Union differ from other unions?

The roles of Jim Larkin, James Connolly and William Martin Murphy

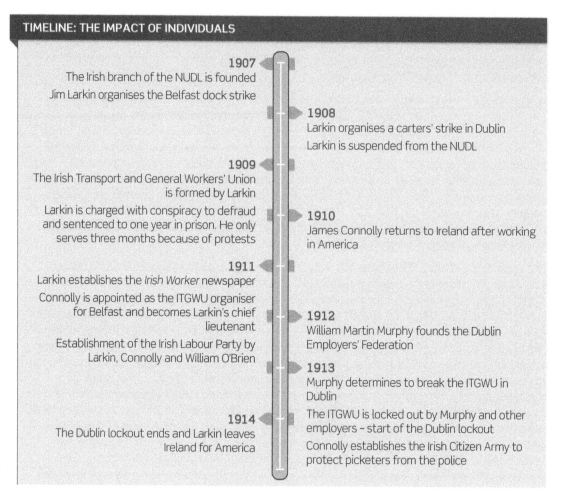

TIMELINE: THE IMPACT OF INDIVIDUALS

1907
The Irish branch of the NUDL is founded
Jim Larkin organises the Belfast dock strike

1908
Larkin organises a carters' strike in Dublin
Larkin is suspended from the NUDL

1909
The Irish Transport and General Workers' Union is formed by Larkin
Larkin is charged with conspiracy to defraud and sentenced to one year in prison. He only serves three months because of protests

1910
James Connolly returns to Ireland after working in America

1911
Larkin establishes the *Irish Worker* newspaper
Connolly is appointed as the ITGWU organiser for Belfast and becomes Larkin's chief lieutenant
Establishment of the Irish Labour Party by Larkin, Connolly and William O'Brien

1912
William Martin Murphy founds the Dublin Employers' Federation

1913
Murphy determines to break the ITGWU in Dublin
The ITGWU is locked out by Murphy and other employers – start of the Dublin lockout
Connolly establishes the Irish Citizen Army to protect picketers from the police

1914
The Dublin lockout ends and Larkin leaves Ireland for America

Jim Larkin (1876–1947)

In the effort to improve working and living conditions for the working classes of Ireland, Jim Larkin was pre-eminent. Unions had existed before his arrival in 1907 but they were primarily for skilled workers, and they were more conservative-minded, feeling that their organisations could only survive if tolerated by the more-powerful employers. This was the attitude that had motivated James Sexton of the NUDL and the other union leaders to force the end of the Belfast dock strike, and it was arguably one that had failed to substantially enhance workers' conditions in Ireland. Larkin, however, had an entirely different approach. Rather than feeding off the scraps that employers were prepared to cast down, he believed that the means to attain greater benefits lay with the working people themselves if only they could instil **solidarity** – as a single unit he felt they would be an unstoppable force for change. To this end, he set about organising the masses of unskilled labour and reached out to the skilled professions also, through the Irish Transport and General Workers' Union. The intention was to create one big union for the workers in Ireland which could take on the employers and, through the threat of united strike action across the related trades, promote better conditions for them.

By pursuing this agenda, Larkin sought to instil a greater militancy within the working classes and create a more assertive attitude towards achieving better conditions – something he felt was lacking in the existing trade unions. To achieve this, he used his exceptional skill and energy as an organiser together with a natural talent for public speaking that was very effective at stirring the people (Source 8). In addition to this medium, in May 1911 he established a weekly newspaper called the

Irish Worker in which to reach out to the broader working classes. The first issue sold 5,000 copies and sales continued to increase, eventually settling at 20,000 copies a week. This level of circulation was mainly confined to the city of Dublin, but it was an effective mouthpiece for the ITGWU and it quickly became an essential organ for the militarisation of the working class in that city.

After 1907, Larkin spent a great deal of time in Dublin organising the unskilled labour in that city. In November 1908, he orchestrated a carters' strike with the intention of having the union recognised and wages increased. This was arguably one of the city's most significant industrial actions and it brought shipping to a halt, with the dockers also supporting their fellow workers together with the brewers. In total, 3,000 men in the city were on strike and when it ended later that year employers had conceded a higher rate of overtime, although basic wages remained the same. Despite the limited tangible success that was achieved by this event, it was nonetheless a significant episode in Ireland's labour history. It saw sympathy strikes in the city and forced arbitration with the employers that did accede to some of the workers' demands. The **black shilling** system for the brewers, for example, was removed and two weeks' notice would be required for dismissal. It also brought Larkin into direct confrontation with Sexton who disapproved of the overtly militant tactics that he encouraged, and the NUDL leader suspended him from the union. In response Larkin set about organising the ITGWU, and this organisation quickly became the largest in Ireland, even though Larkin was briefly imprisoned, with Sexton's help, after being found guilty of fraud. In 1908, Larkin had transferred funds from the Cork branch of the NUDL to support the strike in Dublin, and Sexton used this to accuse Larkin of criminal action. It is generally accepted that this was an attempt by the NUDL leader to undermine Larkin and his new union which had attracted significant NUDL numbers.

Larkin offered something very different from the older trades unions; he was more militant and he believed in the power of the working classes. This belief was fuelled by his unwavering acceptance of socialism and the need to reorganise the economic system in Ireland so that workers could enjoy more rights and better conditions. This could only be achieved through the actions of the working class itself, rising up in collective solidarity against the employers. This was a cornerstone of his philosophy and it is what continued to motivate his actions throughout his lifetime.

James Connolly (1868-1916)

Like Larkin, James Connolly was equally committed to a socialist agenda and upon his arrival in Ireland in 1910 he quickly became involved in the ITGWU. The following year he became an organiser and Larkin's right-hand man. In Belfast, Connolly was successful in winning a pay rise for seamen and firemen whom he organised strike action with and, in 1911, he also established the Irish Textile Workers' Union for the female linen workers. These undertakings contributed very effectively to the growing militancy of the Irish working classes. Due to the efforts of Connolly and Larkin, Irish workers were quickly becoming organised and starting to achieve some improvements to their situations, albeit in small increments.

If Larkin was the engine of the labour movement in Ireland then Connolly was its theoretician and, together with Larkin and William O'Brien, he organised the Irish Labour Party in 1912 as the political wing of the movement. The aim of this party was to represent the working people of Ireland specifically, rather than accepting representation by the mostly middle-class Irish Party that was pressing for home rule. The creation of the Irish Labour Party did not immediately affect the conditions of the working classes because industrial action overtook these political attempts in 1913, but it signalled a clear determination to promote the interests of working people beyond simply union activities. In this regard, Connolly is particularly noteworthy because he added a more rounded approach to the labour movement, contributing greater political understanding to Larkin's militancy and exuberant rank and file leadership. As a thinker, Connolly had a much better grasp of socialist theory, but Larkin had the better personal touch with the ordinary worker and could win over a crowd more easily. In this sense, each man brought different but complimentary skills to the movement and together they offered a strong blend of leadership that was able to organise Irish labour to an extent never before realised.

KEY TERM

Black shilling
This was money deliberately held back each week by employers and only given out at the end of the year if the employee's conduct had been satisfactory.

William Martin Murphy (1844–1919)

Larkin and Connolly were the unrivalled leaders of the growing labour movement in Ireland. Their collective actions after 1907 were very effective in organising the working class and making it a militant body determined to improve their situation. Just as determined, however, were the employers, who viewed the growing militancy with both concern and scorn. In Dublin especially, where the ITGWU had achieved a strong foothold, the employers in that city were keen to destroy the organisation before it began to significantly affect their business interests. Just as the workers rallied to the call of Larkin, the employers also rallied, but to the call of the city's, and Catholic Ireland's, wealthiest businessman – William Martin Murphy.

Murphy had been a Home Rule MP before losing his seat to a Parnellite after the split in 1892 and had made his fortune in the transport business, first the railways and then the tramway system. He had interests throughout Ireland and Britain and even helped to develop the tram system in Buenos Aires. In Dublin, he effectively controlled the United Tramway Company as well as owning the city's largest hotel, Clery's department store and two newspapers – *Irish Catholic* and *Irish Independent*. As an employer, he was generally regarded as one of the better ones in the city, paying fair wages and also tolerating the deferential and moderate trade unions of the skilled workers. He was, however, adamantly opposed to any militancy such as that encouraged by Larkin and Connolly. Having successfully defeated strike action in 1911 by the Amalgamated Society of Railway Servants (ASRS) by threatening them with a **lockout**, he was determined to suffocate the ITGWU in Dublin. To this effect, he founded the Dublin Employers' Federation in 1911 with the intention of getting a blanket decision from the city's employers to not employ members of the ITGWU.

As an employer himself, he was among the first to adopt this action. In July 1913, he called a meeting of his employees in the Dublin United Tramway Company to invite them to form a 'legitimate union', but also to warn them of summary dismissal if anyone sought to recruit for the ITGWU. In August, he went even further and sacked all members of that union from his *Irish Independent* despatch department – 40 men and 20 boys. This resulted in the boycotting of the newspaper and opened the door to further confrontation with the city's working class.

SOURCE

3 From William Martin Murphy's verbal warning at a meeting of his employees in the Dublin United Tramway Company on 19 July 1913.

I want you to clearly understand that the directors of this company have not the slightest objection to the men forming a legitimate Union. And I would think there is talent enough amongst the men in the service to form a Union of their own, without allying themselves to a disreputable organisation, and placing themselves under the feet of an unscrupulous man who claims the right to give you the word of command and issue his orders to you and to use you as tools to make him the labour dictator of Dublin... I am here to tell you that this word of command will never be given, and if it is, that it will be the Waterloo of Mr. Larkin. A strike in the tramway would, no doubt, produce turmoil and disorder created by the roughs and looters, but what chance would the men without funds have in a contest with the Company who could and would spend £100,000 or more. You must recollect when dealing with a company of this kind that every one of the shareholders, to the number of five, six, or seven thousands, will have three meals a day whether the men succeed or not. I don't know if the men who go out can count on this.

WHAT WAS THE IMPACT OF THE GENERAL STRIKE IN 1913–14?

TIMELINE: THE GENERAL STRIKE AND LOCKOUT

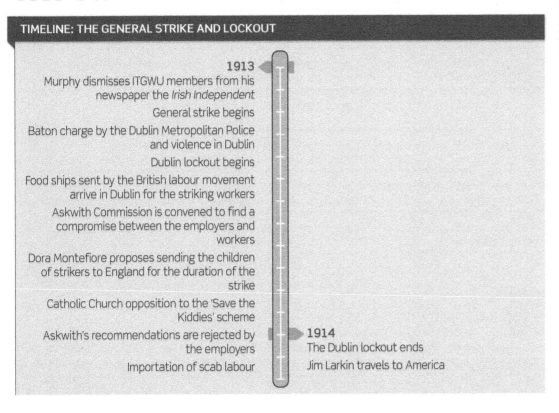

1913

Murphy dismisses ITGWU members from his newspaper the *Irish Independent*

General strike begins

Baton charge by the Dublin Metropolitan Police and violence in Dublin

Dublin lockout begins

Food ships sent by the British labour movement arrive in Dublin for the striking workers

Askwith Commission is convened to find a compromise between the employers and workers

Dora Montefiore proposes sending the children of strikers to England for the duration of the strike

Catholic Church opposition to the 'Save the Kiddies' scheme

Askwith's recommendations are rejected by the employers

Importation of scab labour

1914

The Dublin lockout ends

Jim Larkin travels to America

Events and significance of the Dublin general strike, 1913–14

The actions of William Murphy initiated Ireland's best remembered and most significant industrial action – first a general strike by the ITGWU and then a retaliatory lockout by the employers of Dublin. Beginning in August 1913, these events paralysed the city for six months, bringing business to a halt and even threatening trade as the industrial dispute was extended into Britain. Sympathy came from first Keir Hardie, leader of the Independent Labour Party in Britain who openly supported the ITGWU's actions, and then from the broader labour movement in the form of financial and food aid for Ireland's striking workers as the industrial action deepened.

The general strike began on 26 August 1913 following the dismissal of Murphy's ITGWU employees. The day was deliberately chosen because it was the first day of the Dublin Horse Show and a strike among the transport workers would cause maximum disruption in the city. At 10.00am trams and buses were stopped as drivers and conductors abandoned their vehicles and took to the streets in protest at the actions of William Murphy and the other employers who had targeted the ITGWU. In all, 700 of the Dublin United Tramways Company's 1,700 workers went on strike and were supported by distributors of Murphy's *Irish Independent* who refused to handle the paper. Furthermore, when Eason and Company, Ireland's largest newsagent, refused to refrain from selling the paper when asked to by Larkin, ITGWU members on Dublin's Dun Laoghaire docks refused to handle any of the company's goods. This quickly extended the strike into a broader action with the dockers coming out in sympathy and it also drew an increasingly violent response from the city's metropolitan police force.

The involvement of the Dublin Metropolitan Police

On 28 August, Larkin and the ITGWU leadership were all arrested and charged with seditious libel, conspiracy and assembly, while a union demonstration in O'Connell Street arranged for the following Sunday was banned. In taking this action, the city authorities were clearly throwing their support behind the employers and they used what tools they had at their disposal to destroy the strike as soon as they could. To this end, the Dublin Metropolitan Police were used as strike-breakers. On the weekend of 30–31 August they baton-charged a crowd of workers in O'Connell Street and this resulted in further violence throughout the city. On Burgh and Eden Quays, the police clubbed any union members present and fatally injured two: James Byrne and James Nolan. The conduct of the city's police officers was very brutal and even Bryne's 14-year-old daughter, who was out shopping, received a blow to the head. By late on Saturday night two had died and more than 200 others were badly injured. When the weekend finally came to a close, over 500 people had received hospital attention following police action.

SOURCE 4

From an eyewitness account by Count Casimir Markiewicz, who observed the actions of 31 August 1913. Markiewicz was the husband of Constance Markiewicz, a prominent figure in the Sinn Fein movement and the first woman to be elected to parliament in 1918. His witness account was published in the *Freeman's Journal* on 1 September 1913.

There was no sign of excitement, no attempt at rescue, and no attempt at a breach of the peace, when a savage and cruel order for the baton charge – unprecedented in such circumstances in any privileged country – was given to the police... Scores of well-fed metropolitan policemen pursued a handful of men, women and children running for their lives before them. Round the corner of Princes Street, I saw a young man pursued by a huge policeman, knocked down by a baton stroke, and then, whilst bleeding on the ground, batoned and kicked, not only by this policeman but by his colleagues... When the police had finished their bloodthirsty pursuit, they returned down the street batoning the terror-stricken passers-by who had taken refuge in the doorways. It was a complete triumph for the police... It was, indeed, a bloody Sunday for Ireland.

SOURCE 5

The Dublin Metropolitan Police's baton charge in O'Connell Street (then called Sackville Street) in August 1913. This event took place early into the Dublin lockout and for Irish workers it highlighted the police force's sympathies for the employers. The charge was particularly violent and resulted in the deaths of two strikers.

The British labour movement becomes aware of the general strike

Apart from the wanton aggression of the police and their clear support for Dublin's employers, the events of 30–31 August were also significant because their actions promoted the workers' cause in Britain. Such was the scale of violence and brutality that stories of what was unfolding in Dublin were printed in British newspapers such as the *Daily Herald* which began publication in 1912. The Dublin correspondent for this paper was Francis Sheehy-Skeffington and he graphically conveyed the events in the city to his readers across the Irish Sea in unrelenting terms, both in his own words and also those of the strikers whom he interviewed. The reports he sent back to London brought the situation in Dublin to the forefront of British trade unionists' minds and in September 1913 William Partridge, a member of the ITGWU, travelled to Manchester having been invited to address the Trades Union Congress, where he spoke of his union fighting for its survival and that of wider trade unionism in Ireland. At the same time, the leader of the British Labour Party, Keir Hardie, arrived in Dublin to see the situation for himself. While in the city, he visited Larkin in prison and also attended the funeral of James Nolan – one of the unfortunates who lost his life during the police baton charge on 30 August 1913. In both these instances, the general strike was given significantly greater exposure to the broader labour movement in Britain. This proved very influential in the following months as the employers in Dublin began to take the strain of the industrial action and then dug in their heels in a bid for victory. (See page 168 for more on the British trade union movement.)

The general strike and the Catholic Church

The majority of the ITGWU membership were practising Catholics. Indeed, Larkin himself was a Catholic, and therefore it is worth considering the response of the Church to the events of 1913. The growth of the ITGWU and the militant attitude of its leadership, particularly during the general strike when it was clearly at loggerheads with Dublin's employers, was a source of concern for the Catholic Church because of its socialist leanings. Although Larkin saw no conflict between this ideology and that of Catholicism, Church representatives in Ireland took a very different position. During the mid-19th century, when an emerging middle class became more prominent in Irish society, the Church underwent what the historian Emmet Larkin termed a 'devotional revolution' (see page 124) whereby the traditional and informal practises of the faith were given greater structure. The Church adopted a more formal position that reflected and helped to reinforce a more conservative set of social values which were preferable to the new middle class. Since this period, the Catholic Church had become increasingly more critical of new ideas, including those of socialism and revolutionary nationalism as embodied by the Fenian movement. Essentially, it objected to anything that threatened the status quo and its own position. Given this reactionary stance, the growth of the socialist-leaning ITGWU met with significant criticism from the Church – notably from Father John Condon who wrote several withering attacks in local newspapers decrying the union's socialist tendencies and how it was so incompatible with Catholicism.

The critical nature of the Church was even more marked in October 1913 following the ITGWU's proposed scheme to send the children of strikers to English homes while the dispute endured (see page 165). The Archbishop of Dublin, William Walsh, in an open letter to the Dublin newspapers, condemned the mothers of these children and suggested they had abandoned their faith, accusing them of sending their children away to stay with strangers who may not even be Catholic. Coming from one of the country's most prominent clerics, this was a significant attack against the ITGWU and clearly placed Church support with the employers during the ongoing dispute. Despite this opposition to the strike and the ITGWU generally, the rank and file membership remained focused on their stance and refused to let their faith affect the principle of unionisation for which they were fighting.

The strike began in opposition to the actions of William Murphy and his perceived singular crusade against the ITGWU. However, the actions of the Dublin police force and the general broadening of the strike affected other employers and individuals in the city such that the strike took on a much greater significance: it became a battle between the working classes of the city and their employers. More grandiose, but not altogether exaggerated, it was a struggle for the principle of workers to be able to collectively stand up for their employment rights, and to join unions for their self-protection within a capitalist environment hostile to their interests. As the strike deepened, Murphy was joined by other employers who saw the need to make a stand against the growing aspirations of working-class militancy.

The lock out and implications for workers and employers

In retaliation to the general strike, the employers rallied together in Dublin and agreed to a lockout which began on 2 September with the coal merchants locking their doors to their workforce whether they were union members or not. They were quickly followed by other employers such as the mineral water producers Bewley and Draper who locked out 200 people, and Jacob's Biscuits, which employed more than 2,000 women, of whom only a small percentage were union members. By the end of the September, more than 25,000 employees had been put out of work by over 400 firms. As the lockout developed in early September, employees had been asked to sign a document pledging not to join the ITGWU or even support it, and if they did not then they were summarily dismissed. This was an overt attempt at destroying Larkin's union, which had become the country's largest and most militant, and thousands of workers refused to sign it. Even many of those who were not in the union felt they could not sign on principle, and so the lockout intensified in that month.

SOURCE

6 From an article by James Connolly, remembering the actions of a worker when asked to sign the pledge not to join or support the ITGWU in September 1913. He published this recollection in the socialist magazine *Forward* on 4 October 1913.

A labourer was asked to sign the agreement forswearing the Irish Transport and General Workers' Union, and he told his employer, a small capitalist builder, that he refused to sign. The employer, knowing the man's circumstances, reminded him that he had a wife and six children who would be starving within a week. The reply of this humble labourer rose to the heights of sublimity. 'It is true, sir', he said, 'they will starve; but I would rather see them go out on in their coffins than I should disgrace them by signing that'. And with head erect he walked out to share hunger and privation with his loved ones. Hunger and privation—and honour. Defeat, bah! How can such a people be defeated? His case is typical of thousands more.

The purpose behind the lockout was to break the solidarity of the working class that the militant ITGWU had stimulated. Murphy recognised that the power of this union lay in the collective approach it adopted and that individual employers had found themselves facing the whole organisation when engaged in a dispute. The lockout undermined this tactic by uniting the employers in solidarity and then taking advantage of the superior financial resources they had at their disposal to wage a war of attrition against the union. The 'siege' they laid against the workers began to take effect towards the end of September when many of the strikers had been out for nearly a month and were beginning to suffer the privations of surviving on meagre strike pay. For their part, employers did not go financially unscathed as the overall cost to their profits over the course of the lockout amounted to £300,000. Specifically, Murphy's Dublin Tramway Company, which began the struggle, saw its net profit drop from £142,382 to £119,871. Employers were prepared to absorb these losses since the need to subdue militant unionism was essential for their long-term interests.

The discomfort of the striking workers was given some relief on 28 September when a ship called *The Hare* docked in the city's port carrying 60,000 boxes of food, each capable of feeding a family of five. This aid had come from the British working class who had been made aware of the situation in Ireland following the August police brutality that was publicised in the *Daily Herald*. Over the next few months, further ships arrived with additional food packages. In October £13,000-worth of aid was sent, in November £16,000 and in December £21,000. This support not only physically helped the Dublin workers to maintain their opposition to the lockout, but it also enhanced their morale by showing them that they had the sympathy of their fellow classes in Britain.

The Askwith Commission

In late September, the Board of Trade announced that there was to be an inquiry into the dispute in Dublin and, under the chairmanship of Sir George Askwith, the Commission opened its proceedings on 29 September. The intention of the inquiry was to find a mutually agreeable solution to the industrial dispute which would therefore end both that confrontation and also the paralysis of the city. After meeting with both the employers and representatives of the strikers, the Commission made the following proposals:

- the withdrawal of the employer's ban on ITGWU membership

- the end to sympathy strikes

- the creation of **Conciliation Boards**.

KEY TERM

Conciliation Board
A neutral body that arbitrates between employers and unions during disputes with the aim of finding a mutually agreeable compromise.

These recommendations were very acceptable for the ITGWU, particularly since they endorsed the existence of the union and stated the right of the workers to join it, which had been the Union's primary interest. Furthermore, the provision of Conciliation Boards to arbitrate in any future dispute offered a more impartial means of securing any improvements required. From the perspective of the employers, however, the recommendations were dismissed out of hand. For them, the intention of the lockout was not to simply end the strike but to completely destroy the ITGWU and with it, militant unionism. The recommendations that were offered recognised the ITGWU and therefore were entirely unacceptable to them. On 14 October, they presented their own terms, which demanded that the union's leadership be replaced with men amenable to the employers, and that any striking worker would only get reappointed to their position of employment as and when there was a vacancy. These terms were naturally distasteful to the ITGWU and the dispute continued.

The significance of the Askwith Commission's failure to end the lockout and strike was that it sent a clear message to the country that the intention of the employers was to destroy Larkin and his brand of militant unionism in the city. Furthermore, and perhaps most interestingly, it presented the employers as vindictive and unwilling to compromise, and this turned public opinion against them. The people of Dublin especially had hoped that the Commission would find terms that would bring an end the dispute, but despite the union's unreservedly positive response, it was the employers that sought to continue the trouble. This gave the ITGWU wider public support which enhanced morale but did not necessarily improve its standing in terms of financial and employment benefit.

SOURCE

From the writer George Russell's 'Open Letter to the Masters of Dublin' published in the *Irish Times* on 6 October 1913. Russell was the editor of the co-operative journal *Irish Homestead*, and also a member of the Dublin Industrial Peace Committee which sought to assist in the resolution of industrial disputes.

We read in the Dark Ages of the rack and thumb screw. But these iniquities were hidden and concealed from the knowledge of men in dungeons and torture chambers. Even in the Dark Ages, humanity could not endure the sight of such suffering, and it learnt of such misuse of power by slow degrees, through rumour, and when it was certain it razed its Bastilles to their foundations. It remained for the twentieth century and the capital city of Ireland to see an oligarchy of four hundred masters deciding openly upon starving one hundred thousand people, and refusing to consider any solution except that fixed by their pride. You, masters, asked men to do that which masters of labour in any other city in these islands had not dared to do. You insolently demanded of those men who were members of a trade union that they should resign from that union; and from those who were not members, you insisted on a vow that they would never join it.

Your insolence and ignorance of the rights conceded to workers universally in the modern world were incredible, and as great as your inhumanity. If you had between you collectively a portion of human soul as large as a threepenny bit, you would have sat night and day with the representatives of labour, trying this or that solution of the trouble, mindful of the women and children, who at least were innocent of wrong against you. But no! You reminded labour you could always have your three square meals a day while it went hungry. You went into conference again with representatives of the State, because, dull as you are, you knew public opinion would not stand your holding out. You chose as your spokesman the bitterest tongue that ever wagged in this island, and then, when an award was made by men who have an experience in industrial matters a thousand times transcending yours, who have settled disputes in industries so great that the sum of your petty enterprises would not equal them, you withdrew again, and will not agree to accept their solution, and fall back again on your devilish policy of starvation. Cry aloud to heaven for new souls. The souls you have got cast upon the screens of publicity appear like the horrid and writhing creatures enlarged from the insect world, and revealed to us by the cinematographer

'Save the Kiddies' scheme

A further episode which enhanced the position of the ITGWU was a proposal to send the children of Dublin's striking workers to Britain until the dispute was resolved. This idea was tabled by Dora Montefiore, a British socialist and feminist who sympathised with the Dublin workers and was associated with the *Daily Herald* newspaper, which was covering the lockout. From her perspective, she felt it would be very practical assistance since the longer the strike continued the harder it became for families to feed themselves on the meagre strike pay they received. It would also be a public relations coup that would expose the heartless nature of the employers. To this end, arrangements were made and in October 1913 the union undertook to send the first consignment of children out of Dublin. The attempt was a failure, however, since the Catholic Church, and particularly the Archbishop of Dublin, was opposed to the scheme and had publicly condemned it in the press. The result of this action was that priests and lay opposition to the scheme lined the railway stations to prevent the children from leaving.

The motivation for the Archbishop's objection was his belief that the children would not be going to Catholic homes and that he had heard false rumours that Montefiore and her colleagues were agents of the white slave trade. To overcome this objection, the union tried to send the children to Catholic homes in Belfast. However, even this was objected to, and on the day of embarkation in late October a confrontation developed that eventually saw the police intervene to prevent the children from boarding.

Importing scab labour

With the lockout and strike into its third month, employers began to import **scab** labour, and on 29 October 50 scabs arrived from Manchester to work in the timber yards. With a strong police presence, these men began to make deliveries around the city and a further 160 arrived the following week. The arrival of larger numbers of imported workers undermined the impact of the strike on employers while exacerbating the impact on the striking workers. The prospect of the employers' position having improved not only weakened striker morale, it also saw their jobs disappearing as roles were filled with new labour.

The consequence of this action was an increase in confrontation as the ITGWU tried to picket the scab workers and prevent them from carrying out their tasks. This was intended to force the employers to abandon their policy of bringing in alternative labour. However, in reality it failed to have any substantial effect because the scabs were well protected – many of them carried revolvers in case of attack, and the police were deployed to oversee their work and be around in the event of a problem. Given the already-exhibited willingness of the police to use their batons against the union, workers were not entirely confident to stand against the scabs. Therefore, despite isolated successes, the picketing generally failed to achieve its goal.

More significantly, the importation of alternative labour gave the advantage to the employers, and therefore Larkin and Connolly felt they needed to strengthen their position. For Connolly, this involved the creation of his Irish Citizen Army – a disciplined force of around 300 union members armed with wooden staves and hurling sticks intended as protection against the police in the city. Larkin and Connolly also sought to close the port of Dublin by calling out workers whose employers had not joined the lockout. This was a controversial action which was resented by the dockers involved. Nonetheless they did support their fellow workers. Larkin also sought to spread the strike into Britain by developing greater solidarity with the labour movement there in the hope that collectively they would gain the upper-hand. Without access to scab labour from Britain the Dublin employers would have to come to terms.

The Dublin lockout was arguably the pre-eminent industrial confrontation in Ireland. Prior to 1913, employers had the upper hand and were able to effectively dictate wages and working conditions to a labour force desirous of employment. The growth of Larkin's ITGWU was a threat to this privileged position and therefore had ignited a reactionary, protective instinct among Dublin's employers. In effect, they had recognised the need to stamp out the challenge to their interests which Larkin had encouraged. In this sense, the Dublin lockout was a seminal moment when the interests of each group spurred them to assert their rights and brought them into conflict. Such was the youthfulness of the new Irish trade union militancy that the outcome of this clash would determine the future relationship between labour and employers. With these stakes, the lockout had a lot resting on it for both parties, and therefore it was keenly fought on both sides.

SOURCE 8

From an article in the *Caledonian Mercury* about the trial of the Tolpuddle Martyrs, published 29 March 1834. The six named labourers were all found guilty of unlawful oath-making and were transported to Australia.

At the Dorchester Assizes on Monday, six labourers, names J. Loveless, J. Loveless, T. Stanfield, J. Stanfield, J. Hammett and J. Brine were indicted under the 57th Geo. III c.19 sec.25, for having administered and unlawful oath to John Lock. The prisoners belonged to the "Friendly Society of Agricultural Labourers," which contained provisions among its rules, that if any master attempted to reduce the wages of his workmen, those who were members of the society should quit, and that no member should divulge any secrets, or violate the same; and that if he did, his crime would be communicated to all the lodges in the country, and he would be hunted from the society of the Unionists. Two men, named Lock and Legg, gave evidence that they had joined the Union, and that they were blindfolded in a room at a house in Tolpuddle, and sworn to strike for wages when other did, and to wish that their "souls might be plunged into eternity" if they divulged the secrets of the order.

SOURCE 9

William Longston describing the use of 'The Document' by employers in evidence given to the committee on the bill to regulate the labour of children in the mills and factories of the United Kingdom, 1832.

The operatives were to sign the following words, or not be employed; and thousands of them did so, and were obliged to do so.

'We, the undersigned, agree with Messrs. --- that we will work for them on the following terms;

We declare that we do not belong to the society called the 'Union', or any other society for the support of turn-outs, or which has for its object any interference with the rules laid down for the government of mills or manufactories.

We agree with our said masters, that we will not become members of, or be connected with, any such society, while we remain in our present employ.

That we will not, directly, or indirectly, subscribe or contribute to any such society, or to any turn-out hands whatsoever.

That we will give a fortnight's notice previous to leaving our employ and we will observe all the other rules of this mill, and all special agreements that we may enter into with our masters.

And if we are discovered to act contrary to the above agreement, each of us so offending will forfeit a sum equal to a fortnight's wages; and our masters shall have power to deduct the same from our wages, or discharge us from their employ without any notice, at their own option.'

THINKING HISTORICALLY   Cause and consequence (6c)

Connections

Sources 3, 6, 8 and 9 all provide information on the organisation of labour.

Read Source 8.

1 How might the actions and goals of the Tolpuddle Martyrs be seen as similar to those of the ITGWU?

Read Source 6 and Source 9.

2 What tools were being used by employers to attempt to control the organisation of labour in England in the 1830s?

3 How is this similar to the response of Irish employers in 1913?

Read Source 3.

4 To what extent had the position of some employers with regards to organised labour changed over the course of the 19th century?

5 Why it is important for historians to see these links across time and be able to explain how causal factors can influence situations much later in time?

ACTIVITY
KNOWLEDGE CHECK

The Dublin lockout

1 a) Write out a list of events that you feel were prominent during the lockout in 1913.

   b) Organise these events under the headings: 'Advantageous to the employers'; 'Advantageous to the workers'.

   c) Briefly explain the reasons for your choices.

2 Read Source 6 on page 164 and suggest how valuable it is for understanding the motivations of Irish workers during the lockout.

HOW IMPORTANT WAS THE ROLE PLAYED BY BRITISH TRADES UNIONS IN IRISH INDUSTRIAL AFFAIRS?

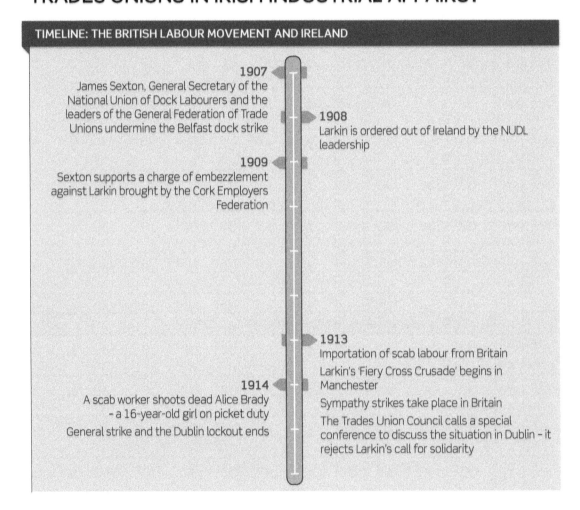

TIMELINE: THE BRITISH LABOUR MOVEMENT AND IRELAND

1907
James Sexton, General Secretary of the National Union of Dock Labourers and the leaders of the General Federation of Trade Unions undermine the Belfast dock strike

1908
Larkin is ordered out of Ireland by the NUDL leadership

1909
Sexton supports a charge of embezzlement against Larkin brought by the Cork Employers Federation

1913
Importation of scab labour from Britain

Larkin's 'Fiery Cross Crusade' begins in Manchester

Sympathy strikes take place in Britain

The Trades Union Council calls a special conference to discuss the situation in Dublin – it rejects Larkin's call for solidarity

1914
A scab worker shoots dead Alice Brady – a 16-year-old girl on picket duty

General strike and the Dublin lockout ends

The role of British trade unions in the attempt to unionise workers in Ireland and in the Dublin general strike

Early British interest in Ireland
The British labour movement had always been connected with Irish labour. Since the creation of the British Trades Union Congress (TUC) in 1868, Irish workers had always been represented alongside their British counterparts, and together they had attempted to secure benefits for each labour force

either side of the Irish Sea. In 1894, however, Irish labour struck out on its own, establishing its own Congress, having concluded that their interests were increasingly becoming marginalised as British industry expanded. After this year, Irish labour adopted a more independent outlook and it was only when Larkin travelled to Ireland in 1907 that the two movements converged once more.

Larkin was a member of the Liverpool-based NUDL and he had been sent to Ireland to organise Irish dockers. With his arrival, the British labour movement began to reach out to Irish workers, and for Larkin such a development was encouraging in terms of collective solidarity. As hopeful as this prospect was, Larkin found himself undermined by the conservatism of the British trade union officials. As a syndicalist, Larkin was motivated by militant, collective action to achieve a better deal for workers and this conflicted with the interests of union officials who envisioned a more collaborative approach with employers. Their agenda was to unionise Irish labour to strengthen their bargaining hand, but Larkin's militancy threatened this objective. Consequently, in the years after 1907 British labour officials sought to temper Larkin's activism. This was first evidenced by the successful attempt by James Sexton of the NUDL and the leaders of another British-based organisation, the General Federation of Trade Unions, to bring the Belfast dock strike to an end.

The conservativism of these individuals undermined early attempts at unionisation in Ireland at the start of the 20th century, perhaps most clearly seen in the city of Cork where Larkin had travelled to arrange further union membership in 1908. Here, Larkin was formally asked to leave the country by his bosses in the NUDL, When he refused, Sexton supported a charge of conspiracy to defraud which had been brought against Larkin by the city's employers' federation in 1909. On the evidence given by Sexton, Larkin was found guilty in June 1910 and received a one-year prison sentence. By actively supporting the employers against Larkin and his attempts to organise trade unions in Ireland, it is clear that British trade unionist leaders, or at least several of them, were hindering the development of a strong Irish organisation out of reactionary fears that Larkin's militancy might affect their own positions.

The British labour movement and the Dublin lockout

British trade unionism had been on the periphery of Ireland's working class dispute with Dublin employers throughout late 1913. It had become aware of the situation as early as August following the police baton charge in O'Connell Street and the subsequent articles published in the *Daily Herald*. The events of that weekend had stimulated a significant sympathy for the plight of the Dublin workers and in the following months food parcels and financial aid were collected on their behalf. For those on strike this was welcome support. However, following the importation of scab labour, the ITGWU needed even more tangible support from the British unions if it was to survive the lockout.

Jim Larkin believed that worker solidarity was the key to success and therefore he embarked upon a tour of Britain to try to encourage the blacking of Dublin traffic – goods and personnel travelling there and back – which would consequently deny Murphy and his allies any scab labour from that country, and also disrupt trade. The tour became known as the 'Fiery Cross Crusade' and it began on 16 November 1913 at the Free Trade Hall in Manchester. At this meeting, he described the situation in Ireland, acknowledged the financial support that British workers had already offered and then urged those present to stand by the men and women of Dublin and not agree to work for, or handle goods from, that city's businesses. He gave similar speeches in London, Leeds, Liverpool, Sheffield and Bristol. At each he encouraged solidarity with the Irish workers and was met with tremendous enthusiasm by the rank and file members present. The tour enjoyed considerable success since Larkin had a strong following in Britain, and as early as 10 November 1913, more than 130 British Nation Union of Railwaymen (NUR) branches had called for joint action with the transport workers and miners to support the Dublin workers. In South Wales two Associated Society of Locomotive Engineers and Firemen (ASLEF) members, drivers James and Reynolds, were dismissed for refusing to move Dublin goods. Following the sacking more than 30,000 railwaymen went out on an unofficial strike in support of the two members.

The growing support amongst British workers for their counterparts in Dublin presented a difficult challenge for their trade union leaders who were keen to build relations with employers rather than be tarnished with radicalism in the manner of Larkin. These men used the same tactics that James Sexton had used during the Belfast dock strike in 1907, preferring to ingratiate themselves with employers so that negotiation would be more achievable instead of using combative industrial action. To address this issue, on 18 November the Parliamentary Committee of the Trades Union Congress (TUC) called a special conference, due to be held in December, to consider the events taking place in Dublin.

Larkin was encouraged by this action and undertook to help convince British trade union leaders to support his cause in Ireland by appealing to their rank and file members in a manifesto which was published in the *Daily Herald* on 22 November. In this document, he encouraged the ordinary worker to demand of their leaders definite solidarity with the Irish and a refusal to be talked out of such action, believing that 1913 was a chance to empower unionism and the working classes of each nation.

SOURCE 10

From Jim Larkin's manifesto to the rank and file members of the British labour movement published in the *Daily Herald* on 22 November 1913.

When you give instructions to those you have elected you mean that they must carry them out; that you, as organised workers, will no longer blackleg on your fellow workers, no matter what Conciliation Boards may say, no matter what contracts may bind you to. There is no clause in a contract, there is no rule laid down by any Conciliation Board that I know of, which compels a man to be a scab. A Trade Union, when it makes an agreement with an employer, makes agreements on the understanding that they are dealing with men who can carry out a bargain made. They do not arrange things for non-union men, but they arrange as union men to work under union conditions and to insist that to blackleg is against the very basic principles of Trade Unionism. Therefore, tell your leaders now and every day until December 9th, and raise your voice upon that date to tell them that they are not there as apologists for the shortcomings of the capitalist system, that they are not there to assist the employers in helping to defeat any such section of workers striving to live, nor to act as a break on the wheel of progress. Tell them that this bloody warfare in Dublin must come to an end, this sacrificing of men, women and children much cease, and if they are not prepared to bring it to an end, then you of the rank and file will see to it that 'finis' shall be written. I leave the cause of the Dublin workers in your strong hands, knowing that your heart and brain will direct them to do the work that is required to lift us from the morass of poverty and degradation, in full confidence that you at long last are realising your powers and that you mean to exercise your powers, and as in the beginning, so we shall continue. Let us make 1913 the year in a new industrial epoch. The greater unionism gives us something to live for.

Yours Fraternally,

Jim Larkin

The Trades Union Congress Special Conference, 9 December 1913

The conference when it convened was not as Larkin expected. He had anticipated a majority of rank and file delegates, but the conference was overwhelmingly union officials with a conservative agenda who wanted an end to militancy. These leaders were concerned for the reputations of their own unions, which in the rank and file were unofficially in favour of supporting more direct militant action on behalf of the workers in Dublin. Fearful that such growing support could jeopardise the positive relationship that they had generated with British employers, British officials sought to undermine Larkin and force an end to the lockout themselves. During the subsequent proceedings, Larkin was criticised for his outwardly hostile approach and his attacks on union officials generally. Such was the antipathy towards Larkin that when a motion by the prominent union leader Ben Tillett was issued condemning his actions it was carried almost unanimously with only six delegates voting against it. This was arguably a personal attack against Larkin rather than an official judgement on the lockout. However, a further motion was proposed by J.W. Kelly which offered no further help to the ITGWU and authorised reopening negotiations with the Dublin employers. To this proposal an amendment was suggested by the Gasworkers' representative Jack Jones regarding the issue of an ultimatum to the employers: that if no satisfactory terms could be agreed then Dublin 'tainted' goods would not be handled. This was a lifeline as far as Larkin was concerned as it would offer some 'muscle' for union negotiators in talks with the employers. However, it was voted down 203,000 for and 2,280,000 against.

The outcome of the conference was that the ITGWU and the Dublin workers out on strike were left isolated by the officials within the British labour movement. These men had sought to undermine militant unionism having been challenged by Larkin's passionate calls for solidarity which had emboldened the British workers and potentially threatened their own relationship with British employers. Consequently, in their attempt to maintain their own relationship they were prepared to cut the Dublin workers adrift, offering them no support beyond sympathy and food aid.

SOURCE 11

From Jim Larkin writing about the TUC special conference on 9 December 1913 in which he was personally attacked and denied industrial support. It was published in the nationalist paper the *Freeman's Journal* on 10 December 1913.

I know the men we have to deal with. All they want to do is delay the negotiations in order that they may weed the men out. The ban against the union has not been withdrawn. The employers of Dublin are neither truthful nor honest, and the only way to deal with them is to deal with them with a strong hand. We have always been able to do that... We say all your money is useful, but money never won a strike. Money can't win a strike. Discipline, solidarity, knowledge of the position and the strength to carry out your will – these are the things.

They could win the Dublin strike tomorrow if they wanted it, and if they didn't mean it they should shut up or put up. If the Union men of this country wanted to win the strike all they had to say was that Dublin should be a self-contained town just now; that she should live upon herself, with the exception that food would be taken in to all the men, women and children in the trenches. All the money and all the leaders would not beat the men they were fighting. He had said hard things, and they had said harder and more bitter things against him. He had done according to his lights. He did not get any thousand a year or any five hundred a year. He had worked in the limelight and the dark had given service that he made no apology to any man there for. He was told coming there that they were going to pass a resolution condemning Larkin and telling him to get out of the road, and that they would settle the strike. You try that on, Larkin will not get out of the road. Larkin will go down fighting.

The impact of the TUC decision

The decision by the British Trades' Union Congress not to support Larkin's call for solidarity left the ITGWU and its workers in a vulnerable position. Isolated from its fellow trade unionists, the organisation continued to resist the lockout and maintained its strike action. However, it was increasingly difficult to maintain an effective resistance with the growing numbers of scab workers arriving from Britain throughout December 1913. Larkin had hoped to secure the support of the British unions, which he felt would have forced the employers to back down since they would have had no source of alternative labour and would have suffered the disruption of trade with one of their largest partners. Without this strong position, the ITGWU had become marginalised. Even though British rank and file members remained enthusiastic towards the plight of the Dublin workers – Larkin still drew an audience of 4,000 in Glasgow the day after the conference – their unions would not countenance any official action beyond donations. Faced with this reality, the ITGWU lost much of its determination and secret advice was given to its members to return to work if they could ensure reasonable terms from their employers. From mid-December, some workers began to go back. However, for the majority the strike continued.

The final months of the strike were desperate and over the Christmas period clashes between strikers and scabs increased, with the one-sided consequences that had characterised the entire dispute. On 11 December, a scab fired into a hostile crowd of picketers but actually wounded the vice-chairman of the Port and Docks Board and, although arrested, was set free. Four days later a scab was fined £2 for firing his revolver in public, while perhaps most tragically, 16-year-old Alice Brady was shot on 18 December and died of her wounds on 2 January 1914. These unfortunate events illustrate the continued high tensions that existed in Dublin even as the strike was quickly disintegrating – the determination of the employers remained absolute while the workers were increasingly desperate to get something out of their crumbling defence. Eventually, however, Larkin had to concede and on 18 January 1914 the ITGWU formally gave instructions for its members to return to work on whatever conditions they could secure for themselves. The general strike was over.

The return to work

The return to work was a gradual process as many were reluctant to go back on the unfavourable terms that many employers were offering. Jacob's Biscuits, for example, only took back 100 of the 672 ITGWU men and cut their wages by between 2 and 4 shillings a week. Equally, many workers could not get their jobs back having been **blacklisted** by their employers and therefore found themselves worse off than before the strike began. In terms of working conditions therefore, the dispute failed to achieve any considerable benefits for the Irish working class. Although the ITGWU was able to survive, the employers of Dublin had won a resounding victory for their interests in that city. They had taken on and defeated the country's largest and most militant trade union, which consequently meant that they had an even more dominant position than the one they had always held.

KEY TERM

Blacklisted
A term applied to someone who has been denied a privilege for a particular reason.

SOURCE 12 From an article written by James Connolly in the *Irish Worker* newspaper on 14 March 1914, describing the manner in which employers treated returning workers after the Dublin lockout. The example he uses is the Jacob's Biscuit factory.

When the girls apply for re-employment this manager after brutally insulting them before the scabs whom he brings in in order that he may parade the applicants before them, compels them to submit to his examination of their clothes, their hats, skirts and blouses, to submit while he pinches their arms, and examines their physical condition and that all through his degrading examination he keeps up a running fire of insulting remarks of which the following are a fair example:- 'So you had to come back when you were starving'

The outcome of the failed general strike and defeat of the ITGWU, therefore, saw few tangible changes that benefited the working class in Dublin or the rest of the country. Militancy had been defeated and Larkin's attempt to use solidarity to enhance the position of workers was unrealised. There had been a glimmer of hope in the early months, but this was quick to fade when the employers rallied together and were able to use Larkin's own tactics against him. The failure of the British labour movement's leaders to offer the support required to counter this strategy proved to be the decisive blow that extinguished the flame of Larkinism, and on 24 October 1914 he travelled to America, not to return to Ireland until 1923.

The failure of Britain's trade unionist leaders to support Larkin and the ITGWU was a momentous personal blow for Larkin because it undermined his central belief in collective solidarity, and it significantly weakened his trade union. This was especially hurtful since he had immense respect for the British labour movement and genuinely believed in the power that it could wield. In this respect, the perceived betrayal he and the Irish workers suffered at the hands of British union officials was particularly hard. Not only was this betrayal bitterly disappointing from an ideological point of view, but it left his membership vulnerable to punitive measures from Dublin's employers. These were hard felt and many ITWGU members struggled to return to work on the same conditions they had before the strike. In this regard, Britain's labour leaders had cost them dearly.

Conclusion

In the years 1907–14, Ireland witnessed a growth in trade union militancy in an attempt to offer the working class of the country a means to improve their own situation. Living conditions for this class were very poor – especially in Dublin where a growth in population was not adequately provided for and left families living in squalid, cramped accommodation that was often unsafe and certainly unhygienic. This experience was enhanced by the generally low wages that Ireland's employers paid to their workforce. These wages were often barely enough to cover rent and food, and children of the poor would be seen searching bins for additional sustenance while wearing sacking in lieu of an overcoat in the wintertime. The general condition of Ireland's working class contrasted sharply with the affluent employers who benefited from their labour. To reconcile these differences, the socialist trade union activist Jim Larkin undertook in 1907 to organise the country's working class into strong unions that could force a change in employment conditions. His belief was that through collective, worker solidarity employers could be made to raise wages. Early attempts to organise strike action offered positive results for this attempt although more conservative union leaders were quick to undermine his militancy. In 1909, his own Irish Transport and General Workers' Union was founded and spread quickly throughout the country, and especially in Dublin where conditions were arguably most bleak. In 1913, the combative nature of Larkin and his powerful union encouraged employers, under the direction of William Martin Murphy, to try to break the organisation so as to ensure the interests of business. These men initiated a lockout against members of the ITGWU and, supported by the government, they were able to gain the upper hand. Reaching out for help from the British labour movement, Larkin became the victim once more of conservative union leaders who refused to offer any assistance beyond financial aid. This was the death knell for Irish industrial militancy and by 1914 the employers had broken the union.

A Level Exam-Style Question Section B

'The lockout was defeated because of the failure of the British labour movement.'

How far do you agree with this statement? (20 marks)

Tip

When answering this question you should consider the dynamics within the British labour movement – did the whole movement fail to support the lockout?

THINKING HISTORICALLY Cause and consequence (7c)

The value of historical explanations

Historical explanations derive from the historian who is investigating the past. Differences in explanations are usually about what the historians think is significant. Historians bring their own attitudes and perspectives to historical questions and see history in the light of these. It is therefore perfectly acceptable to have very different explanations of the same historical phenomenon. The way we judge historical accounts is by looking at how well argued they are and how well evidence has been deployed to support the argument.

Approach A	Approach B	Approach C
The Dublin lockout was caused by the actions of individual men who held opposing ideas and refused to yield any ground to the other.	*The Dublin lockout was an inevitable climax to growing divisions within the Irish economic system. The gap between rich and poor was widening at such a rate that some kind of explosion was going to happen.*	*The attempt to improve working conditions is a natural and evolutionary action taken at a time when the economic environment has developed sufficiently to absorb any change that is necessary.*

Work in groups of between three and five. (You will need an even number of groups in the class.)

1 In your groups, devise a brief explanation of the Dublin lockout of between 200 and 300 words that matches one of the approaches above. Present your explanation to another group, who will decide on two things:

a) Which of the approaches is each explanation trying to demonstrate?

b) Considering the structure and the quality of the argument and use of evidence, which is the best of the three explanations?

2 If you choose a 'best' explanation, should you discount the other two? Explain your answer.

ACTIVITY
KNOWLEDGE CHECK

The role of the British labour movement

1 How did the British labour movement positively affect the Irish working class?

2 Why did the Trades' Union Congress not support the ITGWU in 1913?

3 Discuss whether this decision reflects the attitudes of the rank and file membership of British trade unions.

4 Read Source 10. What does it suggest Larkin hoped to achieve with British Labour support?

 WIDER READING

Greaves, C.D. *The Irish Transport and General Workers' Union: The Formative Years*, Dublin (1982)

Nevin, D. *James Larkin: Lion of the Fold*, Dublin (1998)

Newsinger, J. *Rebel City: Larkin, Connolly and the Dublin Labour Movement*, Merlin Press (2004)

Newsinger, J. *Jim Larkin and the Great Dublin Lockout of 1913*, Bookmarks Publications (2013)

O'Connor, E. *A Labour History of Ireland 1824–2000*, University College Dublin Press (2011)

ACTIVITY
SUMMARY

Trade unionism in Ireland

1 Outline the reasons for the growth of trade unionism in Ireland between the years 1907 and 1914.

2 Using these reasons answer the questions below.

a) How important was the role of individuals in promoting a confrontation such as the Dublin lockout?

b) Why were the reasons you came up with insufficient to win the lockout by 1914?

c) In your opinion what was the main cause for the ITGWU's defeat by 1914?

Preparing for your A Level Paper 3 exam

Advance planning

Draw up a timetable for your revision and try to keep to it. Spend longer on topics that you have found difficult, and revise them several times. Aim to be confident about all aspects of your Paper 3 work, because this will ensure that you have a choice of questions in Sections B and C.

Paper 3 Overview

Paper 3	Time: 2 hours 15 minutes	
Section A	Answer one compulsory question for the option studied, assessing source analysis and evaluation skills.	20 marks
Section B	Answer one question from a choice of two on an aspect in depth for the option studied.	20 marks
Section C	Answer one question from a choice of two on an aspect in breadth for the option studied	20 marks
	Total marks =	60 marks

Section A questions

There is no choice of question in Section A. You will be referred to a source of about 350 words long, printed in a Sources Booklet. The source will be a primary source or one that is contemporary to the period you have studied, and will relate to one of the key topics in the Aspect of Depth. You will be expected to analyse and evaluate the source in its historical context. The question will ask you to assess the value of the source for revealing something specific about the period, and will expect you to explain your answer, using the source, the information given about its origin and your own knowledge about the historical context.

Section B questions

You will have a choice of one from two questions in Section B. They will aim to assess your understanding of one or more of the key topics in the Aspect of Depth you have studied. Questions may relate to a single, momentous year, but will normally cover longer periods. You will be required to write an essay evaluating an aspect of the period. You may be asked about change and continuity, similarity and difference, consequences, significance or causation, or you may be given a quotation and asked to explain how far you agree with it. All questions will require you to reach a substantiated judgement.

Section C questions

You will have a choice of one from two questions in Section C. Questions will relate to the themes of the Aspects of Breadth you have studied, and will aim to assess your understanding of change over time. They will cover a period of not less than 100 years and will relate either to the factors that brought about change, or the extent of change over the period, or patterns of change as demonstrated by turning points.

Use of time

- Do not write solidly for 45 minutes on each question. For Section B and C answers, you should spend a few minutes working out what the question is asking you to do and drawing up a plan of your answer. This is especially important for Section C answers, which cover an extended period of time.

- For Section A, it is essential that you have a clear understanding of the content of the source and its historical context. Pay particular attention to the provenance: was the author in a position to know what he or she was writing about? Read it carefully and underline important points. You might decide to spend up to 10 minutes reading the source and drawing up your plan, and 35 minutes writing your answer.

Preparing for your A Level exams

Paper 3: A Level sample answer with comments

Section A

These questions require you to analyse and evaluate source material with respect to its historical context.

For these questions remember to:

- look at the evidence given in the source and consider how the source could be used in differing ways to provide historical understanding
- use your knowledge of the historical context to discuss any limitations the source may have
- use your historical understanding to evaluate the source, considering how much weight you would give to its argument
- come to a judgement on the overall value of the source in respect to the question.

Study Source 6 (Chapter 3, page 75) before you answer this question.

Assess the value of the source for revealing the tensions in Ireland over Catholic emancipation and the part played by Daniel O'Connell in attempting to deal with these tensions.

Explain your answer, using the source, the information given about its origin and your own knowledge about the historical context. (20 marks)

Average student answer

Source 6 is very useful for revealing the tensions in Ireland over Catholic emancipation and Daniel O'Connell's role in dealing with them because it is a source produced by O'Connell himself. It is his election speech where he is challenging the existing rules about the ban on Catholics sitting in parliament and so it is central to understanding the tensions in the country.

This has some focus on the question demand but the comment about the source being 'central to understanding the tensions' is not really qualified sufficiently and is more of an assertion.

The source is O'Connell's election speech in the by-election for County Clare which took place in 1828 – two years after the general election because his opponent Vesey Fitzgerald had been appointed to a new cabinet position and needed to stand once more. As a source to consider the tensions over Catholic emancipation, therefore, it is really useful because it is focused entirely upon the issue of voting and standing for parliament – the latter being that which Catholics were not allowed to do. In standing as a Catholic, Daniel O'Connell was challenging the penal laws which barred Catholics from enjoying the same rights as Protestants. The fact that he was doing this suggests that there were significant tensions in Ireland over the issue and, therefore, the source is useful because it shows up these tensions quite effectively and also how O'Connell was trying to exploit them in order to confront them.

The points in this paragraph do address the question but not in an explicit way that conveys real focus on the demand. There is some useful contextual material and knowledge displayed, but this is not clearly linked to the point about 'showing up tensions' which is the clearly focused element and which could itself be more developed.

The source is also valuable for considering the tensions in Ireland over emancipation because it is a speech to a public audience – O'Connell refers to 'my fellow countrymen', and this would suggest that what he says would be relevant to that audience. Namely that if he talks about the inability of Catholics to sit in parliament then this is something that the audience would agree with – since he is trying to win their votes. In this sense the source is good because it offers some understanding about how widespread the issue was and, although we do not know how many people he was speaking to, as it is likely to have been a political rally it is reasonable to suggest that the numbers would be quite large.

> This paragraph offers some useful inferences and tries to link them to the content of the source. The material is focused on the value of the source and some provenance is considered in building the point. However, it could be more thoroughly explained.

Furthermore, O'Connell was the leader of the Catholic Association which was set up in 1823 to agitate for reforms to the existing laws and, therefore, the source offers a good insight into the manner of that agitation. Rather than using violence or aggression, O'Connell used constitutional methods such as standing for election. From this it is reasonable to infer that there were other options available but O'Connell felt peaceful means more appropriate; suggesting that because emancipation was quite controversial and tensions were quite high, the demand for reform could have been violent and actually his efforts were intended to avoid such confrontation. In this sense the source is valuable because it not only shows the methods employed by prominent figures to achieve their aims, but also offers some indication as to the extent of the issue.

> This paragraph uses some knowledge about the source's context to develop an inference which is quite appropriate, if a little undeveloped and in need of greater explanation. There is an attempt to focus clearly on the demand in the final sentence.

Overall the source is very useful because it was clearly located at the time of the Catholic emancipation issue – it was produced in 1828 and emancipation was passed in 1829, and it is from a central figure in that debate. It offers some good insight into the methods employed by those seeking to exploit the tensions over emancipation and also implies that that issue was especially prominent during the 1820s. While it is only the view of one man, it is likely he is speaking to a large crowd and, therefore, it is still really valuable for a broader picture.

> The concluding paragraph is a broad sweep of the overall response. It offers new ideas about the source's limitations towards the end and this should really be included in the body as part of the evaluation.

Verdict

This is an average answer because:

- it lacks the substantive judgement the question demands
- although the source's provenance is considered, it lacks detailed explanation or development

- it does not come to a strong reasoned judgement.

Use the feedback on this essay to rewrite it, making as many improvements as you can.

Paper 3: A Level sample answer with comments

Section A

These questions require you to analyse and evaluate source material with respect to its historical context.

For these questions remember to:

- look at the evidence given in the source and consider how the source could be used in differing ways to provide historical understanding
- use your knowledge of the historical context to discuss any limitations the source may have
- use your historical understanding to evaluate the source, considering how much weight you would give to its argument
- come to a judgement on the overall value of the source in respect to the question.

Study Source 6 (Chapter 3, page 75) before you answer this question.

Assess the value of the source for revealing the tensions in Ireland over Catholic emancipation and the part played by Daniel O'Connell in attempting to deal with these tensions.

Explain your answer, using the source, the information given about its origin and your own knowledge about the historical context. (20 marks)

Strong student answer

The source is very valuable for determining the tensions in Ireland over Catholic emancipation and Daniel O'Connells's role in dealing with these tensions because it is clearly focused upon those themes. Emancipation was perhaps the biggest issue in Ireland during the 1820s and O'Connell was the main figure in addressing its surrounding tensions. Since the source is from O'Connell himself and specifically about the issue in question, the source has a lot of useful insight which generally outweighs the limitations of it representing the attitude of only one man.

Like any source, the speech from O'Connell has limitations: it is a subjective commentary from a Catholic intent on addressing the historical issue of Catholic discrimination that had been in place since 1688 and affected him and his co-religionists. In this sense the material offers a one-sided view of the tensions in Ireland from the position of Catholics themselves and does not immediately present a rounded impression of the broader feeling in Ireland. On this basis there is, therefore, some weakness to the source's value overall. However, this is arguably offset by the insight it offers as to the Catholic position specifically. On this theme the source is invaluable because it comes from O'Connell himself. As the leader of the Catholic Association which was established in 1823 for the express purpose of achieving emancipation it, therefore, offers a clear impression of not only his own attitude, but also how he intended to address the tensions among his fellow Catholics about the issue. On this point it is evident from the tone and content of the speech that he is clearly unhappy about the existing discrimination and intended to use the broader ill-feeling towards it to institute change.

This introduction offers a clear argument which is related to the question demand. It also identifies some broad features of the source quality which it uses to support the general argument.

This paragraph considers the source quality effectively and uses the provenance to develop a clear line of argument that is well developed and focused appropriately.

This attempt was via a constitutional approach – standing as a candidate in the County Clare by-election against the incumbent MP, Vesey Fitzgerald, in 1828 following his appointment to a cabinet position in that year. Such an appointment at the time necessitated a by-election, and O'Connell's decision to stand against him in it offers a significant comment about the extent of wider tensions for several reasons – not least the cost of such a challenge. Financially, to stand would be quite an expense so the decision to do so would not have been taken lightly and the cost would have been borne by the association through the monthly subscriptions of its members. In this sense although the speech is only from O'Connell's perspective, it is reasonable to infer that it reflected the views of a wider Catholic community. Furthermore, by standing in an election, O'Connell was reaching out to the public on the issue of emancipation and this would have been intended to both promote the concern and register the Catholic community's demand for it. By promoting the issue the source is, therefore, very useful as a lens through which to consider the extent of feeling in Ireland in regard to Catholic emancipation.

> Appropriate knowledge is used to strengthen this paragraph and help develop a valid inference about wider tensions. Including some figures as to the membership size of the Catholic Association would enhance the point being made here.

Although the source is primarily and obviously from the position of a Catholic, there is the opportunity to elicit some idea of the government position on the issue of emancipation. The source comments on how Fitzgerald claimed to be a 'friend of the Catholics' which in one sense can be dismissed as electoral rhetoric. However, in another it could suggest that the government felt as though it was sympathetic towards Catholics and that emancipation was, therefore, not a significant issue worthy of dispute. This is quite a stretch. However, it would also support the idea that there were indeed significant tensions – if one group did not take seriously the views of another then the issue becomes much greater. On this basis the speech is a valuable source evidencing tensions and also how those tensions might have been exacerbated.

> These paragraphs develop some broader ideas about the tensions in Ireland and make the answer more rounded. They include some useful evidence taken from the source to help support the points being made and also clearly consider the quality of the source.

Finally the quality of the source is still good despite being one-sided: O'Connell was a prominent public figure in Ireland throughout the 1820s and was the cause of the agitation for reform. In this sense it is reasonable to suggest that he was the cause of the tensions that existed – or at least the manner of them being vocalised. On this point in terms of understanding the tensions, the source explains the motives of the instigator of them, which is perhaps one of the most useful forms of evidence to consider. Additionally Catholic emancipation was passed in 1829 following the Clare election and the realisation from government that something was necessary. The speech came only months before this decision and, therefore, is also well placed to convey valuable information as to this action.

Overall, therefore, although the source is limited in that it comes from a Catholic who is the main cause of tension, this subjectivity is also its strength because it offers a clear idea as to how O'Connell used the tensions to stimulate reform, while the public nature of the source offers a noticeably collective impression which reduces the criticism that it is only the opinion of one man.

> This is a clear and well thought out conclusion. It presents a judgement that has largely been substantiated in the body of the response.

Verdict

This is a strong answer because:

- it focuses explicitly upon the source when developing an answer
- the provenance of the source is consistently used to develop well-considered points
- it reaches a clearly substantiated judgement that has been justified in the body.

Paper 3: A Level sample answer with comments

Section B

These questions require you to show your understanding of a period in depth. They will ask you about a quite specific period of time and require you to make a substantiated judgement about a specific aspect you have studied.

For these questions remember to:

- organise your essay and communicate it in a manner that is clear and comprehensible
- use historical knowledge to analyse and evaluate the key aspect of the question
- make a balanced argument that weighs up differing opinions
- make a substantiated overall judgement on the question.

How accurate is it to say that the Land Act of 1870 was largely unsuccessful in answering the land question in Ireland between 1870 and 1880? (20 marks)

Average student answer

The land question was a very complex one in Ireland and it was not easily solved until after the Land War ended in 1882. Given that this was the case, the Land Act of 1870 only went some way to address the problem but it was not enough in its own right.

The land question was a very important one in Ireland because the majority of the country earned its living from the land and ownership was, therefore, very significant. Most of it belonged to Protestant landlords who had benefited from the Penal Laws in the 17th century which did not allow Catholics to buy land and as a result they became big landowners in their own right who simply rented land to the larger Catholic population. This was quite controversial in the 19th century because it meant that Catholics were always at the mercy of Protestant landlords who could set whatever rental price they desired, resulting in many Catholic tenant farmers struggling to manage. This was made worse by the evictions that subsequently took place if tenants could not afford to pay and by 1870 there was considerable discontent among Ireland's agricultural community. This had manifested itself in the form of a Tenant League which was an informal grouping of farmers into a loose organisation for the express aim of demanding land reform. This group was quite vocal and a Land Conference was held in Dublin during 1870 to discuss the issue of land. From this meeting Gladstone got ideas for his Land Act that was passed later in the year.

The Act itself was a great step forward for Irish tenant farmers because it attempted to address their concerns by formalising 'tenant right' and allowing tenants to claim compensation for the improvements they made upon the land in the event of their eviction from it. This was significant progress for the farmers because it was the first time that the British government had actually intervened on their behalf to try to makes things better. In this sense the Act was quite successful because it showed the farmers that the government was thinking of them and was attempting to help them out. The extent to which the actual terms of the Act were successful, however, is open to debate. Firstly the 'tenant right' was only formalised in areas such as Ulster where it had already existed in principle and nowhere else. Secondly it was very difficult to claim compensation after an eviction because it was a long-winded process and also not easy to identify the tangible improvements that many tenants had made. In these cases, therefore, the Act had significant limitations which did not really help the farmers despite the anticipated benefits it had initially promised.

This introduction offers some general argument that is clearly focused on the question demand. However, it is very limited in terms of introducing debate.

This paragraph has lots of useful, relevant, knowledge. However, it is not developed in a particularly analytical way. Rather than relating the material to the set question, it tells a story about the origin of the Land Act that was passed in 1870.

This paragraph starts to focus on the question more clearly by considering the Act itself and its provisions. There is some development of argument about the limits of these but it could be strengthened by using some examples to support the commentary.

It was also very clear that the Act was insufficient to solve the land question because after 1873 depression started to set in and, in 1877, Irish agriculture started to suffer once more. This resulted in a decline in the price of agriculture produce which consequently affected Ireland's tenant farmers because it meant a drop in their income and, therefore, potential eviction from their land. In 1879 the situation got even worse as harvests had been poor for a third year running and people began to fear famine once more. In County Donegal a 'mini-famine' actually took place which saw people go hungry rather than die of starvation. However, this added to the re-emergence of discontent. This manifested itself in the form of the Irish Land League which was set up by a local man from County Mayo, Michael Davitt, in 1879. Davitt was in favour of complete land reform and felt that the 1870 Act was not good enough and, therefore, it was his intention to force greater reform. He did this using the help of Charles Stewart Parnell, the leader of Ireland's Home Rule Party, who was a well-known public figure. Together they organised massive rallies for the farmers which preached boycotting Irish landlords and even the non-payment of rent. This action took off throughout rural Ireland and quickly became known as the 'Land Wars', clearly emphasising how unsuccessful the 1870 Land Act had been.

Given that the decade ended with the beginning of a figurative 'war' in the Irish countryside, it is reasonable to suggest that the 1870 Land Act was not entirely successful. This had been intended to solve the land question but instead had caused a much bigger debate which spilled out into violence after 1880.

> There is an attempt to assess the Land Act once more, which is developed through a wider consideration of the time frame set. There is good general knowledge which could be strengthened with a little more precision – for example, how many people were broadly involved in the Land Wars? This would also help develop the overall point about discontent.

> A short but appropriate conclusion which could be elaborated upon a little further.

Verdict

This is an average answer because:

- it is quite narrative throughout
- although own knowledge is used in support of the answer, this material could be more precise
- it does not evenly consider a counterargument.

Use the feedback on this essay to rewrite it, making as many improvements as you can.

Paper 3: A Level sample answer with comments

Section B

These questions require you to show your understanding of a period in depth. They will ask you about a quite specific period of time and require you to make a substantiated judgement about a specific aspect you have studied.

For these questions remember to:

- organise your essay and communicate it in a manner that is clear and comprehensible
- use historical knowledge to analyse and evaluate the key aspect of the question
- make a balanced argument that weighs up differing opinions
- make a substantiated overall judgement on the question.

How accurate is it to say that the Land Act of 1870 was largely unsuccessful in answering the land question in Ireland between 1870 and 1880? (20 marks)

Strong student answer

To a certain extent, it is reasonable to suggest the Land Act of 1870 was unsuccessful in solving Ireland's land question because at the end of the decade there was a renewed land-based problem which was a substantial threat to stability. However, given the difficulty and deep-rooted nature of the question, the legislation of 1870 was a well-intentioned attempt to at least begin searching for a lasting solution.

Land reform in Ireland was a complicated undertaking because it had such an impact on great swathes of the population. More than 500,000 tenant farmers relied upon the land for their livelihoods while a smaller percentage of Protestant landowners drew considerable profit from them. Given this reliance from both spectrums of society, land was, therefore, a prominent concern that was always going to be a considerable challenge. On the basis of this qualification it is reasonable to suggest that while Gladstone's first Land Act did not solve the question comprehensively, it nonetheless set the wheels in motion by a least acknowledging that there was a problem and trying to offer a solution. It sought to provide this by setting down clear legislation that would protect tenant farmers from unfair landlord practices such as arbitrary eviction and rent increases. In terms of intention, therefore, it was a well-meaning Act that endeavoured to improve the position of farmers. Despite this intention, however, the Act in reality did little to resolve their problems because it was both imprecise and lacking significant provisions.

Foremost the Act attempted to formalise the Ulster custom which gave tenant rights of fixity of tenure, fair rents and freedom of sale. This was undoubtedly a progressive step and something which the tenant farmers themselves sought – the 'three Fs' had been the main focus of the Dublin Land Conference in early 1870. However, the Act was short-sighted in its provision of this right. Rather than extend it across the whole of Ireland, it merely formalised it where it already existed – Ulster and some areas in Donegal. This gave the impression of addressing the issue of land, but in actuality it left the majority of the country unchanged. In this sense the Act was merely 'window-dressing' which covered up some problematic features while failing to offer substantive change. On this point, the Act was especially limited when considering its additional provision of compensation for evicted farmers. This was intended to compensate those forced off their land for the improvements they had made to it – building walls or improving the quality of the soil for example. Although a laudable purpose, the reality of this measure was the very complicated long-winded method by which farmers were to claim their money. It involved courts and also the ability to actually prove they had improved the plot. This was both expensive and often fruitless since landlords often denied the claims and the courts usually sided with them. A final element of the Act that failed to actually enhance the position

---

Comments (right margin):

A clear argument is presented which is focused on the question demand and which also acknowledges that there is a debate surrounding the issue.

This paragraph sets the question in context and develops some clear analysis of the question focus which is supported by precise evidence and begins to advance the presented argument.

This is a well-developed paragraph about the limitations of the Act itself. Using good own knowledge it presents a focused and analytical argument with some clear, qualified evaluation.

of farmers was the so called 'Bright clause' which offered tenants loans of up to two-thirds of the price of land so that they could purchase their plot should they wish to. This was equally unsuccessful because the loans were charged at five percent interest over 35 years and so very few, only 877 people, took advantage of this opportunity. Since the Act lacked a genuinely achievable means of adoption, its measures looked positive but in reality they left considerable room for improvement and were, therefore, largely unsuccessful.

The extent of their failure was most clearly evidenced after 1877 when agriculture suffered depression because of the importation of cheap American wheat and meat products. This challenge removed any sense of success from the Act by encouraging greater numbers of evictions as farmers increasingly could not afford to pay rents because of the stark decline in value of their produce – falling from $1.70 to $0.66 a bushel. Given the extent of decline it is reasonable to suggest that the Act had failed to secure the position of tenant farmers and, while it could be suggested the depression was a circumstance no one could have anticipated, had the Act offered more tangible protection then such an occurrence might have been less traumatic. Indeed, had the Act offered effective support the development of the Irish Land League in 1879 may have been less significant than it actually turned out to be. This organisation co-ordinated rural Ireland's greatest mass movement which pitched farmers in opposition to their landlords in what became known as the Land Wars. This involved an estimated 200,000 by 1881 who were refusing to pay rents and boycotting landlords who had evicted tenants. The development of this movement, which also involved violent actions at times, was the direct result of economic disaffection brought on immediately by the depression, but which was ultimately rooted in the failure of the Land Act to adequately address the land question. In this sense, therefore, it would be appropriate, and accurate, to suggest that the legislation did indeed fail to solve the issue of land.

> Here the argument is continued using further evidence which is precise and well-selected. The focus is clear and at the end of the paragraph there is a good linking sentence which relates nicely back to the question demand. This is a good way to ensure you do not drift away from your point.

Despite these failings after 1877, in the immediate years following 1870 the Act seemed to be successful. Before 1875 in particular, Ireland enjoyed considerable growth with the value of its agricultural output reaching £40.6 million compared to its £28 million 20 years before. Additionally eviction rates remained low during this time because of the increasing income of tenant farmers. With this in mind supporters of the Land Act could suggest that the legislation actually offered some definitive improvement and that it took a global depression before it was ruined. This argument has some merit. However, it also discounts the shortfalls of the Act itself since if incomes were good then eviction was always unlikely because farmers could pay their rent. In this manner, therefore, the underlying weakness of the Act was masked by economic growth and it was the economic environment that unmasked it only two years later. Had the Act been genuinely effective then it should have been more able to stand the declining markets at the end of the decade.

> This paragraph clearly considers a counter-argument which is incorporated in to the overall argument being presented. This is a good way to develop a balanced response that helps to promote evaluation in essays.

In conclusion, therefore, while the Land Act of 1870 did offer some promise of success with regard to answering the Irish land question, this was only in the short term and presented only a superficial notion of improvement. After 1877 when economic conditions declined the frailties of the Act were more pronounced, resulting in the massive agitation known as the Land Wars. In resorting to such action, it was clear that the initial Act was undoubtedly unsuccessful in resolving the deep-rooted land issue.

> This is a reasoned and confident conclusion which has been justified in the main body.

Verdict

This is a strong answer because:

- it is clearly analytical and offers a well-defined argument
- there is good use of precise and well-selected evidence throughout to support the points made
- it considers a counterargument and includes this as part of the overall evaluation, reaching a reasoned conclusion.

Paper 3: A Level sample answer with comments

Section C

These questions require you to show your understanding of a subject over a considerable period of time. They will ask you to assess a long-term historical topic and its development over a period of at least 100 years, and they require you to make a substantiated judgement in relation to the question.

For these questions remember to:

- organise your essay and communicate it in a manner that is clear and comprehensible
- use historical knowledge to analyse and evaluate the key aspect of the question covering the entire period
- make a balanced argument that weighs up differing opinions
- make a substantiated overall judgement on the question.

How far do you agree that Irish nationalism in the years 1774–1891 was ineffective? (20 marks)

Average student answer

To a great extent Irish nationalism can be considered ineffective because it failed to achieve the goal it had set for itself. By 1891 there was no independent state and nor had Dublin gained any greater legislative powers since those taken away after 1801. By its own measure, therefore, nationalism was consequently a failure.

Irish nationalism developed mainly after 1801 when William Pitt's Whig government introduced a successful union bill which resulted in the dissolution of the Dublin parliament and Ireland joining Britain in a much closer partnership. This measure had been intended to improve Irish relations following the United Irishmen uprising in 1798, but in fact the Act only ignited nationalist sentiments and a particular desire to have power back in their own hands once more. Over the course of the early 19th century this desire was generally quiet and little action was taken apart from a brief attempt at rebellion undertaken by Robert Emmett in 1803. This attempt failed when only a few people supported him and it consequently ended with Emmett's execution in Dublin. After this action, nationalism was less active for a number of years – at least until the 1840s when difficult conditions in the country reawakened this desire. The fact that nationalism was only present at the turn of the 19th century and then was quiet until the 1840s suggests that it was generally ineffective because firstly the two uprisings were a failure and secondly they did not stir the nation to support them in great numbers. This apathy is further evidenced by the fact that nationalist agitation did not re-emerge until the 1840s – more than 40 years since the last attempt.

When nationalism did re-emerge it was because of famine in Ireland which made many of the Irish greatly unhappy with the actions of the British government who did very little to support their country. Although Robert Peel bought £100,000 of corn and repealed the Corn Laws in 1846, this was not enough and by 1851 more than one million Irish had died of starvation and hunger-related diseases. Irish nationalists such as John Mitchel and Thomas Davis became increasingly angry with the British for not really helping and they organised a new movement to push for independence. This movement was called Young Ireland and it reawakened militant nationalism once more by carrying out an armed uprising in 1848 with the support of William Smith O'Brien, a local MP. This attempt was a complete failure and Mitchel was transported to Van Diemen's Land having encouraged such action. Here, therefore, Irish nationalist attempts had been ineffective once more after requiring a huge trauma to encourage its revival anyway. In this sense nationalism was not especially potent and even when presented with a devastating event which should have encouraged a lot of support, it failed to achieve its aims.

> This introduction focuses on the question demand and offers some explanation, but it could be strengthened by acknowledging the existence of some debate.

> This paragraph has some general focus and development which is supported by some good knowledge, but the argument could be more sustained. In places the response also drifts into narrative.

> Once again there is some good knowledge, but the material is quite narrative throughout and only really starts to clearly address the question demand at the end of the paragraph. Here the reasoning is good but it could be more developed.

Although Young Ireland was a failure it did have a positive outcome for Irish nationalism in that it encouraged a more permanent organisation that was intent on securing independence. This was the Irish Republican Brotherhood (IRB) which was set up in 1858 by James Stephens. As an organisation it became very large and had an American branch which was populated by Irish Americans who were either emigrants from Ireland or the children of emigrants. The IRB demanded complete separation from Britain and it sought to achieve this through armed rebellion just as the previous attempts by Emmett and Young Ireland. In 1867 it made its attempt, but this was poorly organised and some members were quick to turn against their colleagues when it was clear that the uprising was not going to work. Once more Irish nationalism was defeated and its goal of independence was unrealised. The IRB lost a lot of support after this attempt and the organisation had to go to ground for a few years in order to regroup and avoid British retaliation. It survived and after 1891 began to organise for another attempt at independence. Given that the movement was able to survive suggests that nationalism was beginning to attract more support, but still its militancy was not a successful approach.

The response had slipped into 'listing' points in this paragraph and is chronologically running through the different nationalist organisations. This has resulted in a descriptive retelling of events which only starts to clearly link to the question demand in the final sentence.

In 1870 a more constitutional Irish nationalism developed in the form of the Home Government Association which was established by Isaac Butt. The switch to moderate nationalism – Butt sought to achieve home rule rather than complete independence – was more successful than militancy because this organisation was able to get MPs elected to parliament and gradually its parliamentary strength forced British MPs to consider its demands. After 1875 Charles Stewart Parnell joined the party and his leadership after 1879 made the renamed Irish Parliamentary Party more influential, winning 85 seats in parliament. This encouraged the prime minister William Gladstone to consider home rule and in 1886 he introduced a bill to parliament that offered this. The bill did not pass but at least the government had made the effort and home rule was now being taken seriously by it. In this sense it could be suggested that Irish nationalism was actually quite successful because it got the government to start listening. However, the tangible success of actually having home rule or independence was still missing.

This paragraph offers some counter-argument and also makes the distinction between the types of Irish nationalism. Once again it is quite narrative. However, the last two sentences are more focused and offer analysis of the points being made.

In conclusion, therefore, Irish nationalism was quite prominent during the 19th century, but it failed to achieve anything of real note. By the end of the century it had got some politicians thinking about changes, but nothing actually changed by 1891 and, therefore, nationalism was ineffective.

A brief conclusion that offers a generally balanced judgement.

Verdict

This is an average answer because:

- it is quite narrative throughout
- the points made are developed in a general way albeit with some good own knowledge

- it does not evenly consider a counterargument.

Use the feedback on this essay to rewrite it, making as many improvements as you can.

Paper 3: A Level sample answer with comments

Section C

These questions require you to show your understanding of a subject over a considerable period of time. They will ask you to assess a long-term historical topic and its development over a period of at least 100 years, and they require you to make a substantiated judgement in relation to the question.

For these questions remember to:

- organise your essay and communicate it in a manner that is clear and comprehensible
- use historical knowledge to analyse and evaluate the key aspect of the question covering the entire period
- make a balanced argument that weighs up differing opinions
- make a substantiated overall judgement on the question.

How far do you agree that Irish nationalism in the years 1774–1891 was ineffective? (20 marks)

Strong student answer

To a great extent it is reasonable to suggest Irish nationalism was ineffective because it failed to achieve its desired goal of independence during this period. Despite this failure, however, there were significant inroads made towards this aim such as getting the British government to consider changes by the 1880s. Given the reluctant nature of this government to grant political change in Ireland and its continued efforts to subdue discontent after 1774, being able to change the opinion of British politicians should be regarded as a significant step. That Irish nationalist movements forced this change of opinion is, therefore, evidence of effectiveness in the long term.

> This introduction offers a clear argument that considers both the presence of debate, and also the influence of change over an extended period.

Over the course of the period 1774–1891 there is certainly much to suggest that Irish nationalism was ineffective. In particular it is difficult to ignore the fact that the main goal of greater autonomy was not achieved despite continued attempts by various nationalist movements throughout the period. Neither the actions of Young Ireland in the 1840s nor those of the Irish Republican Brotherhood (IRB) in the 1860s encouraged significant reform, and by the early 1890s Ireland was still closely bound to the British empire and receiving direction from the Westminster parliament. In this literal sense, therefore, it is reasonable to suggest that nationalist attempts were ineffective since they did not yield any marked reform. Despite this rather critical interpretation, however, there were significant inroads that were made in terms of the Irish situation. Certainly independent political power was not achieved, but there were clear improvements for Ireland's population in other ways which in the longer term would pave the way for the converted autonomy that the majority of the country desired. For example, the Catholic Association's victory in gaining Catholic emancipation in 1829 was a substantial improvement and one that gave nationalism the chance of a greater presence in the Westminster parliament which had been legislating for Ireland since 1801. Indeed, after 1870 the Irish Parliamentary Party rapidly gained greater numbers here, 85 seats in 1885, and this was instrumental in encouraging the British government to consider political reform for Ireland. Though in the short term it might not have seemed especially beneficial for Irish nationalism, this success was first a victorious small battle which later helped to win the war after 1891 when home rule became a serious opportunity. Consequently, while perhaps nationalism appeared ineffective before this date, it was actually laying the foundations for future success.

> This paragraph is clearly analytical and offers a reasoned argument that is well supported by appropriate knowledge. It is focused throughout and makes sure to link directly back to the question demand at the end of the paragraph.

The suggestion that Irish nationalism was ineffective came from the failed attempts of various organisations to force change in Ireland: the United Irishmen's uprising in 1798; the 1848 uprising by Young Ireland and the IRB's attempt in 1867 all failed and saw British control

> An analytical argument is being clearly developed in this paragraph. It is quite evaluative and counter-arguments are being integrated into the overall response. This helps to build a clearly evaluated and well-balanced answer that is consistently addressing the question demand.

unaffected. Certainly it is evident these events were not successful and by each organisation's own measure they would accept the failure. However, in each case there was some benefit which would ultimately prove effective. In the first instance each of these attempts registered a growing demand for change and also a determination to achieve it. Despite failure, nationalism was not put off and over the course of the 19th century continued to grow in various forms that eventually forced Britain to consider change, for example the small nationalist uprising attempted by Robert Emmett in 1803. Few people supported him and his efforts resulted in his execution in Dublin, but that did not see the end of nationalism and in the 1840s and 1860s it re-emerged with much greater ferocity and support. Even the 1820s arguably saw the growth of nationalism with first O'Connell's Catholic Association, and then his Repeal Movement 20 years later. Indeed, it was this latter movement which saw the establishment of the more militant Young Ireland organisation after 1842. In this sense what the 19th century actually characterises is not an ineffective nationalist movement but rather one that was growing and developing different approaches to achieve its aims. In doing so each organisation was experimenting and probing the British establishment while also keeping alive the idea of an autonomous Ireland. Though tangibly not effective in some ways, this was effective in the sense of preparation.

No more evident is this preparation than in the success enjoyed by the Irish Parliamentary Party in 1885. Here it won 85 seats, but perhaps more importantly it also won the attention of the prime minister William Gladstone. The victory of Parnell's party encouraged Gladstone to support home rule and actually put forward a bill granting this in 1886. This was arguably a significant achievement for Irish nationalism because for the first time since the Constitution of 1782 a British government was attempting to concede political reform to Ireland. Although the bill was defeated, it marked a transition in the thinking of the British Liberal Party especially and after this time it was increasingly sympathetic to Irish demands. In this manner constitutional nationalist pressure had been very effective in winning British political support which in the future would eventually yield independence for Ireland. The success of Irish constitutionalism was arguably down to the groundwork undertaken by men like O'Connell, John Mitchel and James Stephens, who each in their own way contributed to the environment in which Gladstone was prepared to endorse home rule. O'Connell by achieving Catholic emancipation which allowed Irish Catholics to sit in Westminster, Mitchel by developing a clear and unambiguous nationalist rhetoric, and Stephens by building a militant underground movement that made moderate nationalist demands more attractive to the British establishment. Without these contributions the hard exterior of British imperialist thought might not have been sufficiently softened for home rule to even be considered. Therefore, it is in softening this exterior that Irish nationalism over the period 1774–1891 was actually very effective.

> The argument is maintained and developed effectively here. It uses good knowledge from across the whole period to inform the analytical explanation which is logically deployed. Once again the paragraph ends with a clear reference back to the question, which emphasises the focus that has been consistently maintained.

In conclusion though, it is easy to say that Irish nationalism was ineffective because it did not achieve a tangible outcome such as home rule or independence. This ignores the effective preparation that the various nationalist movements undertook during the 19th century. This helped to prepare the ground for British politicians to start to accept Irish demands for more control over their country and without it, it would have been unlikely that any progress here would ever have been made.

> A clear and reasoned judgement which has been clearly explained in the body of the response.

Verdict

This is a strong answer because:

- it is clearly analytical and offers a well-defined argument
- throughout the response there is good use of precise and well-selected evidence to support the points made
- it considers a counterargument and includes this as part of an overall developed evaluation.

Index

Acknowledgements

Acknowledgements The authors and publisher would like to thank the following individuals and organisations for permission to reproduce photographs and text in this book.

Photographs

(Key: b-bottom; c-centre; l-left; r-right; t-top)

Alamy Images: 19th era 46, Liszt Collection 42, 125, National Geographic Image Collection 6bl, Niday Picture Library 23, Osman Photos.com 162, Pictorial Press 55, Pictorial Press Ltd 74, 77, 112, 118, 144, SOTK2011 84, The Print Collector 100, Timewatch Images 12, World History Archive 36; **Getty Images:** Buyenlarge 9, Topical Press Agency/Hulton Archive 156; **Mary Evans Picture Library:** 134, 147, IIllustrated London News 139, Illustrated London News Ltd 18, 33, 122, London Illustrated News 97, 103, Mary Evans Picture Library 69

Cover image: Mary Evans Picture Library: Epic/Tallandier

All other images © Pearson Education

Figures

Figure 2.1 from *Edexcel GCE History AS Unit 2 D1 Britain and Ireland 1867–1922* (Collier, M. 2008) p.151, Text © Martin Collier, Original illustrations © Pearson Education Ltd. 2008, with permission from Pearson Education Ltd.

Text

Extracts on p.5, p.73, p.81, p.135 from *The Making of Modern Ireland 1603–1923*, published by Faber & Faber (Beckett, J.C. 2011), with permission from Charles Gray, Queen's University Belfast; Extracts on p.5, p.135 from *Great Britain and the Irish Question, 1798–1921*, Hodder Education (Adelman, P. and Pearce, R., 2005), reproduced by permission of Hodder Education; Extract on p.14 from *An Argument on Behalf of the Catholics of Ireland* by Theobald Wolfe Tone, www.ucc.ie/celt/published/E790002/index.html, with permission from Corpus of Electronic Texts (CELT); Extract on p.22 from Social Aspects of Fenianism in Connacht and Leinster, *Eire-Ireland*, vol. xxi, no. 1, Spring, pp.29–30 (Griffin, B. 1986), with permission from Irish American Cultural Institute and Brian Griffin; Extract on p.26 from Motion for Leave [First Night] HC Deb 08 April 1886 vol 304 cc1036-141, http·//hansard.millbanksystems.com/commons/1886/apr/08/motion-for-leave-first-night, Contains Parliamentary information licensed under the Open Parliament Licence v3.0; Extract on p.31 from Ulster Covenant, www.proni.gov.uk/index/search_the_archives/ulster_covenant.htm, Contains public sector information licensed under the Open Government Licence v2.0; Extract on p.41 from Union with Ireland Act 1800, www.legislation.gov.uk/apgb/Geo3/39-40/67/contents, Contains public sector information licensed under the Open Government Licence (OGL) v3.0. www.nationalarchives.gov.uk/doc/open-government-licence; Extract on p.49 from Constitution of the Irish Free State (Saorstát Eireann) Act, 1922, www.irishstatutebook.ie/eli/1922/act/1/enacted/en/html © The Office of the Attorney General, reproduced under the terms of the PSI licence, www.psi.gov.ie; Extract on p.51 from *Gladstone: 1809–1874*, Clarendon Press (Matthew, H.C.G. 1998) p.147, © H.C.G. Matthew 1997, by permission of Oxford University Press; Extract on p.57 from *Ireland in the Twentieth Century* Macmillan (Harkness, D. 1996) p.15, reproduced with permission of Palgrave Macmillan; Extract on p.59 from *Edexcel GCE History AS Unit 2 D1 Britain and Ireland 1867–1922*, Pearson (Collier, M. 2008) p.132, Text © Martin Collier, Original illustrations © Pearson Education Ltd. 2008, with permission from Pearson Education Ltd; Extract on page 61 from Letter from the Prime Minister to Sir James Craig and Mr de Valera, http://filestore.nationalarchives.gov.uk/pdfs/small/cab-24-128-CP-3331.pdf, Contains public sector information licensed under the Open Government Licence (OGL) v3.0; Extract on p.67 from The Catholic Relief Act in Ireland, 1778, *Church History*, Vol.32, No.2, June, pp.181–206 (abstract) (Burns, R. E. 1963), with permission from Cambridge University Press; Extract on p.67 from Quebec and the Irish Catholic Relief Act of 1778: An Institutional Approach, *Journal of Historical Sociology*, Volume 16, Issue 3, September, p.375 (Stanbridge, K. 2003), Copyright © 2003, John Wiley and Sons; Extract on p.68 from The Catholic Question in the Eighteenth Century, *History Ireland*, Vol.1, Issue 1, Spring (Bartlett, T. 2003), with permission from Thomas Bartlett; Extract on p.78 from A Web of English History, www.historyhome.co.uk/peel/ireland/emancip.htm, with permission from Marjie Bloy; Extract on p.89 from *An Economic History of Ulster*, Manchester University Press (Kennedy, L. and Ollerenshaw, P., 1985) p.67, with permission from the authors; Extracts on p.90, p.102 from *Victorian Belfast*, Ulster Historical Foundation (Johnson, J. 1993), courtesy of Ulster Historical Foundation (www.ancestryireland.com); Extract on page 91 from *Ireland and the Industrial Revolution: The Impact of the Industrial Revolution on Irish Industry, 1801–1922*, 1st ed., Routledge (Bielenberg, A. 2009), copyright © 2009 Routledge, reproduced by permission of Taylor & Francis Books UK; Extract on p.93 from *An Unlikely Success Story: The Belfast Shipbuilding Industry 1880–1935*, Ulster Historical Foundation (Lynch, J. 2001), courtesy of Ulster Historical Foundation (www.ancestryireland.com); Extracts on p.96, p.98, p.100 from *Belfast Shipbuilders: A Titanic Tale*, Colourpoint Books (Cameron, S. 2011), with permission from Colourpoint Books; Extract on p.99 from MacCall writing From Dunleath Papers (D1167 and D4179), Public Record Office of Northern Ireland, www.proni.gov.uk © The Office of the Attorney General, reproduced under the terms of the PSI licence, www.psi.gov.ie; Extract on p.110 from *The Great Hunger* by Cecil Woodham-Smith (Copyright © Cecil Woodham-Smith, 1962) Reprinted by permission of A.M. Heath & Co Ltd; Extract on p.113 from *Victorian Literature: A Sourcebook*, Palgrave Macmillan (Plunkett, J., Parejo Vadillo, A., Gagnier, R., Richardson, A., Rylance, R., Young, P. 2011) pp.30–31, reproduced with permission of Palgrave Macmillan; Extract on p.116 from Famine and Disease in Ireland, HC Deb, 9 March 1846, vol. 84 cc780-4, http://hansard.millbanksystems.com/commons/1846/mar/09/famine-and-disease-in-ireland, Contains Parliamentary information licensed under the Open Parliament Licence v3.0; Extract on p.120 from Food Exports from Ireland 1846–47, *18th–19th-Century History*, Features, Issue 1, Spring 1997, The Famine, Volume 5 (Kinealy, C. 1997), with permission from the author, Professor Christine Kinealy is author of a number of books on Ireland's Great Famine, including a graphic novel, *The Bad Times. An Drochshaol* (Quinnipiac University Press, 2015); Extract on p.133 from Landlord and Tenant (Ireland) Act, 1870, www.legislation.gov.uk/ukpga/Vict/33-34/46/contents/enacted, Contains public sector information licensed under the Open Government Licence (OGL) v3.0; Extract on page 148 from *Ireland and the Land Question 1800–1922*, 1st ed., Methuen (Winstanley, M.J. 1984) p.43, copyright © 1984 Methuen, reproduced by permission of Taylor & Francis Books UK; Extract on page 149 from *The Course of Irish History*, Mercier Press (Moody, T.W. and Martin, F.X. (eds) 1994) p.288, with permission from Mercier Press and reproduced with permission of Roberts Rinehart Publishers in the format Republish in a book via Copyright Clearance; Extract on p.154 from *Dublin Made Me*, Mercier Press (Andrews, C.S. 1979) republished by The Lilliput Press in 2001, with permission from The Lilliput Press; Extracts on p.162, p.170, p.171, p.172 from *Rebel City: Larkin, Connolly and the Dublin Labour Movement* Merlin Press (Newsinger, J. 2004), with permission from The Merlin Press Ltd; Extract on p.167 from 27f. The Southern Argument for Slavery, http://www.ushistory.org/us/27f.asp, Copyright © 2016 ushistory.org; Extract on p.167 from Parliamentary Papers 1831–2, XV, pp.428–30, Contains Parliamentary information licensed under the Open Parliament Licence v3.0; Extract on page 167 from Shelfmark: British Library Newspaper Archive: Caledonian Mercury about the trial of the Tolpuddle Martyrs published 29 March 1834, © The British Library Board, Caledonian Mercury 29 March 1834, (The trial of the Tolpuddle Martyrs).